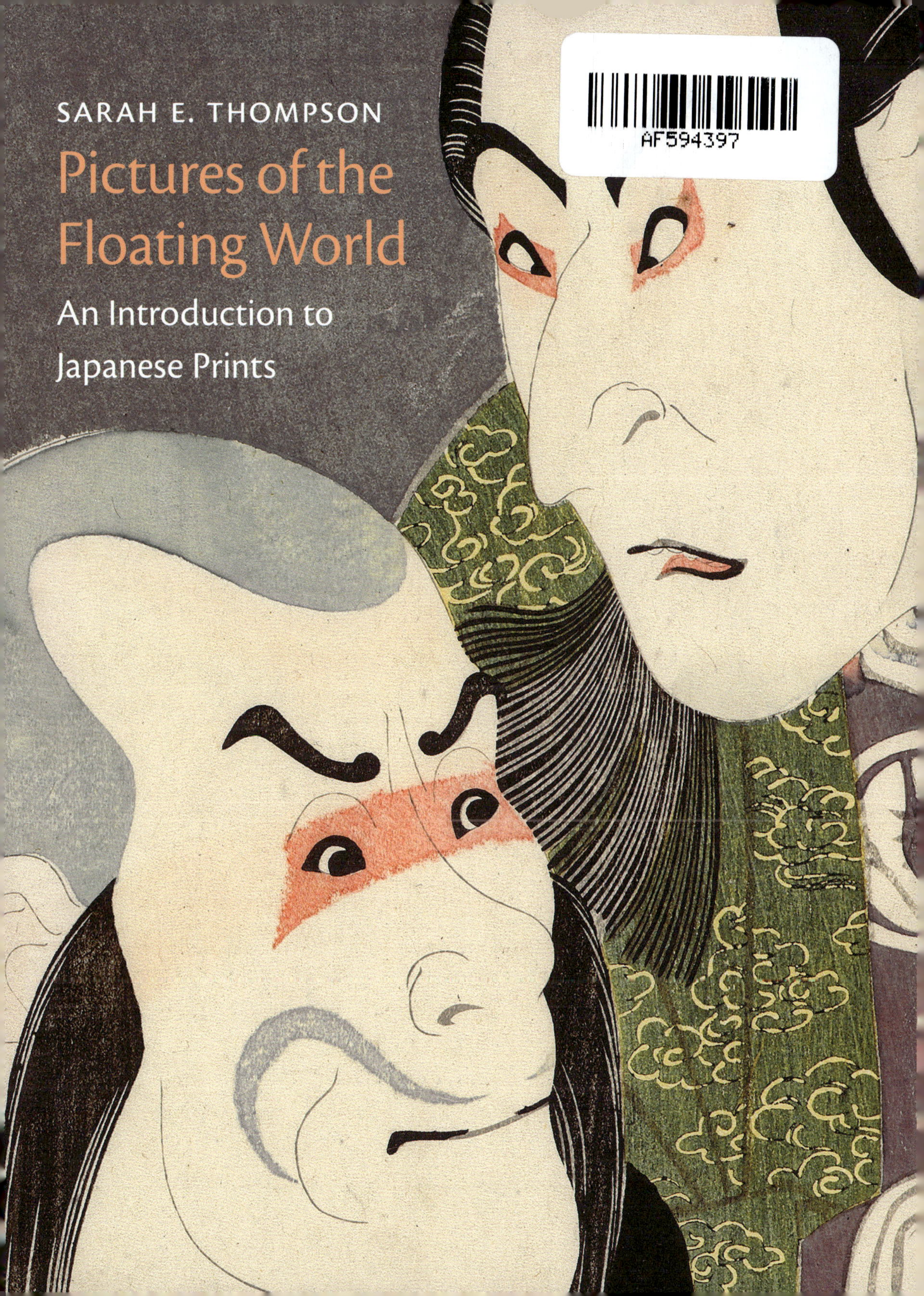

SARAH E. THOMPSON

Pictures of the Floating World

An Introduction to Japanese Prints

Pictures of the Floating World

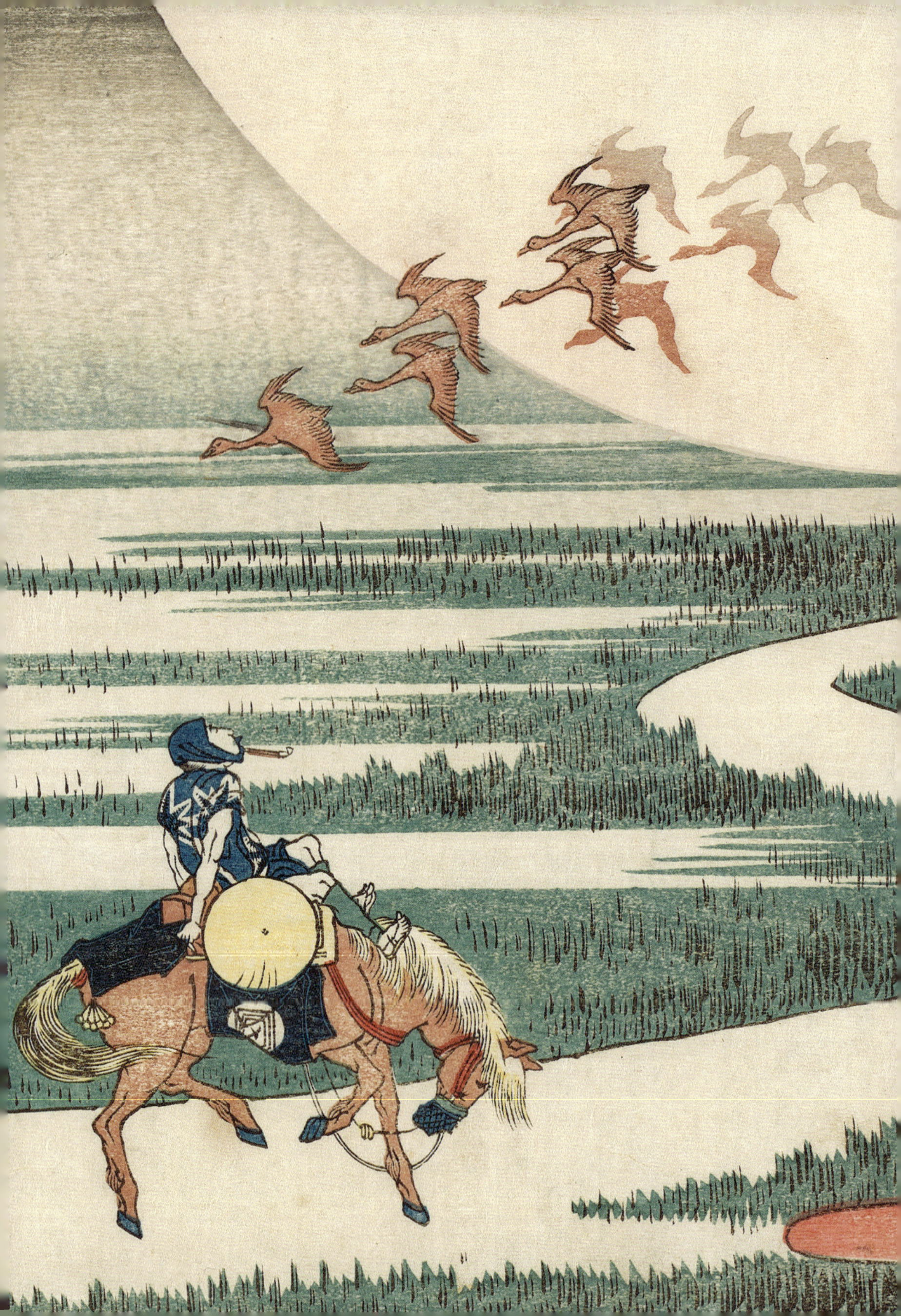

SARAH E. THOMPSON

Pictures of the Floating World

An Introduction to Japanese Prints

MUSEUM OF FINE ARTS, BOSTON

ABBEVILLE PRESS PUBLISHERS

New York London

SLIPCASE: Katsushika Hokusai (1760–1849). *Bellflower and Dragonfly*, c. 1833–34 (Tenpo 4–5); see page 101.
FRONT COVER: Toshusai Sharaku (active 1794–1795). *Actors Sawamura Yodogoro II as Kawatsura Hogen and Bando Zenji as Oninosadobo* (detail), 1794 (Kansei 6), 5th month; see page 54.
BACK COVER: Katsushika Hokusai (1760–1849). Publisher: Nishimuraya Yohachi (Eijudo). *The Falling Mist Waterfall at Mount Kurokami in Shimotsuke Province (Shimotsuke Kurokamiyama Kirifuri no taki)* (detail), c. 1832 (Tenpo 3); see page 82.

PAGE 2: Totoya Hokkei (1780–1850). *Musashi Plain (Musashino)* (detail), c. 1834–35 (Tenpo 5–6); see page 84.
PAGE 6: Utagawa Hiroshige I (1797–1858). *Night View of Saruwakamachi (Saruwaka-machi your no kei)* (detail), 1856 (Ansei 3), 9th month; see page 89.
PAGE 18: Kitagawa Utamaro I (early 1750s–1806). *Three Beauties of the Present Day (Toji san bijin): Tomimoto Toyohina, Naniwaya Kita, Takashima Hisa* (detail), c. 1793 (Kansei 5); see page 31.
PAGE 44: *Actor Ichikawa Ebizo as Usui Arataro Sadamitsu in a Shibaraku Scene* (detail), 1796 (Kansei 8), 11th month; see page 57.
PAGE 68: Utagawa Hiroshige I (1797–1858). *The Sea off Satta in Suruga Province (Suruga Satta kaijo)* (detail), 1858 (Ansei 5), 4th month; see page 94.
PAGE 96: Utagawa Hiroshige I (1797–1858). *Kingfisher and Hydrangea* (detail), c. 1832 (Tenpo 3); see page 111.
PAGE 122: Utagawa Kuniyoshi (1797–1861). *Ruan Xiaowu, the Short-lived Second Son (Tanmeijiro Genshogo)* (detail), c. 1827–30 (Bunsei 10–Tenpo 1); see page 135.

Project editor: Lauren Bucca
Copy editor: Ashley Benning
Production director: Louise Kurtz
Design: Misha Beletsky and Julia Sedykh

MFABoston

 The text of this book was set in Ten Oldstyle. Printed in China.

First edition
10 9 8 7 6 5 4 3

Library of Congress Cataloging-in-Publication Data
Names: Thompson, Sarah E. (Sarah Elizabeth), 1951– author.
Title: Pictures of the floating world : an introduction to Japanese prints / Sarah E. Thompson.
Description: New York : Abbeville Press Publishers, [2022] | "Museum of Fine Arts, Boston." | Includes bibliographical references and index. |
Summary: "An illustrated history of Japanese prints"—Provided by publisher.
Identifiers: LCCN 2022018471 |
ISBN 9780789214393 (paperback)
Subjects: LCSH: Ukiyoe—Themes, motives. | Ukiyoe—Massachusetts—Boston. | Museum of Fine Arts, Boston.
Classification: LCC NE1321.8 .T477 2022 | DDC 769.952—dc23/eng/20220611
LC record available at https://lccn.loc.gov/2022018471

For bulk and premium sales and for text adoption procedures, write to Customer Service Manager, Abbeville Press, 655 Third Avenue, New York, NY 10017, or call 1-800-ARTBOOK.

Visit Abbeville Press online at www.abbeville.com.

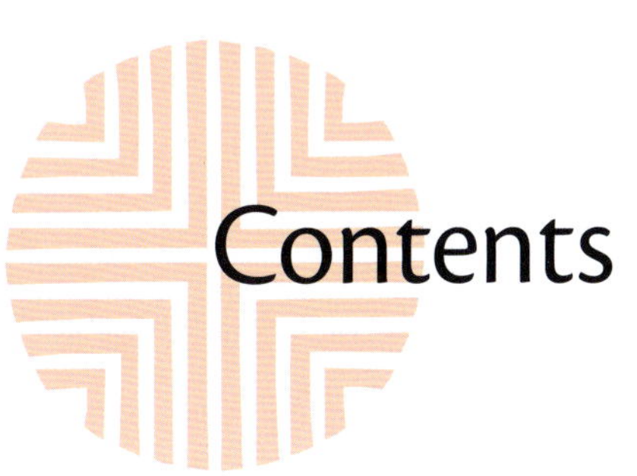

Contents

INTRODUCTION 7

1

Beauty and Fashion

19

2

The Kabuki Theater

45

3

Landscapes and Cityscapes

69

4

The Natural World

97

5

History and Literature

123

6

Fantasy

151

ARTIST BIOGRAPHIES 180

GLOSSARY 186

FURTHER READING 187

INDEX OF ARTISTS AND TITLES 188

IMAGE CREDITS 192

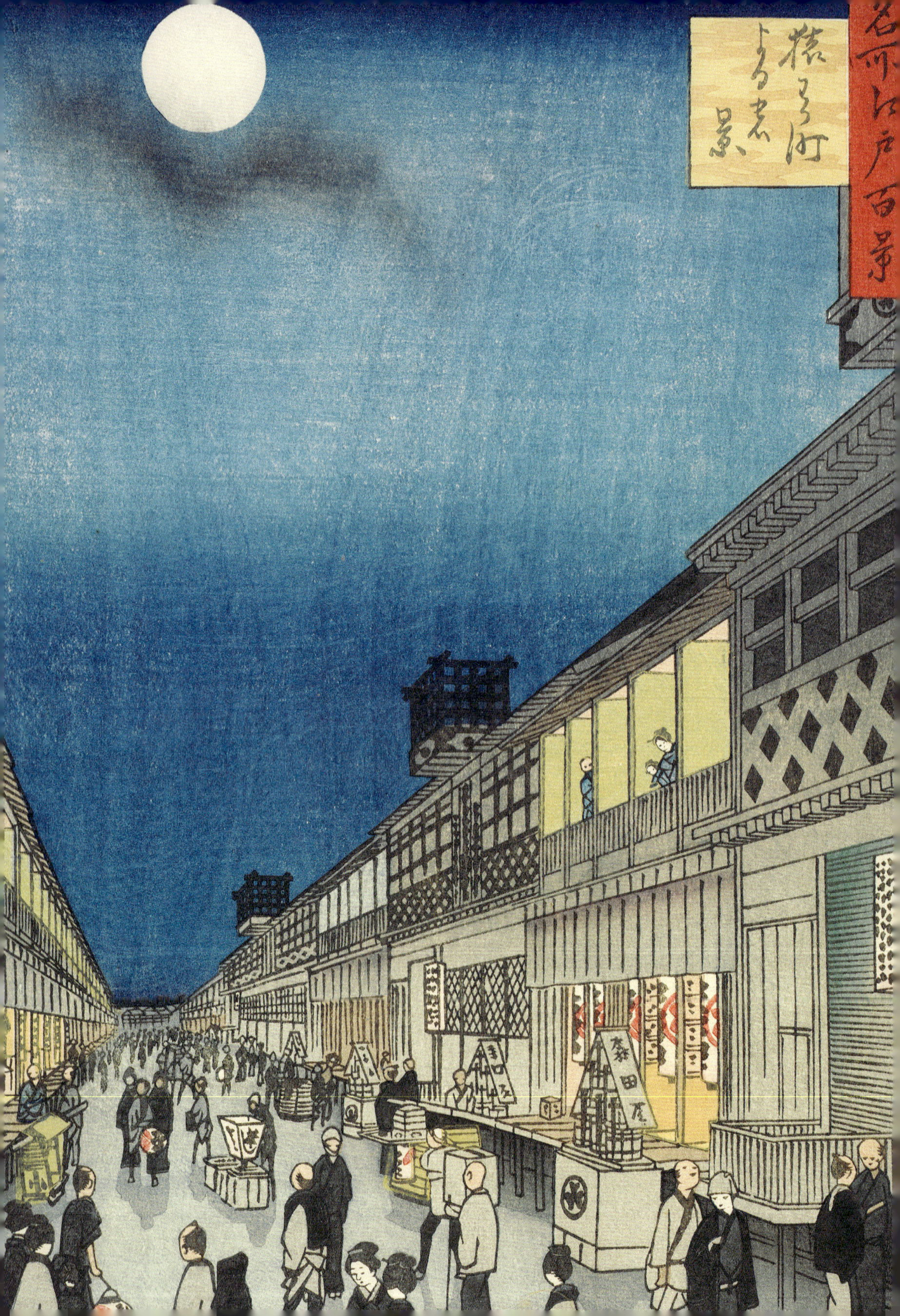

名所江戸百景

Introduction

The printed pictures made in Japan from the late seventeenth century through the beginning of the twentieth century revolutionized visual culture by making it possible for ordinary people who were not part of the ruling elite to enjoy professionally produced art in their homes. Sold in stores to the general public at very affordable prices, woodblock prints chronicled the urban entertainment culture of the time, known as the Floating World (*ukiyo*). Artists of the school called *ukiyo-e* (literally "pictures of the Floating World") depicted current fashions and amusements in paintings, book illustrations, and prints, but the term is most strongly associated with the woodblock prints. The artists and publishers strove to make commercial products that would appeal to the widest possible range of potential customers, and in the long run they were even more successful than they had ever dreamed. In the mid-nineteenth century, the prints began to find an appreciative audience outside Japan as well, and today they are enthusiastically collected and enjoyed around the world.

Ukiyo-e prints began to be made during the Edo period, also called the Tokugawa period, when Japan was largely—though not completely—isolated from the outside world and controlled by the Tokugawa clan of shoguns, hereditary military dictators who ruled from the city of Edo (now Tokyo) in the name of the emperor, who still resided in the old capital city of Kyoto. Book publishing flourished in all the major cities of Japan at the time, but the prints were especially associated with Edo. Woodblock prints continued to be made by the same method, though with some changes in subject matter and drawing style, for most of the Meiji era (1868–1912), when a new government promoted rapid modernization, leading to Japan becoming one of the world's major industrial powers by the beginning of the twentieth century. Prints of this period docu-

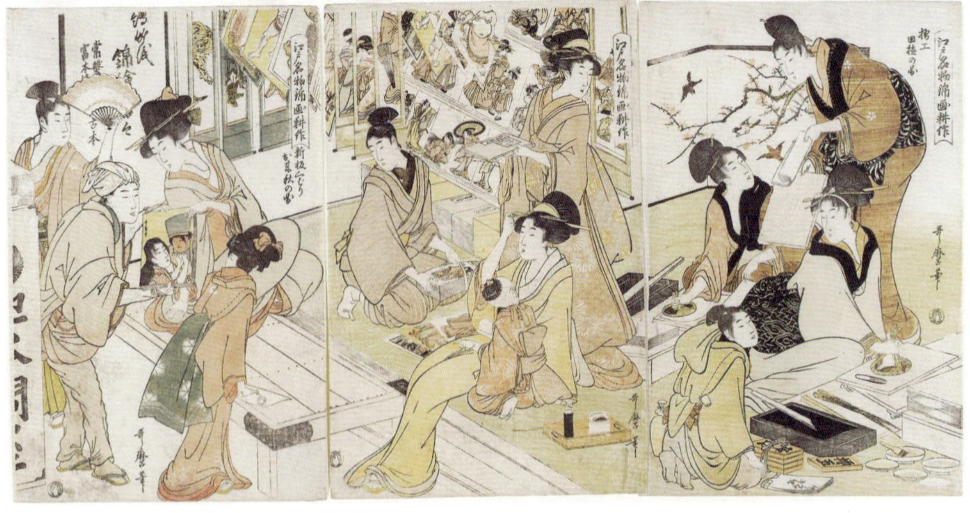

Kitagawa Utamaro I (early 1750s–1806)
Publisher: Tsuruya Kiemon (Senkakudo)
Woodblock Printer (Suriko), Print Shop, Distributing New Prints (Shinpan kubari), from the series the Cultivation of Brocade Prints, a Famous Product of Edo (*Edo meibutsu nishiki-e kosaku*), c. 1803 (Kyowa 3)
Woodblock print (nishiki-e); ink and color on paper
Vertical oban triptych; 29¾ × 14¾ in. (75.6 × 38 cm)

In this gender-bending parody print, Utamaro depicts a printing studio and retail outlet mainly staffed by women, with some boy assistants. In reality the two activities would be in separate locations, and most—if not all—of the staff would be male.

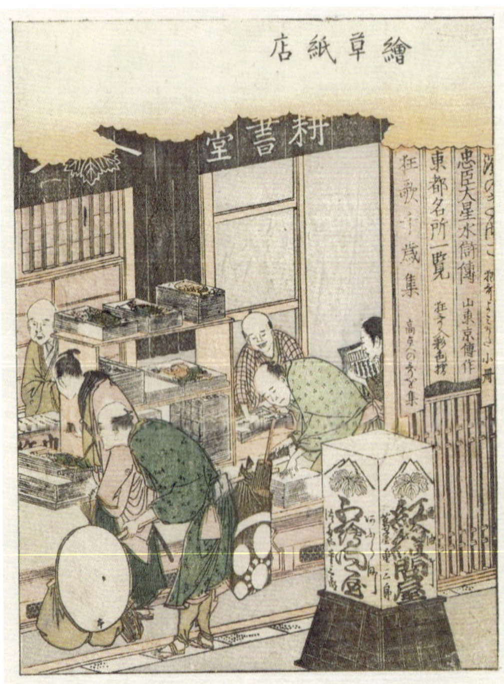

Katsushika Hokusai (1760–1849)
Publisher: Tsutaya Juzaburo (Koshodo)
Print and Book Store (Ezoshi ten): The Store of Tsutaya Juzaburo, from the book *Illustrated Pleasures of the East (Ehon Azuma Asobi)*, c. 1802 (Kyowa 2)
Woodblock printed book page; ink and color on paper, 6 × 7⅞ in. (15.1 × 20 cm)

Prints and books are stacked on shelves near the front of the store to be perused by customers standing at the entrance. Vertical placards outside advertise the titles of some of the books currently available.

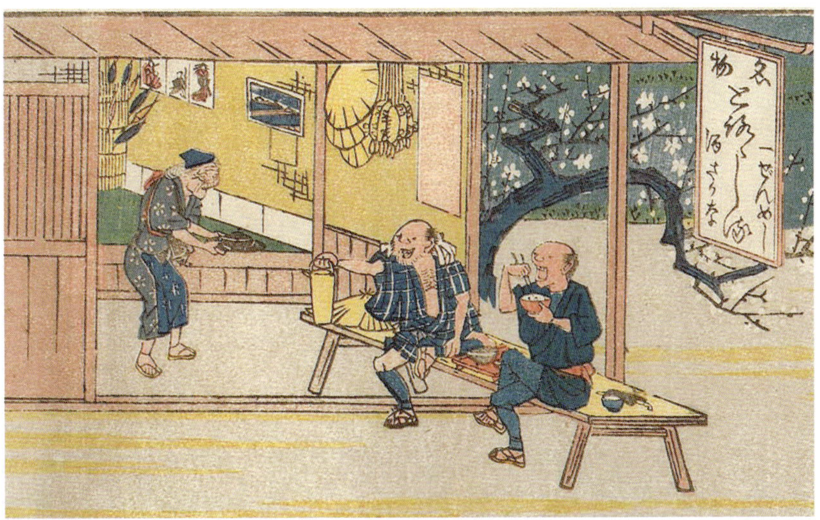

Utagawa Hiroshige I (1797–1858)
Mariko, from the series Fifty-three Stations of the Tokaido Road (*Tokaido gojusan tsugi no uchi*), also known as the First Tokaido or Great Tokaido (detail), c. 1841–44 (Tenpo 12–Koka 1)
Horizontal aiban; 13¾ × 8⅞ in.
(35 × 22.4 cm)

In this scene from one of Hiroshige's many series depicting stops along the Tokaido highway, travelers take a break at a roadside teahouse that is decorated with inexpensive prints pasted to the wall, strategically placed to cover deteriorating plaster.

ment the many changes taking place in Japan, while also continuing to depict traditional subjects.

The original consumers of the prints were the new middle class that appeared in the major Japanese cities, especially Edo, during the seventeenth century. The rule of the Tokugawa shoguns was for the most part peaceful and prosperous, and social developments took place in Japan that were very similar to trends in Europe at around the same time: the growth of major cities, the development of a cash economy and beginning of a banking system, and above all, the rise of a new class of potential consumers with varying amounts of disposable income. Only members of the ruling warrior class, the samurai, could participate in government. No Japanese at all were permitted to travel abroad, and even travel within the country was strictly regulated. Wealthy merchants, whose income often exceeded that of the lower-ranking samurai, spent their money instead on the pleasures of the Floating World, including the kabuki theater and the Yoshiwara brothel district. Woodblock prints served as souvenirs of these experiences or as vicarious entertainment for those who could not afford the real thing.

The basic technology of printing by hand from carved wooden blocks had been employed in Japan since the eighth century CE to make multiple copies of Buddhist prayers and images. With the growth of urban populations

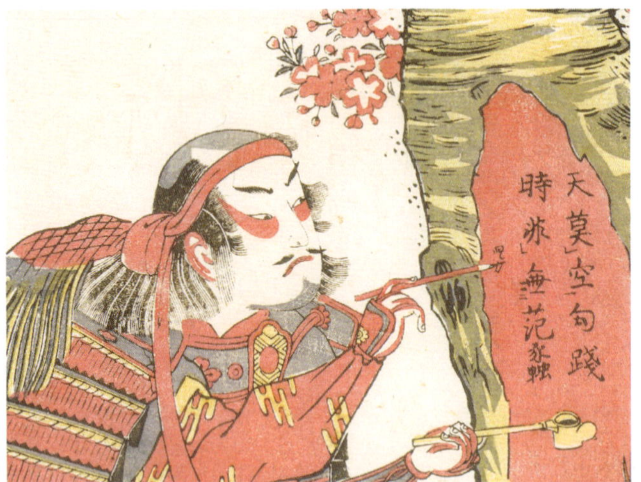

Suzuki Harunobu (1725–1770)
Publisher: Sakaiya Kurobei
Kojima Bingo no Saburo Takanori,
c. 1762–64 (Horeki 12–Meiwa 1)
Woodblock print (benizuri-e);
ink and limited color on paper
Vertical oban; 10⅞ × 15½ in.
(27.6 × 39.3 cm)
Detail of page 130

Shortly before he designed the first ukiyo-e prints to be produced in full color, Harunobu skillfully deployed just three printed colors—red, yellow, and blue.

and the accompanying rise of literacy in the seventeenth century, commercial publishing for a general audience became a viable business endeavor. Early seventeenth-century printed books reproduced literature that already existed in manuscript form with woodcut versions of the painted illustrations, but in the second half of the century, original fiction about the adventures of fashionable men and women of the Floating World appeared with illustrations in the new ukiyo-e style. Single-sheet woodblock prints began to be made in the 1680s, as a new product line manufactured by the same method as the printed books and sold alongside them in the bookstores.

The prints were mass-produced commercial products, created by a team of skilled workers. The process began with an artist's drawing, which would, however, be destroyed in the process of making the prints. This drawing was handed over to a professional blockcutter, who glued it facedown to a block usually made of cherry wood, which is soft enough to cut easily but hard enough to withstand the pressure of many printings. The blockcutter cut through the paper to create a reversed design with the parts to be printed left in relief. A printer then inked the block, placed a piece of paper facedown on it, and rubbed the back of the paper with a smooth, round pad to create an impression identical to the original drawing. In the case of multicolor prints, a separate block would be used for each color. Thousands of impressions could be made before the block became too worn to use. The entire process was controlled by the publisher, who then sold the finished prints in his store. Thus at least four different people—artist, blockcutter, printer, and publisher—participated in the production of each print, and there might well be assistants or apprentices involved also.

The Early Prints

Artists: Hishikawa Moronobu, Sugimura Jihei, Torii Kiyonobu I, Torii Kiyomasu I, Okumura Masanobu, Nishimura Shigenaga, Torii Kiyoshige

The first single-sheet prints were black-and-white works made from a single block, like the book illustrations that were their prototypes. Produced in a horizontal format similar to a two-page spread in a printed book, they were often issued in a series—usually a set of twelve prints, but sometimes eight or ten. The subject matter included scenes from traditional stories and current plays, as well as views of fashionable life in the Floating World. The latter sometimes included explicit erotica, which did not become illegal until the 1720s. Although the prints were sold uncolored, purchasers sometimes added hand-painted color to them.

Other early prints were larger in size and made in a vertical format that suggested a hanging scroll painting, and in fact they were probably seen as less expensive substitutes for paintings. These larger prints usually depicted famous actors

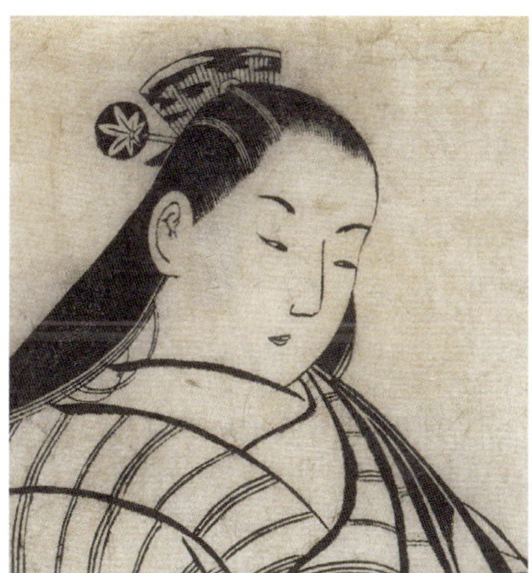

Torii Kiyomasu I (active c. 1696–1716)
Publisher: Igaya Kan'emon (Bunkido)
Standing Courtesan, c. 1705–7
Woodblock print (sumizuri-e); ink on paper
Vertical o-oban; 10½ × 21⅞ in. (26.3 × 55.6 cm)
Detail of page 21

The earliest prints, like this one of a courtesan, were made in black and white.

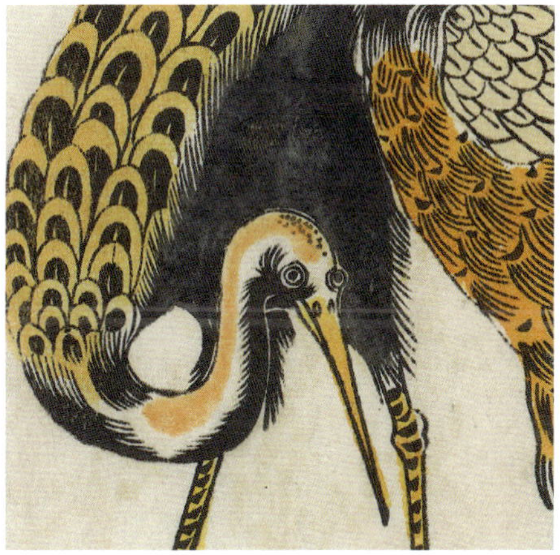

Nishimura Shigenaga (1697?–1756)
Publisher: Igaya Kan'emon (Bunkido)
Cranes and Chrysanthemums, from a bird-and-flower series with the title Kashinsai (?), 1730 (Kyoho 15)
Woodblock print (urushi-e); ink on paper, with hand-applied color and nikawa
Hosoban; 6¼ × 12¼ in. (15.9 × 31.1 cm)
Detail of page 98

Adding hand-painted colors to prints helped to make them more visually appealing to customers.

or courtesans. Often, though not always, they had hand coloring added by the publishers, who competed with one another to make their products more visually attractive to customers. The hand-colored prints featured a bright orange-red color made from red lead (*tan* in Japanese), which was applied here and there as an accent, sometimes with additional hand coloring in yellow and green.

A new, more elaborate type of hand coloring became popular from the late 1710s to the mid-1740s, featuring a bright, pinkish-red color called *beni,* derived from safflower, as well as vegetal blues, yellows, and sometimes greens. Some of the prints also included special embellishments such as sprinkled brass filings whose bright golden color suggested the actual gold used in expensive paintings, or a hand-applied black color with glue mixed into the ink so that it would dry to a shiny finish; the latter are sometimes called *urushi-e* (lacquer pictures) even though no actual lacquer is involved. These prints were smaller in size than earlier works, usually in a vertical format equivalent to one-third of a horizontal sheet. The most common subject was scenes from current kabuki plays, which, if they can be identified, enable us to date the prints. And young women modeling the latest fashions—both Yoshiwara courtesans and other kinds of women—were still very popular. Other prints showed scenes from classical literature or nature subjects called "bird-and-flower pictures" (*kacho-ga*), a theme derived from the Chinese painting tradition.

The publishing industry came under scrutiny by the shogunate in the 1720s, resulting in a major overhaul of the laws regulating it. This was the first of three

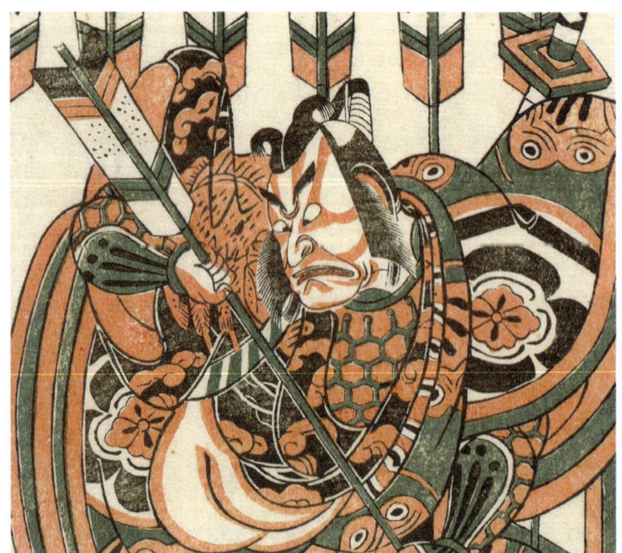

Torii Kiyoshige (active 1720–1760)
Publisher: Sakaiya Kurobei
Actor Ichikawa Ebizo II as Bunshin Yanone Goro, 1754 (Horeki 4), 1st month
Woodblock print (benizuri-e); ink and limited color on paper
Hosoban; 5¾ × 12½ in. (14.6 × 31.6 cm)
Detail of page 50

Red and green were among the first colors applied by printing from separately carved woodblocks rather than by hand painting. Here they enhance the portrayal of a kabuki actor.

major incidents of heightened censorship of prints during the Edo period. Every print was now required by law to include identification of both the artist and the publisher, a practice that was already common as a form of advertising. Explicit erotica was made illegal, although the law does not seem to have been strictly enforced and erotic prints continued to be made and sold on a discreet, under-the-counter basis. Any reference to current events other than entertainment was strictly forbidden, perhaps in order to avoid any possible criticism of the government, and the ban was extended back as far as 1573, the time when the Tokugawa clan began its rise to power. In prints, books, and stage plays, any reference to events after 1573 had to be disguised with fictional settings in older periods.

Another legal change at this time affected printmaking in a more positive way, though only slowly. This was the lifting of the ban on the importation of European books and prints—provided that they made no mention of Christianity, which was still strictly illegal. Western images were brought to Japan by Dutch traders, who were the only Europeans allowed into the country and confined to an island in the harbor of the port city of Nagasaki, and also secondhand via Chinese merchants. Japanese artists gradually became aware of these exotic pictures, and in the 1740s ukiyo-e print designers began to experiment with Western-style vanishing point perspective, leading eventually to the boom in landscape prints that started almost a century later.

The most important innovation in printing technology in the mid-eighteenth century was the development of color printing. Full-color woodblock printing—with five or more color blocks in addition to a black outline block (which might even sometimes be omitted)—had already been done in the seventeenth century in China, where it was used to produce elegant art books with reproductions of paintings. Some of these books had found their way to Japan so that the Japanese knew full-color printing was possible, but because of the ban on foreign travel, they were unable to go to China to study printing and the Chinese who came to Japan were merchants, not printers. Color printing technology was reverse-engineered in Japan over a period of several decades, from the early 1740s to the mid-1760s.

The earliest color prints generally used the two colors of red and green in addition to a black key block. Impressions taken from the key block made from the artist's drawing were used in the same way as the drawing to carve a block for each color. The colors were kept in alignment during printing by raised guide marks in one corner and along one side of each block, so that the printer could position the paper in exactly the right place every time. For a while, printed images and hand-painted ones were in competition with each other, and some very beautiful, large hand-painted prints were produced. Eventually, however, color printing replaced hand coloring.

The Rise of Full-Color Printing

Artists: Suzuki Harunobu, Katsukawa Shunsho, Isoda Koryusai, Kitao Shigemasa, Torii Kiyonaga, Kitagawa Utamaro I, Chobunsai Eishi, Eishosai Choki, Toshusai Sharaku, Utagawa Toyokuni I, Utagawa Kunimasa

In the 1750s and early 1760s color prints became increasingly elaborate, often utilizing three or even four colors, and sometimes overlapping the printed colors to create the illusion of additional hues. As in the age of hand-colored prints, kabuki plays and fashionable young women were the main subjects, but other themes also appeared, such as scenes from history. The final breakthrough into full-color printing came in 1765—or possibly at the very end of 1764—when the wealthy members of amateur poetry-writing clubs pooled their resources to fund the making of full-color printed pictorial calendars, probably to be used as gifts for their friends at the New Year holiday for the year corresponding to 1765. These gorgeous full-color prints became known as *nishiki-e* or "brocade pictures." The technology was so effective that it continued to be used in much the same form until the beginning of the twentieth century.

The availability of full-color printing at reasonable prices led to what is often considered a golden age of printmaking over the next few decades, with a number of outstanding artists taking advantage of the new medium. In kabuki prints, the Torii school that had dominated the field since the 1690s was now overtaken by the Katsukawa school, which produced accurate, recognizable likenesses of actors. From the 1760s to the 1790s, human figures in prints—especially women in fashionable kimono—became more and more elongated,

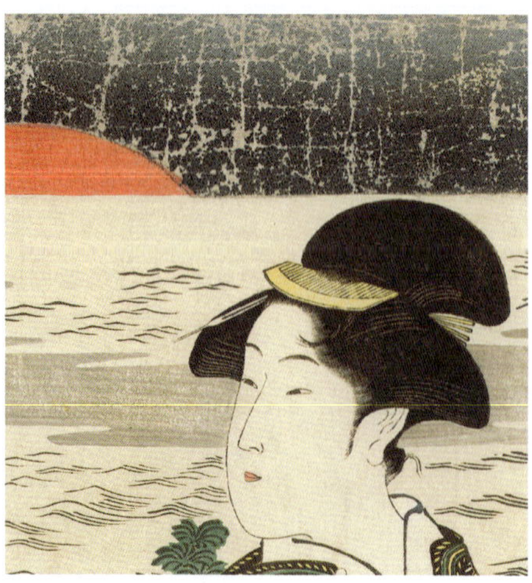

Eishosai Choki (active c. 1780–1810)
Publisher: Tsutaya Juzaburo (Koshodo)
Sunrise on New Year's Morning, late 1790s (mid-Kansei era)
Woodblock print (nishiki-e); ink, color, and mica on paper
Vertical oban; 10⅛ × 15¼ in. (25.5 × 38.6 cm)
Detail of page 34

The silvery gray parts of this print are made with mica.

a look that was unrealistic but extremely elegant. In the 1790s, both actors and women were sometimes depicted in close-up bust portraits, which might be embellished with backgrounds of ground mica painted on after the printing was completed for a silvery, glittering effect.

A second wave of censorship of the printing industry began in 1790, again as part of a widespread governmental attempt to correct economic problems by a general tightening up and reorganization, known as the Kansei Reforms after the era in the Japanese dating system when they occurred. From 1790 on, all legally published prints were required to include not only the names or marks of both the artist and the publisher, but also a censor's seal indicating that the preliminary drawing had been cleared for publication; this seal was stamped onto the drawing and then carved into the printing block as part of the design. Other provisions of the 1790 publishing law repeated the earlier edict of 1722: no erotica, no depictions of current events, no excessively luxurious works. A number of prominent artists, book authors, and publishers were punished under the new regulations, with large fines and/or short but humiliating jail terms. Ukiyo-e prints were also indirectly affected by regulations applied not to publishing but to the Floating World itself, with new restrictions on both the kabuki theater and especially the Yoshiwara, so that these institutions lost some of their former exuberance.

In the early decades of the nineteenth century, print publishing was somewhat subdued as artists and publishers sought to avoid any possible difficulties with the government. Although prints of Yoshiwara courtesans continued to be made, increasing numbers of prints now showed fashions modeled by ordinary middle-class women, who were less likely to arouse the disapproval of the censors. Close-up portraits of actors became illegal in 1801, although they made a quiet comeback in the 1810s after enforcement of the ban dropped off; in compensation, kabuki prints put increasing emphasis on dynamic action scenes and detailed stage settings.

Later Works: The Nineteenth Century

Artists: Katsushika Hokusai, Shotei Hokuju, Totoya Hokkei, Utagawa Kunisada I, Keisai Eisen, Utagawa Hiroshige I, Utagawa Kuniyoshi, Utagawa Yoshitora, Utagawa Yoshitsuya, Kawanabe Kyosai, Toyohara Kunichika, Tsukioka Yoshitoshi

Around 1830, several new subjects became enormously popular, giving serious competition to the two traditional favorites of actors and women. These included warrior prints (*musha-e*), a category that included not only warriors but historical figures in general; landscapes and cityscapes (*fukei-ga*); and bird-and-flower pictures (*kacho-ga*), the traditional term used in East Asian painting for nature sub-

jects in general, including insects, fish, and animals as well. All of these subjects had been part of the repertoire of ukiyo-e artists from the beginning, but only as minor themes; now, however, they became potential bestsellers on their own. A major technological development in printmaking at the time was the introduction of Prussian blue—called Berlin blue in Japan—a synthetic colorant imported from Europe that had been known in Japan for some time but had only now become cheap enough for practical use in making prints. It was much more resistant to fading than earlier blue pigments and may have contributed to the sudden rise of landscape prints, which made extensive use of blue tones for water and sky.

Like all other areas of life in Japan, printmaking was severely affected by the economic depression that struck in the mid- to late 1830s, following several years of poor harvests due to weather conditions. As in earlier periods, the economic problems led to a broad reform movement by the Tokugawa shogunate, which included new, stricter regulations on publishing. The Tenpo Reforms were the third episode of heightened censorship during the Edo period, and the severest of all. The publishing edict of 1842 reinforced all of the existing prohibitions and introduced a new system of censorship seals; it also banned composite images with more than three sheets and prints using more than eight colors. Most shockingly of all, images of kabuki actors and courtesans—traditionally the two most popular subjects—were banned.

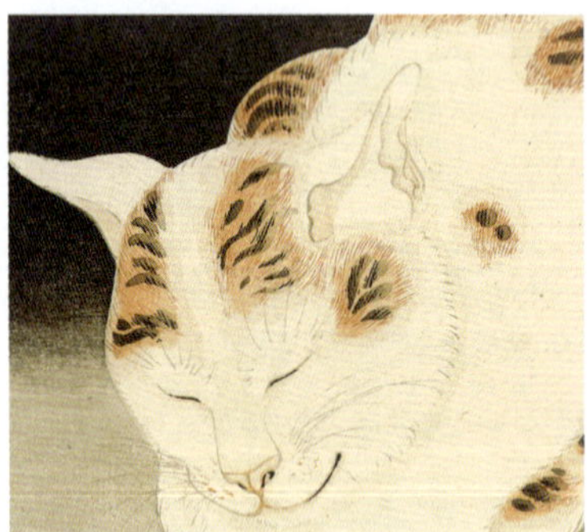

Kawanabe Kyosai (1831–1889)
Sleeping Cat, 1885–89 (Meiji 18–22)
Woodblock print (nishiki-e);
ink and color on paper
Shikishiban, 10⅛ × 9¾ in. (25.5 × 24.4 cm)
Detail of page 119

Animals, like this sleepy cat, became a popular subject in nineteenth-century prints.

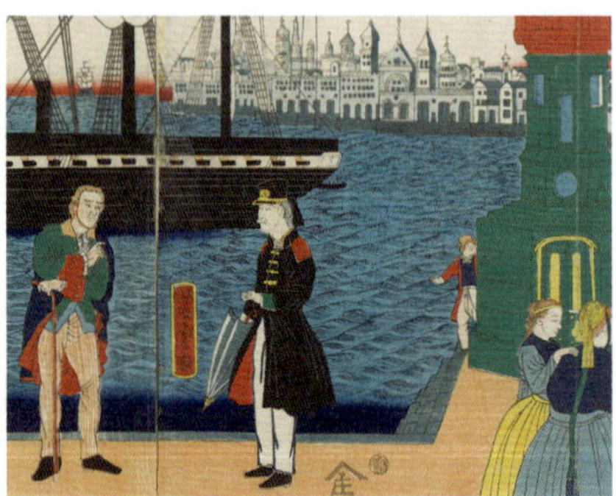

Utagawa Yoshitora (active c. 1836–1887)
Publisher: Yamadaya Shojiro
The City of Paris, France (Furansu Parisu no fu), 1862 (Bunkyu 2), 6th month
Woodblock print (nishiki-e); ink and color on paper
Vertical oban triptych; 29¼ × 14¼ in. (74.2 × 36.2 cm)
Detail of page 95

The 1860 opening of Yokohama as a treaty port for foreign trade led to the rise of "Yokohama prints," often showing foreigners as artists imagined them.

Fortunately for artists and publishers, the newer history, landscape, and nature prints were still permissible, and fashions could be modeled by ordinary women instead of courtesans. Opposition to the reforms was so great, however, that some artists and publishers even produced scenes allegedly illustrating traditional stories or humorous imaginary scenes, embellished with mysterious details hinting at some deeper meaning—presumably a criticism of government policies—but in such an ambiguous manner that nothing could be proven. The severest aspects of the regulations were soon dropped. For example, from late 1846 on, kabuki prints were again permitted, provided that the actors' names were not mentioned. But the kind of heavily veiled political commentary inspired by the reforms themselves continued to appear from time to time.

In the 1850s and 1860s, the Tokugawa shogunate had much more serious problems than regulating print production. The arrival of the American fleet under Matthew Perry in Japan in 1853 and the trade agreement reached in 1854 ended the policy of near-isolation that had lasted for over two centuries. Other Western nations also signed treaties of commerce with Japan, and the port of Yokohama opened for international trade in 1860. Prints made at the time show the exotic appearance of the foreigners in Yokohama, and sometimes include highly fanciful depictions of their home countries as imagined by Japanese artists.

The Tokugawa shogunate was overthrown in 1867 and replaced with a new government supposedly headed by the Meiji emperor but actually by politicians acting in his name, who spearheaded an ambitious and successful campaign of modernization along Western lines. By the end of the Meiji era in 1912, Japan had achieved a level of technological development comparable to the other major world powers of the time. Ukiyo-e woodblock prints continued to be made throughout the Meiji era, since they were still the most effective method for producing images in full color at reasonable prices. The main technological innovation in woodblock print publishing was the introduction of synthetic aniline dyes that produced brilliant reds, purples, and greens, but otherwise, production methods and formats remained the same.

From about 1905 to 1910, the function handmade woodblock prints had as the primary visual expression of popular culture was taken over by more recently introduced media such as photography and lithography, and in new formats including postcards and pictorial magazines. Woodblock printing was revived as a fine art form in the 1910s and has continued in that role until the present, now as one of many possible print media that an artist might choose to use. Ever since the late nineteenth century, when they inspired the Japonisme movement in France, the older ukiyo-e prints have remained enormously popular with collectors and connoisseurs around the world. Today, they continue to exert a global influence on contemporary artists.

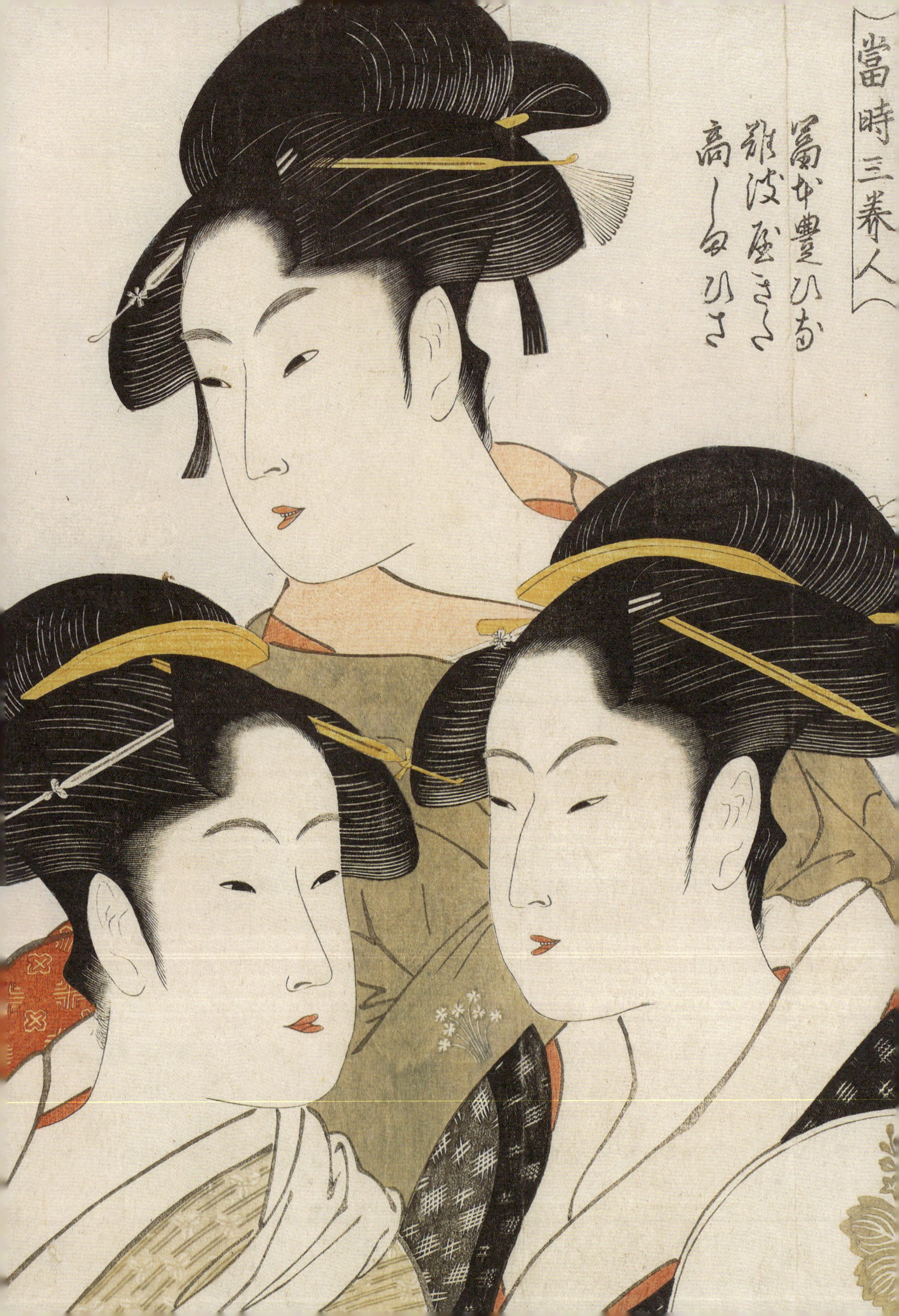
當時三美人
冨本豊ひな
難波屋きた
高しまひさ

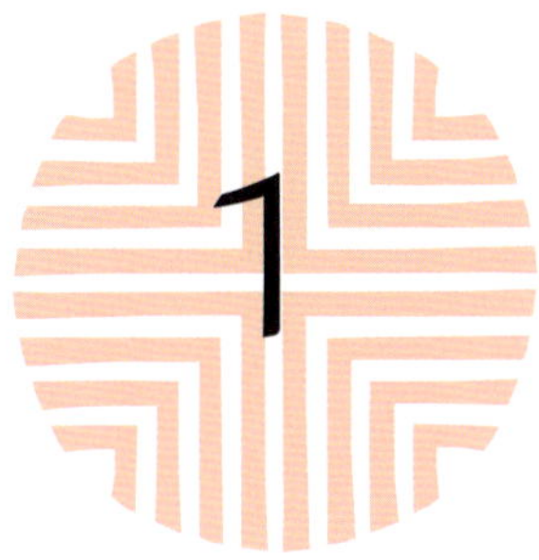

Beauty and Fashion

Images of fashionable young people, especially women, were the main subject of early ukiyo-e prints and remained one of the most important throughout the history of the field. Many, though by no means all, of the women in the prints are high-ranking courtesans of the Yoshiwara, the legal, licensed brothel district of Edo, who wore a specialized costume featuring layers of elaborate kimono, many hairpins, and a sash called an obi tied in the front instead of the back. Also seen often in prints are geisha, who though associated with the Yoshiwara were not sex workers but rather professional party entertainers skilled in music and dance, and ordinary women of various social classes, often beautifully dressed for some special occasion. Attractive young men are also sometimes included in the category of prints known as *bijin-ga*, literally "pictures of beautiful people."

The prints can be roughly dated both by the drawing style known to be popular in a given period and by the fashions shown—especially the hairstyles. Harunobu, the artist who designed the first commercial prints to be produced in full color, drew small, charming, somewhat childlike figures. Artists such as Koryusai in the 1770s and Kiyonaga in the 1780s began to draw taller, more adult-looking figures, and women's hairstyles became increasingly puffy at the sides as well as the back. In the 1790s, Utamaro and Eishi drew extremely tall, attenuated figures resembling modern fashion illustrations—unrealistic but very beautiful. By about 1800, women's hairstyles featured buns protruding at the top as well as the sides. In the early nineteenth century, figures gradually returned to more realistic proportions. During the Meiji era in the 1880s, ladies of the imperial court began to wear Western styles on some occasions, although this new fashion did not trickle down to the general population until the twentieth century.

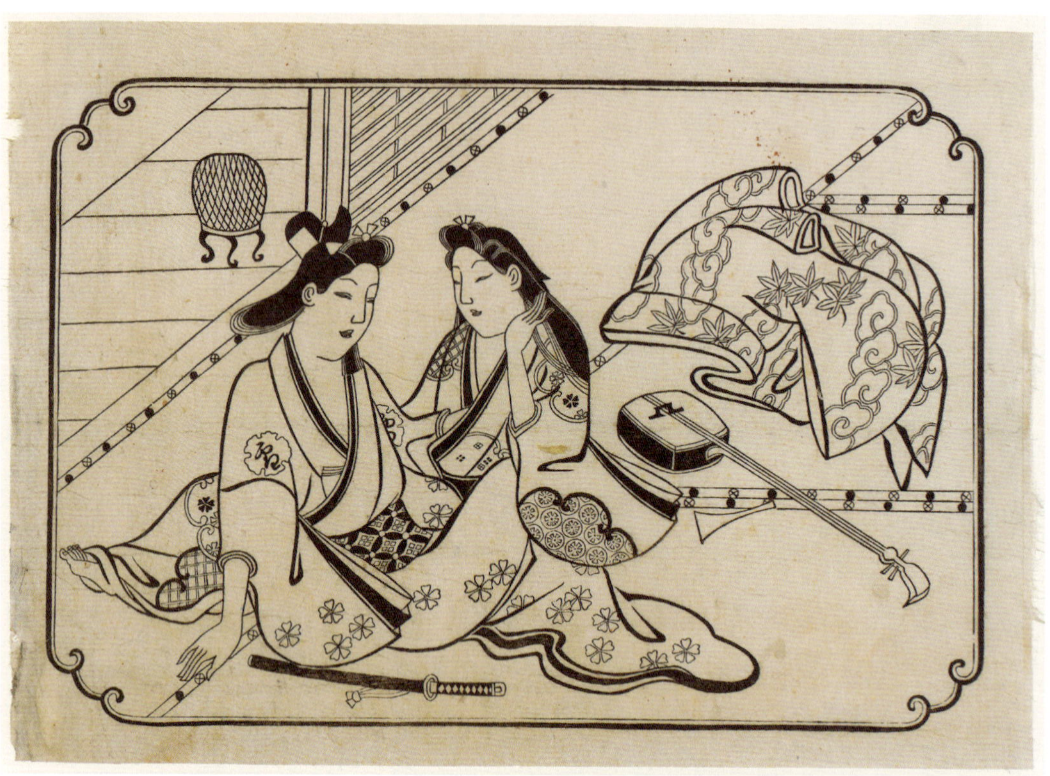

Attributed to Hishikawa Moronobu (died 1694)
A Young Man Dallying with a Courtesan, from an untitled series of twelve erotic prints, c. 1680 (Enpo 8)
Woodblock print (sumizuri-e); ink on paper
Horizontal oban; 14½ × 10¼ in. (36.8 × 26 cm)

In a palatial brothel resembling an upper-class mansion, a fashionable young man—either a high-ranking samurai or the son of a wealthy merchant family—becomes acquainted with a courtesan. This nonexplicit print was the first of a set of twelve erotic prints that mixed explicit and nonexplicit images, both of which were legal at the time. The beautifully delineated textile patterns and accessories such as his sword, her shamisen, and the incense burner create an image of luxurious leisure.

Torii Kiyomasu I (active c. 1696–1716)
Publisher: Igaya Kan'emon (Bunkido)
Standing Courtesan, c. 1705–7
Woodblock print (sumizuri-e);
ink on paper
Vertical o-oban; 10½ × 21⅞ in.
(26.7 × 55.6 cm)

Large, vertical prints such as this one were similar in appearance to the more expensive one-of-a-kind paintings made by the same artists. The attention lavished on the fashionable costumes of top courtesans in both prints and paintings suggest that these works were intended to appeal to male and female viewers alike. This courtesan's outer robe—so long that she must lift it to step forward—is decorated with the personal crests of famous kabuki actors.

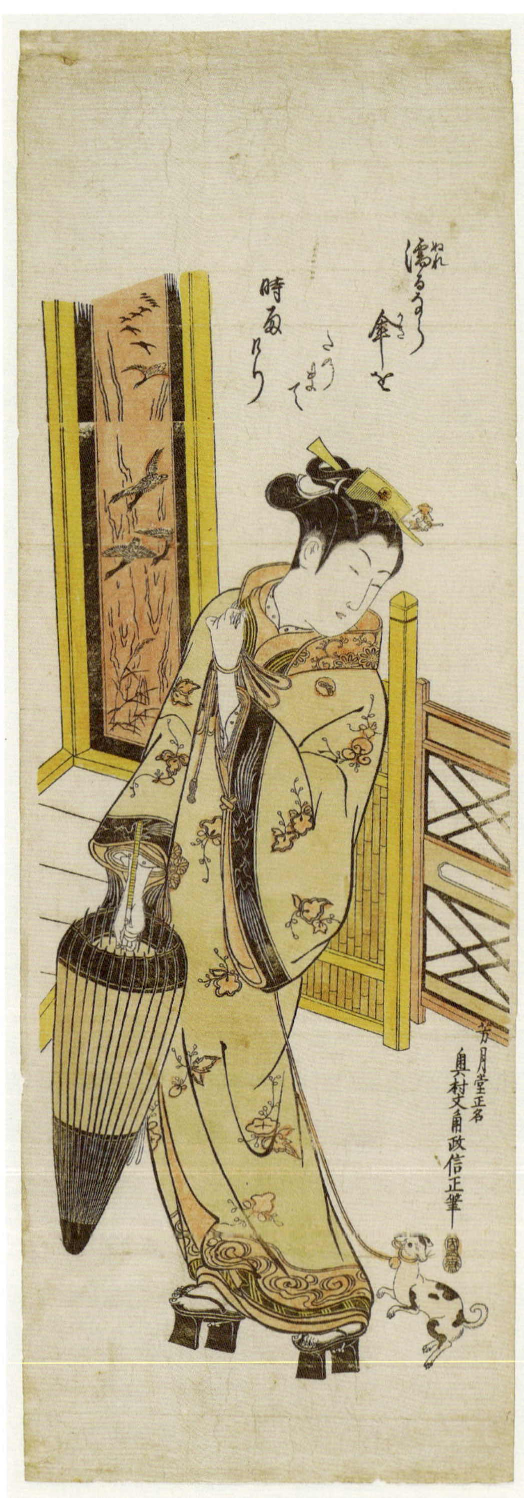

Okumura Masanobu (1686–1764)
Woman with Umbrella and Dog on Leash, c. 1744–48
Woodblock print (beni-e); ink on paper, with hand-applied color
Wide hashira-e; 10 × 28½ in. (25.4 × 72.4 cm)

Hand-colored prints became increasingly popular in the first half of the eighteenth century, reaching a peak in the 1740s when they had to compete with early color prints. In this elegant example, a fashionable young woman, wearing a raincoat and high clogs and carrying an umbrella, sets out on a walk with her small, lively puppy. The humorous poem inscribed above warns her to be cautious in autumn showers—a metaphor for falling in love.

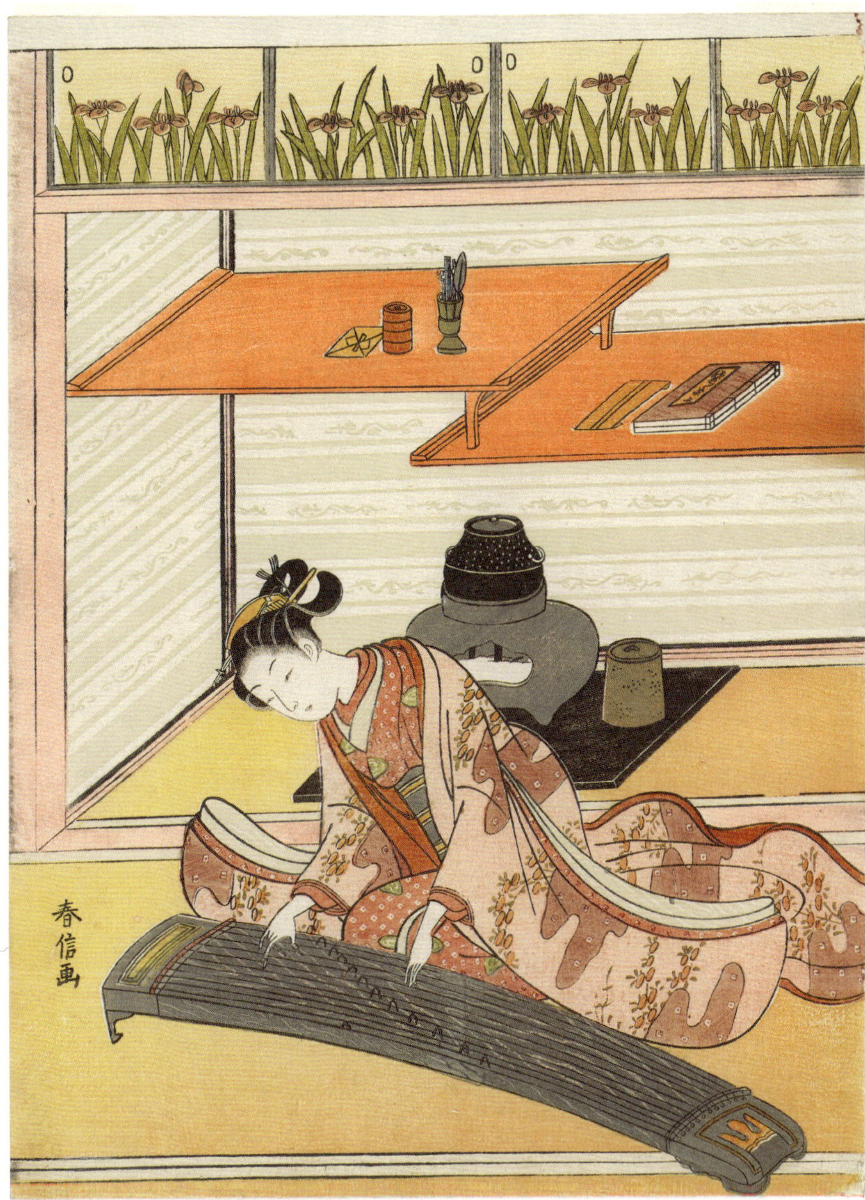

Suzuki Harunobu (1725–1770)
The Koto Player, c. 1767–68
(Meiwa 4–5)
Woodblock print (nishiki-e);
ink and color on paper
Vertical chuban; 8¼ × 11⅛ in.
(21 × 28.3 cm)

Harunobu, the first artist to design mass-produced prints in full color, drew sweet, youthful, almost childlike figures. Here, a well-bred young lady, whose long sleeves show that she is not yet married, plays the zither-like musical instrument known as the koto. In the alcove behind her are a kettle and brazier to heat water for the tea ceremony, and on the shelves, equipment for the incense-guessing game, with books that may contain poetry.

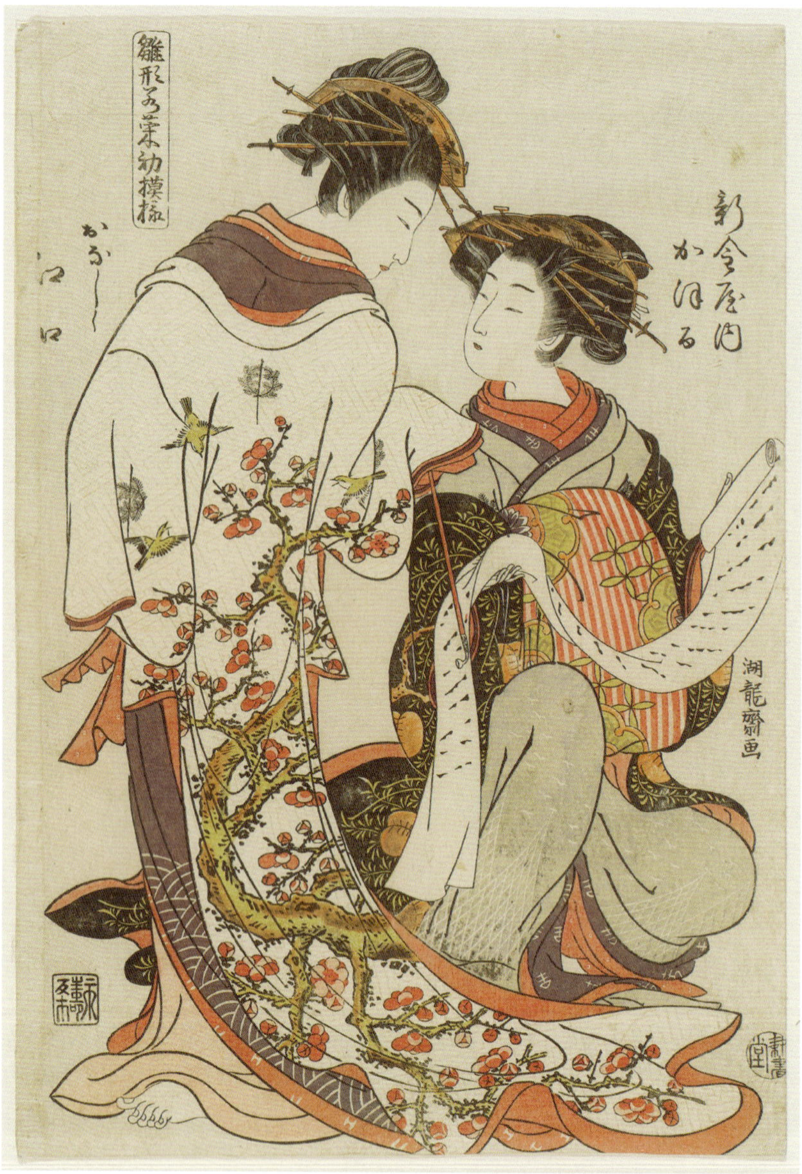

Isoda Koryusai (1735–1790)
Publisher: Nishimuraya Yohachi (Eijudo)
Kaoru and Eguchi of the Shin-Kanaya, from the series Models for Fashion: New Year Designs as Fresh as Young Leaves (*Hinagata wakana no hatsu moyo*), 1776 (An'ei 5), fall
Woodblock print (nishiki-e); ink and color on paper
Vertical oban; 9⅞ × 14¼ in. (25 × 36 cm)

This long-running series presented the courtesans of the Yoshiwara posing in the elegant new clothes that they wore for the first time at the New Year, setting fashions for the coming year. Figures were now drawn in a more elongated style ideal for showing off kimono patterns. In this design, two courtesans are dressing for the New Year fashion parade along the main street of the quarter; one is distracted by a love letter from a favorite client.

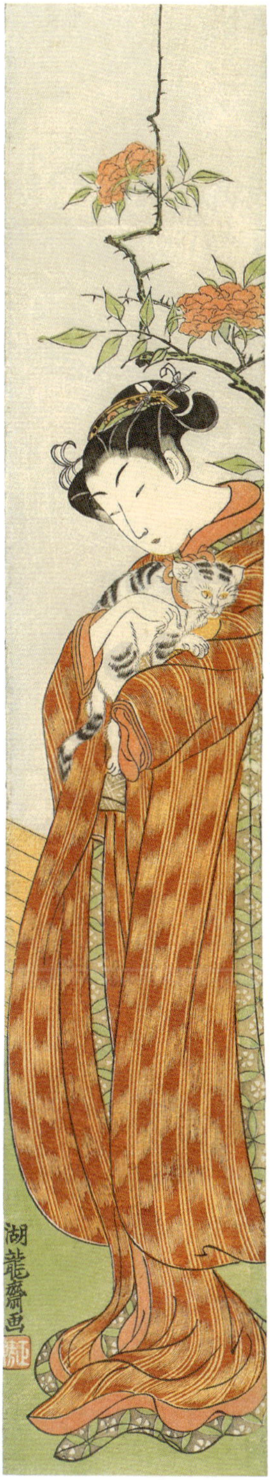

Isoda Koryusai (1735–1790)
Young Woman Holding a Cat, c. 1770
Woodblock print (nishiki-e); ink and color on paper
Hashira-e; 4¾ × 25¾ in. (12 × 65.4 cm)

Tall, narrow prints such as this one are known as "pillar prints" (*hashira-e*) because they were intended to be hung from the interior pillars of a Japanese room. Often they were sold already mounted as hanging scrolls, in the same manner as paintings but using less expensive materials. Artists took advantage of the format to create interesting compositions, with figures sometimes cropped at the sides to emphasize verticality. Here, a statuesque beauty cuddles a pet cat.

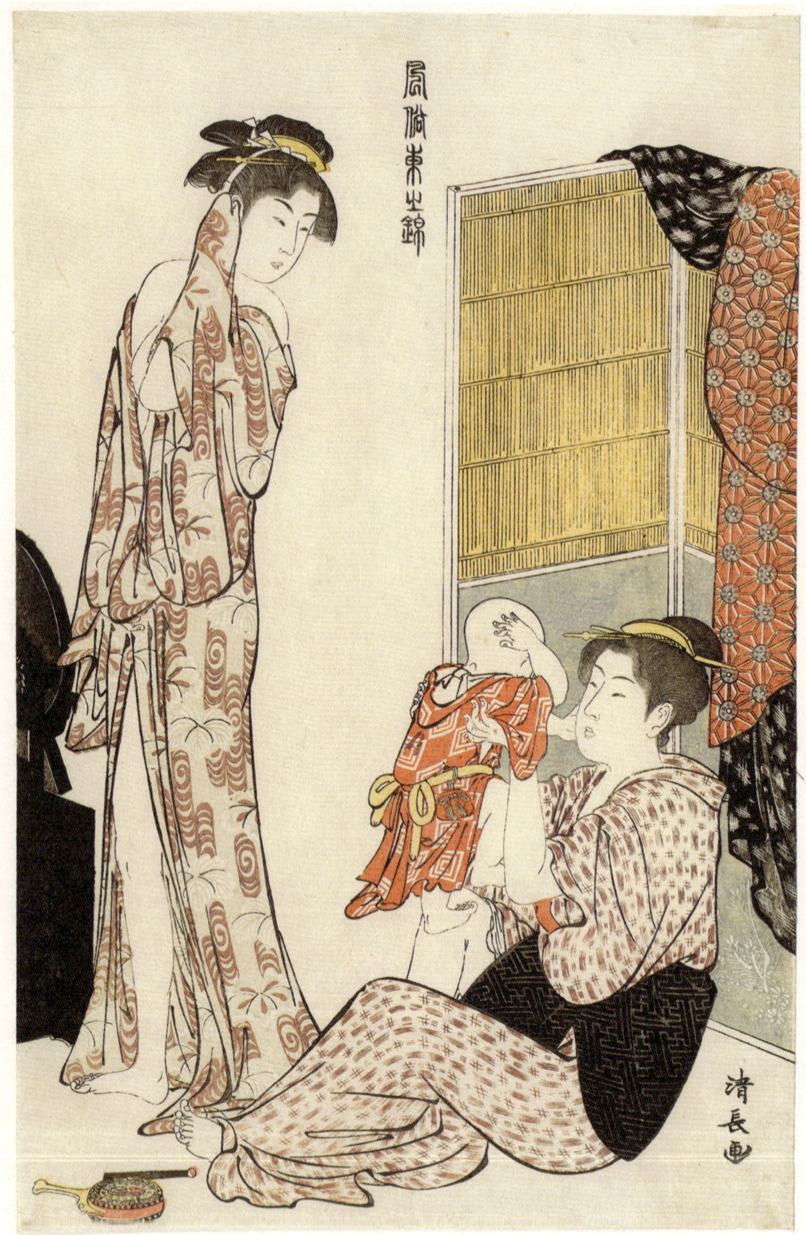

Torii Kiyonaga (1752–1815)
Woman in Bathrobe and Mother Playing with Baby, from the series Current Manners in Eastern Brocade (*Fuzoku Azuma no nishiki*), c. 1785 (Tenmei 5)
Woodblock print (nishiki-e); ink and color on paper
Vertical oban; 10 × 15¼ in. (25.5 × 38.9 cm)

Kiyonaga, the leading designer of prints of women in the 1780s, drew elegantly elongated figures in many appealing scenes from everyday life, often delicately suggestive. Here, a young woman who has just come from the bath wipes her ear with the sleeve of her thin cotton bathrobe, clutching it loosely around her body in a way that allows alluring glimpses of skin. Another woman lounges on the floor playing with a baby, also posed in a somewhat revealing position.

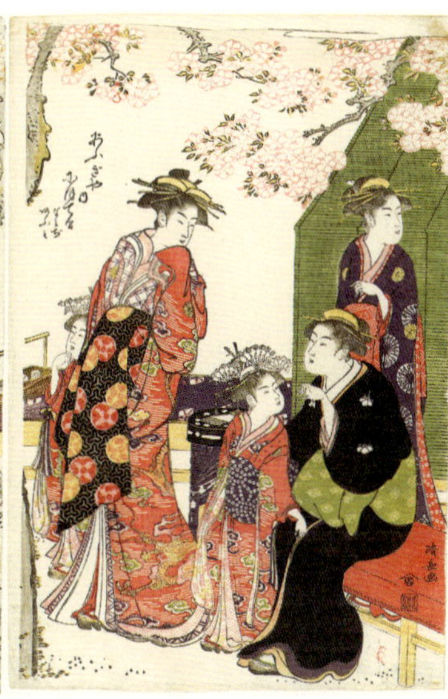
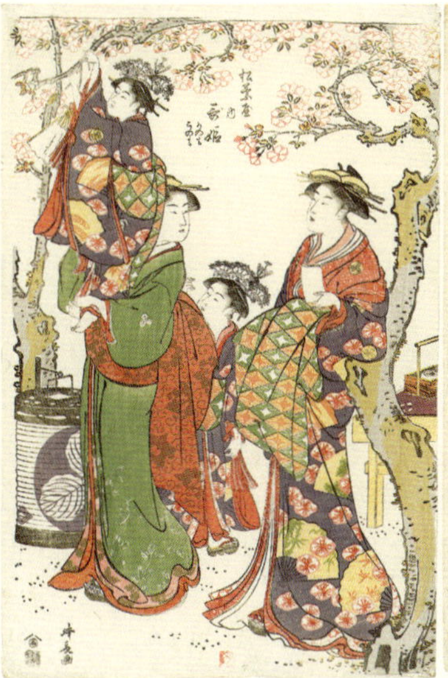
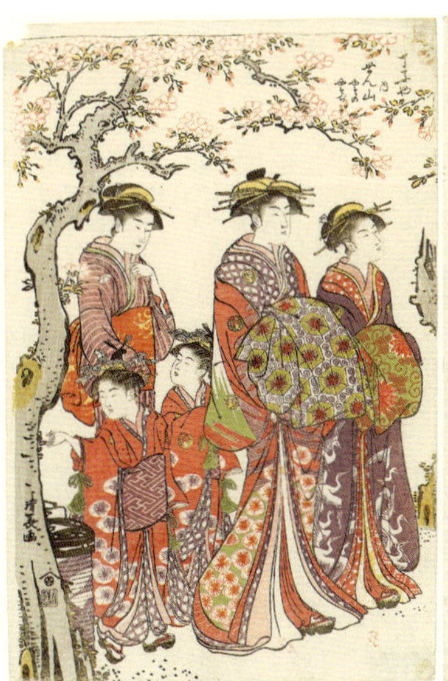

Torii Kiyonaga (1752–1815)
Publisher: Nishimuraya Yohachi (Eijudo)
Courtesans Viewing Cherry Blossoms: Nioteru of the Ogiya, kamuro Namiji and Omi (R); Utahime of the Matsubaya, kamuro Kanomo and Konomo (C); Senzan of the Chojiya, kamuro Yasono and Yasoji (L), 1785 (Tenmei 5)
Woodblock print (nishiki-e); ink and color on paper
Vertical oban triptych; 30¾ × 15½ in. (78.1 × 39.4 cm)

Every spring, live cherry trees were planted along the main street of the Yoshiwara for the duration of the blossoming season; the beauty of the courtesans was often compared to the beauty of the flowers. This triptych—one scene spread over three sheets of paper—shows three of the most prominent courtesans, each dressed in elaborate finery and accompanied by two *kamuro* (child attendants) in matching costumes, as well as other attendants. In the center sheet, a *kamuro* ties a fan inscribed with a poem to one of the flowering branches.

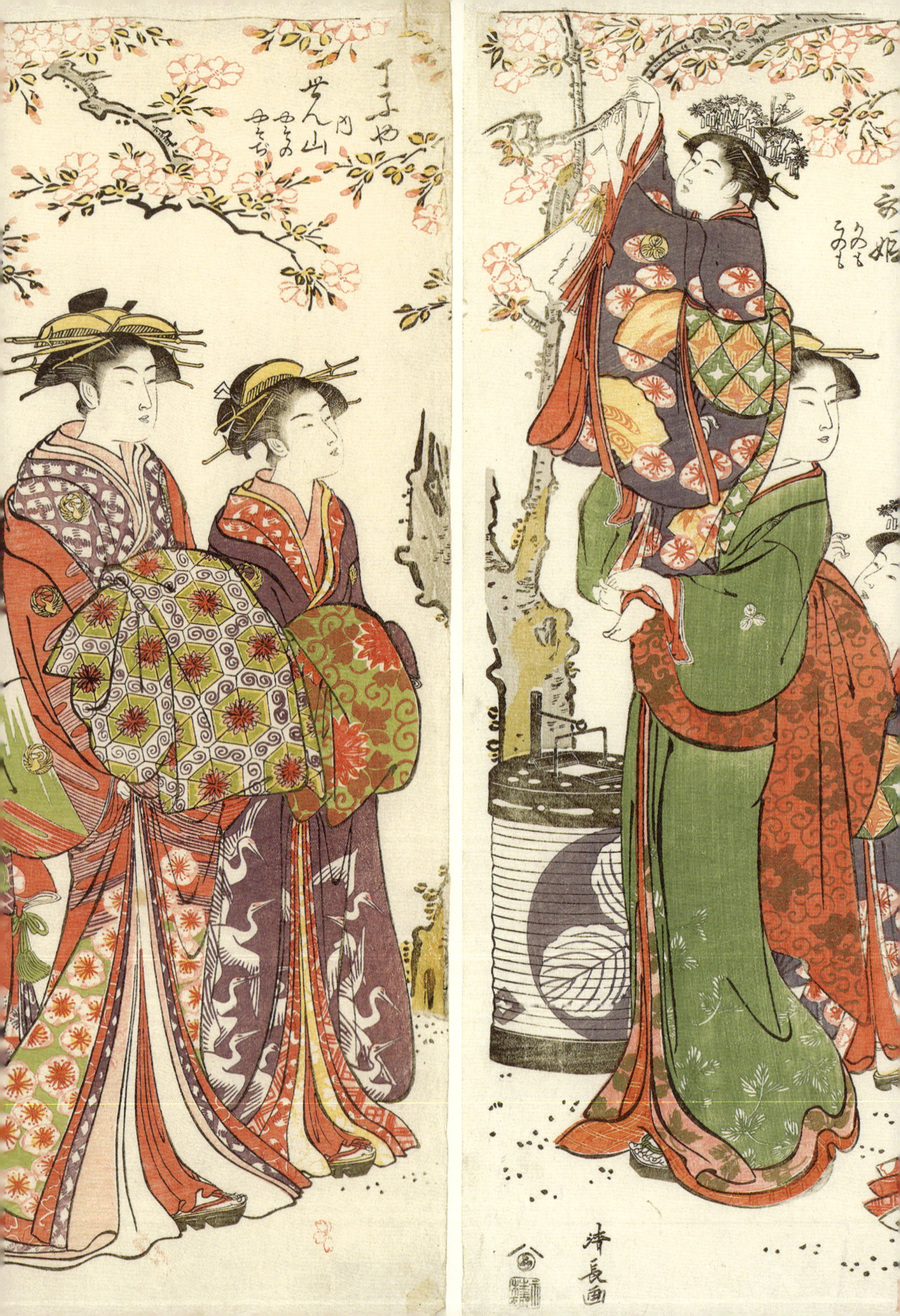
丁子や
内
せん山
清長画

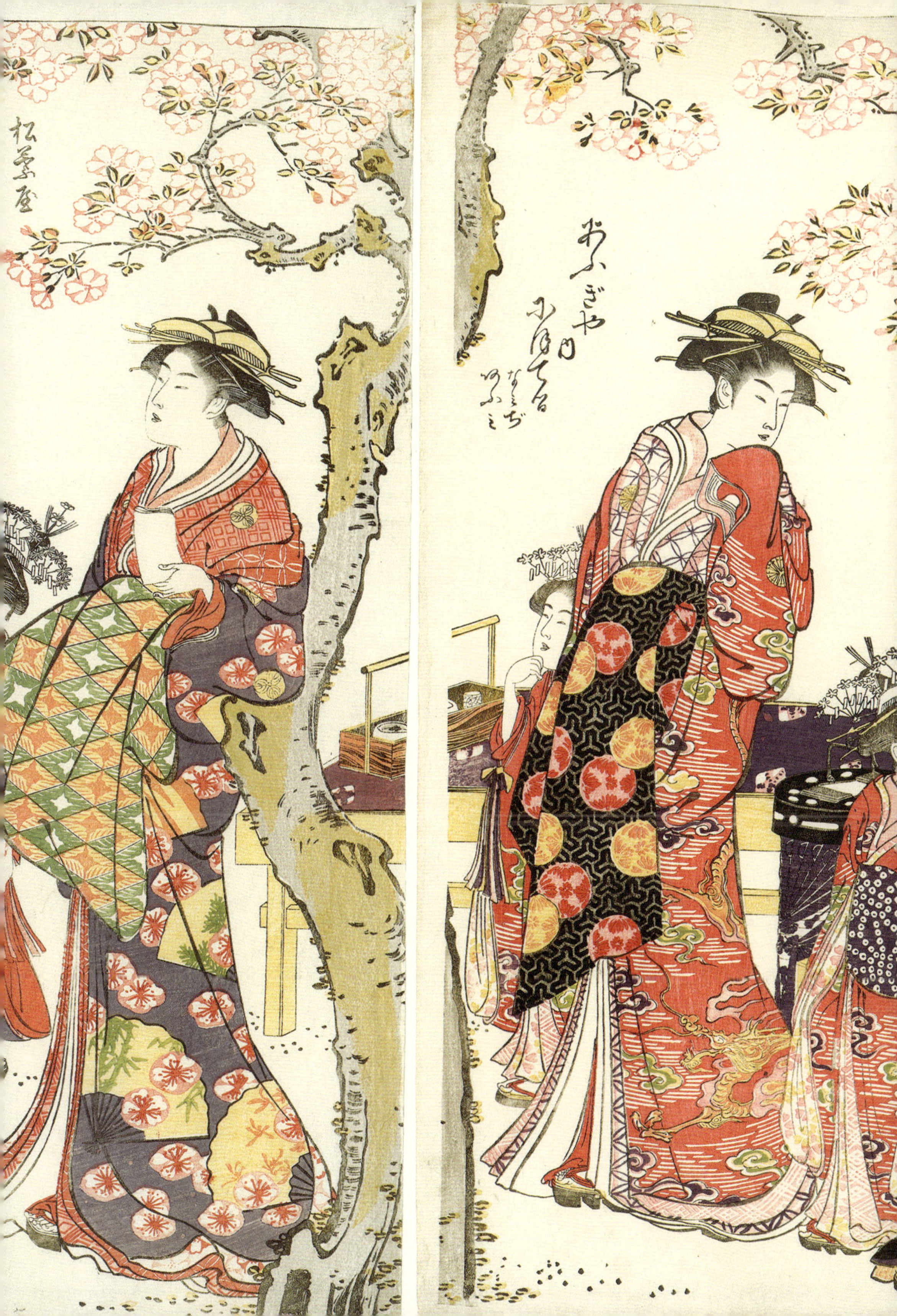
松葉屋
おふぎや

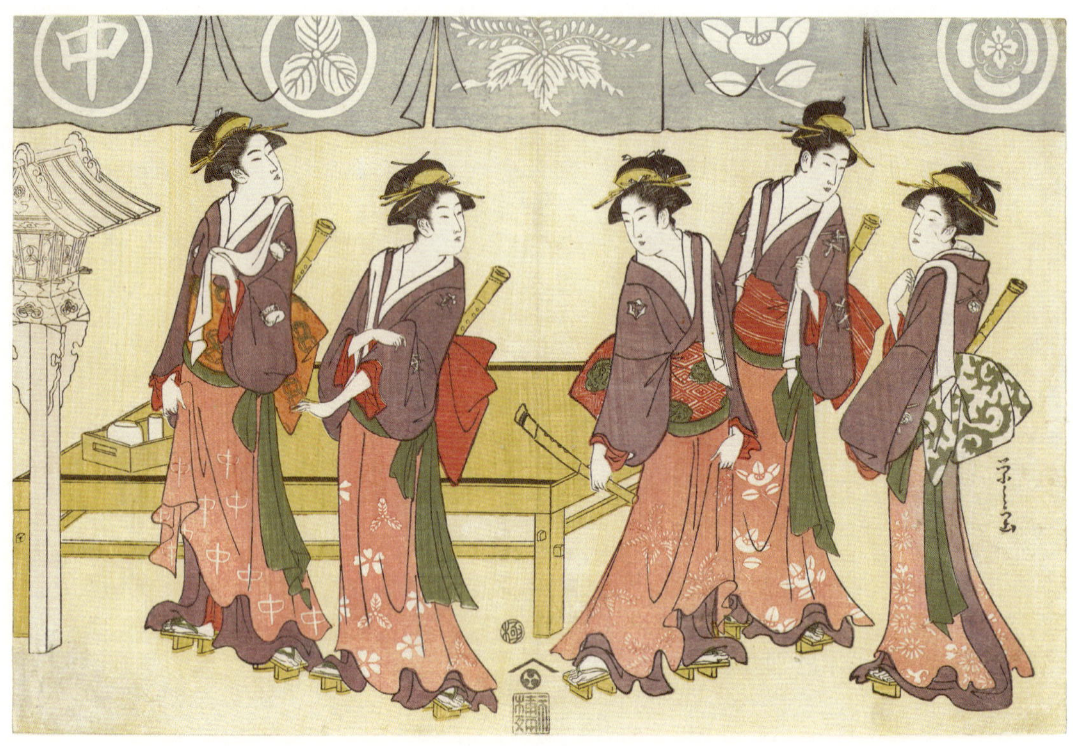

Chobunsai Eishi (1756–1829)
Publisher: Nishimuraya Yohachi (Eijudo)
Five Teahouse Waitresses as the Five Men of the Karigane Gang, c. 1793 (Kansei 5)
Woodblock print (nishiki-e); ink and color on paper
Horizontal oban; 14⅞ × 9¾ in. (37.6 × 24.8 cm)

The five men of Karigane Bunshichi's criminal gang, executed in Osaka in 1701, were romanticized as swashbuckling heroes in later kabuki plays. In Eishi's joking reference to the popular theme, five lovely young women who worked as waitresses in Edo teahouses in his own day are compared to the legendary outlaws. They wear their teahouse aprons and carry the bamboo flutes that were a fashion accessory for the original five men, with identifying crests on their clothing and on the curtains overhead.

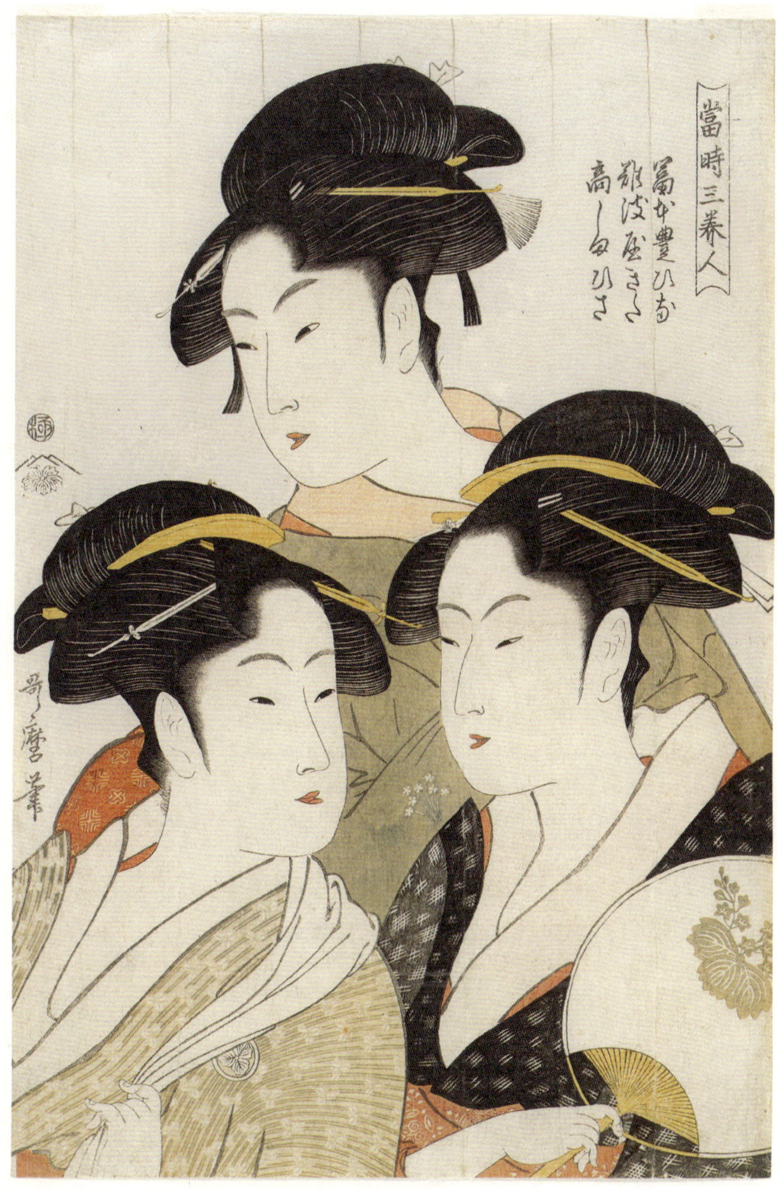

Kitagawa Utamaro I
(early 1750s–1806)
Publisher: Tsutaya
Juzaburo (Koshodo)
Three Beauties of the Present Day (Toji san bijin): Tomimoto Toyohina, Naniwaya Kita, Takashima Hisa, c. 1793 (Kansei 5)
Woodblock print (nishiki-e); ink and color on paper
Vertical oban; 9⅞ × 14¾ in. (25 × 37.5 cm)

Most beautiful women in ukiyo-e are drawn with generic pretty faces, but Utamaro sometimes experimented with individualized portraiture for women as well as kabuki actors. In this comparison of three young women considered to be among the greatest beauties in Edo at the time—a musician and two teahouse waitresses—there are subtle differences in the outlines of their faces and the shape of their features. The portraits are set off by a background of shiny mica.

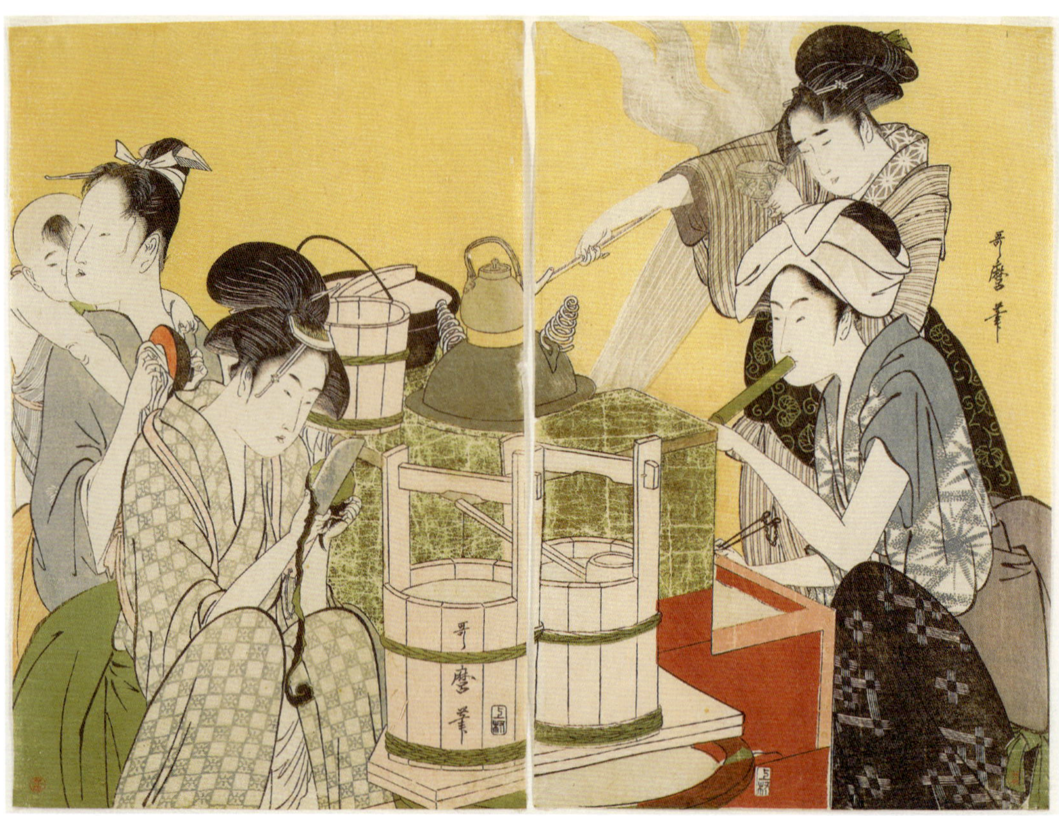

Kitagawa Utamaro I
(early 1750s–1806)
Publisher: Uemura Yohei
Kitchen Scene, c. 1794–95
(Kansei 6–7)
Woodblock print (nishiki-e);
ink and color on paper
Vertical oban diptych;
20¼ × 15 in. (51.3 × 38 cm)

Utamaro's women are so attractive that they make even kitchen work look glamorous. To the right, a woman whose hair is protected by a white scarf heats up the stove by blowing through a bamboo tube onto the fire inside, while another woman winces away from the smoke. In the left sheet of the diptych, another woman peels a piece of fruit, and a young mother is distracted by her child as she wipes a lacquer bowl.

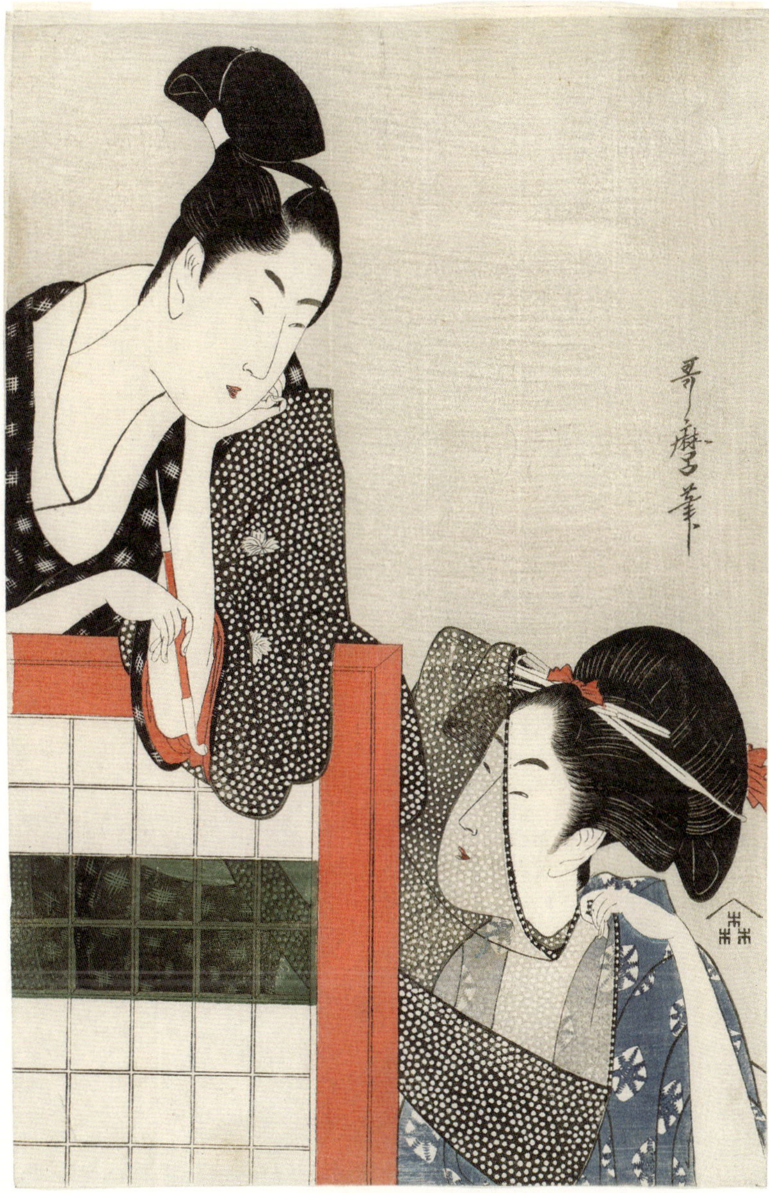

Kitagawa Utamaro I
(early 1750s–1806)
Publisher: Moriya Jihei (Kinshindo)
Couple with a Standing Screen, c. 1797 (Kansei 9)
Woodblock print (nishiki-e); ink and color on paper
Vertical oban; 9⅞ × 15 in. (25.1 × 38 cm)

In this charming scene of a flirtatious young couple, Utamaro plays with themes of peeping and transparency. The girl peers up at the boy through the trailing end of his translucent outer jacket, which catches on her hairpins as she holds it to her face. He leans against a standing screen with a green gauze panel through which the pattern of his clothing can be seen, a tribute to the amazing skill of the blockcutters and printers who turned Utamaro's vision into printed reality.

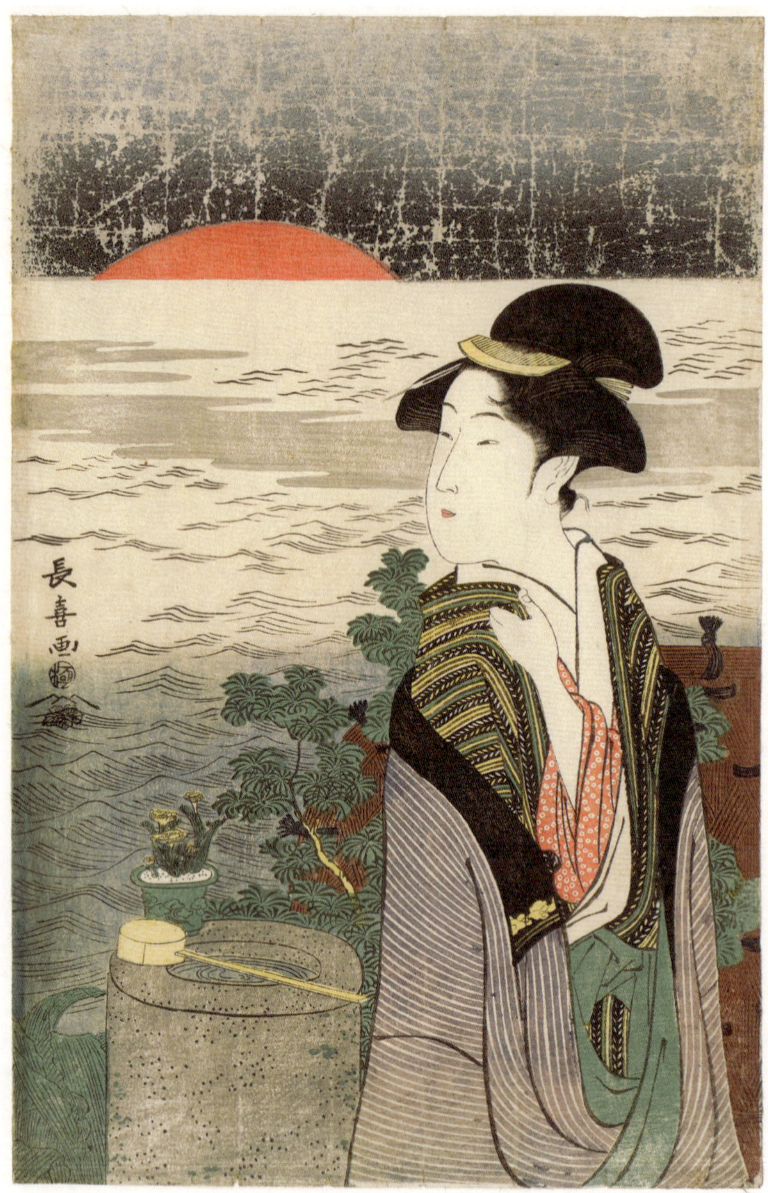

Eishosai Choki (active c. 1780–1810)
Publisher: Tsutaya
Juzaburo (Koshodo)
Sunrise on New Year's Morning,
late 1790s (mid-Kansei era)
Woodblock print (nishiki-e);
ink, color, and mica on paper
Vertical oban; 10⅛ × 15¼ in.
(25.5 × 38.6 cm)

A New Year custom still practiced in Japan today is getting up early on the first day of the year to watch the sun rise. In the chilly air of early morning, a young woman standing in a garden pulls her clothes more tightly around herself as she watches the sun rising from the eastern sea. On the stone washbasin beside her is a potted Adonis plant, a popular New Year decoration that symbolizes long life and good fortune.

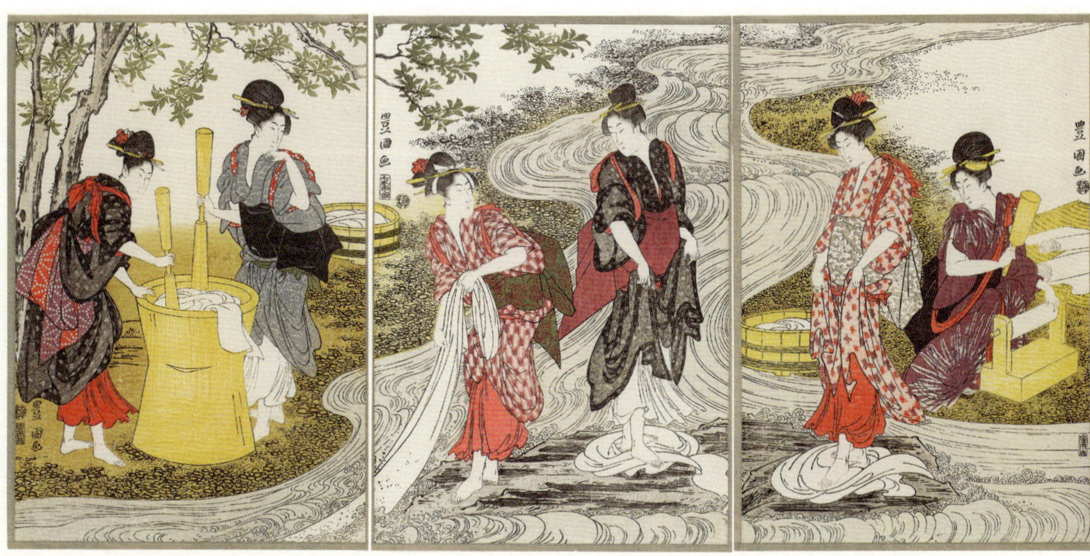

Utagawa Toyokuni I (1769–1825)
Publisher: Izumiya
Ichibei (Kansendo)
The Chofu Jewel River (Chofu no Tamagawa), c. 1795–1801 (late Kansei era)
Woodblock print (nishiki-e); ink and color on paper
Vertical oban triptych,
29¾ × 14¼ in. (75.5 × 36.1 cm)

Toyokuni is best known for his prints of kabuki actors, but he also designed many lovely images of women. This scene of improbably well-dressed beauties rinsing white cloth in a river—and showing off their shapely white legs in the process—plays on the theme of the Six Jewel Rivers, a set of rivers in various parts of Japan that were all named "Jewel River" (Tamagawa) for their clear waters. Chofu, to the west of Edo, was known for producing bleached cloth.

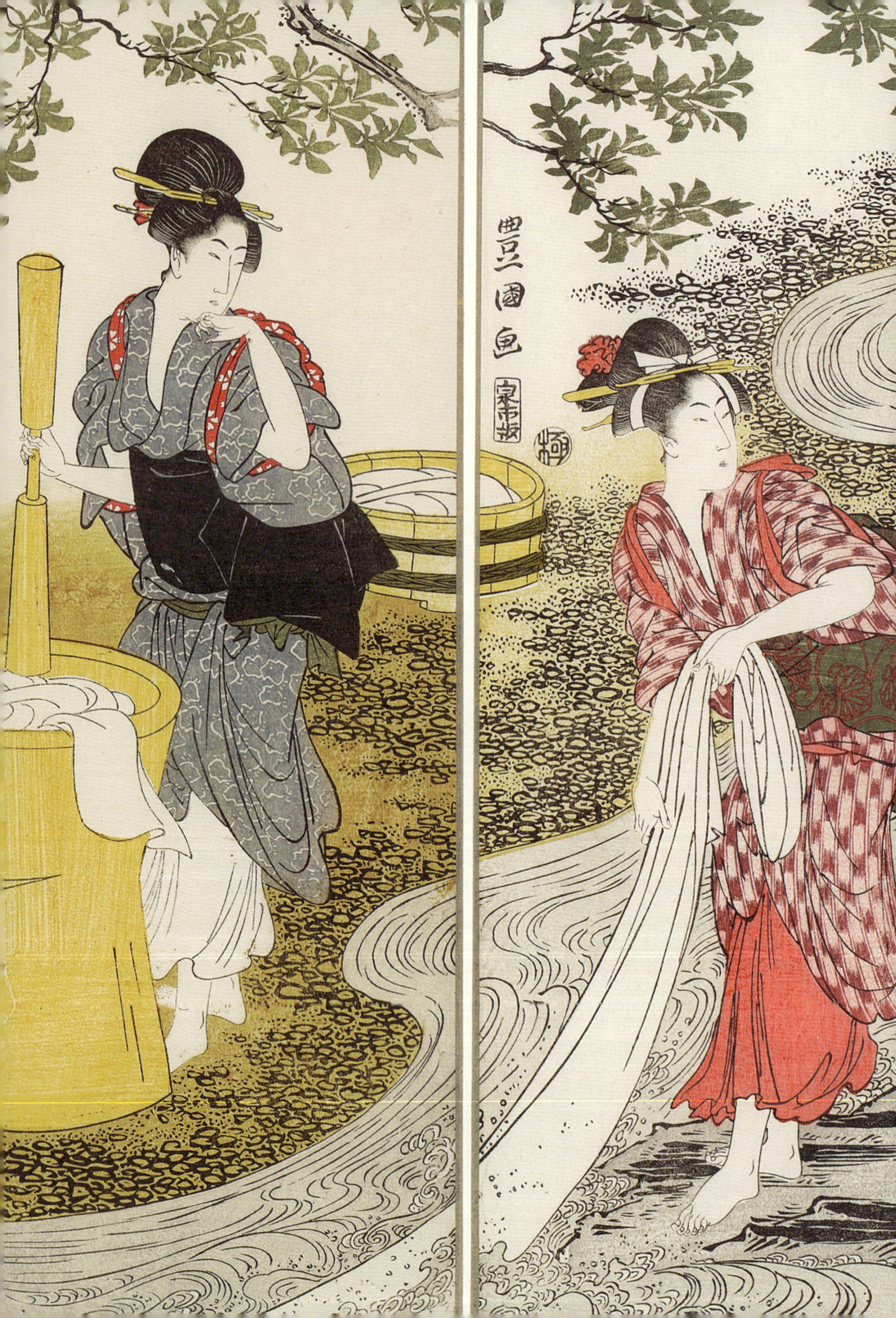
豊国画
泉市板
極

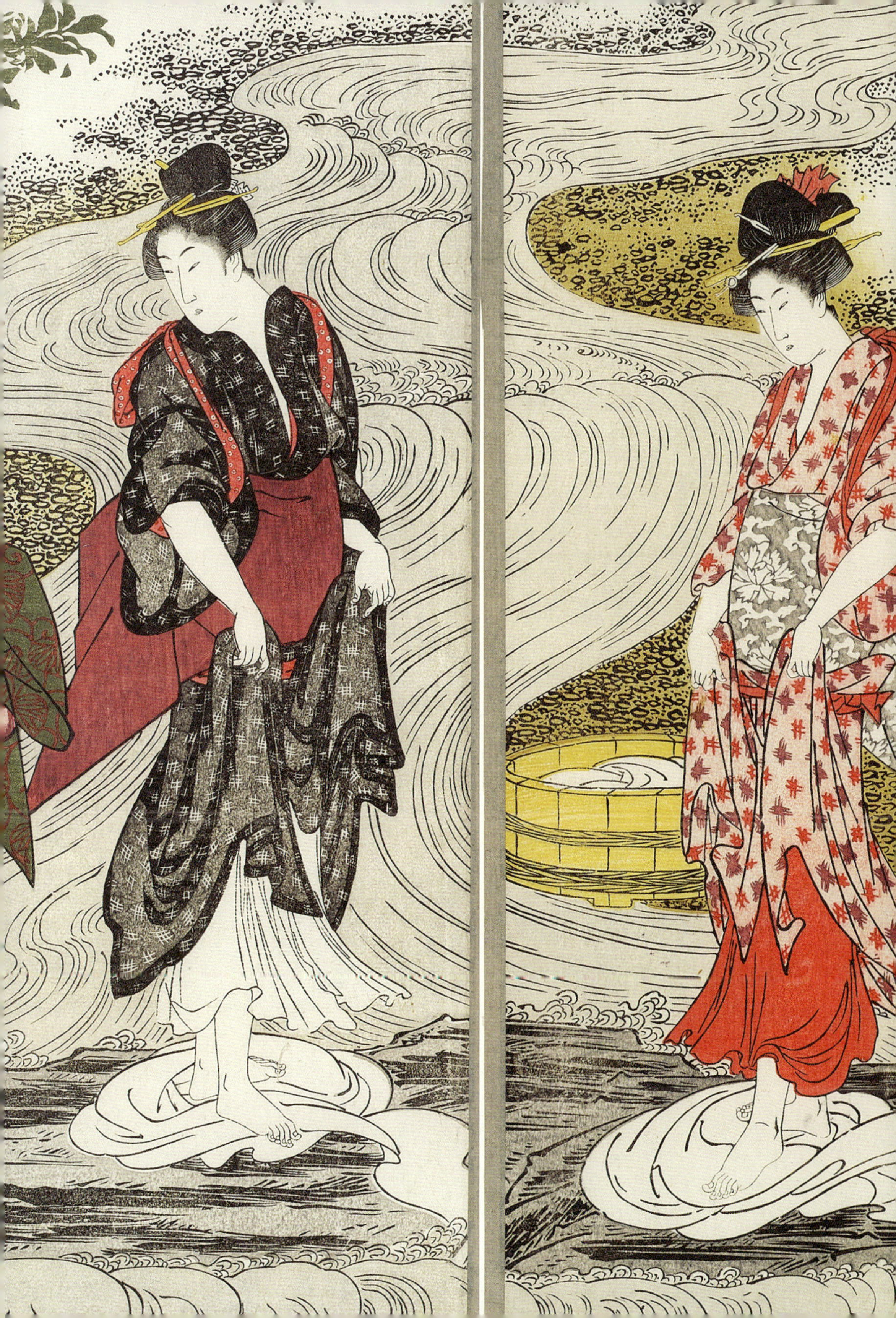

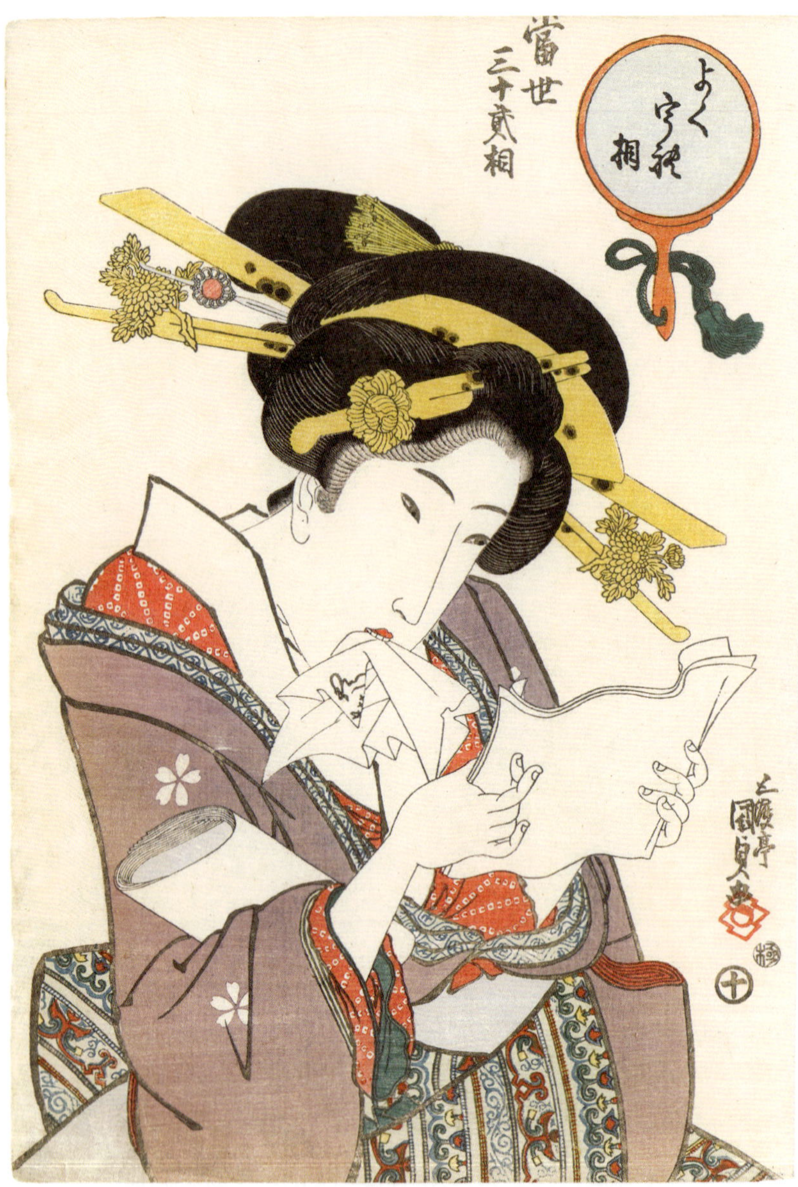

Utagawa Kunisada I
(Toyokuni III) (1786–1864)
Publisher: Nishinomiya Shinroku
The In-demand Type (Yoku ureso), from the series
Thirty-two Physiognomic Types in the Modern World
(*Tosei sanjuni so*), c. 1820
Woodblock print (nishiki-e); ink and color on paper
Vertical oban; 11⅛ × 14½ in.
(28.3 × 36.8 cm)

The design of a magnifying glass that frames the title suggests the instrument used by a professional physiognomist to examine the people whose futures he will predict based on their facial features. This elegantly dressed young woman is most likely a geisha, whose services as a musician, dancer, and party hostess would be in demand for private entertainments. She looks anxious as she scans the letter in her hands—perhaps bad news from a boyfriend.

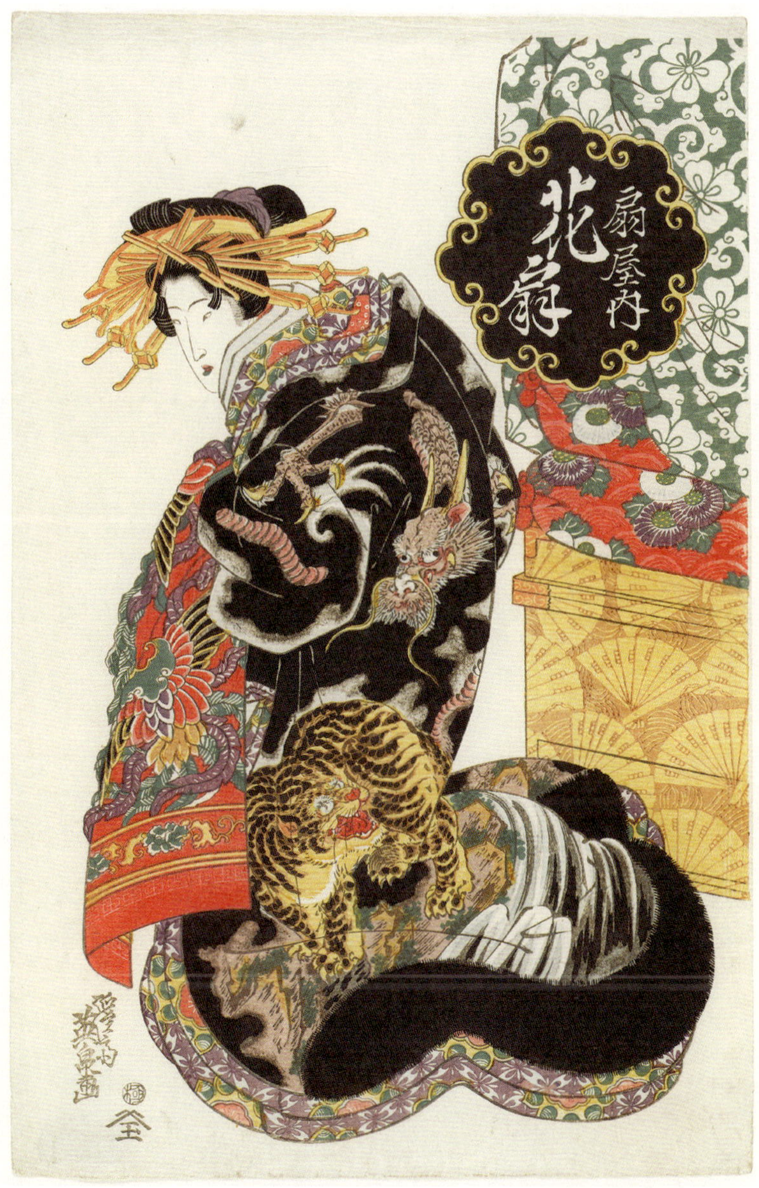

Keisai Eisen (1790–1848)
Hanaogi of the Ogiya, c. 1830
Woodblock print (nishiki-e); ink and color on paper
Vertical oban; 10¼ × 15¾ in. (25.9 × 40 cm)

The professional name Hanaogi (Flower Fan) was traditionally used by the leading courtesan of the Ogiya (House of the Fan). This Hanaogi shows off an especially elaborate costume, which she will probably wear for the New Year parade in which the courtesans showed off their new clothes in the latest fashions. Her *uchikake* (surcoat) is decorated with both a tiger and a dragon, and her red obi is so heavily embroidered that the design stands out in relief.

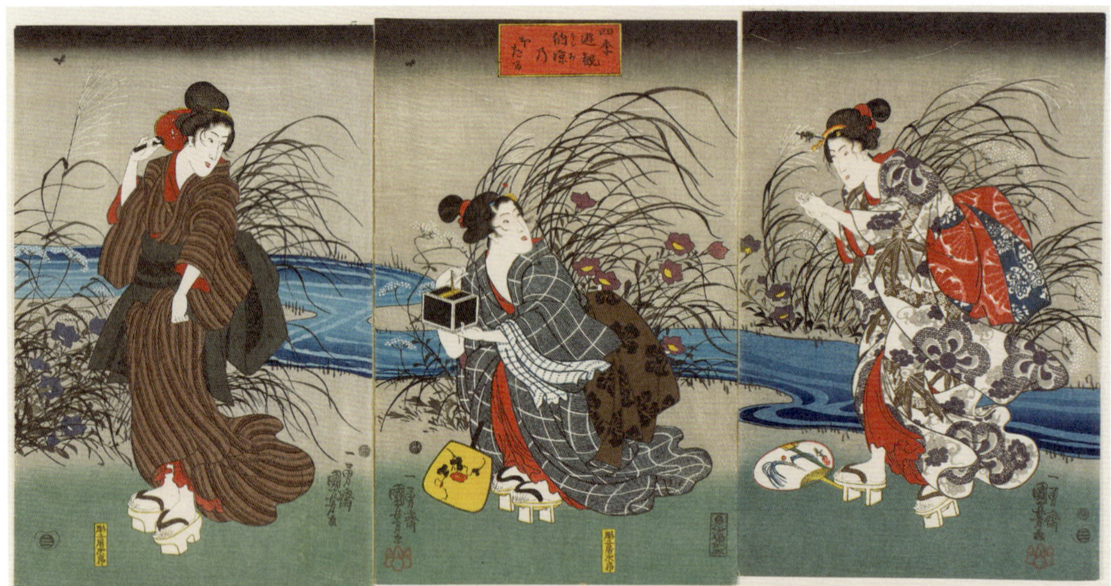

Utagawa Kuniyoshi (1797–1861)
Publisher: Ibaya Senzaburo (Dansendo)
Blockcutter: Matsushima Fusajiro (Horiko Fusajiro, Hori Fusa)
Catching Fireflies in the Cool of the Evening (Suzumi no hotaru), from the series Excursions in the Four Seasons (*Shiki yukan*), 1843–47 (Tenpo 14–Koka 4)
Woodblock print (nishiki-e); ink and color on paper
Vertical oban triptych; 27⅞ × 14¼ in. (70.8 × 36.1 cm)

By the side of a stream on a summer evening, three beautifully dressed young women hunt for fireflies to keep in small bamboo cages. The usual method was to hold out a fan for the insects to light on and then catch them in one's hands. The fan at the lower right, apparently dropped by the young woman who has just made a catch, is signed by the painter and lacquer artist Zeshin, a friend of Kuniyoshi.

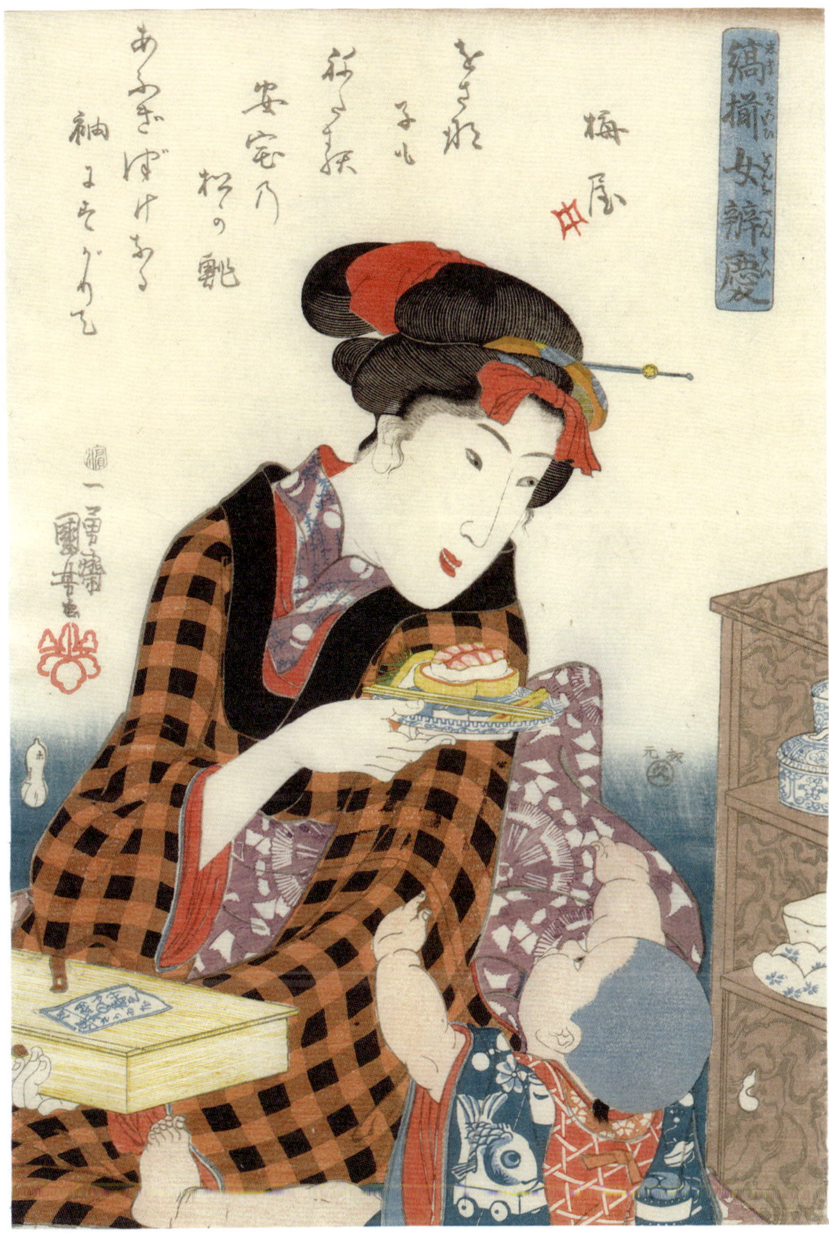

Utagawa Kuniyoshi (1797–1861)
Publisher: Ibaya Kyubei
Takeout Sushi Suggesting Ataka, from the series Women in Benkei-checked Fabrics (*Shimazoroi onna Benkei*), c. 1844 (Tenpo 15/Koka 1)
Woodblock print (nishiki-e); ink and color on paper
Vertical oban; 9¾ × 14 in. (24.6 × 35.5 cm)

A teenage girl with a fashionable red hair bow offers her baby brother a plate of takeout sushi. The checked fabric pattern used for her kimono was named for the historical warrior-priest Benkei, a retainer of Minamoto no Yoshitsune, and this series presents young women wearing checked kimono in situations that suggest incidents in Benkei's life. The address of the sushi shop, written on the box, sounds similar to Ataka, where one of Benkei's most famous adventures took place.

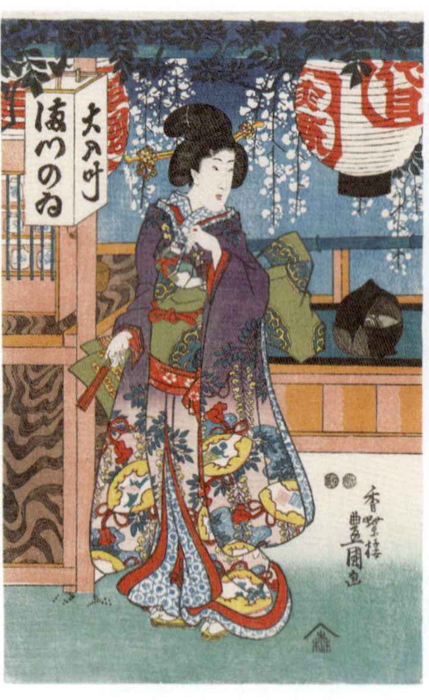

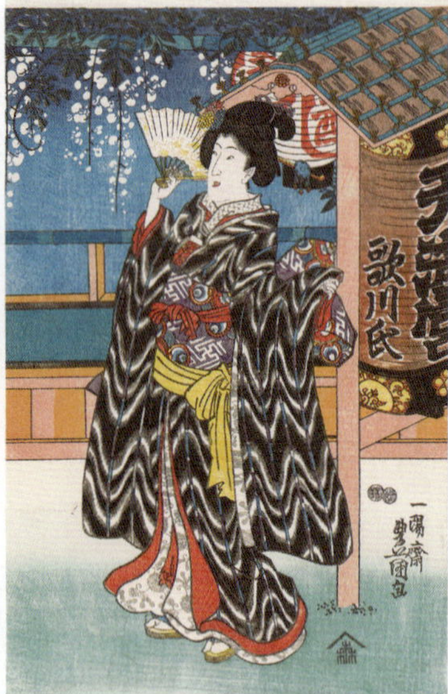

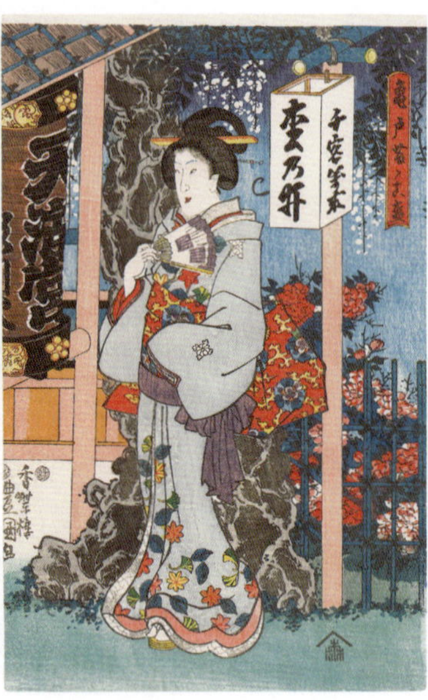

Utagawa Kunisada I
(Toyokuni III) (1786–1864)
Publisher: Moriya Jihei (Kinshindo)
Wisteria in Full Bloom at Kameido
(Kameido fuji no shinsei),
1847–52 (Koka 4–Kaei 5)
Woodblock print (nishiki-e);
ink and color on paper
Vertical oban triptych;
27⅞ × 14½ in. (70.6 × 36.9 cm)

Three young women show off their gorgeous costumes in front of the Matsunoi Teahouse on the grounds of the Kameido Tenjin Shrine, famed for its spectacular wisteria blossoms. The shrine was in the same neighborhood where the artist himself lived at the time, and the two votive lanterns displayed under their own small roof are gifts from the Utagawa family. To the left are two unmarried women in long-sleeved kimono (*furisode*), accompanied by a married woman at the right, who wears shorter sleeves.

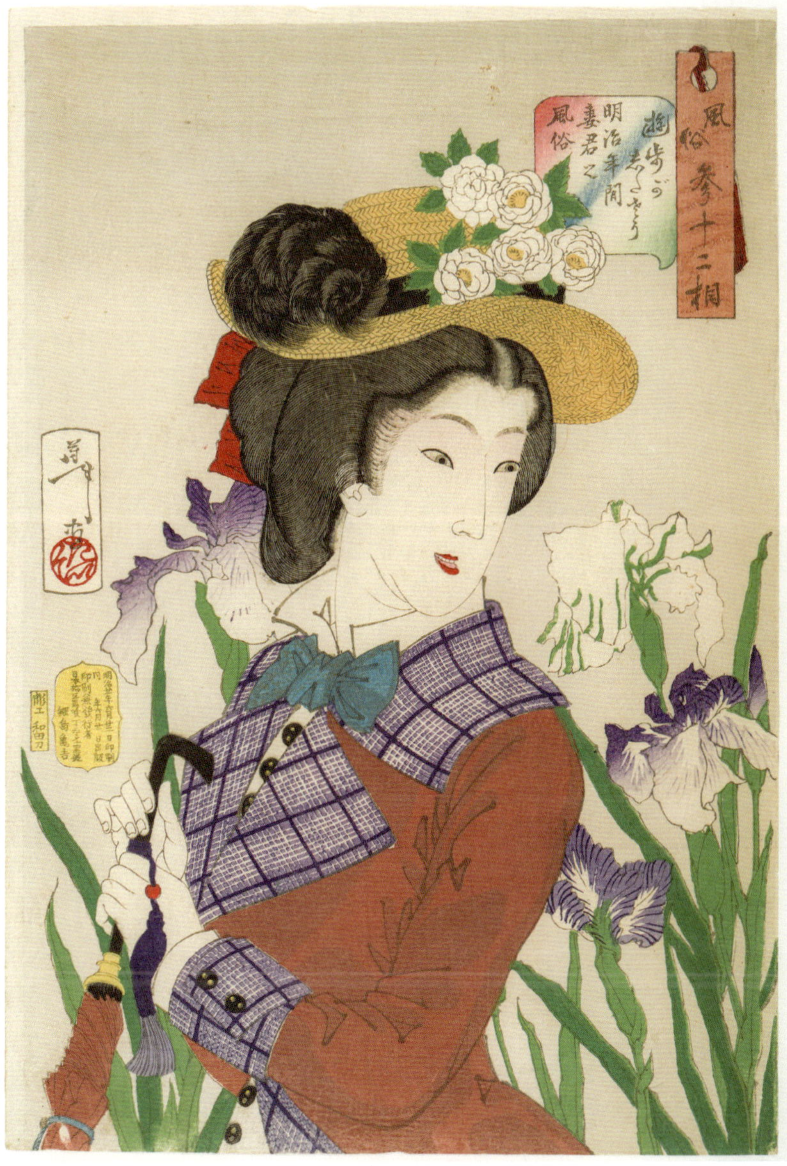

Tsukioka Yoshitoshi (1839–1892)
Publisher: Tsunajima Kamekichi
Looking as if She Wants to Go for a Walk: The Fashion of a Married Woman of the Meiji Era (Yuho ga shitaso, Meiji nenkan saikun no fuzoku), from the series Thirty-two Appearances of Fashion (*Fuzoku sanjuni so*), 1888 (Meiji 21), June 22
Woodblock print (nishiki-e); ink and color on paper
Vertical oban; 9⅞ × 14½ in. (25.1 × 36.8 cm)

By the late 1880s, a few upper-class Japanese women were beginning to wear Western-style clothing occasionally. The fashion was encouraged by the Meiji empress, who wanted foreign women such as the wives of diplomats at the court to see what gorgeous clothing could be made from Japanese silk, her country's most important export. Yoshitoshi's elegant lady holds a parasol as she poses in a garden, in front of purple irises that match the lapels of her jacket.

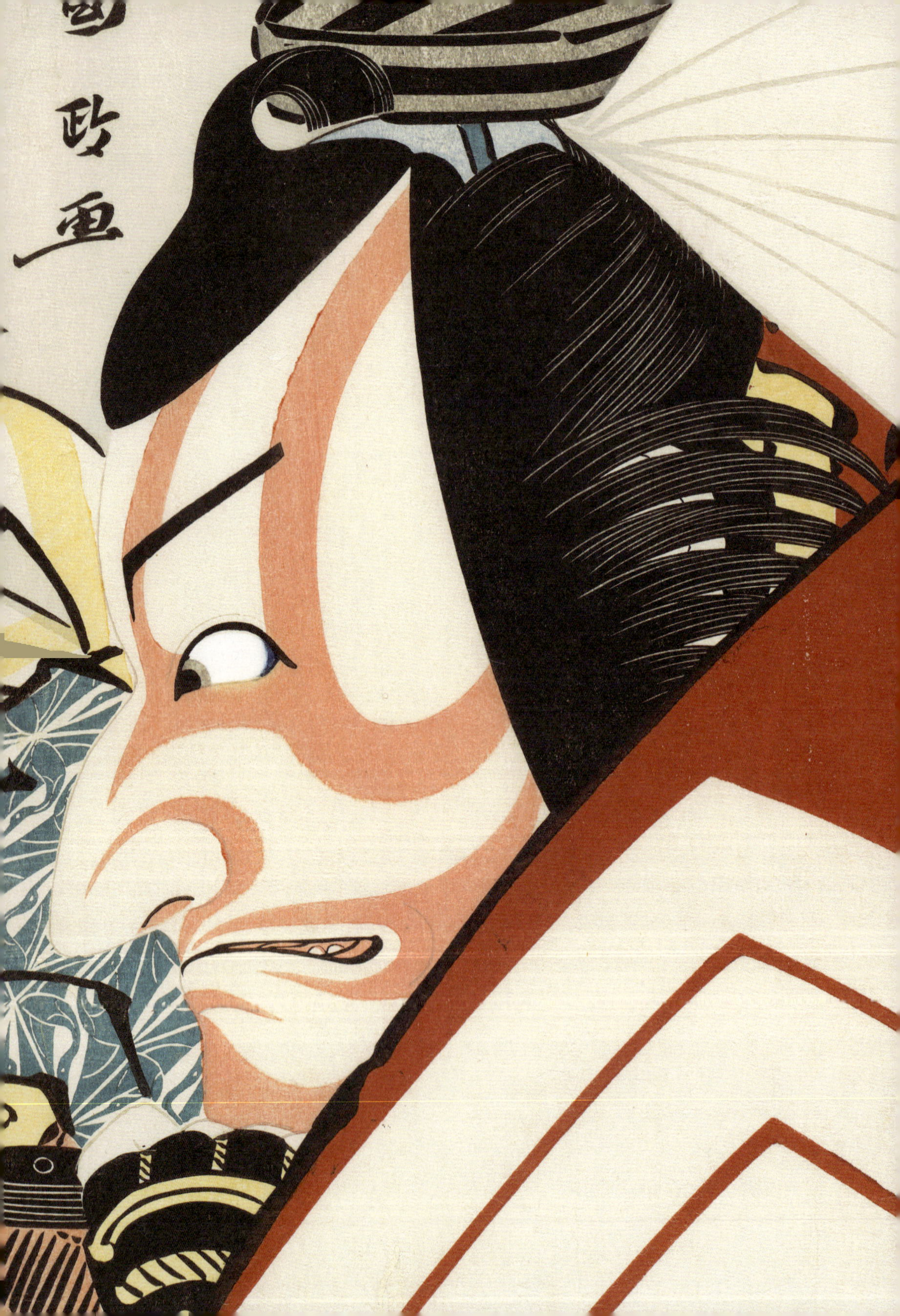
政画

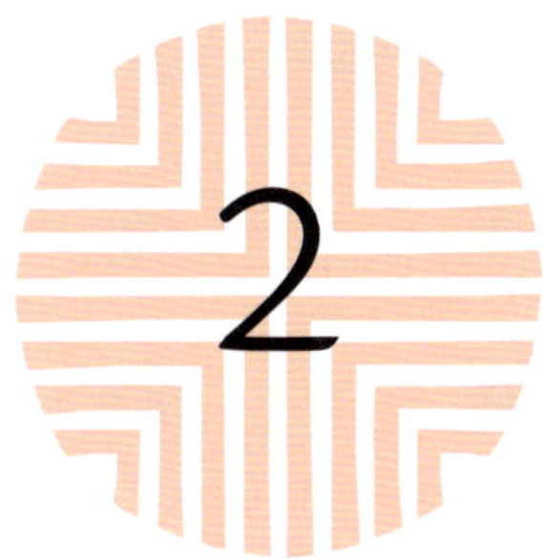

The Kabuki Theater

By far the most common subject matter in woodblock prints of the Edo period was the kabuki theater, which combined the appeal of movies, television, stage plays, and popular music all rolled into one glorious, flamboyant package. Woodblock prints were the perfect souvenir for fans to recall favorite past performances, dream happily of performances to come, or perhaps imagine meeting a favorite star in real life.

Kabuki was founded in Kyoto at the beginning of the seventeenth century by a woman: the renowned dancer Okuni of Izumo, whose troupe of both women and men performed popular variety shows with musical numbers and comic skits. Many changes took place as kabuki evolved over the following decades, and by the 1690s when kabuki prints began to be made, it had become an all-male theatrical form featuring lengthy plays with complex plots, elaborate costuming, and ingenious special effects. Performances lasted all day and usually included several different featured plays, with music-and-dance interludes sometimes inserted into other, longer plays.

Women were permitted to act only in private theatricals; in public performances, all parts were filled by men who wore the standard adult male hairstyle of a shaved forehead and crown. When playing female roles, they used wigs, often with a purple scarf across the forehead to symbolize the shaven head beneath. Actors used stage names indicating their affiliation with an acting family, a lineage to which they were related by blood, adoption, or both. These names would be passed on to worthy successors, so that one actor might have several names during his career and the same name might be used in succession by a series of actors, indicated by generational numbers.

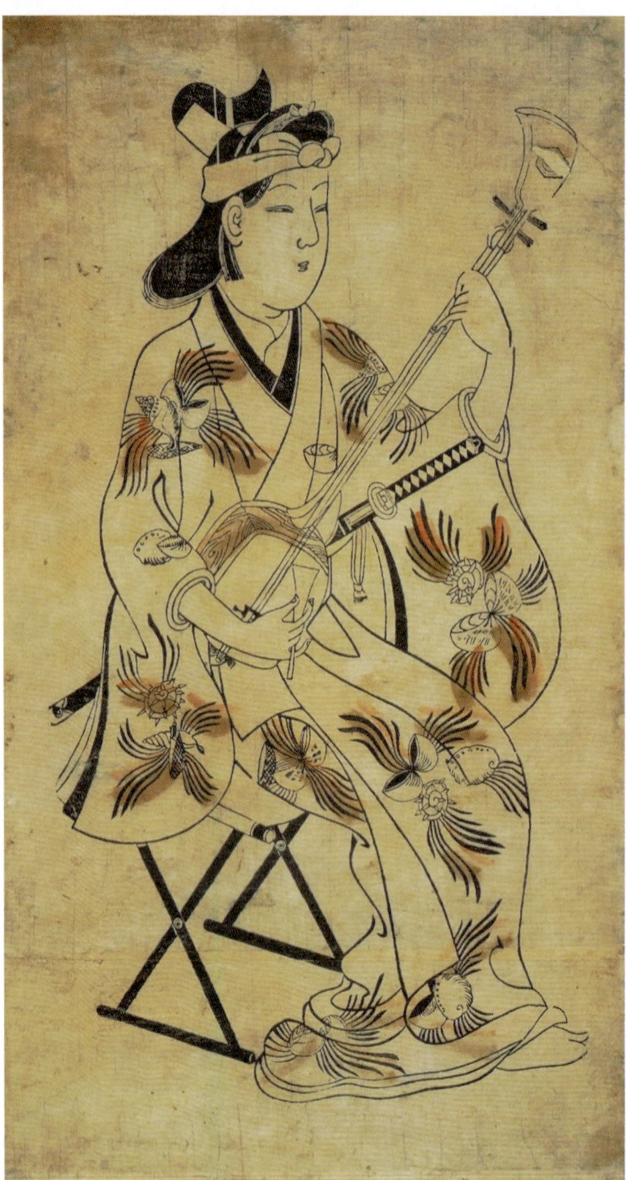

Unknown artist
Young Kabuki Actor Playing a Shamisen, c. 1680–90
Woodblock print (tan-e); ink on paper, with hand-applied color
Vertical o-oban; 12½ × 23⅛ in. (37.1 × 58.7 cm)

In the 1630s and '40s, attractive teenage boys such as this one, who shaved the top of the head but not the forelock, were the top stars of kabuki. But by the time this print was made decades later, only adult men with shaven foreheads could legally become actors. The handsome young musician providing background music may be in a private theatrical performance rather than a public one; he may be wearing a wig; or the print may be a nostalgic reference to the earlier days of kabuki.

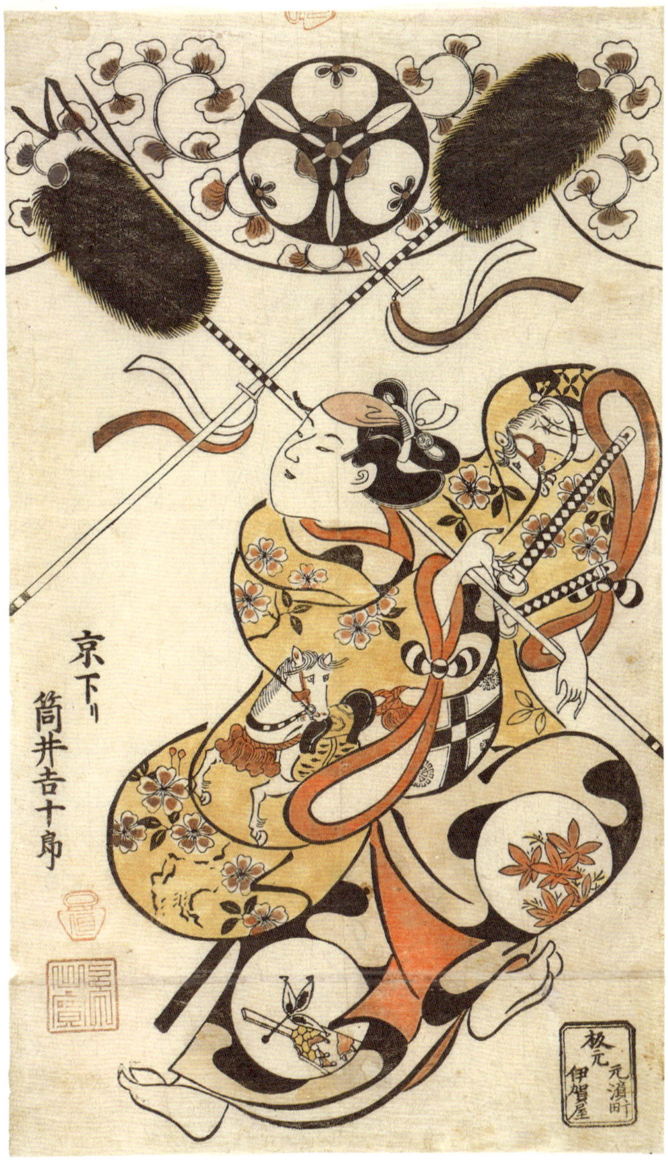

Attributed to Torii Kiyonobu I, 1664–1729
Publisher: Igaya Kan'emon (Bunkido)
Actor Tsutsui Kichijuro in the Spear Dance, 1704 (Genroku 17/Hoei 1), 11th month
Woodblock print (tan-e); ink on paper, with hand-applied color
Vertical o-oban; 12½ × 21 in. (31.8 × 53.5 cm)

This unsigned work is attributed to the founder of the Torii school, which dominated the field of actor prints throughout the first half of the eighteenth century. Large works such as this one served as affordable substitutes for more expensive paintings. The actor's headscarf—originally purple in color but now somewhat faded—conceals his shaven forehead as he dances energetically with two spears, their points covered with decorative pompoms. His personal crest appears on the curtain overhead.

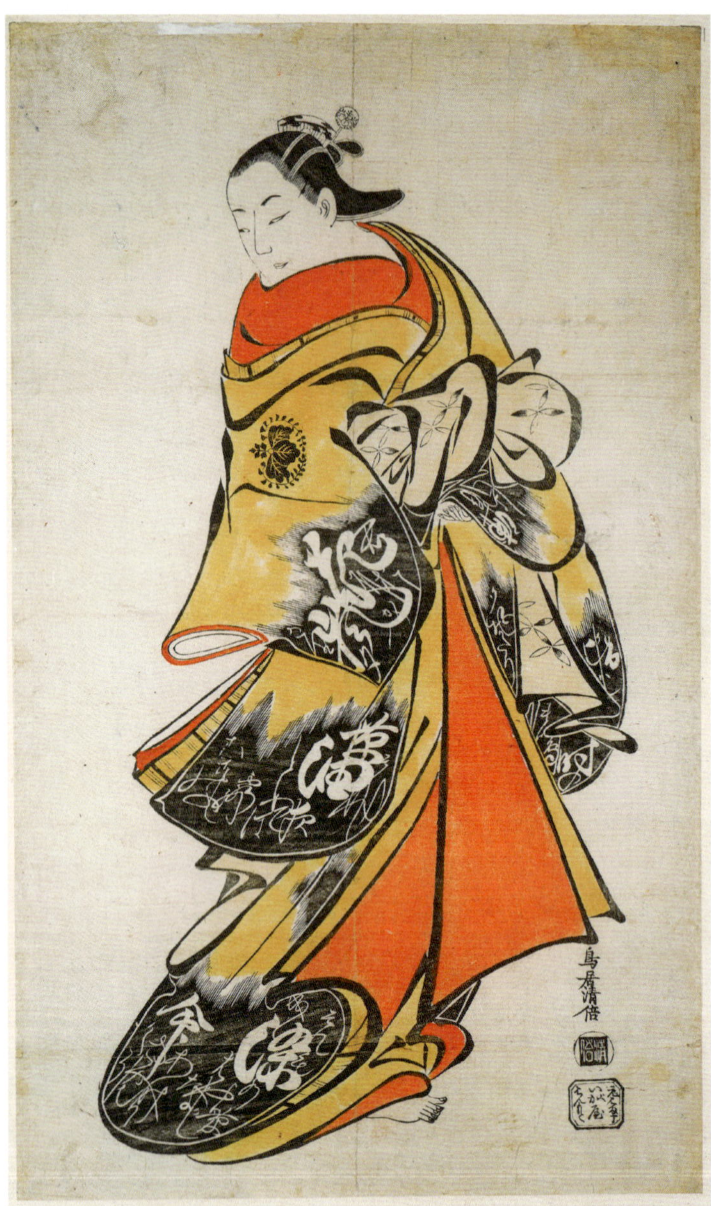

Torii Kiyomasu I (active c. 1696–1716)
Publisher: Igaya Kan'emon (Bunkido)
Actor Fujimura Handayu II as Oiso no Tora, c. 1715 (Shotoku 5)
Woodblock print (tan-e); ink on paper, with hand-applied color
Vertical o-oban; 12½ × 20½ in. (31.7 × 52 cm)

The print appears to show a beautiful courtesan glancing seductively back over her shoulder; but the crest on the sleeve—a paulownia leaf in a garland of flowers—is that of the kabuki actor Fujimura Handayu II, who specialized in female roles. He is most likely playing the courtesan Oiso no Tora, the lover of the young warrior Soga no Juro, in a production for the New Year of 1715. The kimono is decorated with elegant phrases found in love letters.

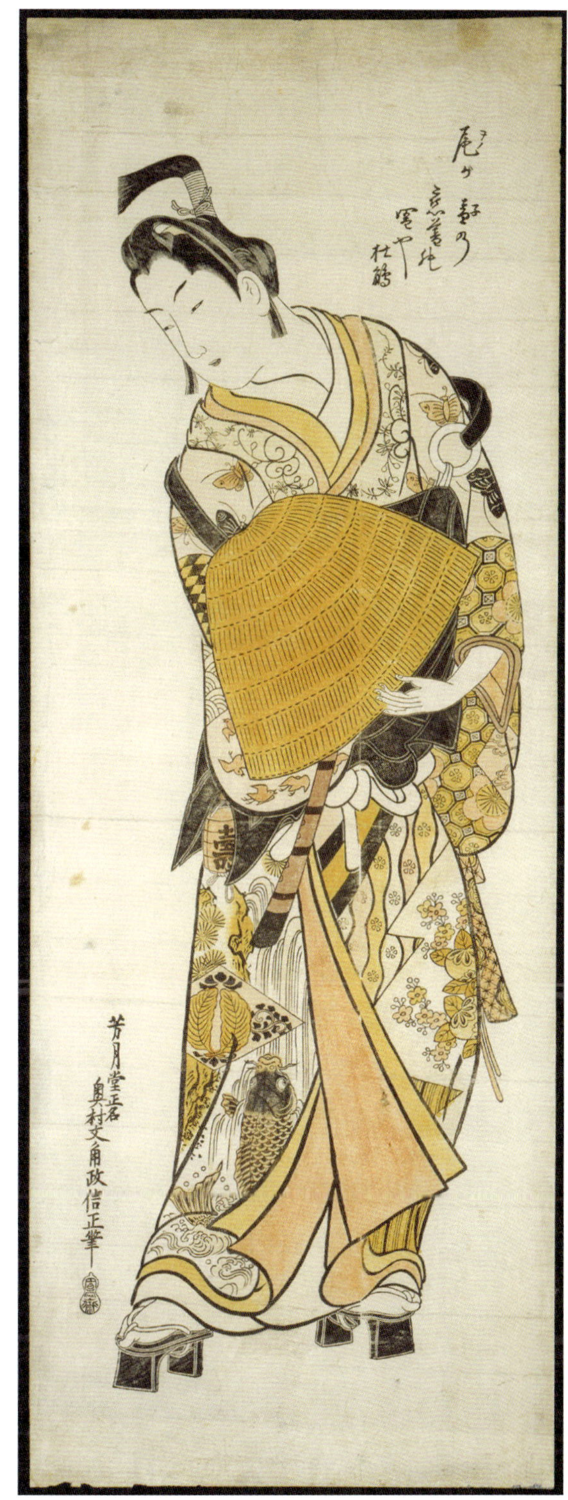

Okumura Masanobu (1686–1764)
Actor Onoe Kikugoro I as Soga no Goro dressed as a Komuso, c. 1744–51 (Enkyo 1–Kan'en 4)
Woodblock print (beni-e); ink on paper, with hand-applied color
Wide hashira-e; 10 × 27¼ in. (25.6 × 69.2 cm)

In the 1740s, hand-painted prints became especially elaborate because they were now in competition with early color printing. This beautiful example shows heartthrob actor Onoe Kikugoro I as the young warrior Soga no Goro, disguised as a mendicant priest (*komuso*) with a black priest's stole, a basket-weave hat, and a bamboo flute. He played this role in at least three different productions. The short poem at the upper right suggests that the flute plays a melody of love.

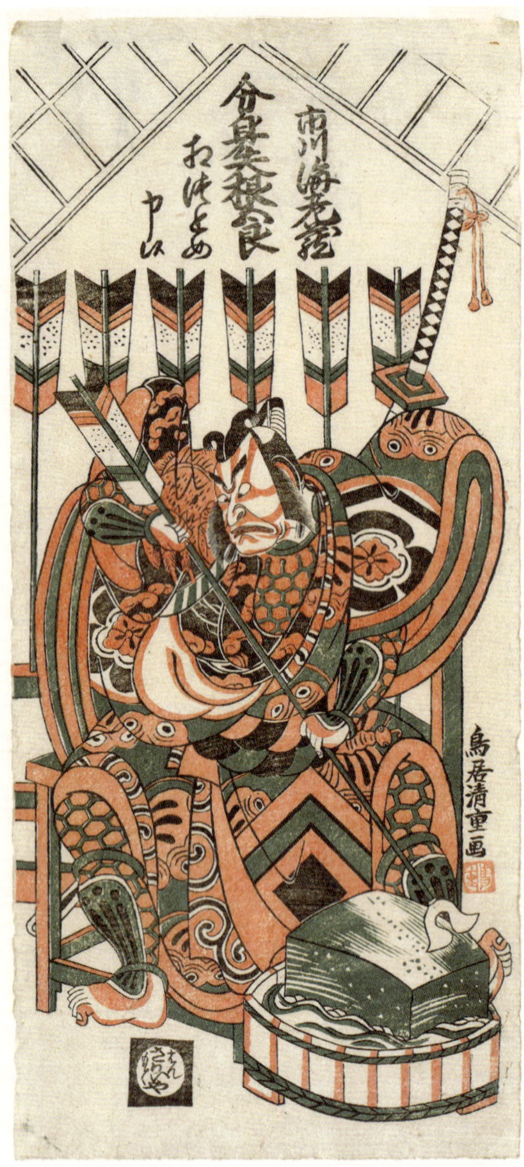

Torii Kiyoshige (active 1720–1760)
Publisher: Sakaiya Kurobei
Actor Ichikawa Ebizo II as Bunshin Yanone Goro, 1754 (Horeki 4), 1st month
Woodblock print (benizuri-e); ink and limited color on paper
Hosoban; 5¾ × 12½ in. (14.6 × 31.6 cm)

From the 1740s to the 1760s, simple color printing became increasingly prominent in ukiyo-e, gradually replacing hand-painted prints. Vividly colored in red and green, this print shows a scene from the well-known tale of the Soga brothers, who devoted their lives to avenging the murder of their father. Goro, the impetuous younger brother, is using a whetstone in a tub of water to sharpen a gigantic arrow. The "Arrow Sharpening" scene, used in various Soga plays, became a specialty of the Ichikawa acting family.

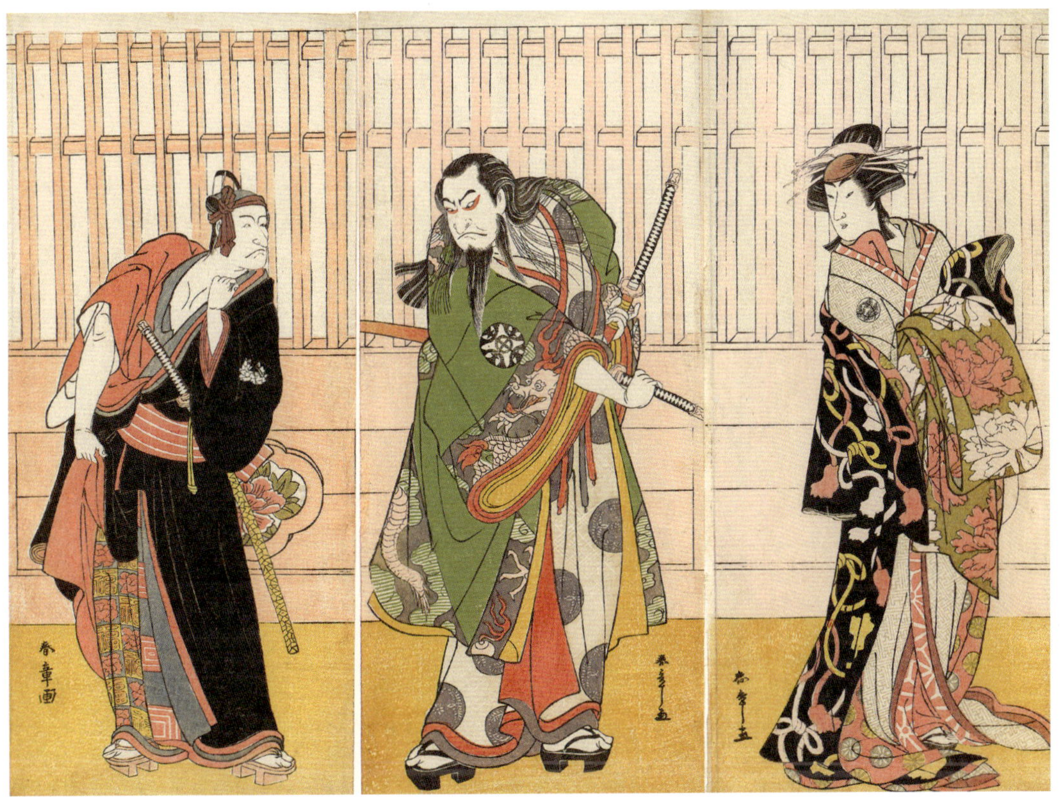

Katsukawa Shunsho (1726–1792)
Actors, from right: Nakamura Riko I as Agemaki, Nakamura Nakazo I as Hige no Ikyu, and Ichikawa Danjuro V as Sukeroku, 1782 (Tenmei 2), 1st month or 5th month
Woodblock print (nishiki-e); ink and color on paper
Hosoban triptych; 17 × 12¼ in. (43.1 × 31.3 cm)

In the age of full-color prints, Katsukawa Shunsho rose to prominence as the leading designer of actor prints, and his Katsukawa school became dominant in place of the Torii school. Shunsho emphasized the individual facial features of the actors. He often designed sets of prints showing actors from the same play with a continuous background that could be assembled in different ways. Here we see the beautiful courtesan Agemaki (right) and the two men contending for her favors, the villainous samurai Ikyu (center) and the dashing playboy hero Sukeroku (left).

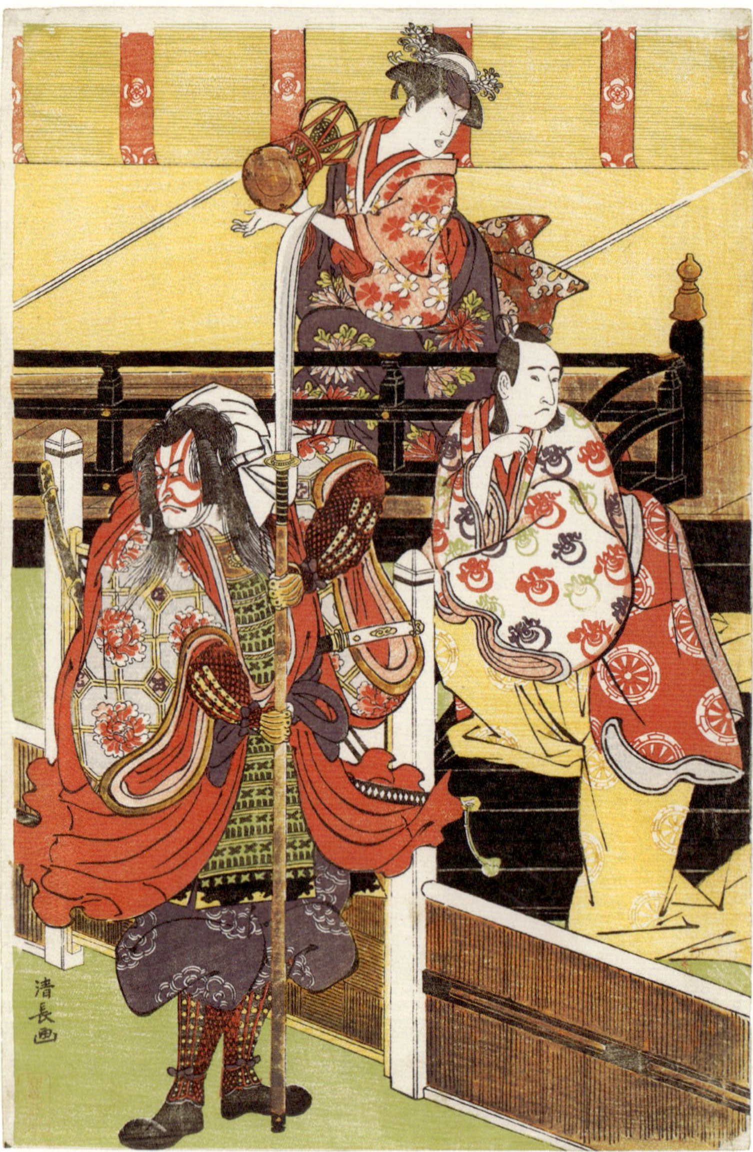

Torii Kiyonaga (1752–1815)
Actors Sawamura Sojuro III as the Fox Tadanobu, Nakayama Tomisaburo I as Shizuka, and Ichikawa Danjuro V as Yokawa Kakuhan, 1784 (Tenmei 4), 7th month
Woodblock print (nishiki-e); ink and color on paper
Vertical oban; 10½ × 15½ in. (26.5 × 39.2 cm)

Kiyonaga was most famous for his prints of beautiful women, but as a leading member of the Torii school, he designed some outstanding actor prints as well. This unusually well-preserved example shows three characters from *The Thousand Cherry Trees of Yoshitsune* (*Yoshitsune senbon zakura*), all searching for the general Minamoto no Yoshitsune, who is in hiding in the mountains of Yoshino: his retainer Tadanobu, actually a shapeshifting fox; his lover, the dancer Shizuka; and the evil priest Kakuhan, actually an enemy general in disguise.

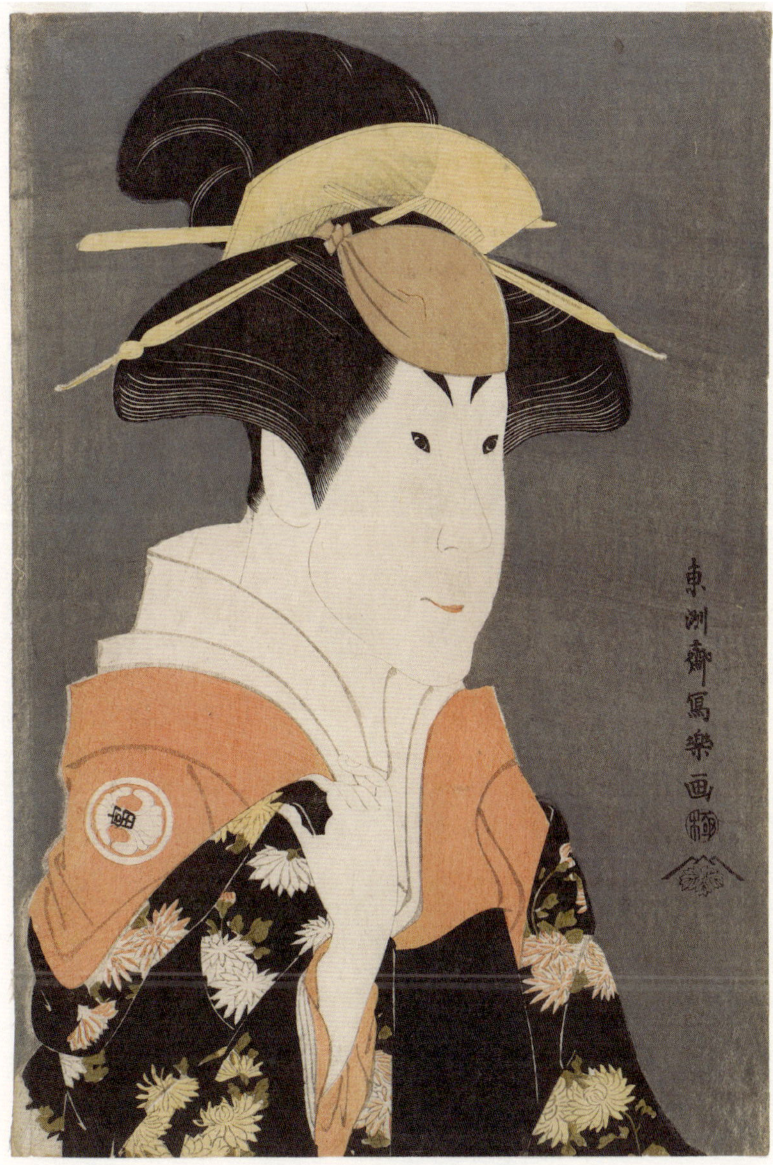

Toshusai Sharaku (active 1794–1795)
Publisher: Tsutaya
Juzaburo (Koshodo)
Actor Segawa Tomisaburo II as Yadorigi, Wife of Ogishi Kurando,
1794 (Kansei 6), 5th month
Woodblock print (nishiki-e);
ink, color, and mica on paper
Vertical oban; 10 × 14¾ in.
(25.5 × 37.3 cm)

The most highly admired of all designers of actor prints is the enigmatic Sharaku, active for under a year, whose true identity is still not certain. In his work, the trend toward increasingly realistic renditions of actors' faces goes beyond realism into caricature, resulting in an eye-catching, surprisingly modern-looking style. Rather than drawing the female-role actors as if they were women, he clearly showed their individual, masculine facial features. Tomisaburo's bright eyes and pert little nose contrast with his angular jawline and jutting chin.

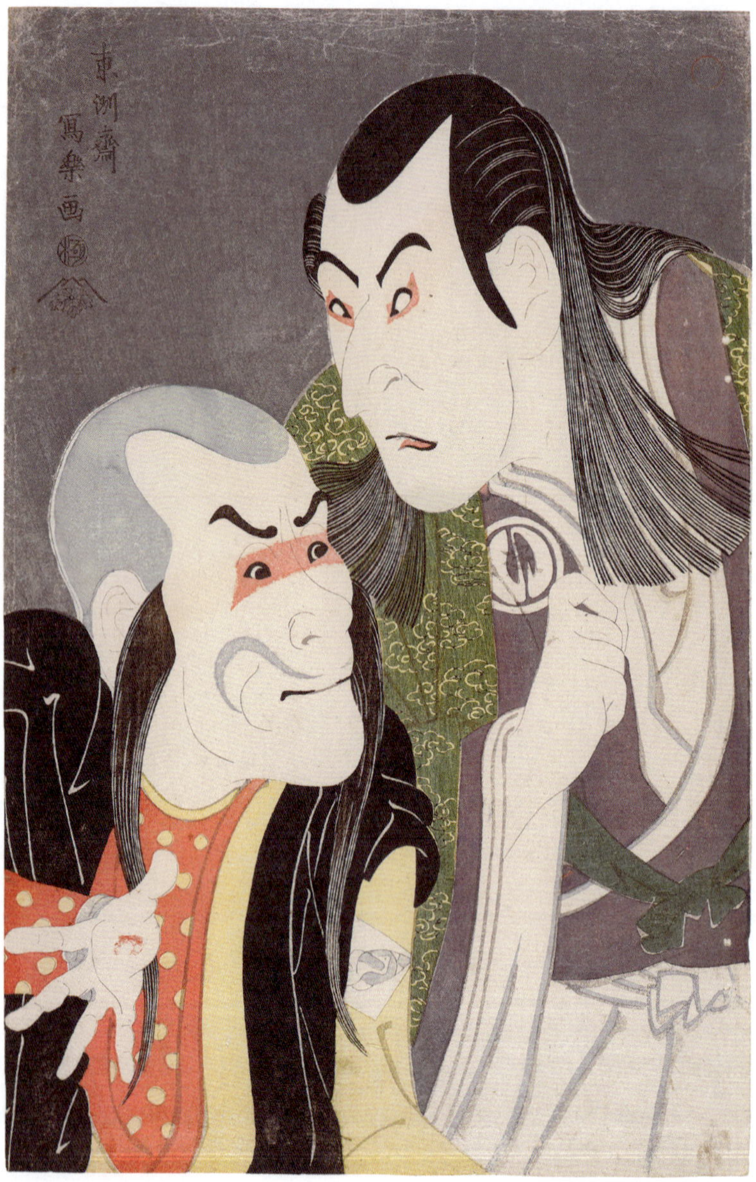

Toshusai Sharaku
(active 1794–1795)
Publisher: Tsutaya Juzaburo (Koshodo)
Actors Sawamura Yodogoro II as Kawatsura Hogen and Bando Zenji as Oninosadobo,
1794 (Kansei 6), 5th month
Woodblock print (nishiki-e); ink, color, and mica on paper
Vertical oban; 10 × 15 in.
(25.2 × 38.3 cm)

Sharaku sometimes designed double portraits contrasting good and bad characters within the same play. In this scene from *The Thousand Cherry Trees of Yoshitsune*, the virtuous Kawatsura Hogen, who is helping Minamoto no Yoshitsune and his followers hide from the enemies pursuing them, listens in horror as a wicked priest with trailing "catfish whiskers" suggests that they turn in the fugitives for a lucrative reward. The portraits are set off by a background of glittering mica.

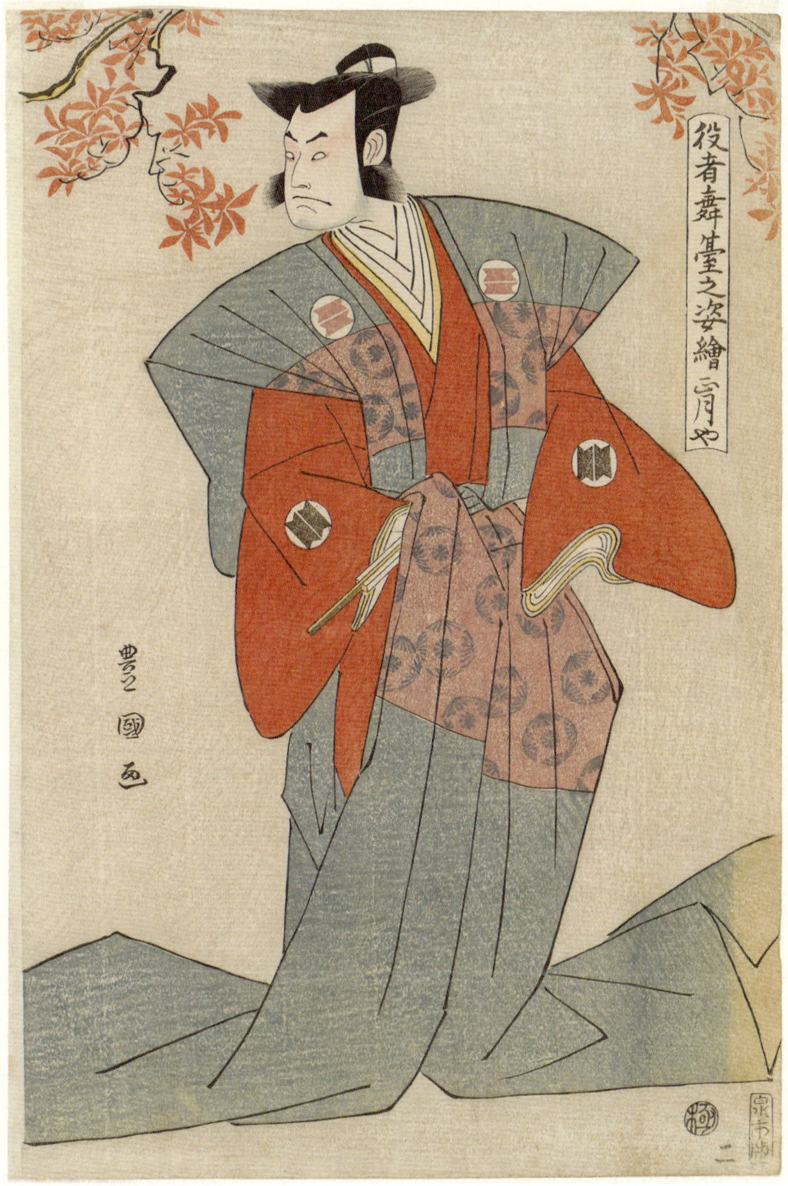

Utagawa Toyokuni I (1769–1825)
Publisher: Izumiya
Ichibei (Kansendo)
Shogatsuya (Actor Sakata Hangoro III as Abe no Muneto), from the series Portraits of Actors on Stage (*Yakusha butai no ugata-e*), 1794 (Kansei 6), 11th month
Woodblock print (nishiki-e); ink and color on paper
Vertical oban; 10 × 14¾ in. (25.5 × 37.5 cm)

At the beginning of his illustrious career, the young Toyokuni made a splash with a striking series of full-length actor portraits showing the stars in their current stage roles, with simplified backgrounds that emphasize the figures. The actors are identified only by their guild names (*yago*), but audiences could recognize them easily thanks to Toyokuni's skillful rendition of their facial features and characteristic poses. Sakata Hangoro III, known for his villain roles, appears here as a proud eleventh-century warrior in formal attire.

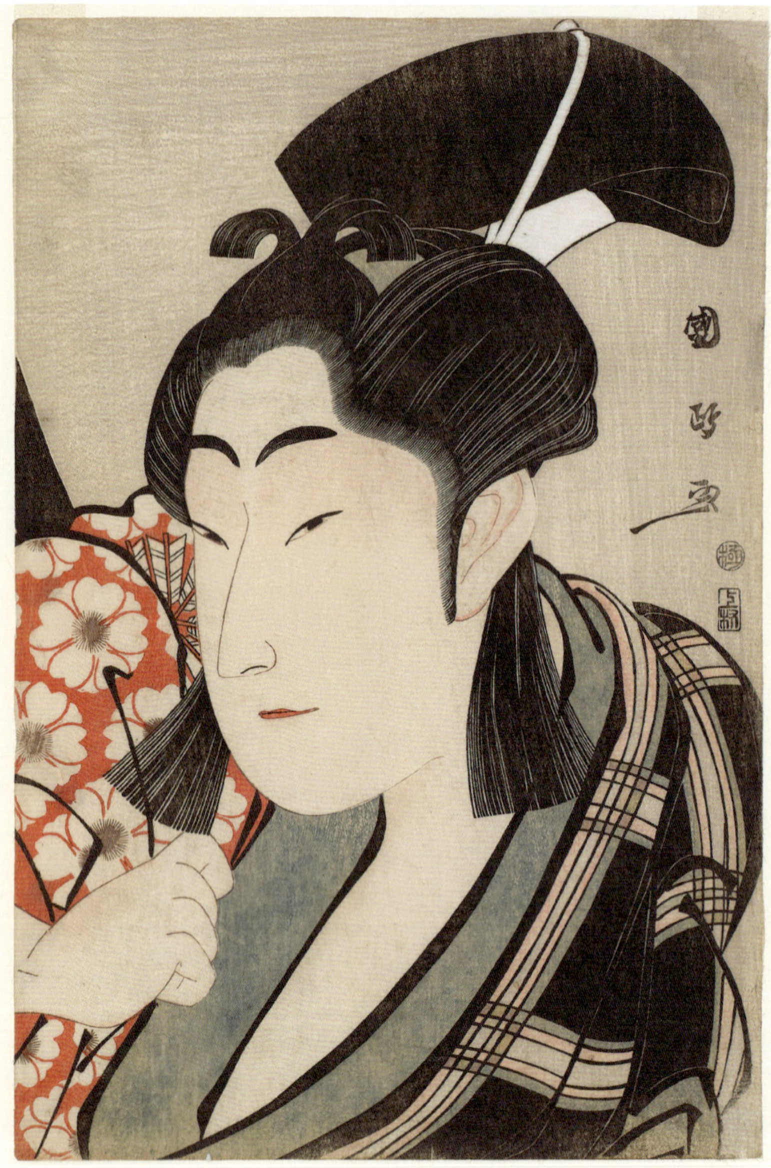

Utagawa Kunimasa (1773–1810)
Publisher: Uemura Yohei
Actor Nakamura Noshio II as Sakuramaru, 1796 (Kansei 8), 7th month
Woodblock print (nishiki-e); ink and color on paper
Vertical oban; 10 × 15 in. (25.5 × 38 cm)

By the end of the eighteenth century, the Utagawa school headed by Utagawa Toyokuni was a serious competitor for the Katsukawa school in the field of actor prints. Toyokuni's first student, Utagawa Kunimasa, designed some outstanding close-up portraits similar in style to the work of Sharaku. The actor Nakamura Noshio II specialized in female roles, but here he plays a handsome young man, one of the triplet brothers in the very popular play *Sugawara and the Secrets of Calligraphy* (*Sugawara denju tenarai kagami*).

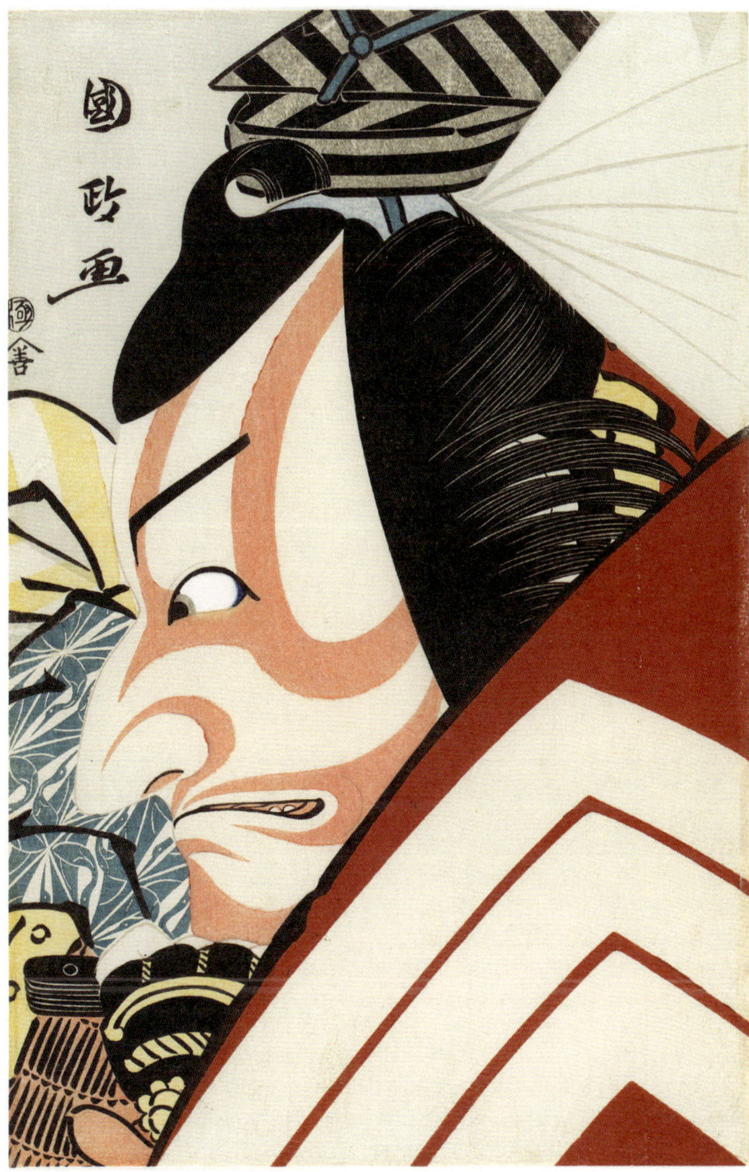

Utagawa Kunimasa (1773–1810)
Actor Ichikawa Ebizo as Usui Arataro Sadamitsu in a Shibaraku Scene, 1796 (Kansei 8), 11th month
Woodblock print (nishiki-e); ink and color on paper
Vertical oban; 9¾ × 14½ in. (24.8 × 36.8 cm)

A favorite kabuki scene that was inserted into a number of different plays is entitled "Wait a Minute!" (*Shibaraku*). This expression is shouted by the protagonist as he makes his entrance, spectacularly costumed in a robe with enormous sleeves resembling the cape of a superhero, in order to disrupt the evil plans just announced by a gloating villain. Among the many depictions of this scene, a specialty of the Ichikawa family of actors, Kunimasa's profile portrait is a standout.

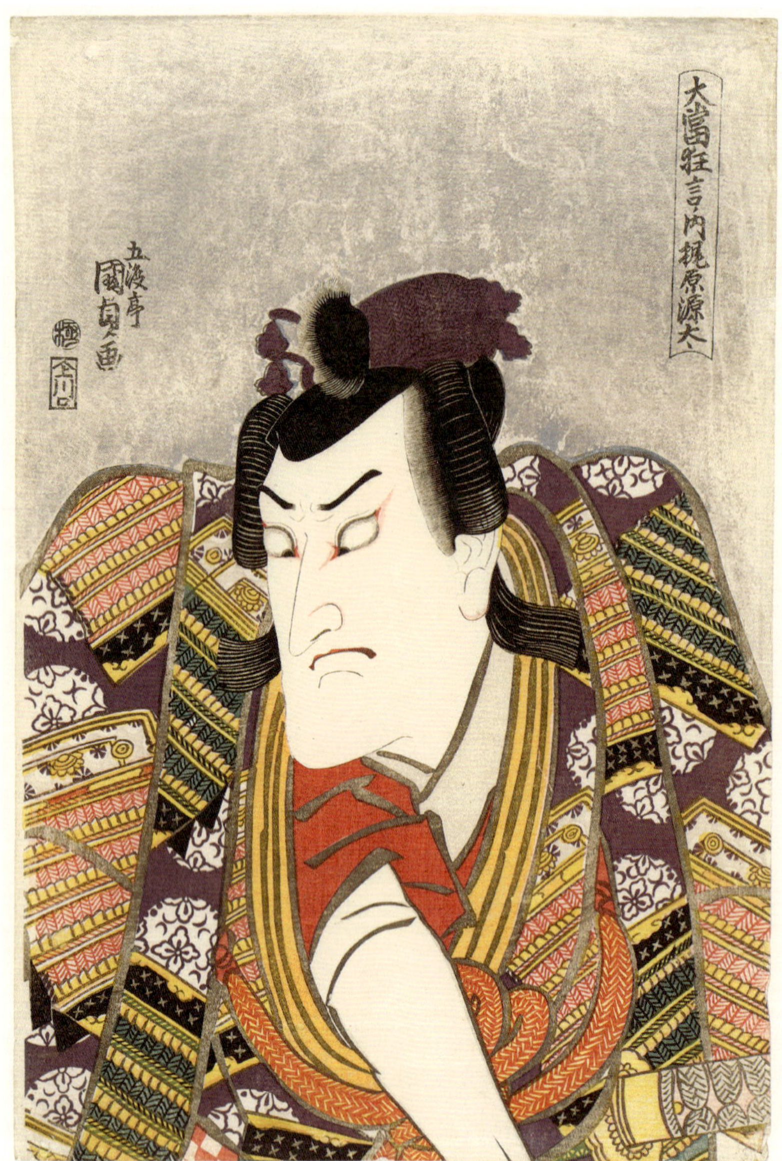

Utagawa Kunisada I (Toyokuni III) (1786–1864)
Publisher: Kawaguchiya Uhei (Fukusendo)
Actor Bando Mitsugoro III as Kajiwara Genta, from the series Great Hit Plays (*Oatari kyogen no uchi*), c. 1814 (Bunka 11)
Woodblock print (nishiki-e); ink and color on paper
Vertical oban; 10½ × 15½ in. (26.5 × 39.4 cm)

Close-up bust portraits, known as "big head pictures" (*okubi-e*), were declared illegal in 1801 because they glorified lowly people such as actors and courtesans. A decade later when the edict had fallen into disuse, Kunisada, the top student of Utagawa Toyokuni, dared to design new prints in the format used earlier by Sharaku, even using silvery mica backgrounds. Mitsugoro III is shown as a young warrior in a Dance of Seven Changes, wearing a kimono patterned with the sleeves of a suit of armor.

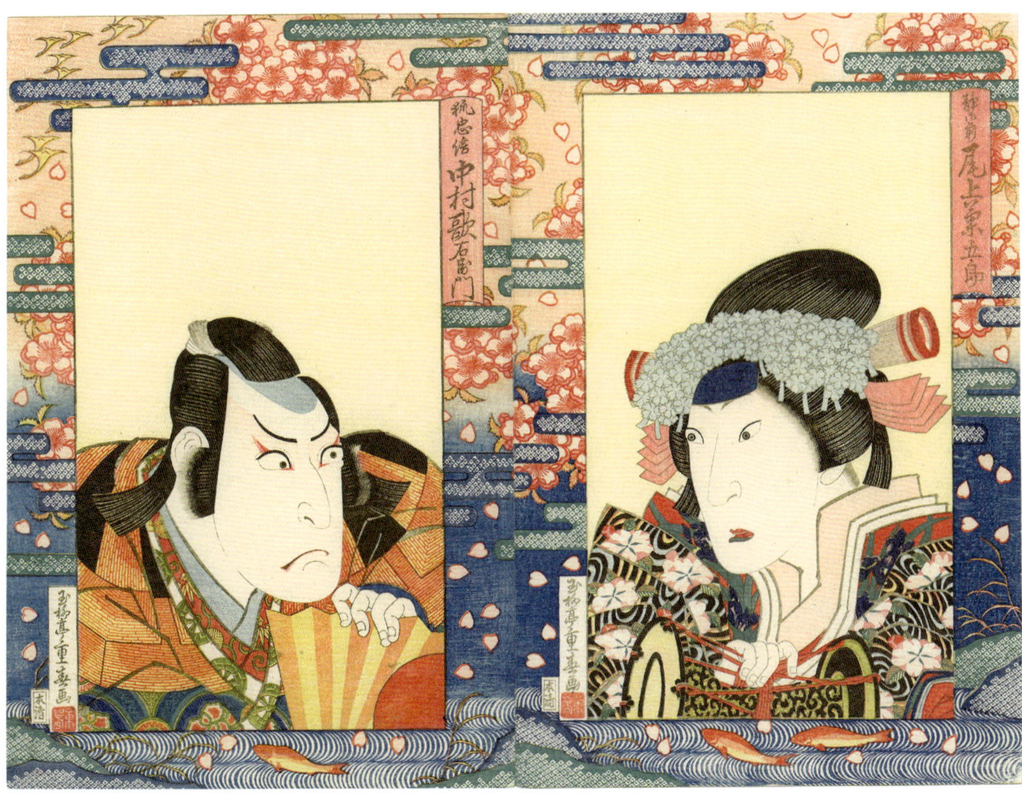

Ryusai Shigeharu (1803–1853)
Publisher: Shohonya
Seishichi (Honsei)
Actors Onoe Kikugoro III as Shizuka Gozen (R) and Nakamura Utaemon III as the Fox Tadanobu (L), 1830
(Bunsei 13/Tenpo 1), 10th month
Woodblock print (nishiki-e);
ink and color on paper
Vertical oban diptych;
$20\frac{1}{8} \times 14\frac{3}{4}$ in. (51×37.5 cm)

Beginning in the late eighteenth century, single-sheet color woodblock prints began to be produced in Osaka as well as in Edo. This diptych, with printed borders that imitate the kind of brocade mounting used for hanging scroll paintings, shows two characters from *The Thousand Cherry Trees of Yoshitsune*. The magical fox disguised as Tadanobu wants Shizuka's hand drum because it was made from the skins of his parents. When kindhearted Shizuka gives him the drum, he helps Yoshitsune's group to escape from their enemies.

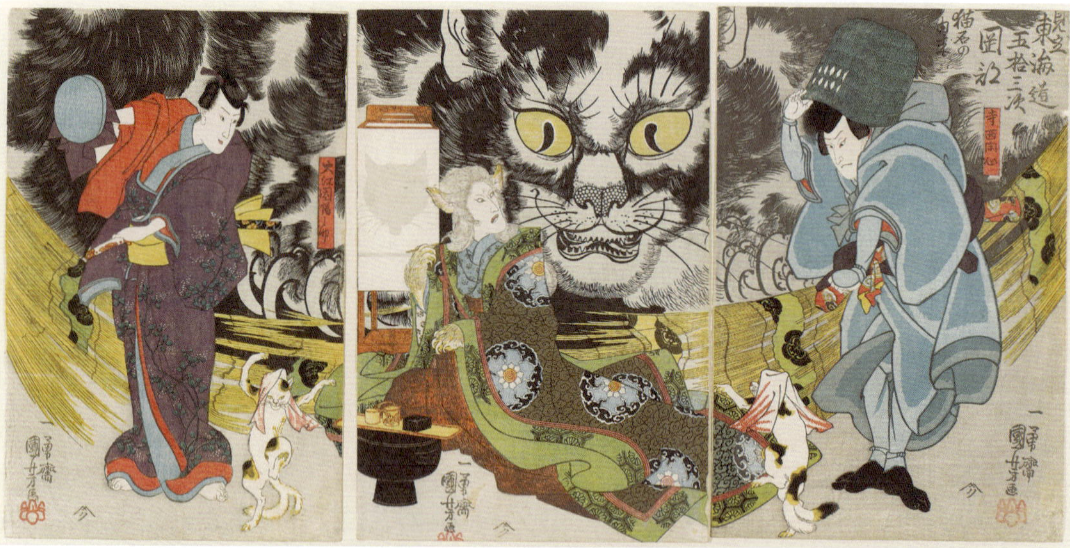

Utagawa Kuniyoshi (1797–1861)
Publisher: Yama-Ku
The Origin Story of the Cat Stone at Okabe, Representing One of the Fifty-three Stations of the Tokaido Road (Mitate Tokaido goju-san tsugi Okabe neko ishi no yurai): Actors Sawamura Sojuro V as Teranishi Kanshin (R), Onoe Kikugoro III as the Cat Monster (C), and Ichimura Uzaemon XII as Oe Inabanosuke (L), 1847 (Koka 4), 7th month
Woodblock print (nishiki-e); ink and color on paper
Vertical oban triptych; 29 × 14½ in. (73.6 × 36.8 cm)

The retirement performance of Onoe Kikugoro III in 1847 included a medley of scenes from his greatest hits, including the role of the cat monster that he had first performed twenty years before. Travelers spending the night in a ruined temple encounter a sweet old lady with long white hair who is actually a giant, human-eating cat, here just beginning to revert to her true form. Small cats with forked tails dance with towels on their heads, on the verge of becoming demons themselves.

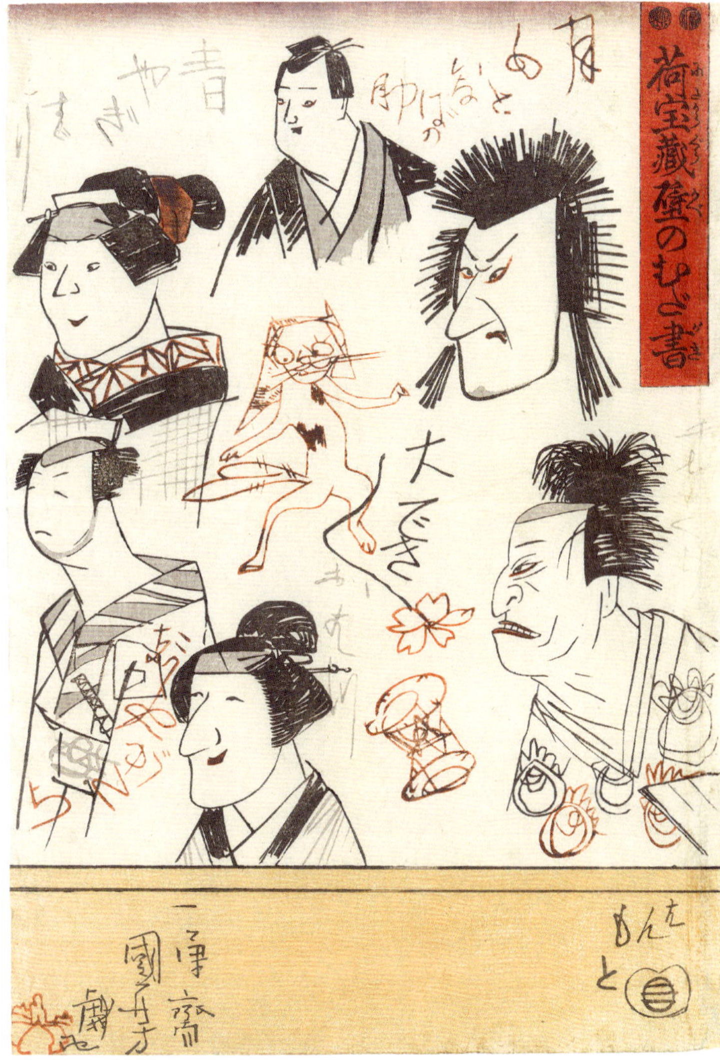

Utagawa Kuniyoshi (1797–1861)
Publisher: Ibaya Senzaburo (Dansendo)
Actor Caricatures: Matsumoto Kinsho I (TR), Ichimura Uzaemon XII (TC), Ichikawa Shinsha I (TL), Nakamura Utaemon IV (BR), Bando Shuka I (BC), Sawamura Ujuro II (?) (BL), from the series Scribbles on a Storehouse Wall (*Nitakaragura kabe no mudagaki*), c. 1848 (Koka 5/Kaei 1)
Woodblock print (nishiki-e); ink and color on paper
Vertical oban; 9¾ × 14 in. (24.7 × 35.5 cm)

In the 1840s, actor prints were technically illegal and had to be presented without the names of the actors and disguised as illustrations of history or literature or in some other way. Perhaps the most ingenious response of all was a set of prints by Kuniyoshi showing actor caricatures that purport to be graffiti scribbled on the white plaster wall of a storehouse. In addition to human actors, a cartoon cat recalls the dancing demon cats of Kikugoro's farewell performance in the previous year.

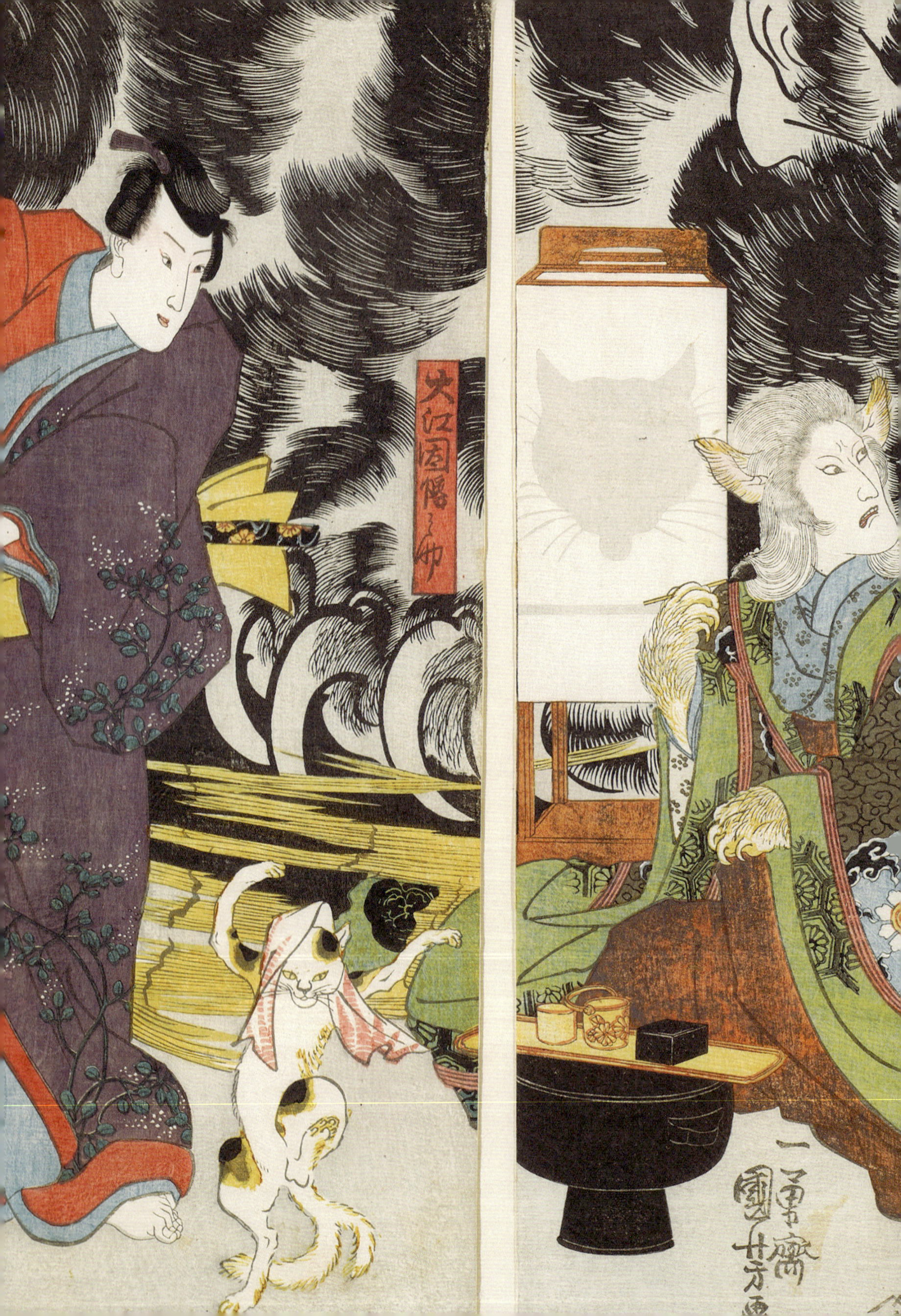
一勇斎国芳画

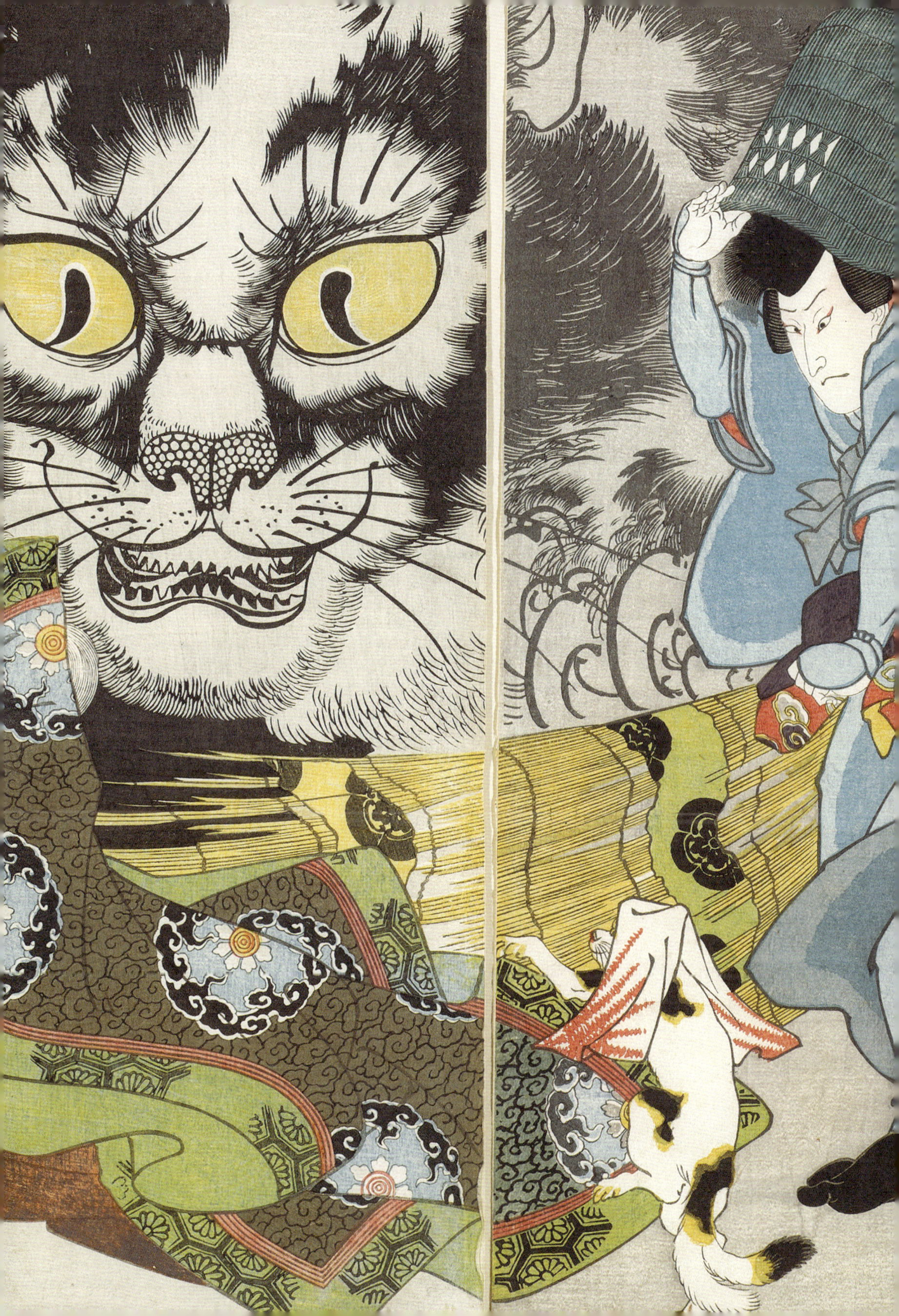

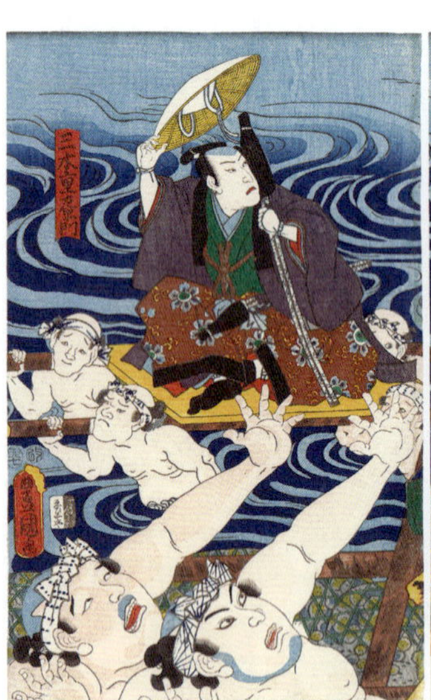
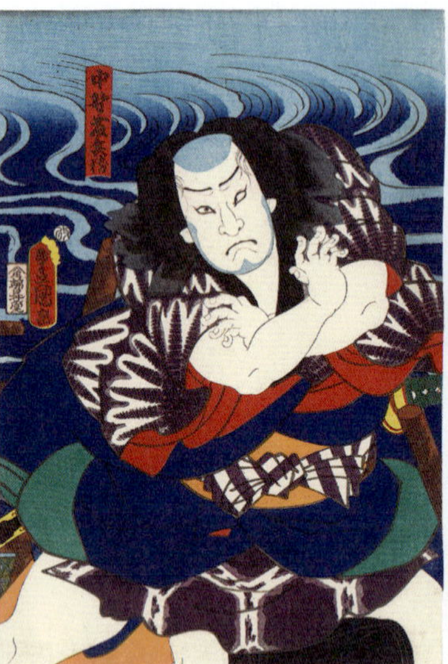
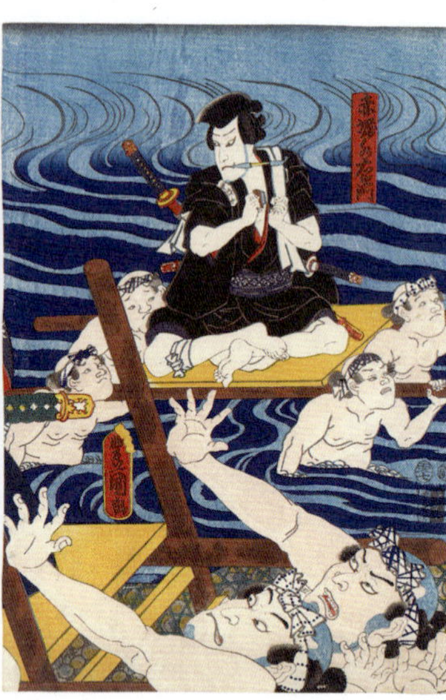

Utagawa Kunisada I (Toyokuni III) (1786–1864)
Publisher: Ebisuya Shoshichi (Kinshodo)
Actors Arashi Kichisaburo III as Akabori Mizuemon, with Matsumoto Kunigoro and Arashi Kangoro (R); Arashi Rikan III as Nakano Tobei (C); and Kataoka Gado II as Miki Juzaemon, with Naritaya Sobei II (?) and Otani Tokuji II (L), 1855 (Ansei 2), 7th month
Woodblock print (nishiki-e); ink and color on paper
Vertical oban triptych;
28¾ × 14¼ in. (72.9 × 36.1 cm)

In this spectacular triptych, Kunisada shows a scene from a kabuki play set at the Oi River on the Tokaido Road, so shallow that travelers crossed it by riding on rafts carried by porters. In the right sheet, a murderer makes his escape, having bribed the river porters to help him. In the center sheet, more porters fight with a loyal retainer of the murdered man, while to the left another would-be avenger is carried in the opposite direction.

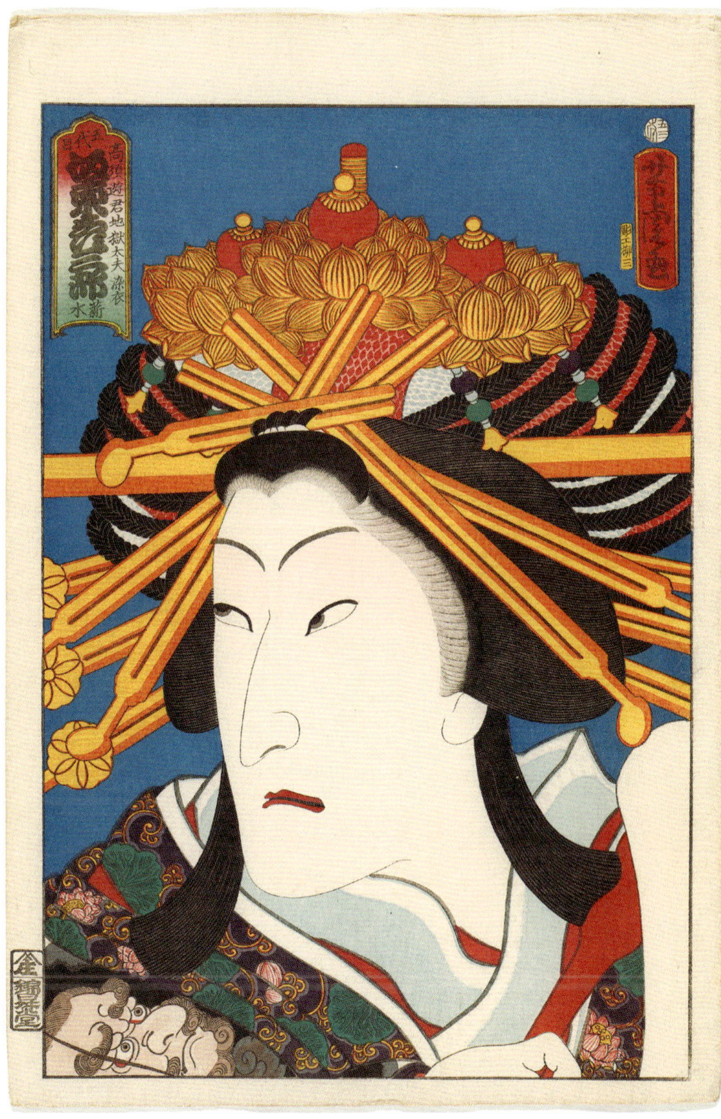

Utagawa Yoshitora
(active c. 1836–1887)
Publisher: Ebisuya Shoshichi (Kinshodo)
Blockcutter: Shimizu Ryuzo
Actor Bando Hikosaburo V as Jigoku Dayu, from an untitled series of actors, 1865 (Genji 2/Keio 1), 3rd month
Woodblock print (nishiki-e); ink and color on paper
Vertical oban; 10 × 15 in. (25.2 × 38 cm)

Toward the end of his long career, Kunisada designed a spectacular series of close-up actor portraits, beautifully printed in brilliant colors. He was assisted by a junior Utagawa school artist, Yoshitora, who was inspired by the master's example to produce some of the best designs in his own oeuvre. Jigoku Dayu, the Hell Courtesan, was said to have worn robes decorated with scenes from the Buddhist hells; this stage costume also features hair ornaments in the shape of lotuses, the sacred flower of Buddhism.

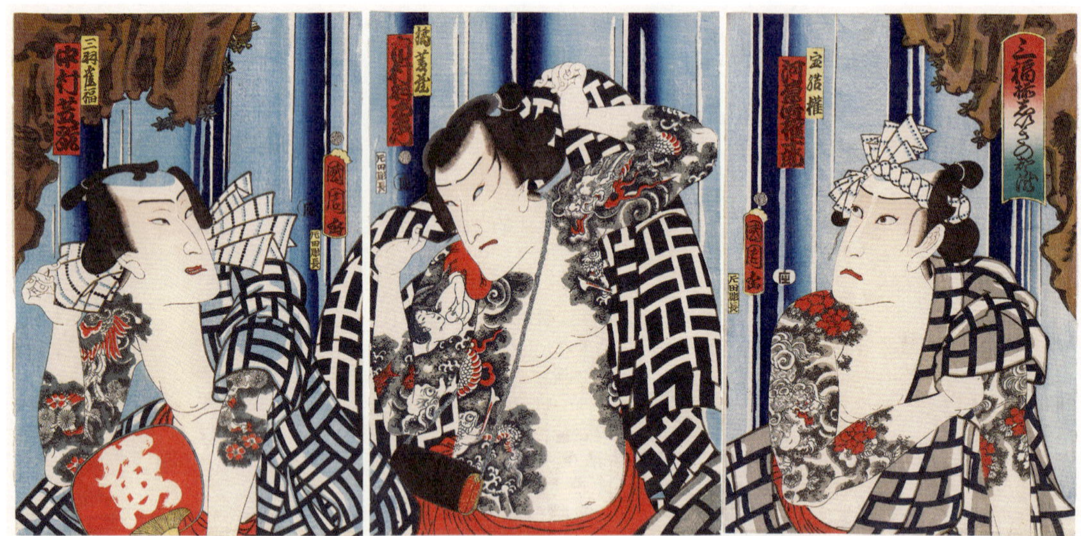

Toyohara Kunichika (1835–1900)
Publisher: Hayashiya Shogoro
Blockcutter: Katada Chojiro (Hori Cho)
Actors Kawarazaki Gonjuro as Takaramusubi no Gon (R), Ichimura Uzaemon XIII as Tachibana Hishizo (C), and Nakamura Shikan IV as Sanba Jafuku (L), in Unity of Three Happinesses: Favorite Actors Before a White Waterfall (Sanpuku soroe shiiki no shirataki), 1863 (Bunkyu 3), 6th month
Woodblock print (nishiki-e); ink and color on paper
Vertical oban triptych; 29 × 13¾ in. (73.6 × 35 cm)

This triptych is an especially fine example of prints that purport to show actors in private life; they are apparently making a pilgrimage to the sacred waterfall at Mount Oyama, not far from Edo. It is possible that such a pilgrimage may have occurred in real life, but the spectacular tattoos displayed by the actors are almost certainly products of the artist's imagination, since actors—who had to play many different kinds of parts—did not usually have tattoos, a fashion limited to trendy young urban men.

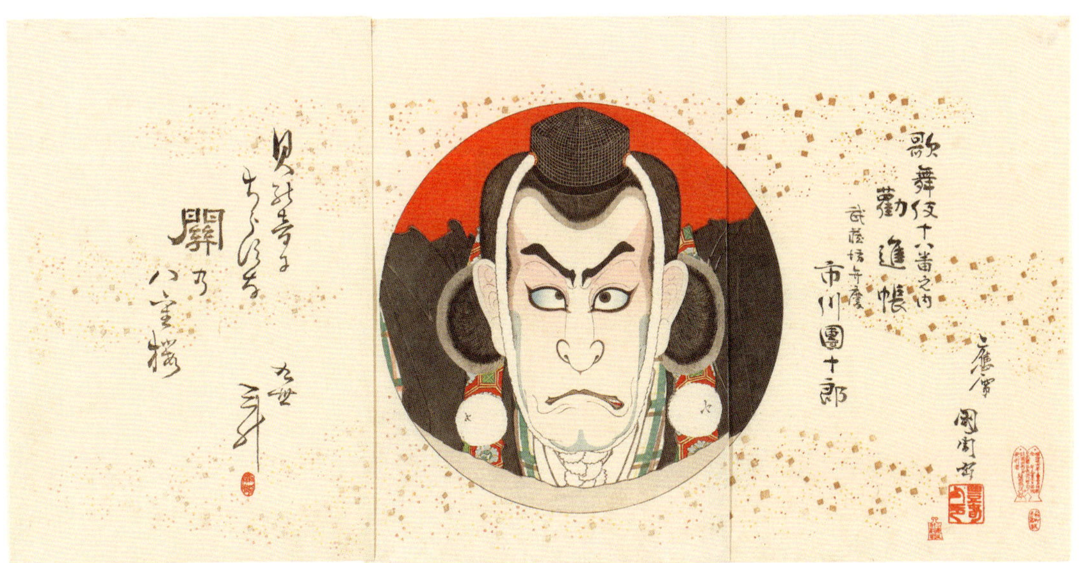

Toyohara Kunichika (1835–1900)
Publisher: Fukuda Kumajiro
Actor Ichikawa Danjuro IX as Musashibo Benkei in The Subscription List (Kanjincho), one of the Eighteen Great Kabuki Plays (Kabuki juhachiban no uchi), 1893 (Meiji 26), May 7
Woodblock print (nishiki-e); ink, color, and metallic powder on paper
Vertical oban triptych; 29¾ × 14½ in. (75.6 × 36.8 cm)

The crossed eyes seen in kabuki prints are an acting technique used to indicate highly focused intensity and determination. In this production of *The Subscription List*, one of the eighteen plays selected as the greatest works performed by the Ichikawa lineage of actors, the Meiji-era star Danjuro IX plays Benkei, the retainer of Minamoto no Yoshitsune. Yoshitsune's group is making their escape disguised as traveling ascetics collecting pledges for temple funds. When they are challenged, Benkei convincingly "reads" names of donors from a blank scroll.

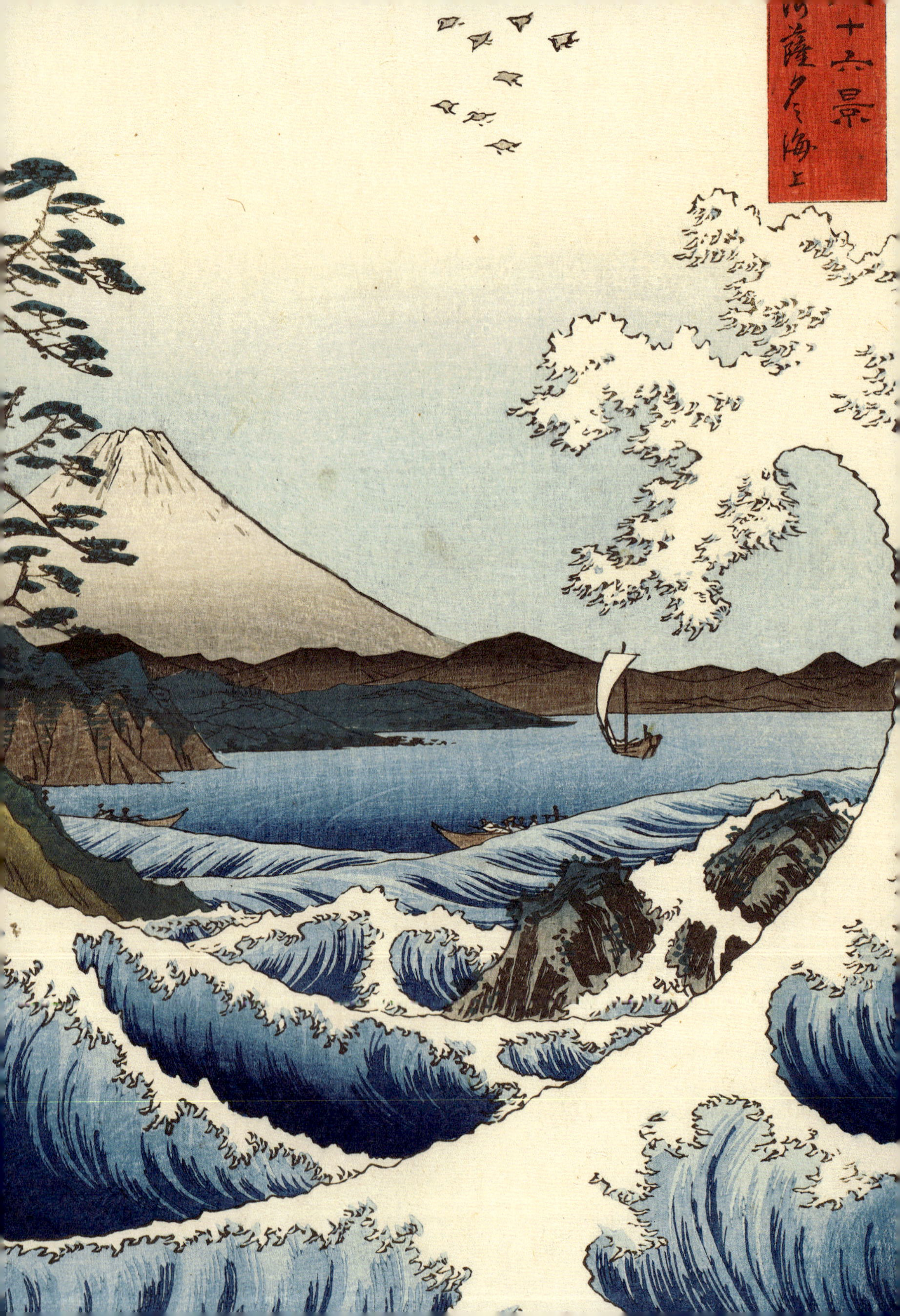
十六景
河薩タ海上

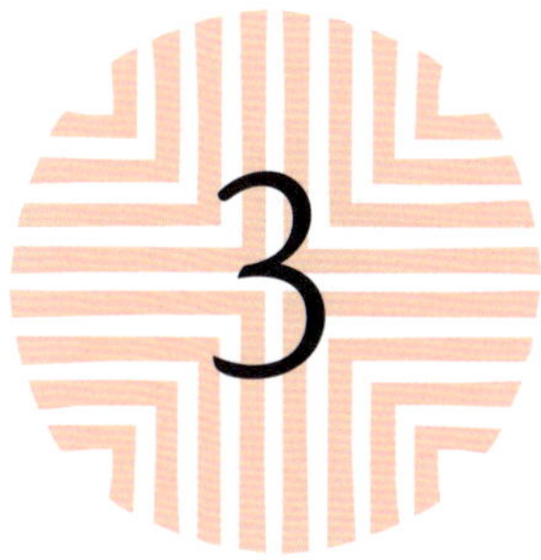

Landscapes and Cityscapes

In Japanese both landscapes and cityscapes are called *fukei-ga*, loosely translated as "views." Works with this subject matter were occasionally made even in the early days of ukiyo-e, depicting famous scenic spots mentioned in classical poetry or notable Floating World locations in Edo. The early works utilize traditional Asian perspective, in which receding lines are parallel and distant objects are drawn higher in the picture plane. In the 1740s, Japanese artists became familiar with Western-style vanishing point perspective, in which receding lines converge at a point on the horizon, through the study of imported European illustrated books as well as Chinese books and prints that referred to the Western drawing method. There were several waves of popularity for "floating pictures" (*uki-e*), as perspective prints were called, sometimes viewed in peep-show devices that used imported glass lenses to give an especially realistic effect.

Print designers and their viewing public gradually became accustomed to this new way of seeing the world, though artists always felt free to adjust the rules to make a better picture or to combine Western and Asian perspective systems. By the 1780s, landscapes were being featured as backgrounds for figure prints of actors or fashionable women, still the most important genres within ukiyo-e. The first pure landscape prints to become runaway best sellers in their own right were Hokusai's Thirty-six Views of Mount Fuji, published beginning in about 1830 and followed a few years later by Hiroshige's Fifty-three Stations of the Tokaido Road. The success of these two series made landscape one of the major genres of ukiyo-e, designed by many different artists. Views of scenic spots in various provinces, which print buyers might someday visit and could at least dream about in the meantime, helped to encourage a popular vision of Japan as a unified nation.

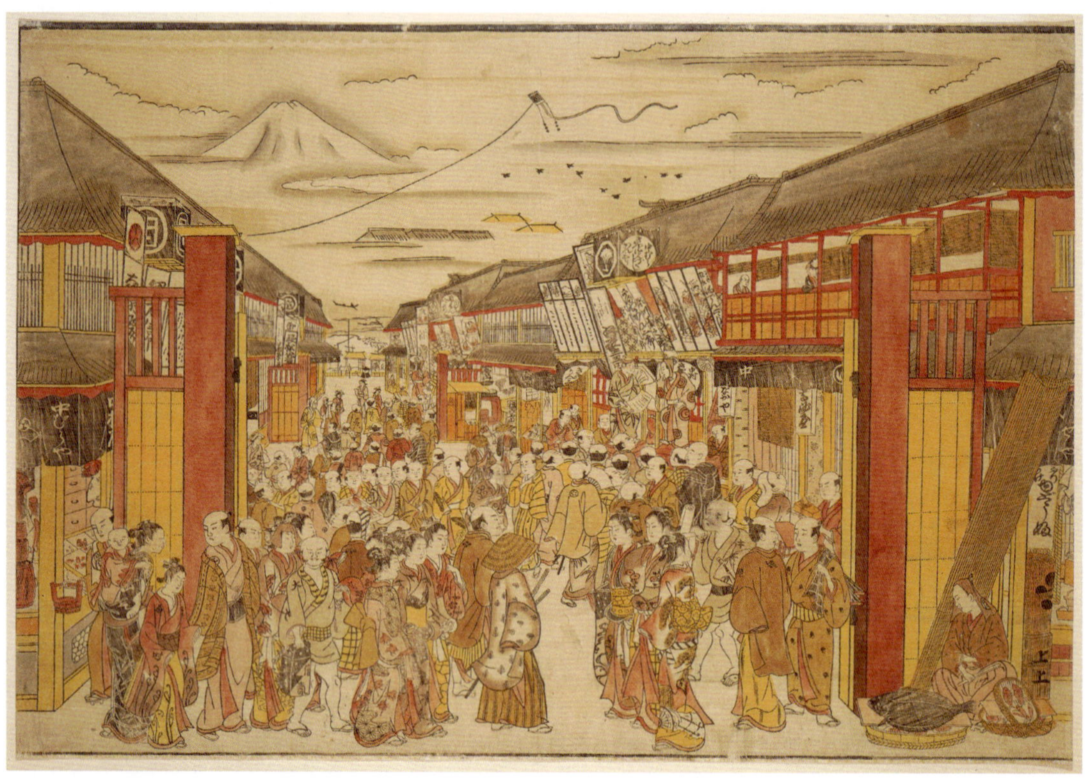

Okumura Masanobu (1686–1764)
Large Perspective Picture of the Kabuki Theater District in Sakai-cho and Fukiya-cho, c. 1745 (Enkyo 2)
Woodblock print; ink on paper, with hand-applied color
Horizontal double oban;
25½ × 17¼ in. (64.8 × 43.8 cm)

The prolific and inventive Okumura Masanobu, one of the first Japanese artists to experiment with vanishing point perspective, uses the magical new technique to transport his viewers to a street in the bustling theater district of Edo, with box-shaped marquees over the theater entrances and painted billboards advertising the stars currently performing. Fashionably dressed theatergoers mingle with street vendors offering snacks, while Mount Fuji rises in the distance, much larger than it would appear in real life.

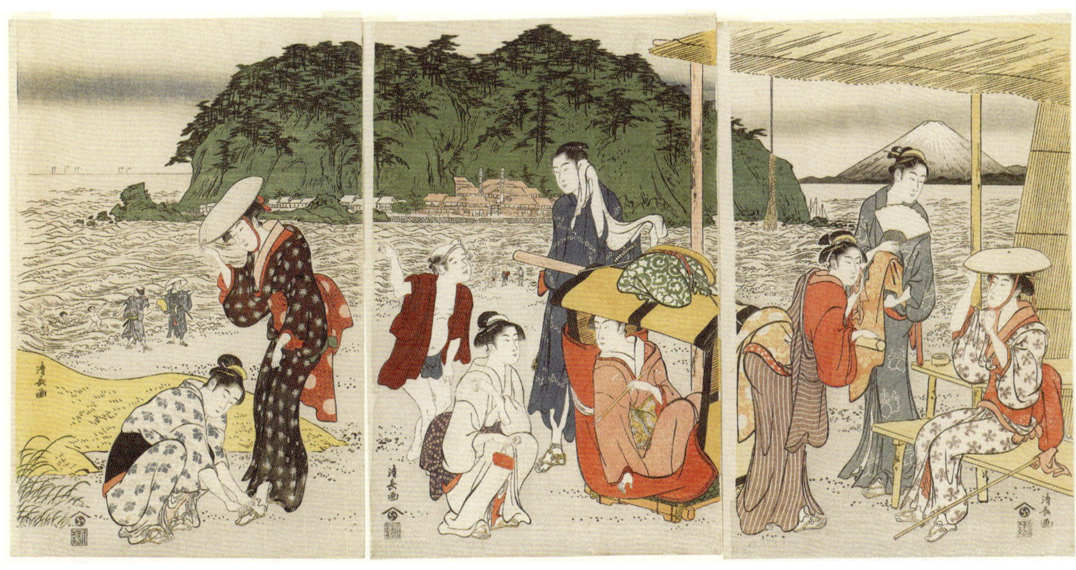

Torii Kiyonaga (1752–1815)
Publisher: Nishimuraya Yohachi (Eijudo)
A Pilgrimage to Enoshima, c. 1789 (Tenmei 9/Kansei 1)
Woodblock print (nishiki-e); ink and color on paper
Vertical oban triptych;
30$\frac{7}{8}$ × 15$\frac{1}{2}$ in. (78.2 × 39.4 cm)

Kiyonaga's depictions of slim, elegant women in fashionable clothes often included landscape backgrounds, as in this view of the sacred island of Enoshima, a popular pilgrimage site close to the city of Edo. Visitors could walk to the island at low tide or pay porters to carry them through the shallow water at other times. In this triptych, a high-ranking lady and her attendants rest at an open-air teahouse on the beach before proceeding to the island.

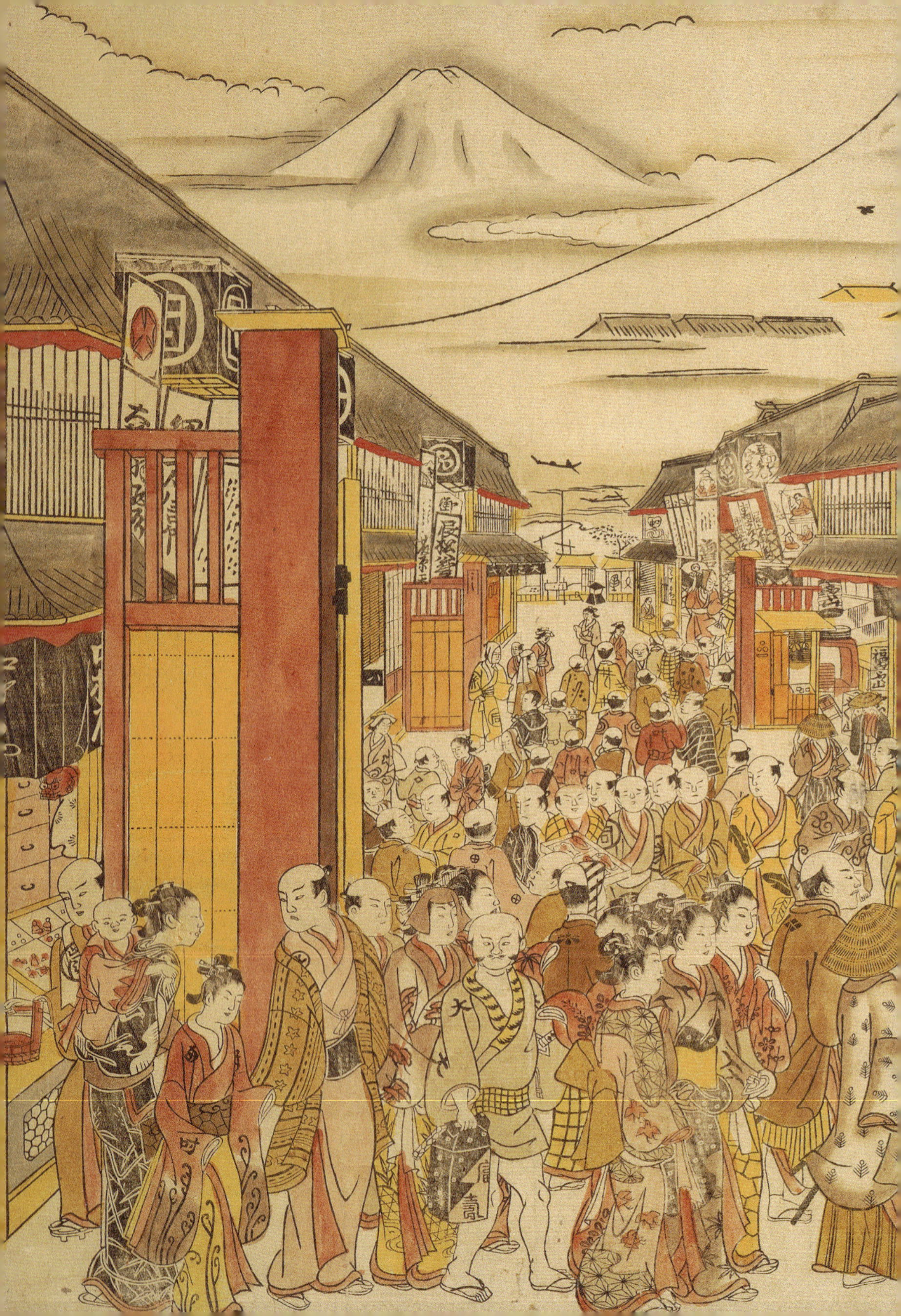

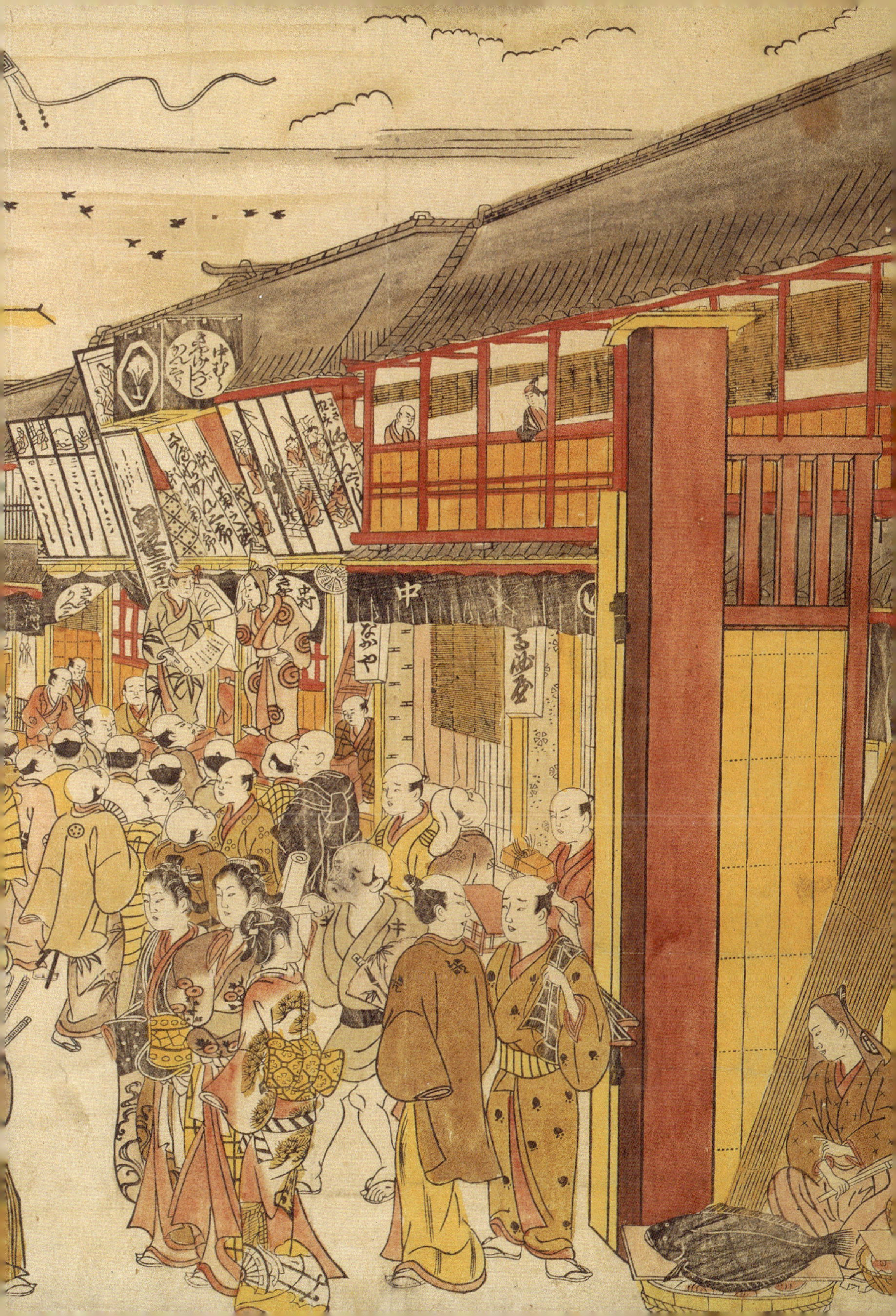
中
なかや

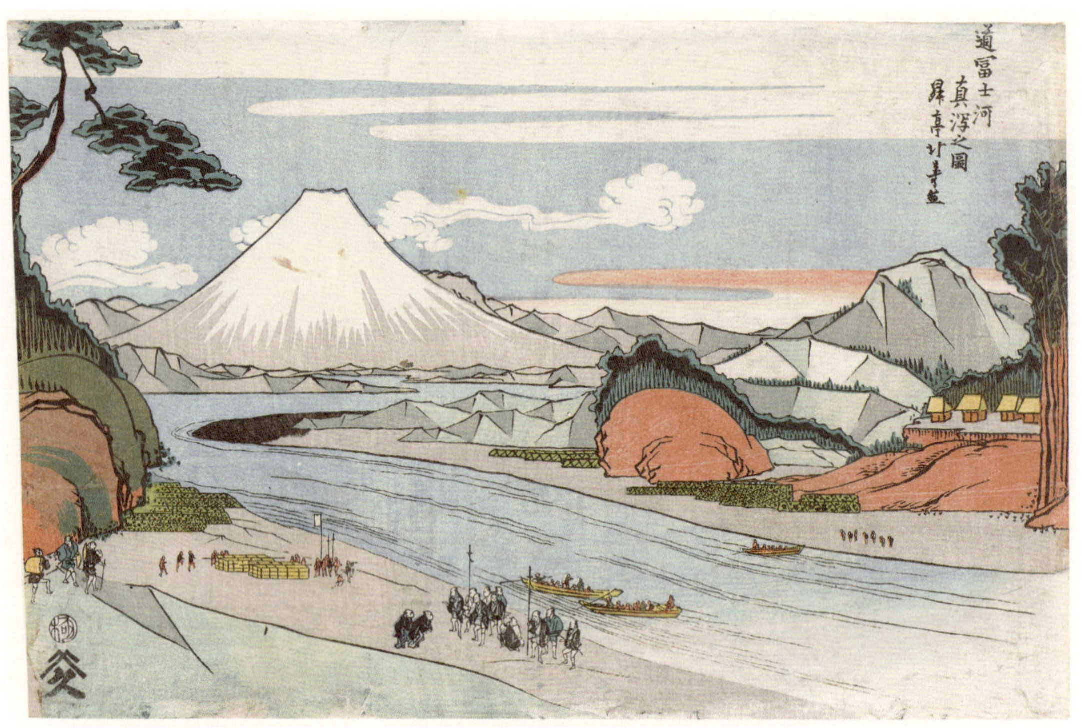

Shotei Hokuju (1763–1824)
Publisher: Yamamotoya Heikichi (Eikyudo)
True Depiction of the Fuji River (Fujikawa shinsha no zu), from the series The Tokaido Road (*Tokaido*), c. 1810–20
Woodblock print (nishiki-e); ink and color on paper
Horizontal oban; 14¼ × 9¼ in. (36 × 23.3 cm)

Hokusai's student Hokuju was designing single-sheet landscape prints in the full-size oban format even before his teacher popularized the genre. His works were reasonably successful but did not become best sellers, and so landscape remained a minor genre within ukiyo-e until later. Hokuju's drawing style is especially interesting to modern viewers because he built up landscape forms by using geometric shapes, in a manner somewhat similar to much later Cubist techniques.

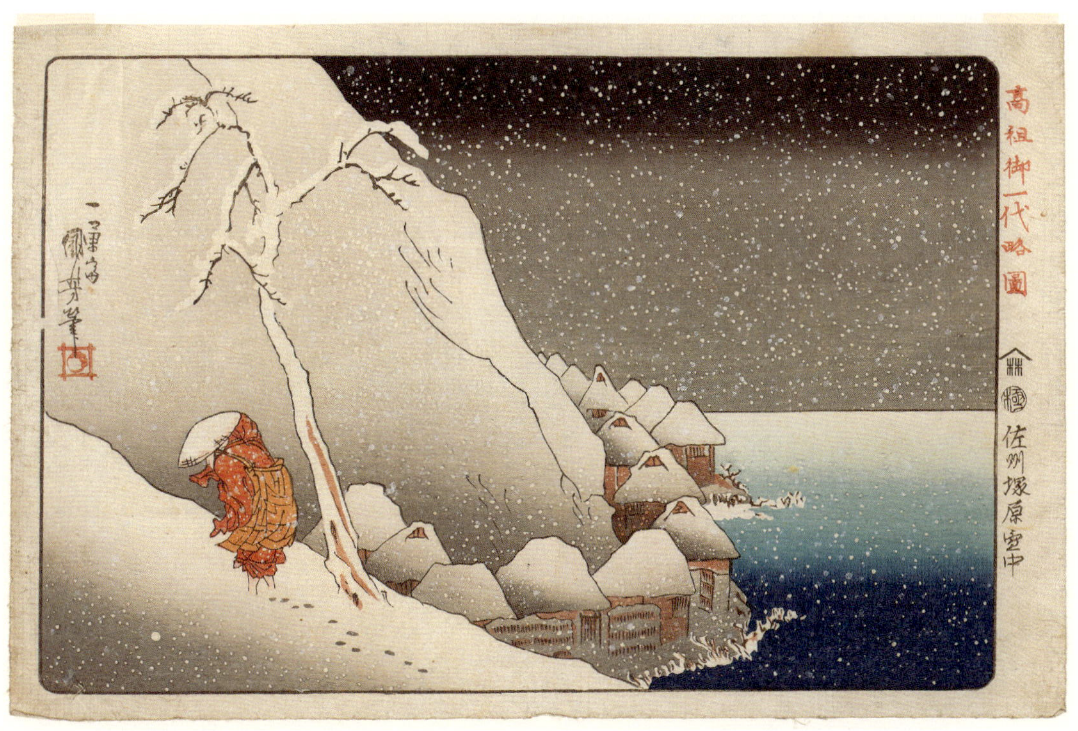

Utagawa Kuniyoshi (1797–1861)
Publisher: Iseya Rihei (Kinjudo)
Nichiren in the Snow at Tsukahara on Sado Island (Sashu Tsukahara setchu), from the series Sketches of the Life of Nichiren (*Koso goichidai ryakuzu*), c. 1830–35 (Tenpo 1–6)
Woodblock print (nishiki-e); ink and color on paper
Horizontal oban; 15⅛ × 9¾ in. (38.3 × 24.8 cm)

Kuniyoshi was known primarily for historical depictions, but he was also capable of designing dramatic landscapes such as this scene from the life of the thirteenth-century priest Nichiren, the founder of a major sect of Japanese Buddhism. Persecution by other sects led to Nichiren's temporary exile to Sado Island in northern Japan. Kuniyoshi shows a solitary figure in the red robes of a high-ranking priest, making his way uphill through a blizzard.

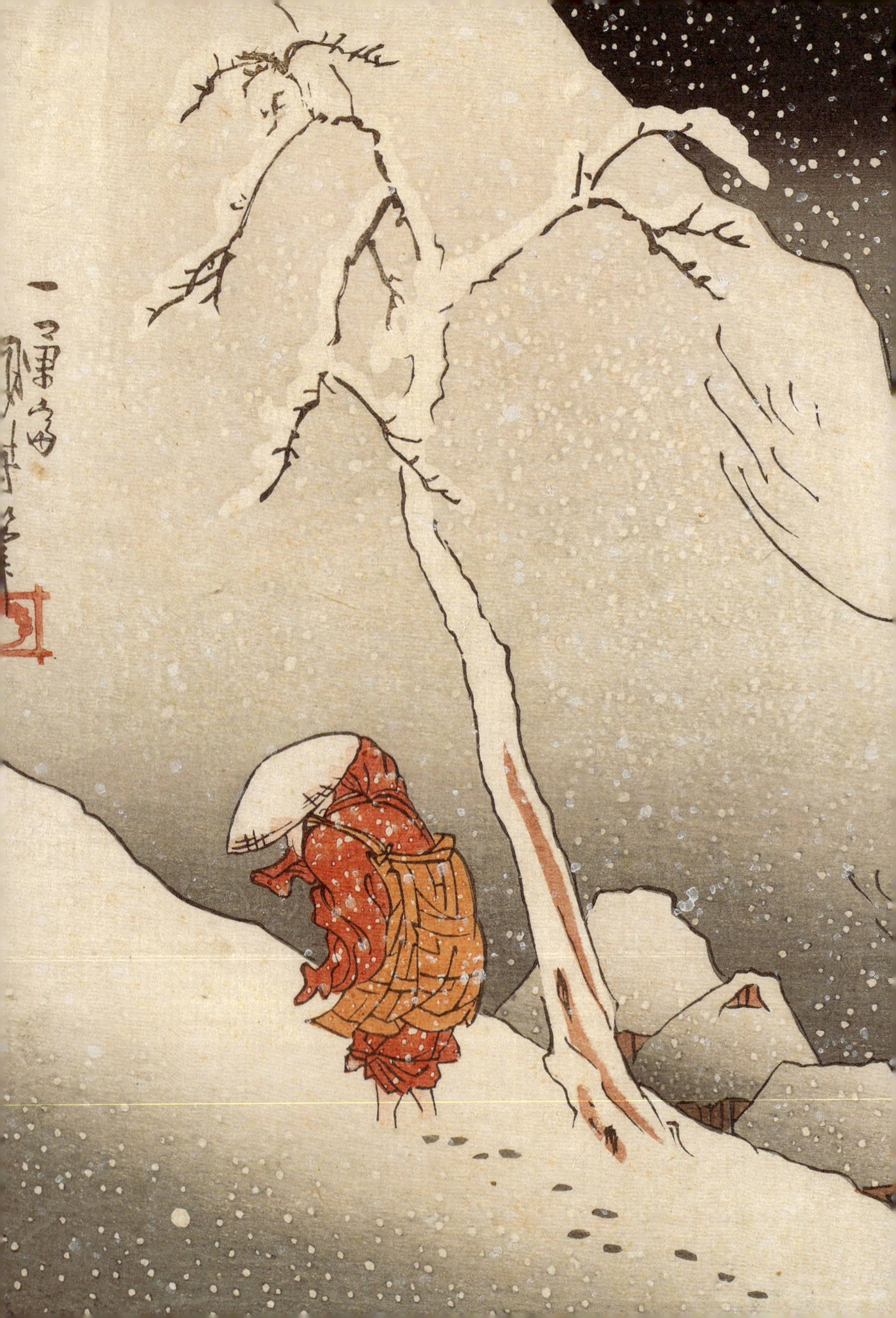

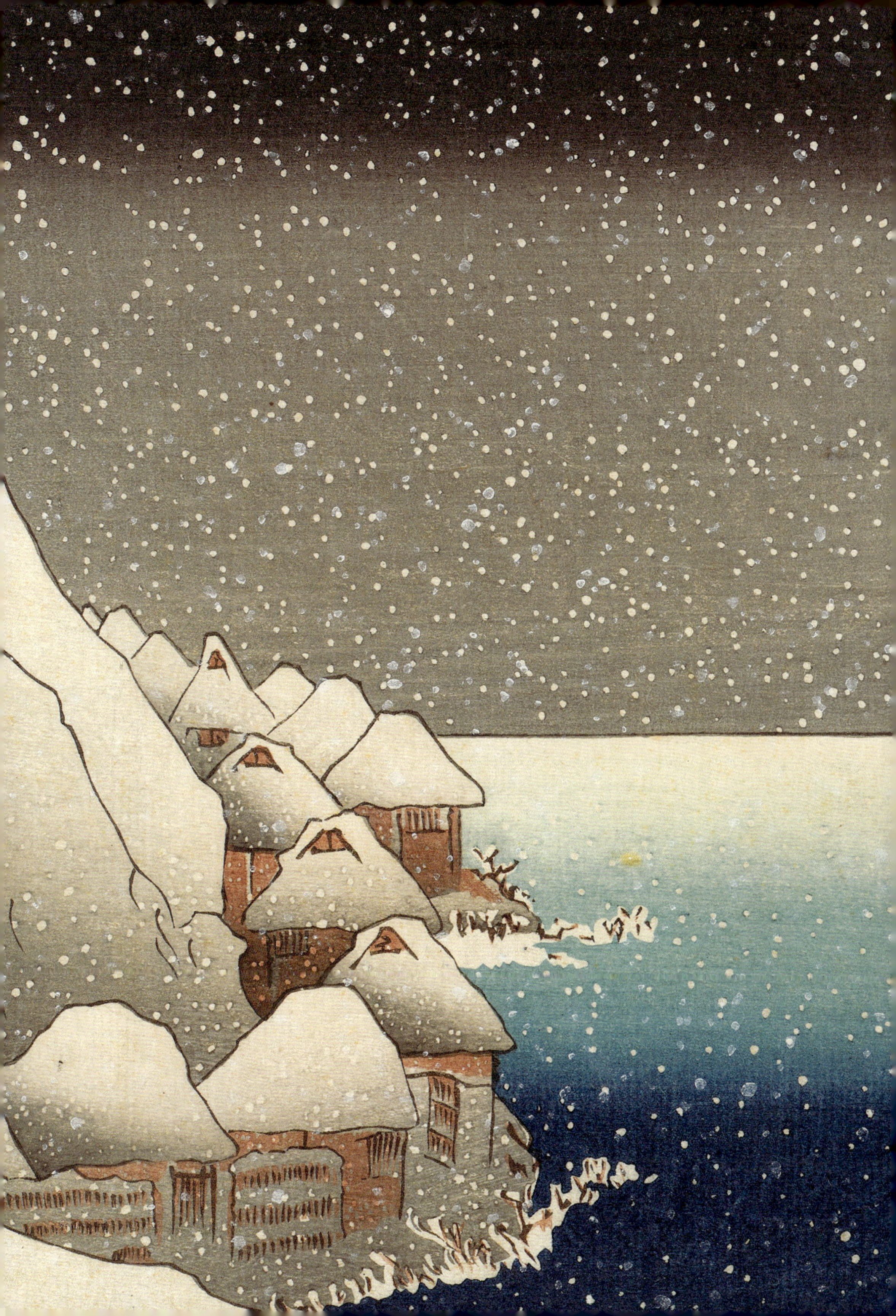

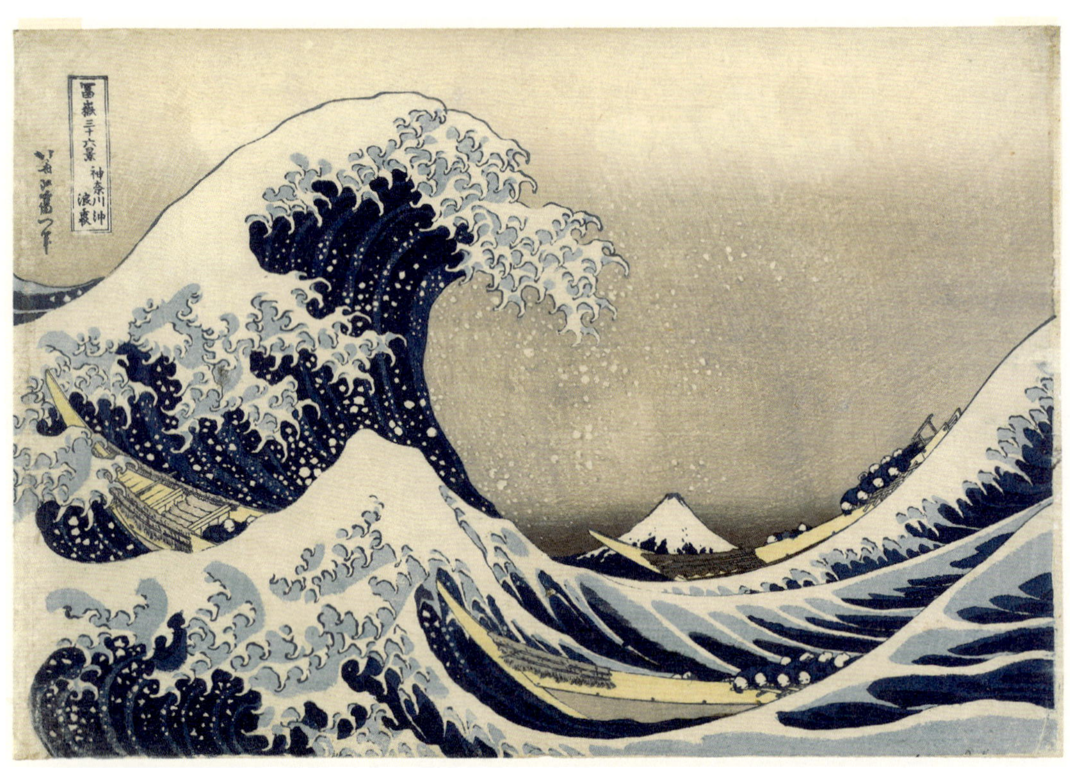

Katsushika Hokusai (1760–1849)
Publisher: Nishimuraya Yohachi (Eijudo)
Under the Wave off Kanagawa (Kanagawa-oki nami-ura), also known as *The Great Wave*, from the series Thirty-six Views of Mount Fuji (*Fugaku sanjurokkei*), c. 1830–31 (Tenpo 1–2)
Woodblock print (nishiki-e); ink and color on paper
Horizontal oban; 15 × 10¼ in. (38 × 25.8 cm)

Hokusai's best-selling series Thirty-six Views of Mount Fuji made landscape prints an important genre for the first time. (It actually includes forty-six prints, because he added ten extra designs.) The most dramatic design in the series shows three of the express fish-delivery boats that supplied the city of Edo, on their way home to the area of present-day Yokohama, threatened by an unusually large wave. Their fate is uncertain, but the auspicious mountain in the background hints that they will get through it safely.

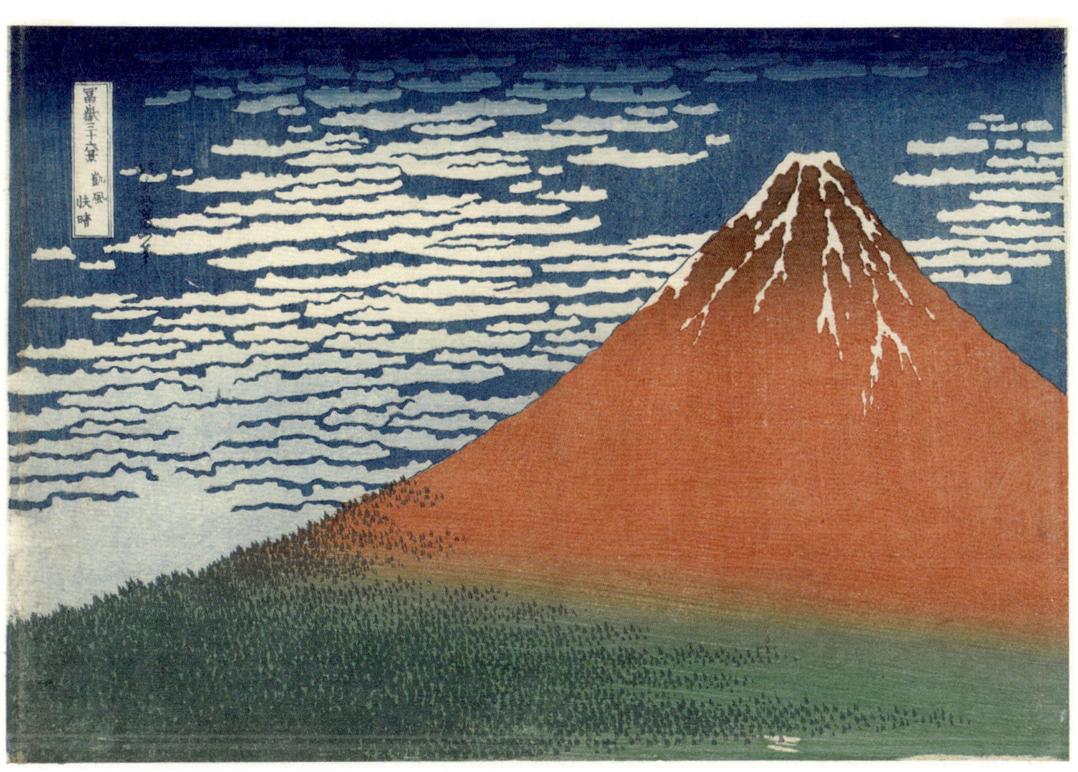

Katsushika Hokusai (1760–1849)
Publisher: Nishimuraya Yohachi (Eijudo)
Fine Wind, Clear Weather (Gaifu kaisei), also known as *Red Fuji*, from the series Thirty-six Views of Mount Fuji (*Fugaku sanjurokkei*), c. 1830–31 (Tenpo 1–2)
Woodblock print (nishiki-e); ink and color on paper
Horizontal oban; 15 × 9¾ in. (38.1 × 24.8 cm)

This iconic view of the great mountain is almost as famous as the print nicknamed *The Great Wave*. The reddish-brown color of the mountain contrasts strikingly with the blue tones used extensively in the rest of the print. In early printings of the Fuji series, even the basic outlines are printed in dark indigo blue, rather than the usual black. The brilliant blue of the sky is a synthetic pigment imported from Europe known as Prussian blue and prized because it did not fade quickly.

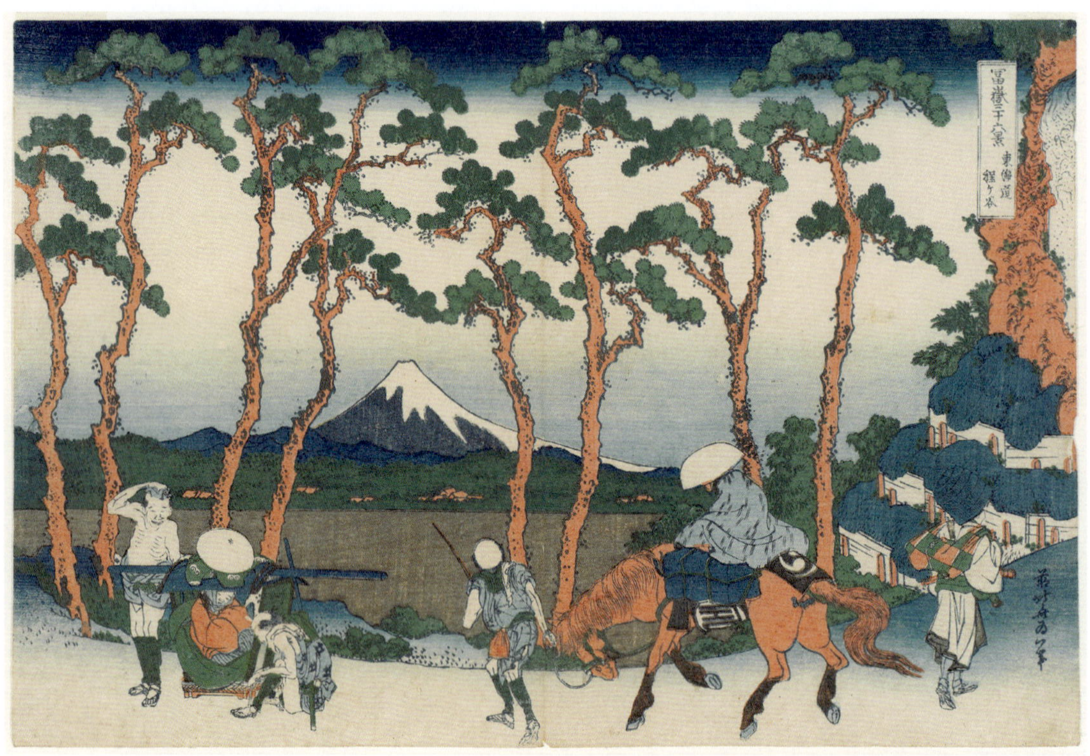

Katsushika Hokusai (1760–1849)
Publisher: Nishimuraya Yohachi (Eijudo)
Hodogaya on the Tokaido (Tokaido Hodogaya), from the series Thirty-six Views of Mount Fuji (*Fugaku sanjurokkei*), c. 1830–31 (Tenpo 1–2)
Woodblock print (nishiki-e); ink and color on paper
Horizontal oban; 14¾ × 9⅞ in. (37.5 × 24.9 cm)

Travelers on the great Tokaido Road pass along a high ridge with a row of trees, gazing through their trunks toward the sacred mountain in the distance. This type of composition was echoed in a number of European paintings of the late nineteenth century. Figures are shown walking, riding a packhorse led by a driver, or riding in a palanquin (whose bearers have stopped for a short break), while to the right is the edge of a roadside religious image on a reinforced slope.

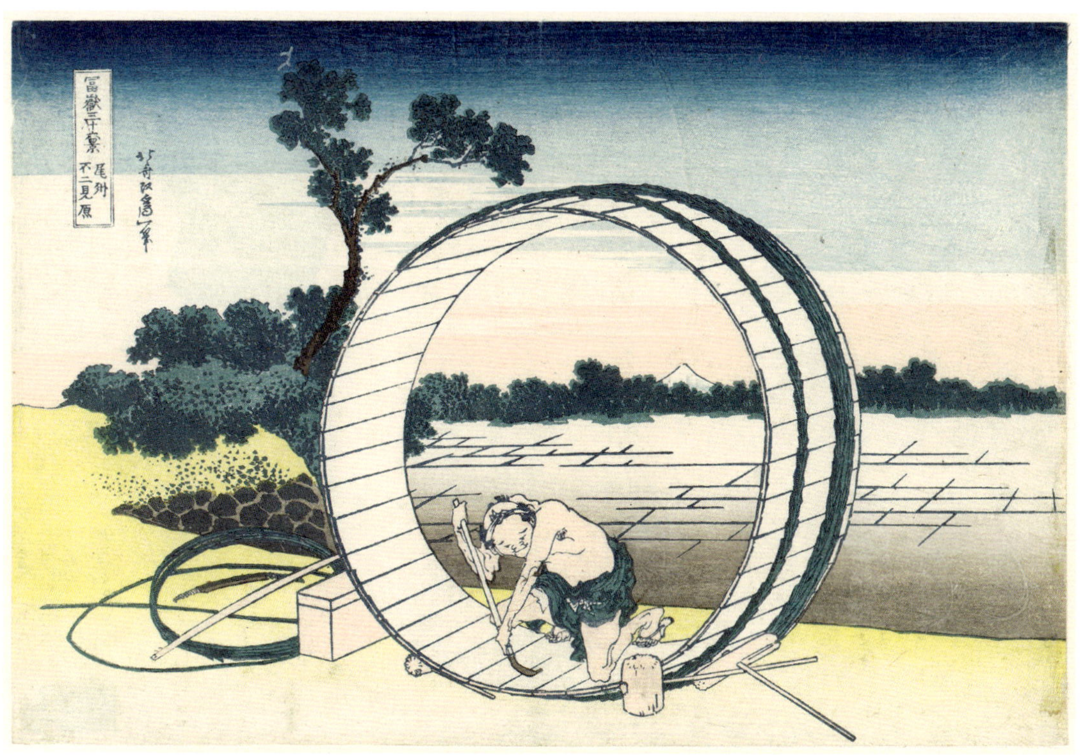

Katsushika Hokusai (1760–1849)
Publisher: Nishimuraya Yohachi (Eijudo)
Fuji View Plain in Owari Province (Bishu Fujimi-ga-hara), from the series Thirty-six Views of Mount Fuji (*Fugaku sanjurokkei*), c. 1830–31 (Tenpo 1–2)
Woodblock print (nishiki-e); ink and color on paper
Horizontal oban; 14⅞ × 10 in. (37.7 × 25.2 cm)

Of all the locations illustrated in the Fuji series, this one is the most distant from Edo, on the far side of the mountain. The huge circle of the barrel that the cooper is constructing frames the tiny triangle of the distant mountain, with the rectangular shapes of fields between them. The area shown still has the name Fuji View (*Fujimi*), but it is now part of downtown Nagoya, surrounded by tall buildings that block the once-famous vista.

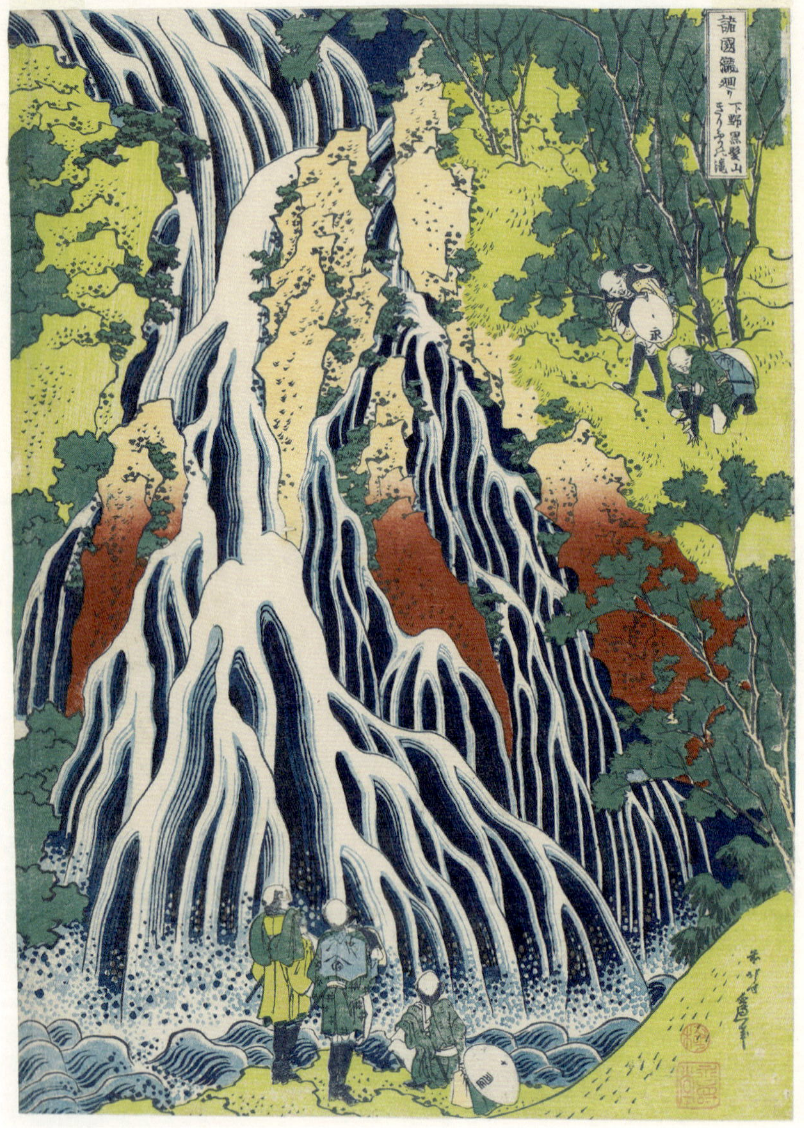

Katsushika Hokusai (1760–1849)
Publisher: Nishimuraya Yohachi (Eijudo)
The Falling Mist Waterfall at Mount Kurokami in Shimotsuke Province (Shimotsuke Kurokamiyama Kirifuri no taki), from the series A Tour of Waterfalls in Various Provinces (*Shokoku taki meguri*), c. 1832 (Tenpo 3)
Woodblock print (nishiki-e); ink and color on paper
Vertical oban; 10¼ × 14 in. (26 × 35.7 cm)

Hokusai's second landscape series after the Views of Mount Fuji was this vertical set of eight waterfalls scattered around the country, selected for variety in appearance so that he could show off different ways of drawing water. The spectacular Falling Mist (*Kirifuri*) waterfall was one of the sights enjoyed by pilgrims on their way to Nikko to visit the Toshogu Shrine dedicated to the deified founder of the Tokugawa shogunate. Hokusai included an inside joke: the name and trademark of the publisher is on the clothing of the figures.

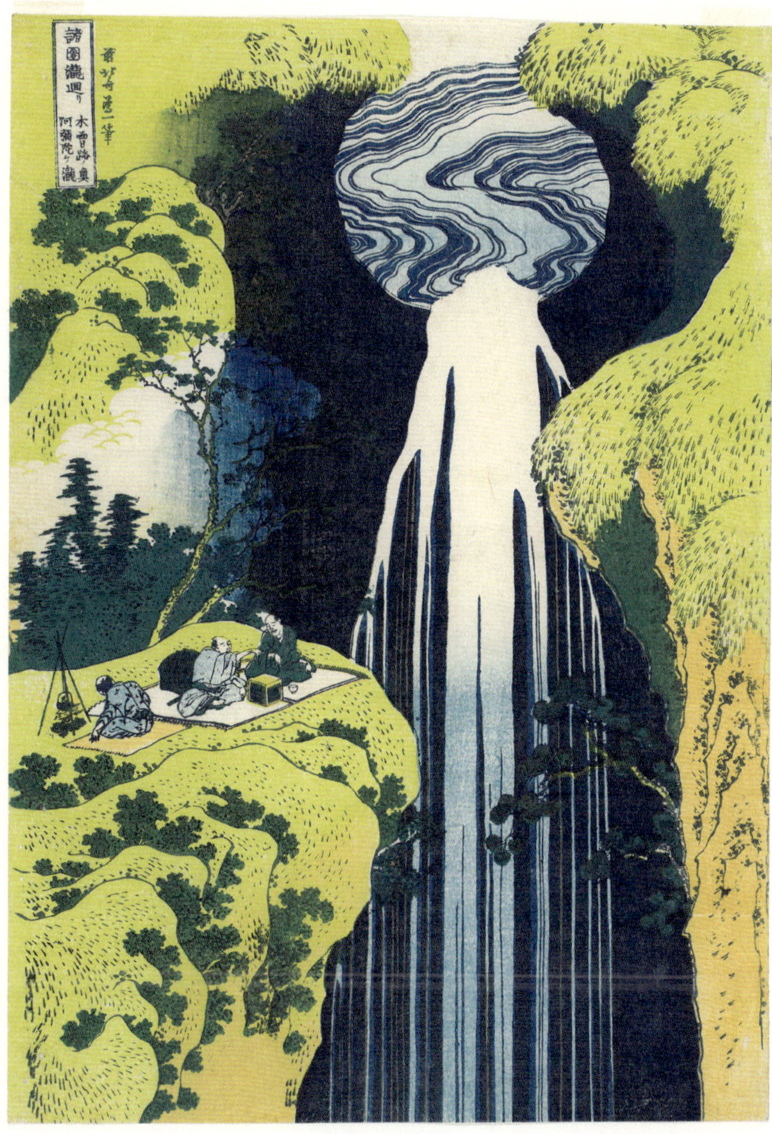

Katsushika Hokusai (1760–1849)
Publisher: Nishimuraya Yohachi (Eijudo)
The Amida Falls in the Far Reaches of the Kiso Road (Kisoji no oku Amida-ga-taki), from the series A Tour of Waterfalls in Various Provinces (*Shokoku taki meguri*), c. 1832 (Tenpo 3)
Woodblock print (nishiki-e); ink and color on paper
Vertical oban; 10⅛ × 14¼ in. (25.7 × 36.1 cm)

The Amida Falls were named for a vision of Amida Buddha seen by a priest who once visited the spot, and the rounded rock formation through which the water flows does indeed resemble the halo of a Buddha. Hokusai probably never visited the site himself but used book illustrations as his models. He deliberately distorted the perspective to make a more interesting picture: the falls are seen from the side, but the stream flowing toward the round opening is drawn as if viewed from above.

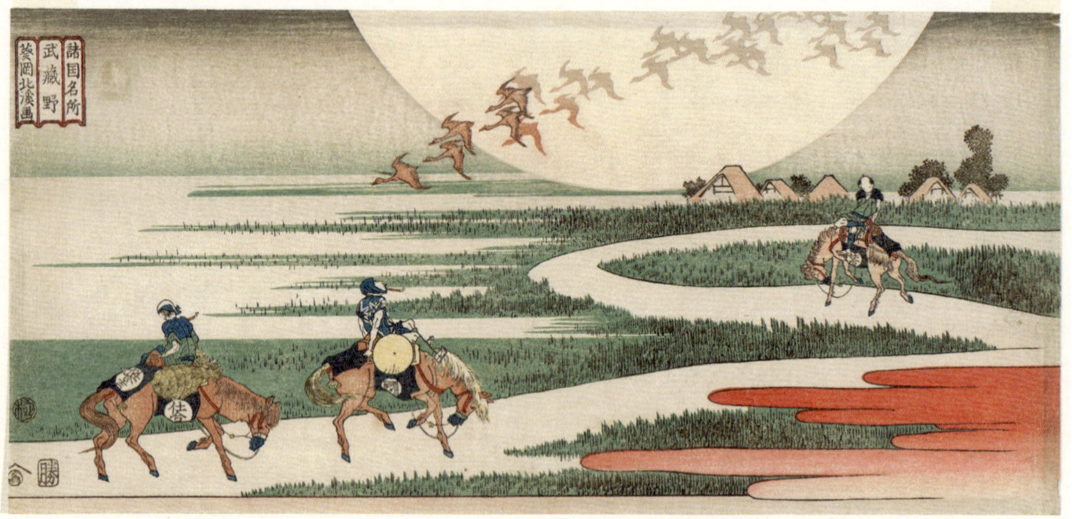

Totoya Hokkei (1780–1850)
Publishers: Nishimuraya Yohachi (Eijudo) and Nakamuraya Katsugoro
Musashi Plain (Musashino), from the series Famous Places in the Provinces (*Shokoku meisho*), c. 1834–35 (Tenpo 5–6)
Woodblock print (nishiki-e); ink and color on paper
Horizontal otanzaku; 14¾ × 6⅞ in. (37.2 × 17.4 cm)

In addition to his many drawings for *surimono* (privately commissioned prints), Hokusai's student Hokkei also designed a few outstanding commercial landscape prints, such as this view of the Musashi Plain to the west of Edo. At the time, the area now covered by Tokyo suburbs was a vast, grassy plain, famous for an optical illusion that made the full moon rising above it look enormous. Hokkei exaggerated the size of the moon still further in this evocative autumn scene.

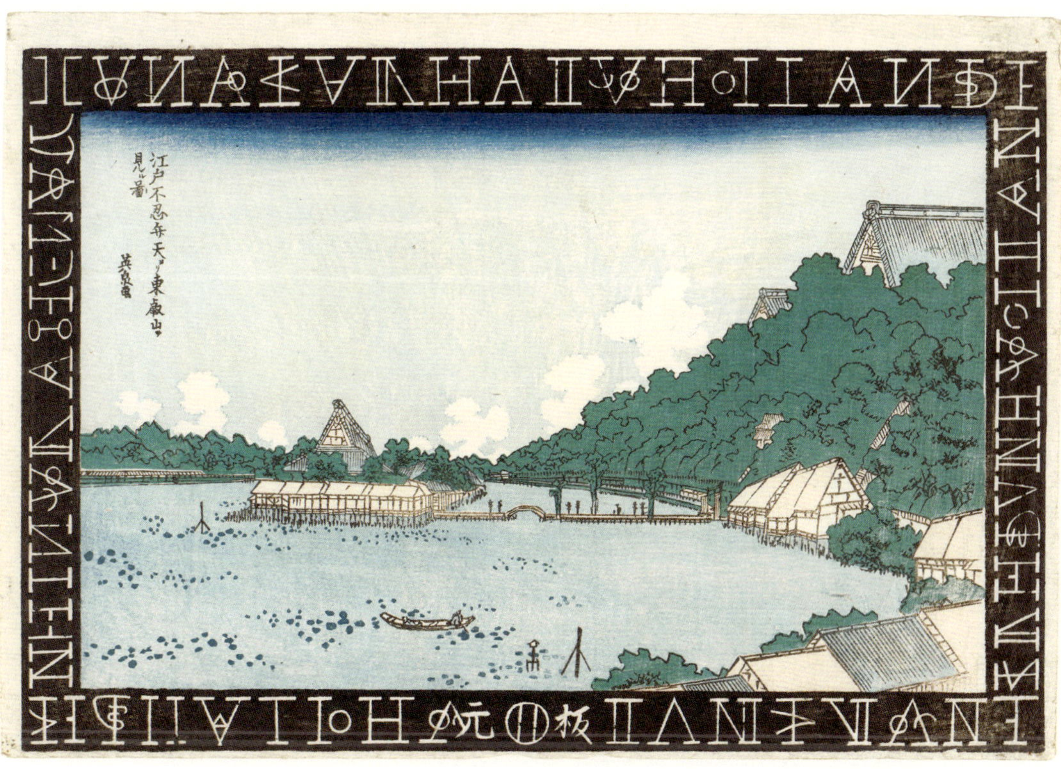

Keisai Eisen (1790–1848)
Publisher: Ezakiya Kichibei (Tenjudo)
Toeizan Temple Seen from Shinobazu Benten Shrine in Edo (Edo Shinobazu Benten yori Toeizan o miru zu), from a series of famous places in Edo with frames of Western letters, c. 1830–35
Woodblock print (nishiki-e); ink and color on paper
Horizontal oban; 15⅛ × 10½ in. (38.4 × 26.7 cm)

Today the Edo-period temple grounds are the site of Tokyo's extensive Ueno Park, and the pond at the foot of the slope leading up to the temple is still very recognizable, though now with a background of skyscrapers. Eisen's view of the pond and its island shrine is done in the Westernized style of the perspective prints that had been popular in the late eighteenth century, complemented by printed frames featuring letters of the roman alphabet as decorations.

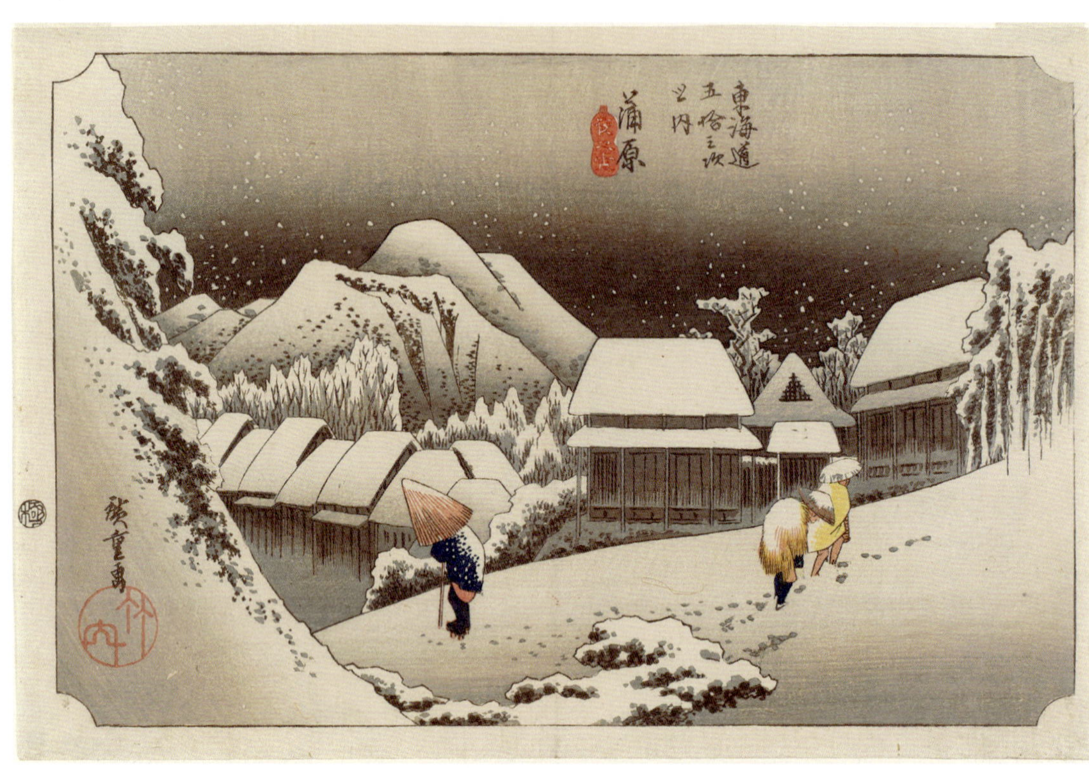

Utagawa Hiroshige I (1797–1858)
Publisher: Takenouchi Magohachi (Hoeido)
Kanbara: Night Snow (Kanbara, yoru no yuki), second state, from the series Fifty-three Stations of the Tokaido Road (*Tokaido gojusan tsugi no uchi*), also known as the First Tokaido or Great Tokaido
c. 1833–34 (Tenpo 4–5)
Woodblock print (nishiki-e); ink and color on paper
Horizontal oban; 14¾ × 9¾ in. (37.5 × 24.8 cm)

Clearly inspired by Hokusai's Thirty-six Views of Mount Fuji, Hiroshige's Fifty-three Stations of the Tokaido Road follows the great coastal highway from Edo to Kyoto with a view of each of the fifty-three highway rest stops between the two cities. In this second version of the print for Kanbara station, an alteration in the placement of the dark shading of the sky—along the horizon rather than along the top of the print—enhances the effect of a chilly evening.

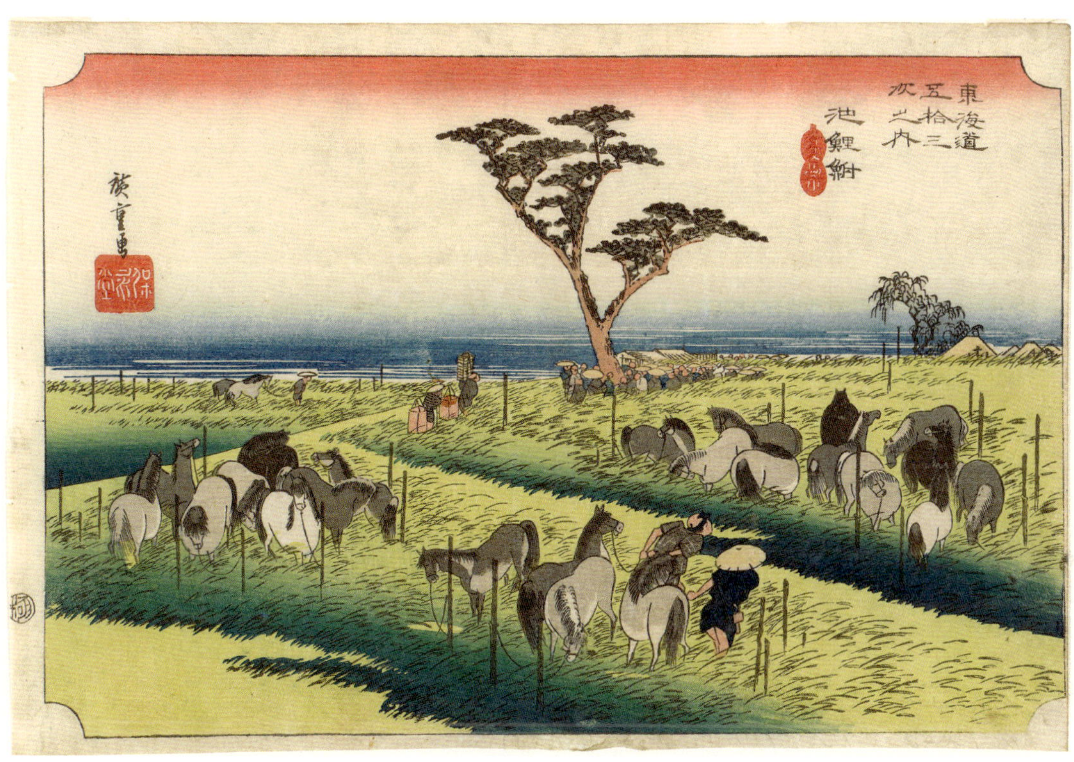

Utagawa Hiroshige I (1797–1858)
Publisher: Takenouchi Magohachi (Hoeido)
Chiryu: Early Summer Horse Fair (Chiryu, shuka uma ichi), second (?) state, from the series Fifty-three Stations of the Tokaido (*Tokaido gojusan tsugi no uchi*), also known as the First Tokaido or Great Tokaido, c. 1833–34 (Tenpo 4–5)
Woodblock print (nishiki-e); ink and color on paper
Horizontal oban; 14½ × 9¾ in. (36.8 × 24.7 cm)

Plump horses standing in windblown grass await new owners at the summer horse fair in the town of Chiryu. This stop on the Tokaido was better known for a classical poem about irises written by a great poet as he passed through the area, but Hiroshige chose to show a modern scene instead. While the horses enjoy the grass, two men carry boxes of food toward the waiting human crowd. A small hill in the background was removed for the second edition of the print.

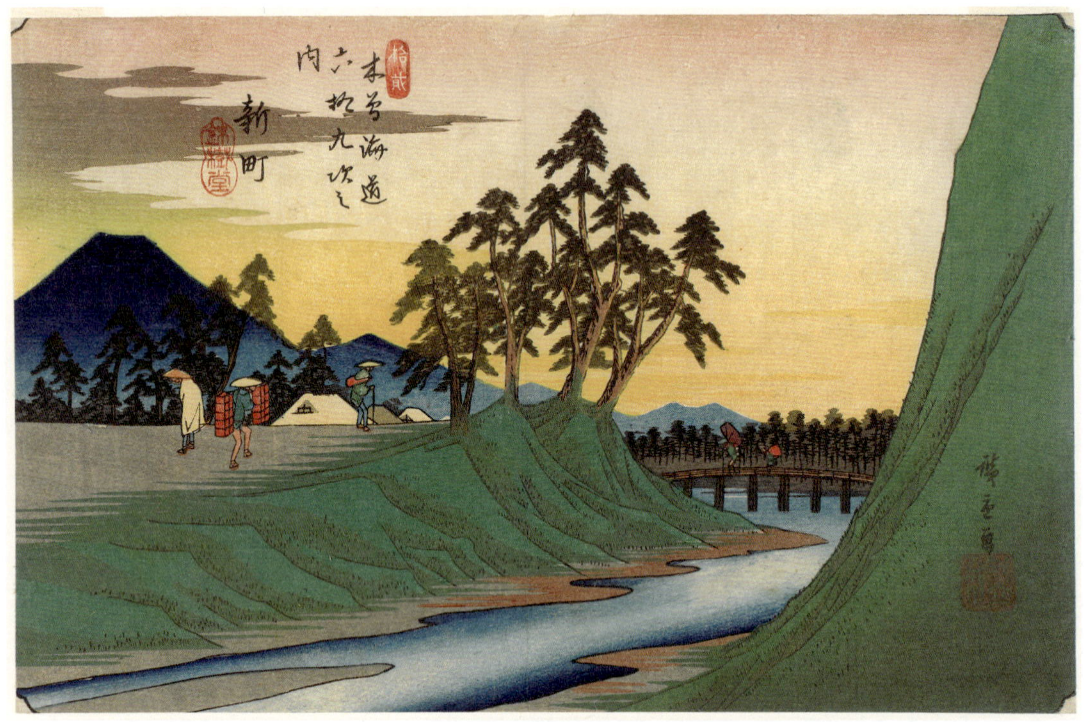

Utagawa Hiroshige I (1797–1858)
Publisher: Iseya Rihei (Kinjudo)
No. 12, Shinmachi, from the series Sixty-nine Stations of the Kisokaido Road (*Kisokaido rokujukyu tsugi no uchi*), c. 1835–38 (Tenpo 6–9)
Woodblock print (nishiki-e); ink and color on paper
Horizontal oban; 13¾ × 8¾ in. (34.9 × 22.3 cm)

One of the five major highways of Edo-period Japan, the Kisokaido Road ran from Edo to Kyoto along the mountainous interior route, rather than the coastal path followed by the more famous Tokaido. In addition to numerous series showing the Tokaido, Hiroshige did just one showing the Kisokaido, in collaboration with Keisai Eisen. The beautiful colors of the sunset sky in this scene underscore the importance of the skill of the printers in realizing Hiroshige's atmospheric vision of the Japanese landscape.

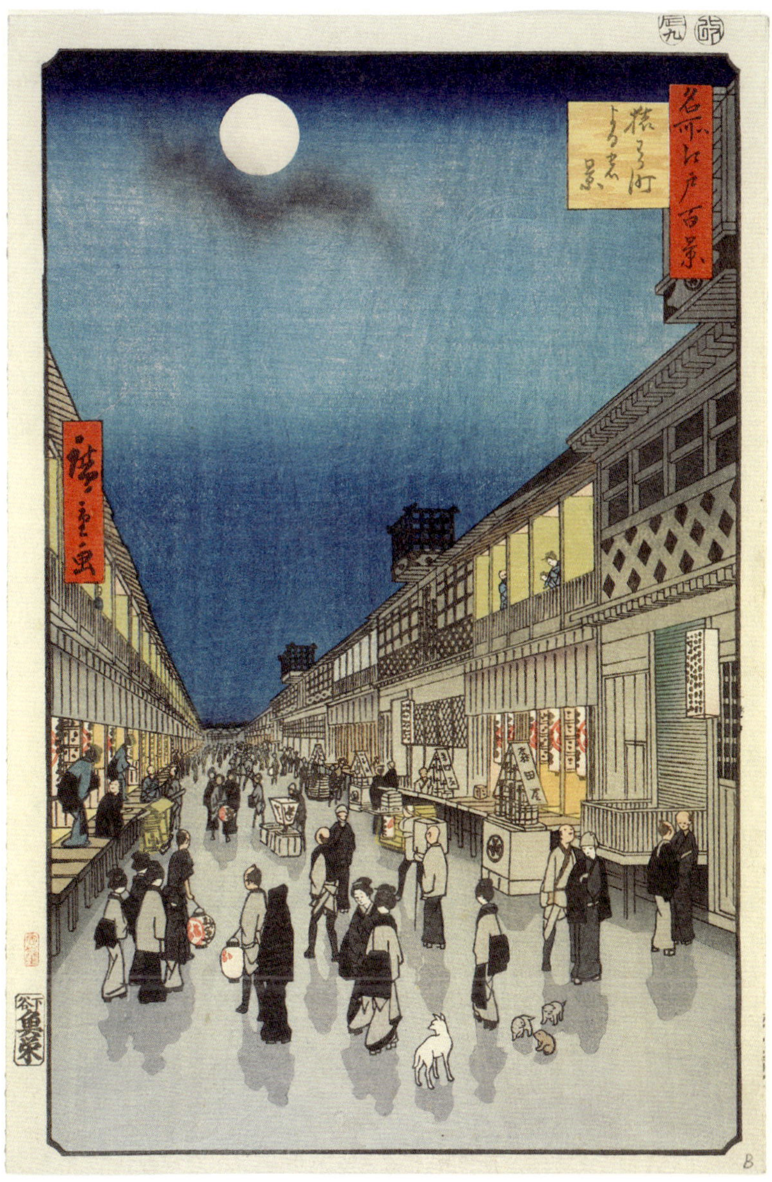

Utagawa Hiroshige I (1797–1858)
Publisher: Uoya Eikichi
Night View of Saruwaka-machi (Saruwaka-machi yoru no kei), from the series One Hundred Famous Views of Edo (*Meisho Edo hyakkei*), 1856 (Ansei 3), 9th month
Woodblock print (nishiki-e); ink and color on paper
Vertical oban; 9½ × 14⅛ in. (24 × 35.7 cm)

Hiroshige's final masterpiece, nearing completion at the time of his death, was the series One Hundred Famous Views of Edo. In this rendition of the theater district, the full moon is so bright it casts shadows, an unusual detail in ukiyo-e prints. Another special feature seen only in deluxe editions is the wisp of cloud across the moon, which was hand-painted onto the printing block so that it is slightly different in each impression of the print.

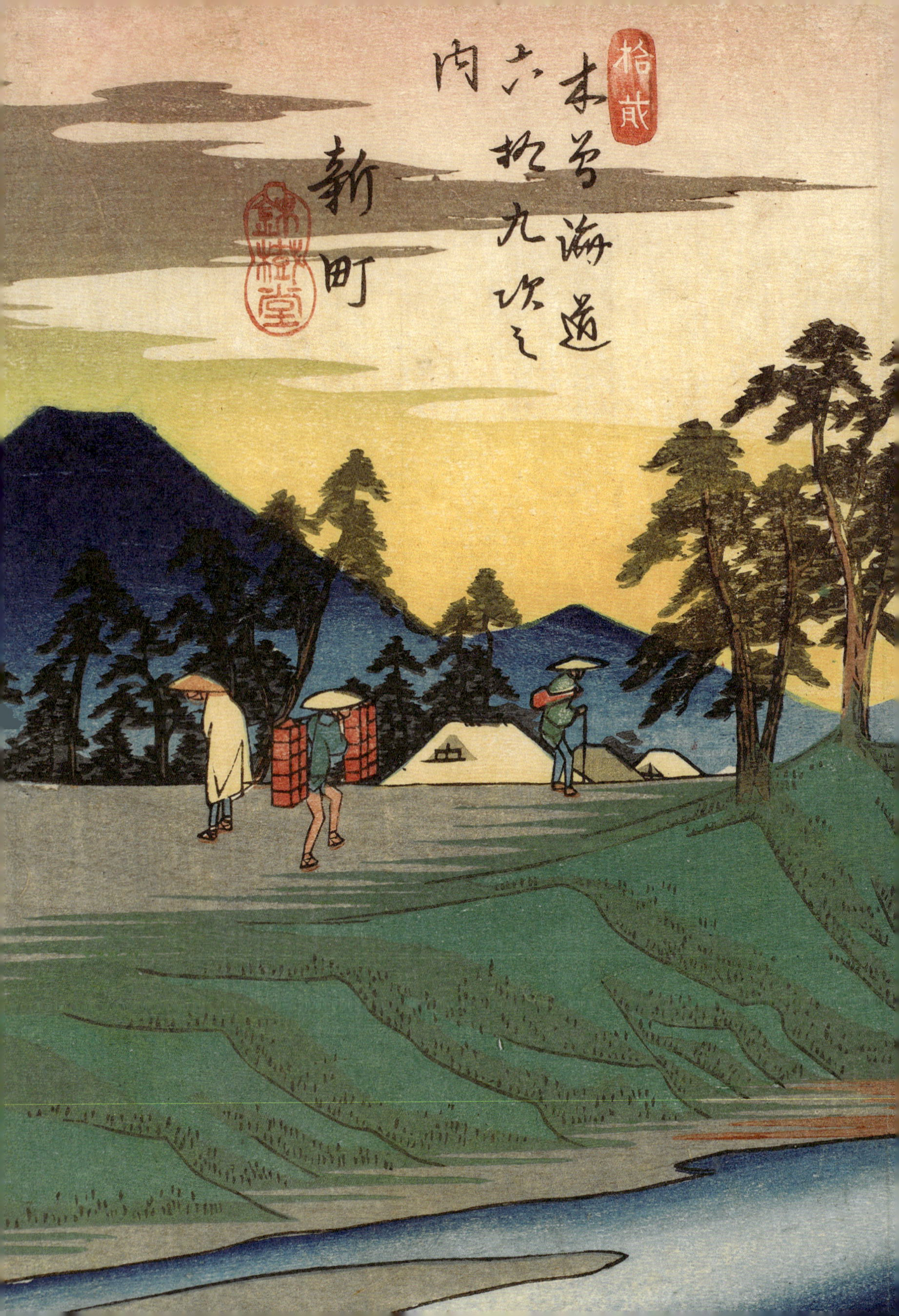
木曽海道六拾九次之内
新町
錦樹堂

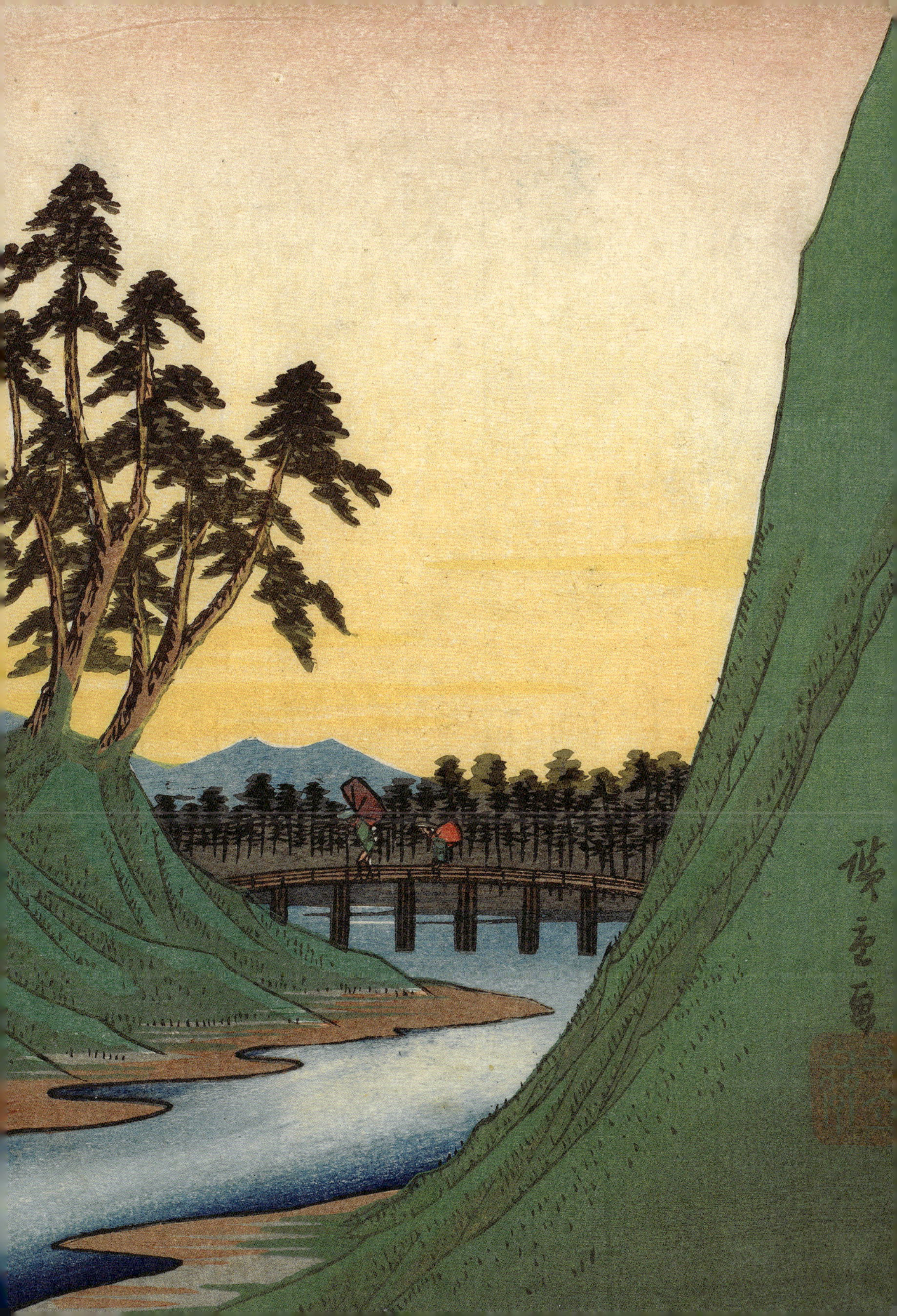
廣重画

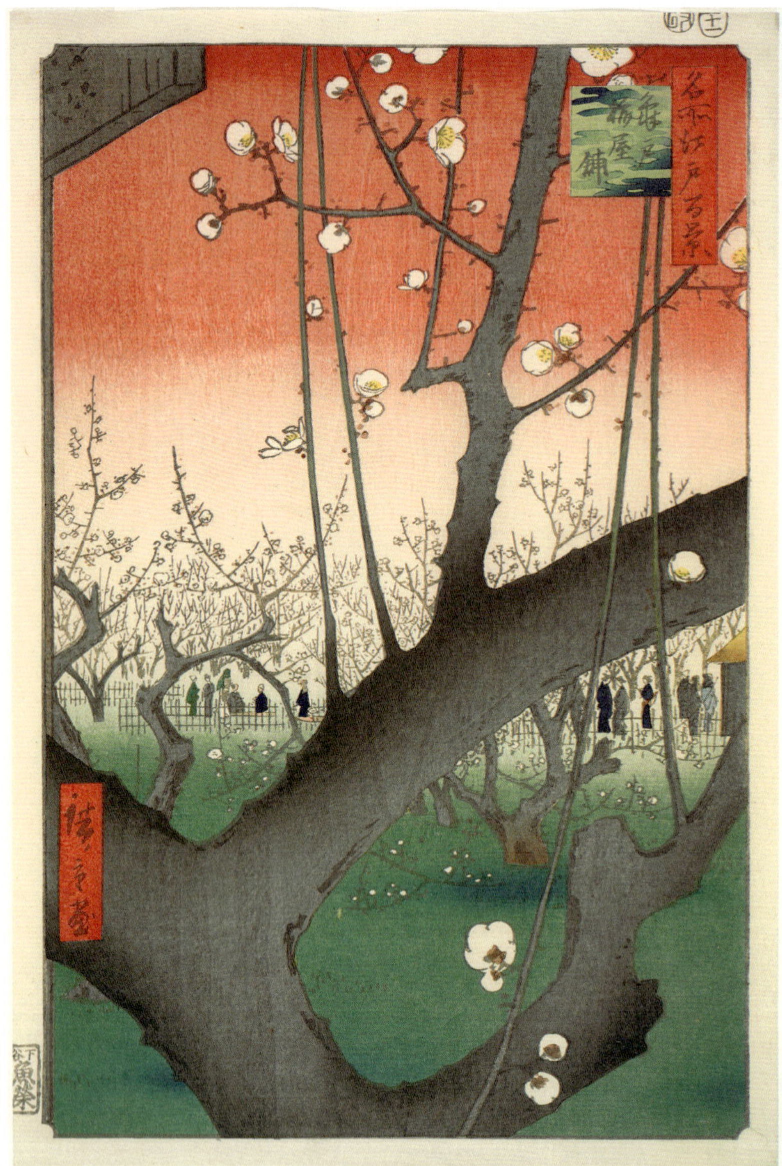

Utagawa Hiroshige I (1797–1858)
Publisher: Uoya Eikichi
Plum Estate, Kameido (Kameido Umeyashiki), from the series One Hundred Famous Views of Edo (*Meisho Edo hyakkei*), 1857 (Ansei 4), 11th month
Woodblock print (nishiki-e); ink and color on paper
Vertical oban; 9¾ × 14⅛ in. (24.8 × 35.9 cm)

The series One Hundred Famous Views of Edo is noteworthy for its extensive use of unusual viewpoints, often combining near and far views in interesting juxtapositions, as in this view of a garden of flowering plum trees seen through the branches of one of the trees. The wooden label identifying the tree is visible at the left edge. European artists of the late nineteenth century found Hiroshige's innovative compositions very intriguing, and this example was copied in oils by Van Gogh.

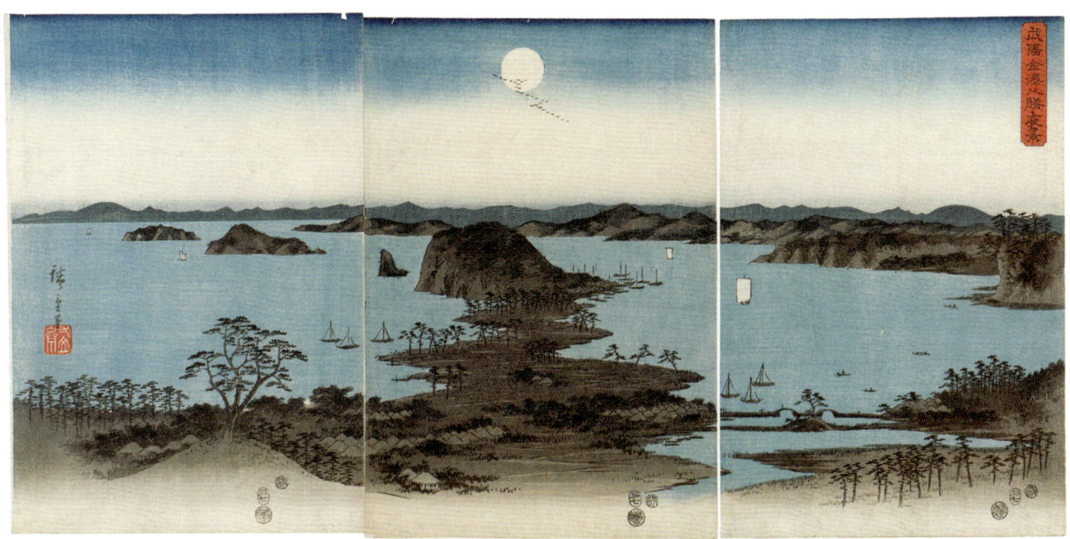

Utagawa Hiroshige I (1797–1858)
Publisher: Okazawaya Taheiji
Eight Views of Kanazawa at Night (Buyo Kanazawa hassho yakei), from an untitled set of three triptychs, 1857 (Ansei 4), 7th month
Woodblock print (nishiki-e); ink and color on paper
Vertical oban triptych;
29⅞ × 14½ in. (75.9 × 36.8 cm)

Late in his career Hiroshige designed three spectacular landscape triptychs suggesting the traditional theme of snow, moon, and flowers—the most beautiful things in the world according to an ancient Chinese poem. For the moon, he chose the coastal scenery of the area known as Kanazawa or Kanesawa, now part of the city of Yokohama (not to be confused with the city of Kanazawa in distant Kaga Province), which was said to have eight especially fine views similar to the Eight Views of Omi near Kyoto.

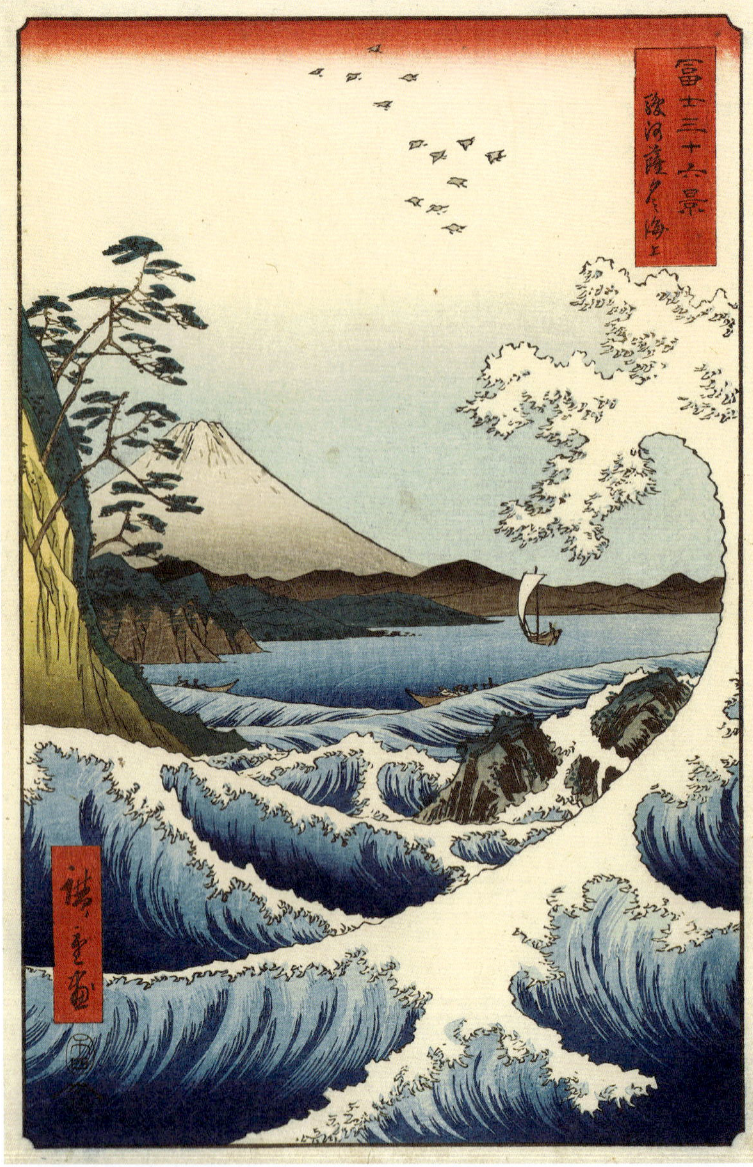

Utagawa Hiroshige I (1797–1858)
Publisher: Tsutaya
Kichizo (Koeido)
The Sea off Satta in Suruga Province (Suruga Satta kaijo), from the series Thirty-six Views of Mount Fuji (*Fuji sanjurokkei*), 1858 (Ansei 5), 4th month
Woodblock print (nishiki-e); ink and color on paper
Vertical oban; 10 × 14¾ in. (25.3 × 37.4 cm)

Almost a decade after Hokusai's death, his onetime rival Hiroshige did his own version of the theme made famous by the older master, using a vertical format rather than a horizontal one. This gorgeous design clearly owes a debt to Hokusai's *Great Wave*. It is even more similar to one of the illustrations in Hokusai's picture book *One Hundred Views of Mount Fuji*, published shortly after his color print series.

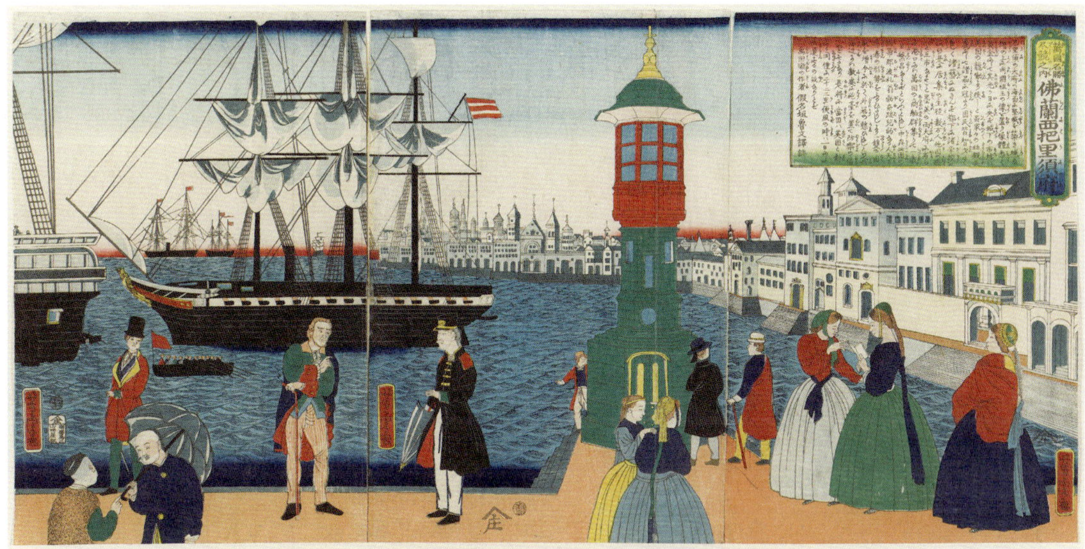

Utagawa Yoshitora
(active c. 1836–1887)
Publisher: Yamadaya Shojiro
The City of Paris, France
(Furansu Parisu no fu), 1862
(Bunkyu 2), 6th month
Woodblock print (nishiki-e);
ink and color on paper
Vertical oban triptych;
29¼ × 14¼ in. (74.2 × 36.2 cm)

The opening of Yokohama as a treaty port for foreign trade in 1860 led to the rise of "Yokohama prints," works showing the newly arrived foreigners either as they actually appeared or as the artists—who were working in Edo rather than Yokohama itself—imagined them. Illustrations in European books, newspapers, and magazines provided raw material for works such as this vivid imaginary depiction of one of the cities from which the foreign merchants and their families had come.

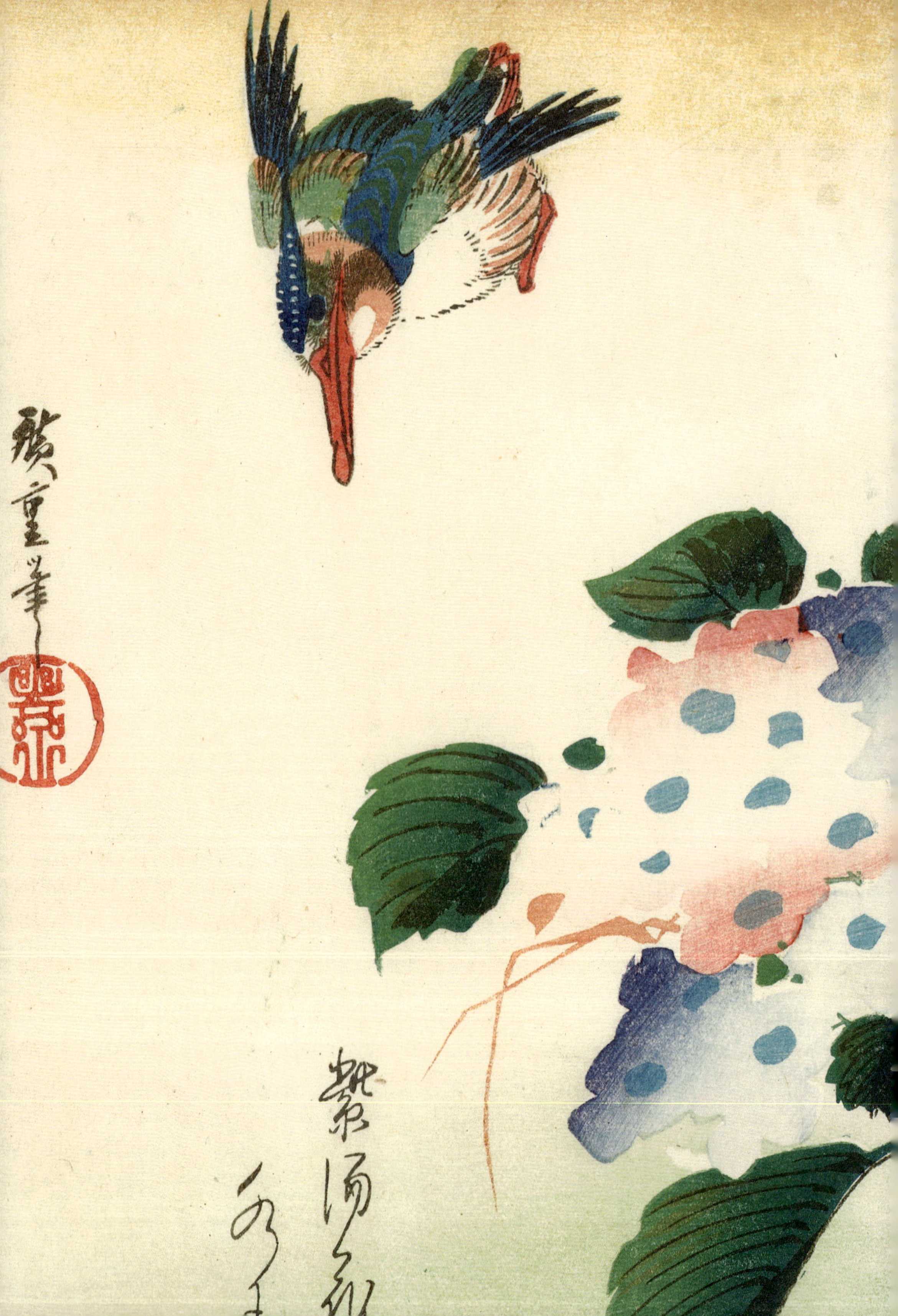

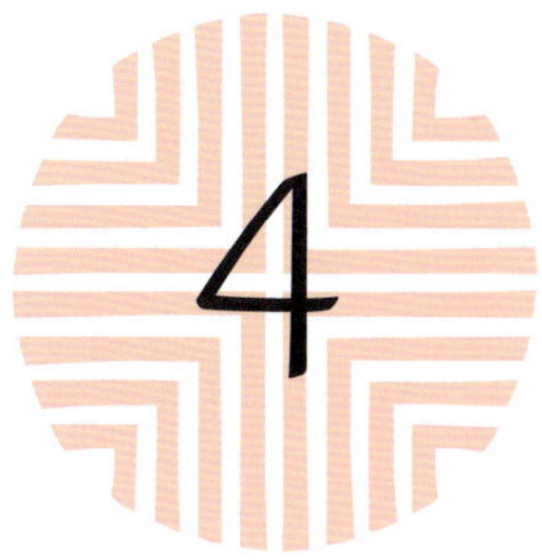

4 The Natural World

The genre of East Asian painting known as "bird-and-flower pictures" originated in China during the Song dynasty (960–1279) and spread to Japan in the fourteenth to sixteenth centuries. Although birds and flowers are indeed the most common subjects, the genre encompasses all kinds of nature studies, including animals, insects, and marine life. Sometimes depictions of flora and fauna have symbolic meanings: for example, cranes are auspicious symbols of longevity, as are pine trees and turtles; bamboo symbolizes resilience. Floral motifs are strongly associated with the changing seasons.

The Kano school, official painters to the shogun, often used nature motifs—painted either in monochrome or brilliant color—blown up to a large scale on folding screens or sliding-door panels as interior decoration for temples and palaces. Nature studies also appeared in the form of book-shaped albums of small paintings, with individual works pasted onto the pages. These painted albums provided inspiration for early printed books of the same themes. Chinese-printed painting manuals were also influential.

In single-sheet prints, there are scattered examples of bird-and-flower prints throughout the history of ukiyo-e, and some especially lovely ones were made in the early days of full-color printing by artists such as Harunobu and Koryusai. But as in the case of landscape prints, the true breakthrough came only in the 1830s, with the work of Hokusai and Hiroshige. Nature, like landscapes and historical events, became a major genre of ukiyo-e printmaking at this time, comparable in popularity to the long-established genres of actors and women.

Often bird-and-flower prints are embellished with poetry of various kinds, recalling the genre's origins in elegant Chinese painting.

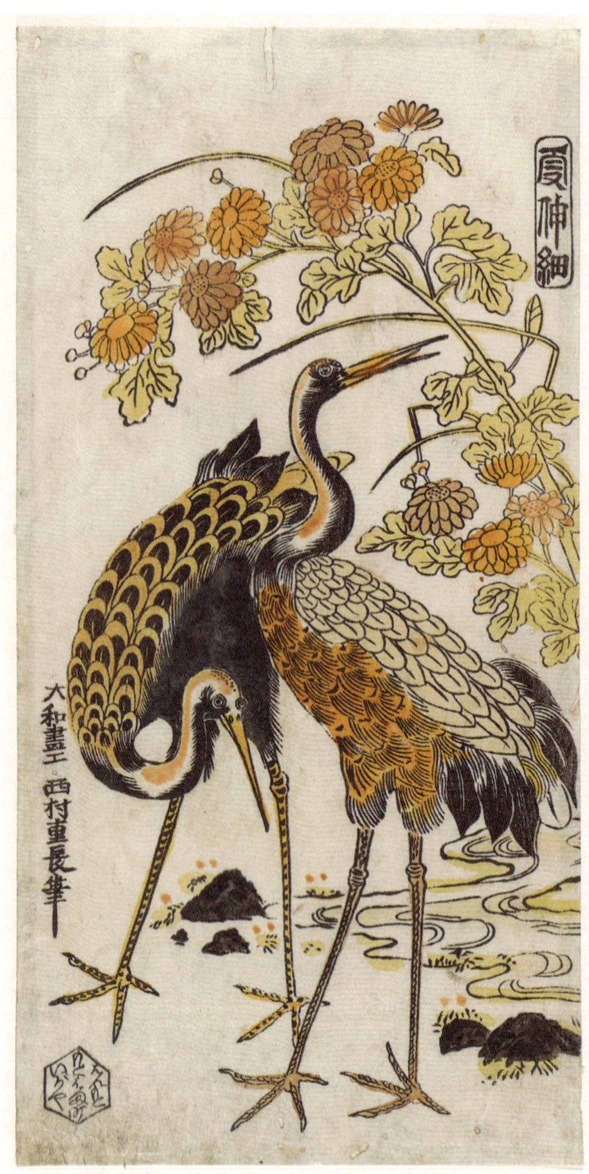

Nishimura Shigenaga (1697?–1756)
Publisher: Igaya Kan'emon (Bunkido)
Cranes and Chrysanthemums, from a bird-and-flower series with the title Kashinsai (?), 1730 (Kyoho 15)
Woodblock print (urushi-e); ink on paper, with hand-applied color and nikawa
Hosoban; 6¼ × 12¼ in. (15.9 × 31.1 cm)

Bird-and-flower prints are not common in early ukiyo-e, but there are a few beautiful examples, such as the prints in this series, whose title remains undeciphered. Two cranes, symbols of long life and good fortune, pose in front of a chrysanthemum bush with multicolored flowers. Hand-colored prints of this type are sometimes called "lacquer prints" (*urushi-e*) because the hand-applied colors include black ink mixed with glue (*nikawa*), making it look shiny and lacquer-like when it dries.

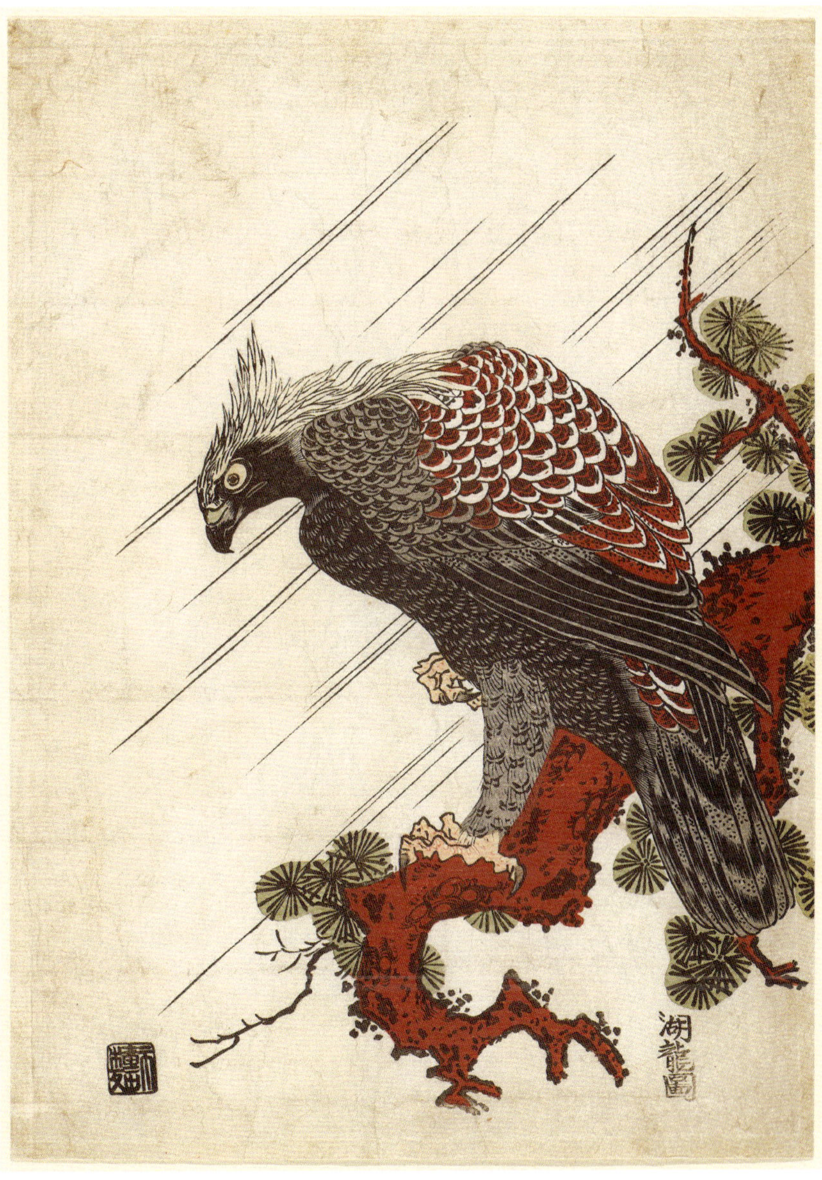

Isoda Koryusai (1735–1790)
Publisher: Nishimuraya Yohachi (Eijudo)
Eagle on a Pine Branch in the Rain, c. 1770
Woodblock print (nishiki-e); ink and color on paper
Vertical chuban; 7½ × 10¼ in. (19 × 25.8 cm)

Unlike most ukiyo-e artists, Koryusai was born into the samurai class and so enjoyed an elite education whose influence can sometimes be seen in his work. Birds of prey, symbolizing the warlike character aspired to by the samurai, were favored subject matter for the painted-door panels, folding screens, and hanging scrolls that decorated upper-class homes. Koryusai's print of the mighty bird unfazed by bad weather showcases his drawing skills and brings the status-laden subject within financial reach of the average townsperson.

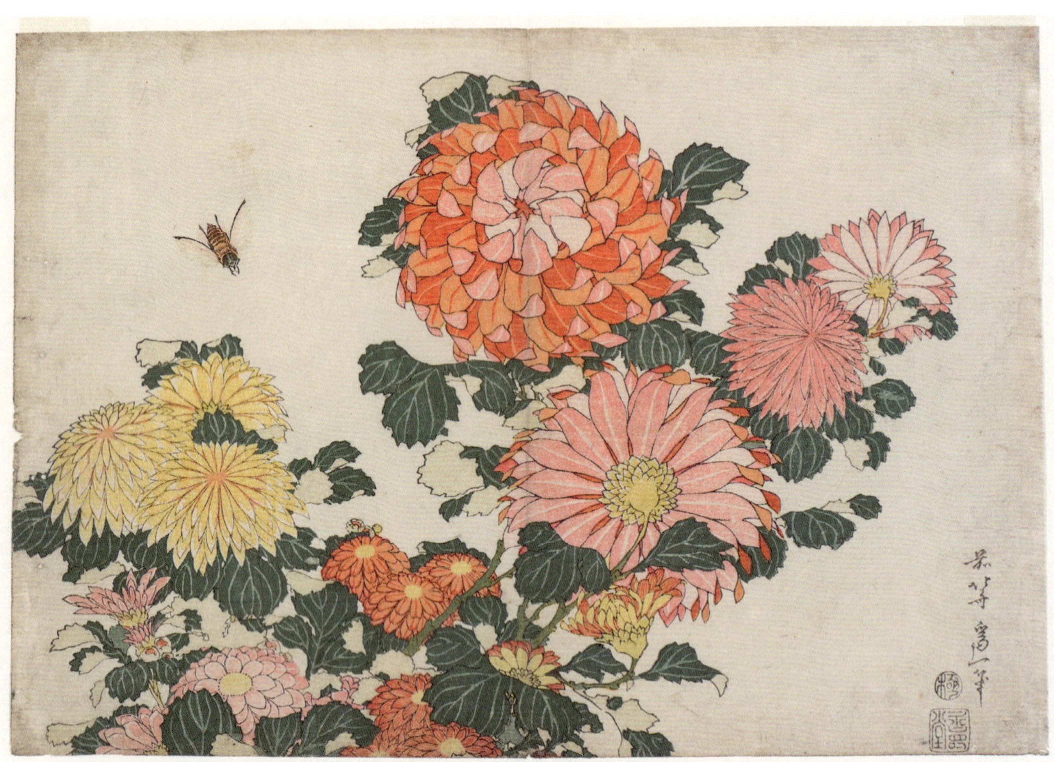

Katsushika Hokusai (1760–1849)
Publisher: Nishimuraya Yohachi (Eijudo)
Chrysanthemums and Horsefly, from an untitled series known as Large Flowers, c. 1833–34 (Tenpo 4–5)
Woodblock print (nishiki-e); ink and color on paper
Horizontal oban; 14¾ × 10 in. (37.5 × 25.3 cm)

Hokusai's untitled series known as Large Flowers did for bird-and-flower prints what his Fuji series had done for landscape just a few years earlier: take a minor subject area in ukiyo-e and turn it into a major one through the brilliance of his designs. The flowers are shown close-up, at eye level, so that they come to life as if the viewer were on the ground beside them. Many of the designs in the series include birds or insects that add to the impression of life and motion.

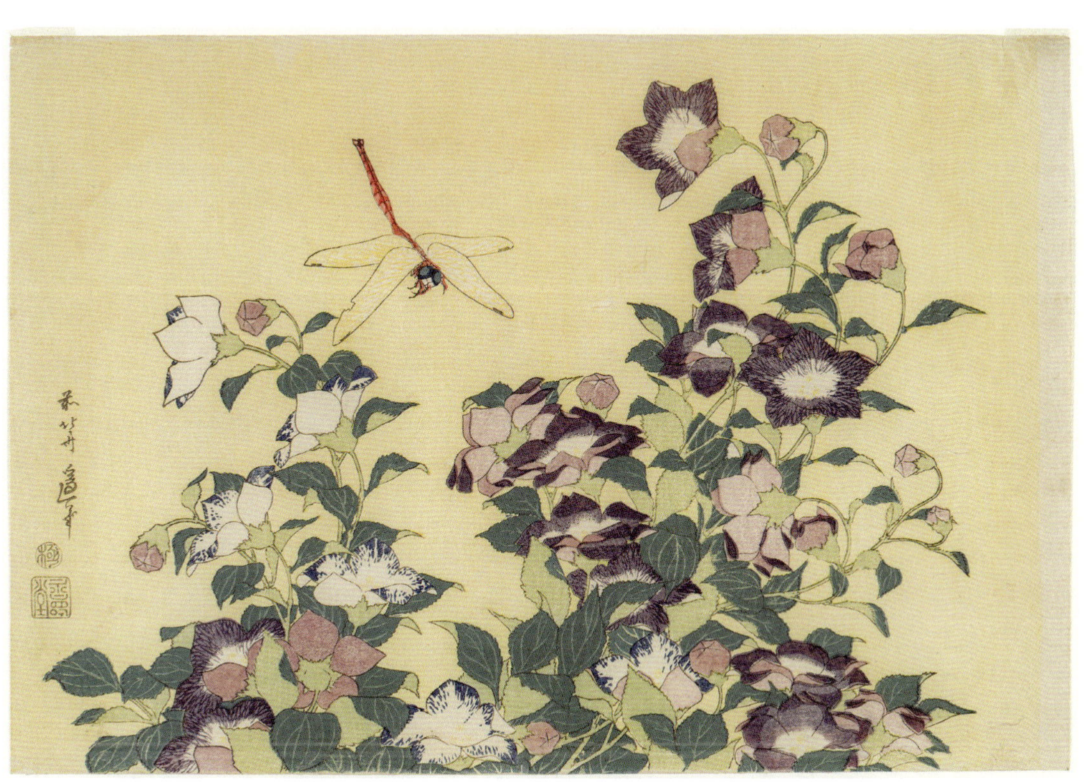

Katsushika Hokusai (1760–1849)
Publisher: Nishimuraya Yohachi (Eijudo)
Bellflower and Dragonfly, from an untitled series known as Large Flowers, c. 1833–34 (Tenpo 4–5)
Woodblock print (nishiki-e); ink and color on paper
Horizontal oban; 15½ × 10½ in. (39.4 × 26.6 cm)

Because they bloom at the end of the summer, bellflowers were traditionally regarded as one of the Seven Plants of Autumn celebrated in Japanese poetry. Their usual color is a dark blue-purple, but as Hokusai shows, other varieties also exist. The addition of the dragonfly suggests that Hokusai may have been influenced by an image of a dragonfly and bellflowers in a poetry album by Utamaro, *Selected Insects* (*Mushi erabi*), published in 1788 when Hokusai was still an aspiring young artist of the Katsukawa school.

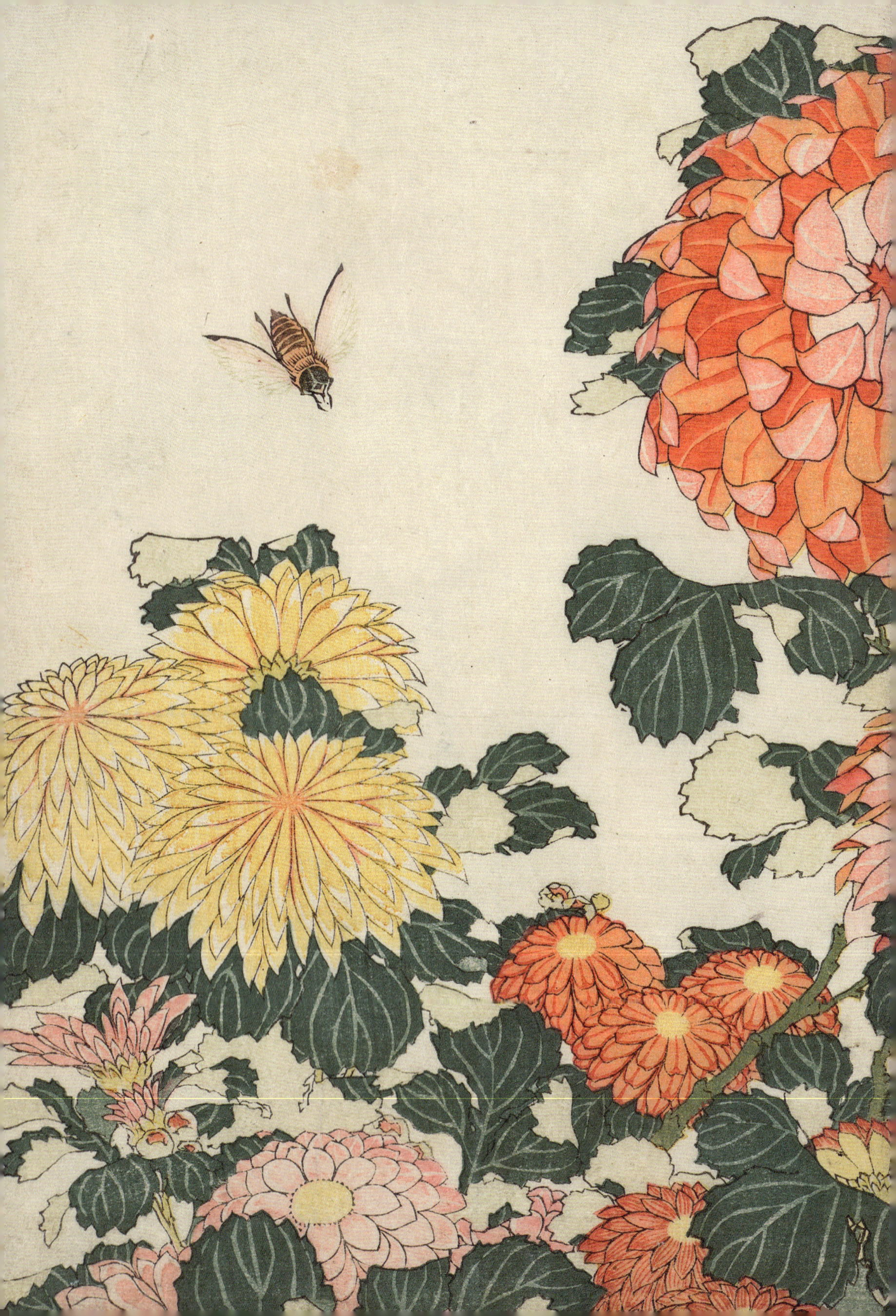

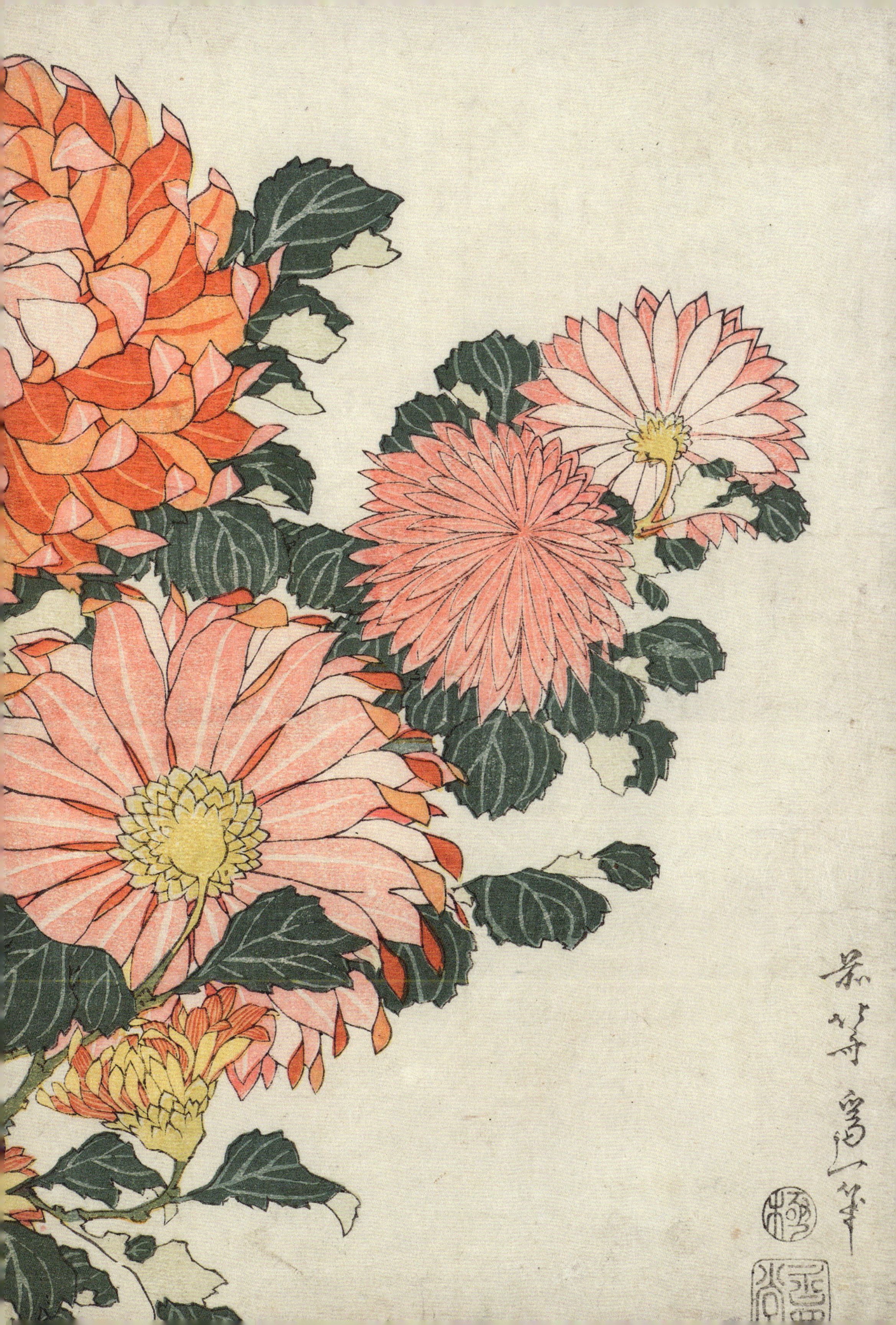
前北斎為一筆

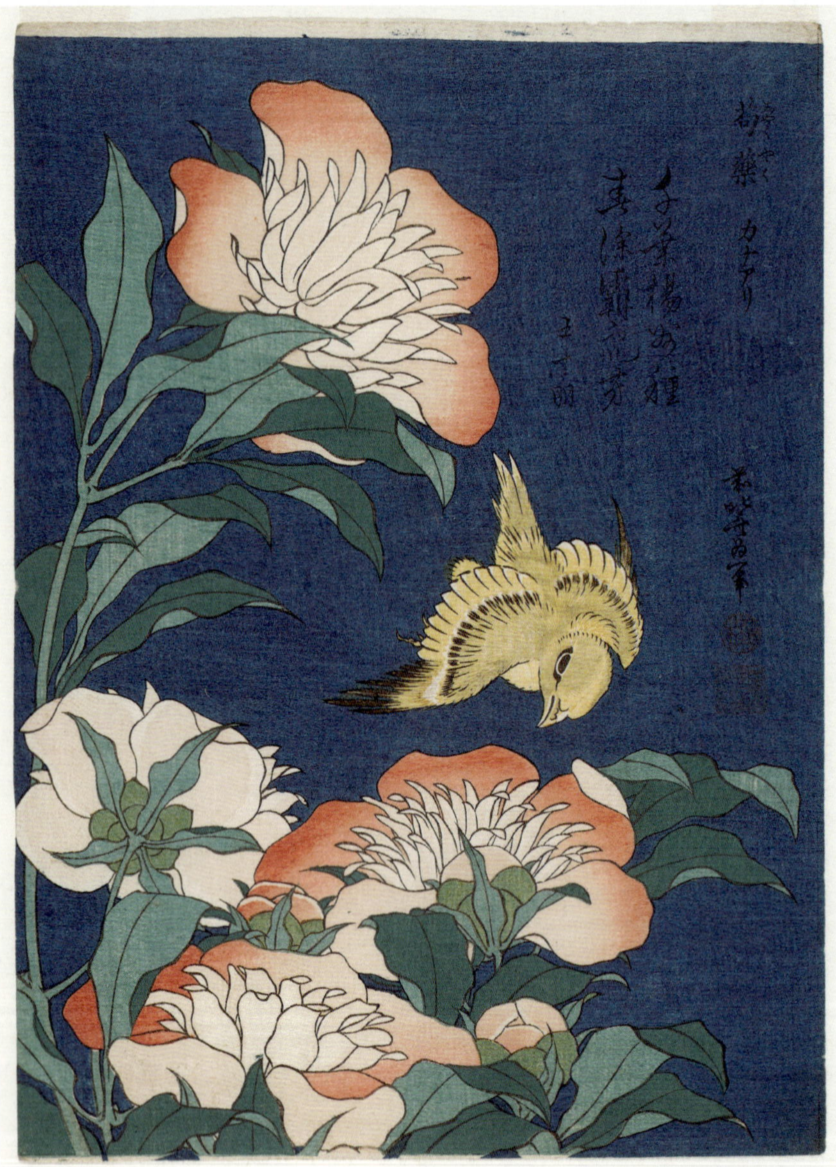

Katsushika Hokusai (1760–1849)
Publisher: Nishimuraya Yohachi (Eijudo)
Peonies and Canary (Shakuyaku, kanaari), from an untitled series known as Small Flowers, c. 1834 (Tenpo 5)
Woodblock print (nishiki-e); ink and color on paper
Vertical chuban; 7¾ × 10¼ in. (19.7 × 26 cm)

According to a Chinese saying, tree peonies were at their finest in the city of Loyang and herbaceous peonies (the type shown here) in Yangzhou. The brilliant yellow canary is an exotic songbird that originated in the islands of the Atlantic and was imported into Japan by Dutch traders. The Chinese couplet inscribed on the print is by the Northern Song dynasty poet Wang Shiming (1112–1171): "The Yangzhou peony with its thousand leaves, / supreme among the fragrances of spring."

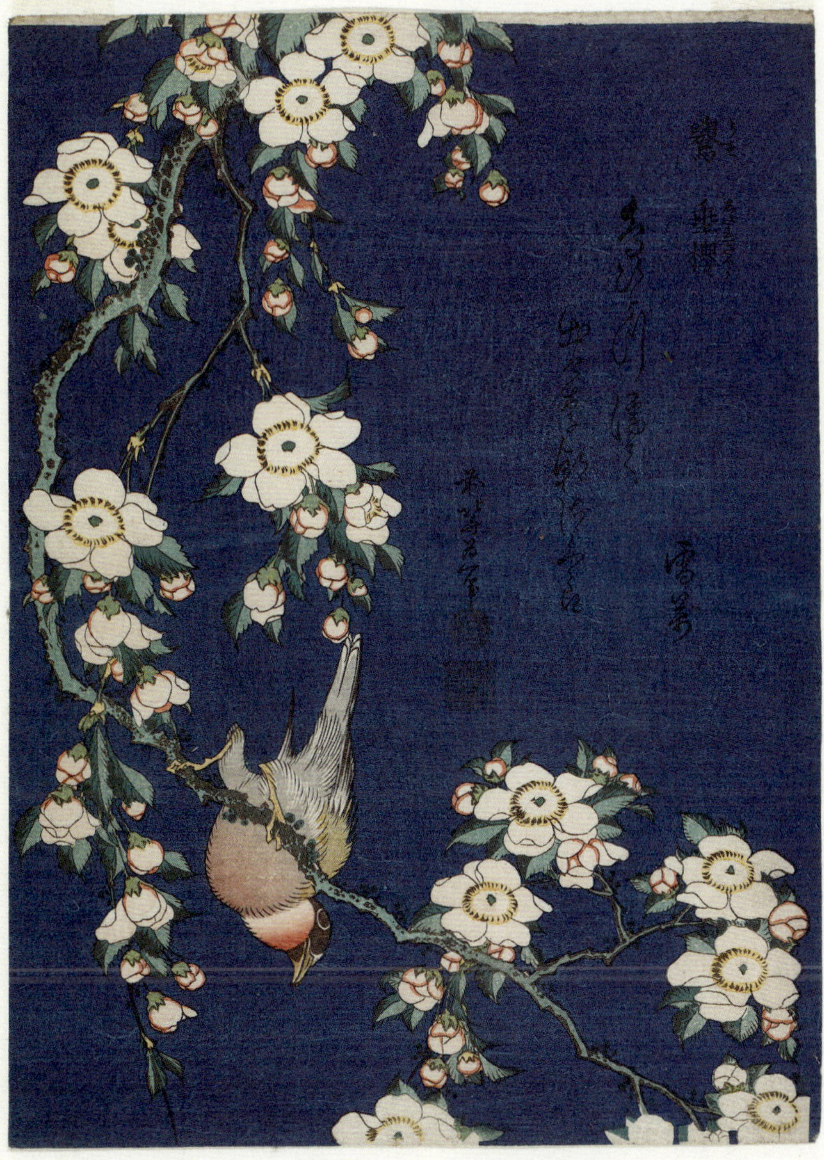

Katsushika Hokusai (1760–1849)
Publisher: Nishimuraya Yohachi (Eijudo)
Bullfinch and Weeping Cherry (Uso, shidarezakura), from an untitled series known as Small Flowers, c. 1834 (Tenpo 5)
Woodblock print (nishiki-e); ink and color on paper
Vertical chuban; 7½ × 10 in. (19 × 25.5 cm)

A sparrow-sized bird with a distinctive red throat and a whistling call, the bullfinch perches on a dangling branch with both buds and blossoms. The haikai poem is by Senraian Setsuman, the poetry name of the shamisen master Sugano Joyu II (1784–1841): "Just a single bird / emerging in morning damp / from cherry blossoms." In addition to his music and poetry, he was also a painter and a tea master, and he may have been a personal acquaintance of Hokusai.

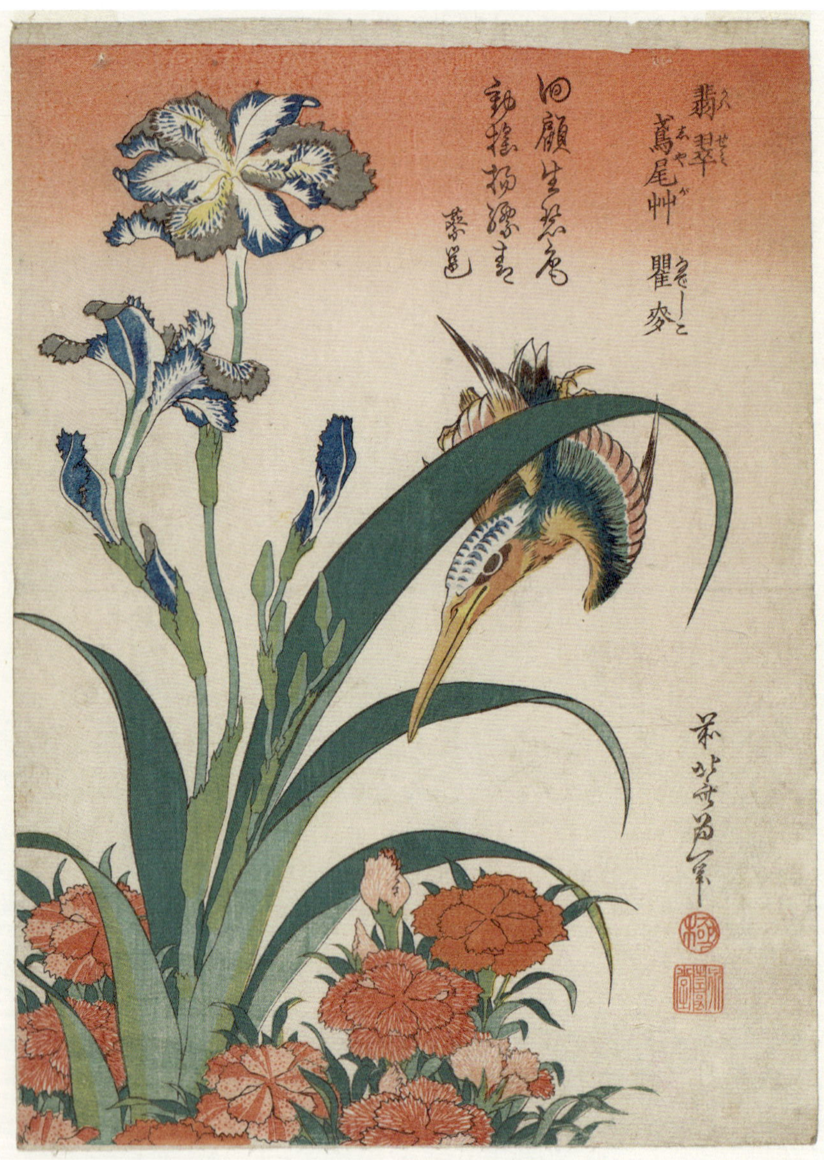

Katsushika Hokusai (1760–1849)
Publisher: Nishimuraya Yohachi (Eijudo)
Kingfisher with Iris and Wild Pinks (Kawasemi, shaga, nadeshiko), from an untitled series known as Small Flowers, c. 1834 (Tenpo 5)
Woodblock print (nishiki-e); ink and color on paper
Vertical chuban; 7½ × 10¼ in. (19 × 25.8 cm)

In one of Hokusai's most colorful compositions, a tiny, brightly colored kingfisher darts under one of the iris leaves. The Chinese poet Cai Yong (AD 132–192) was a scholar, calligrapher, and politician of the Eastern Han dynasty, also known for his interests in mathematics and astronomy. The couplet at the upper right is from his poem on the kingfisher, describing the brilliant feathers that resemble the water it flies over: "Turning, a brilliant green; / in motion, a delicate blue."

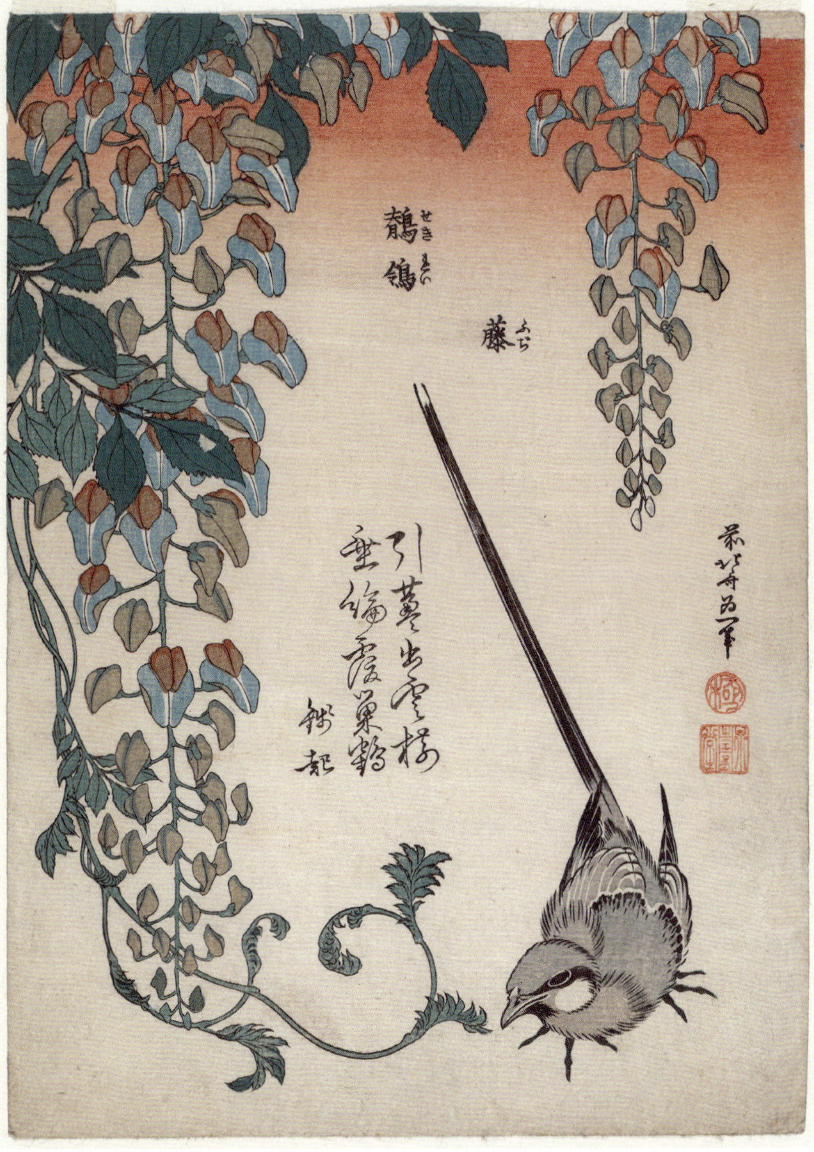

Katsushika Hokusai (1760–1849)
Publisher: Nishimuraya Yohachi (Eijudo)
Wisteria and Wagtail (Fuji, sekirei), from an untitled series known as Small Flowers, c. 1834 (Tenpo 5)
Woodblock print (nishiki-e); ink and color on paper
Vertical chuban; 7½ × 10⅛ in. (19 × 25.7 cm)

The wagtail's English name comes from the way that it moves its long tail up and down, and in Japanese mythology these movements are said to have inspired the gods to invent sexual intercourse. Here, the upturned tail of the bird contrasts amusingly with the drooping wisteria blossoms. The Chinese couplet, describing another interaction between plants and birds, is by the Tang-dynasty poet Qian Qi (c. 722–780): "Vines dangle from the cloud-high trees; / their strands overhang the crane on its nest."

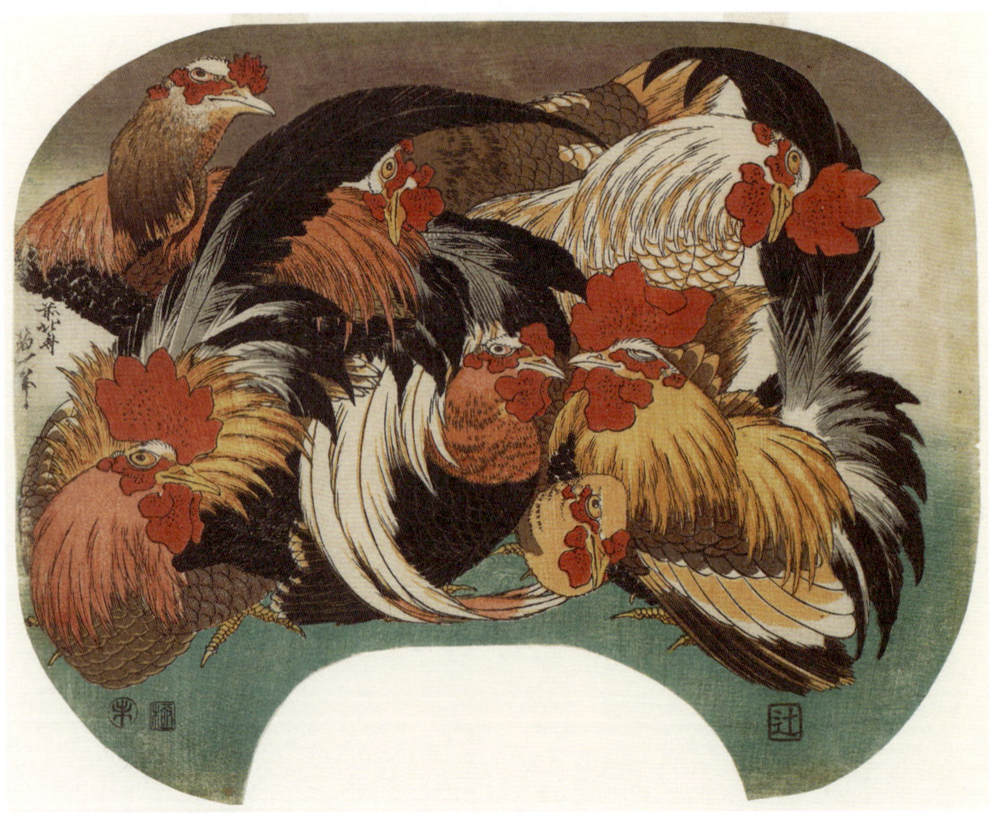

Katsushika Hokusai (1760–1849)
Flock of Chickens, 1835 (Tenpo 6)
Woodblock print (nishiki-e);
ink and color on paper
Uchiwa-e on horizontal aiban
sheet; 11 × 8¾ in. (28 × 22 cm)

Chickens are traditionally admired in East Asia, where they are among the twelve animals of the zodiac; they often appear in paintings and decorative arts. The seven bright-eyed birds crowding together for a group portrait in this fan print include several with fine black tail plumage and one white rooster with a very long tail that is draped over the birds in front of him. Japanese chicken breeders developed a number of special breeds found only in Japan.

Katsushika Hokusai (1760–1849)
Publisher: Moriya Jihei (Kinshindo)
Cranes on a Snow-covered Pine Tree, c. 1834 (Tenpo 5)
Woodblock print (nishiki-e); ink and color on paper
Vertical nagaban; 9¼ × 20½ in. (23.6 × 52 cm)

Both cranes and pine trees are symbols of long life and so are frequently depicted in East Asian art. In the context of this beautifully composed snow scene, they suggest good wishes for the New Year. The print is one of a set of five large-format works that were probably made as a group, although they lack any series titles. All five show natural subjects with auspicious symbolism, much like the hanging scroll paintings that decorated the homes of the wealthy.

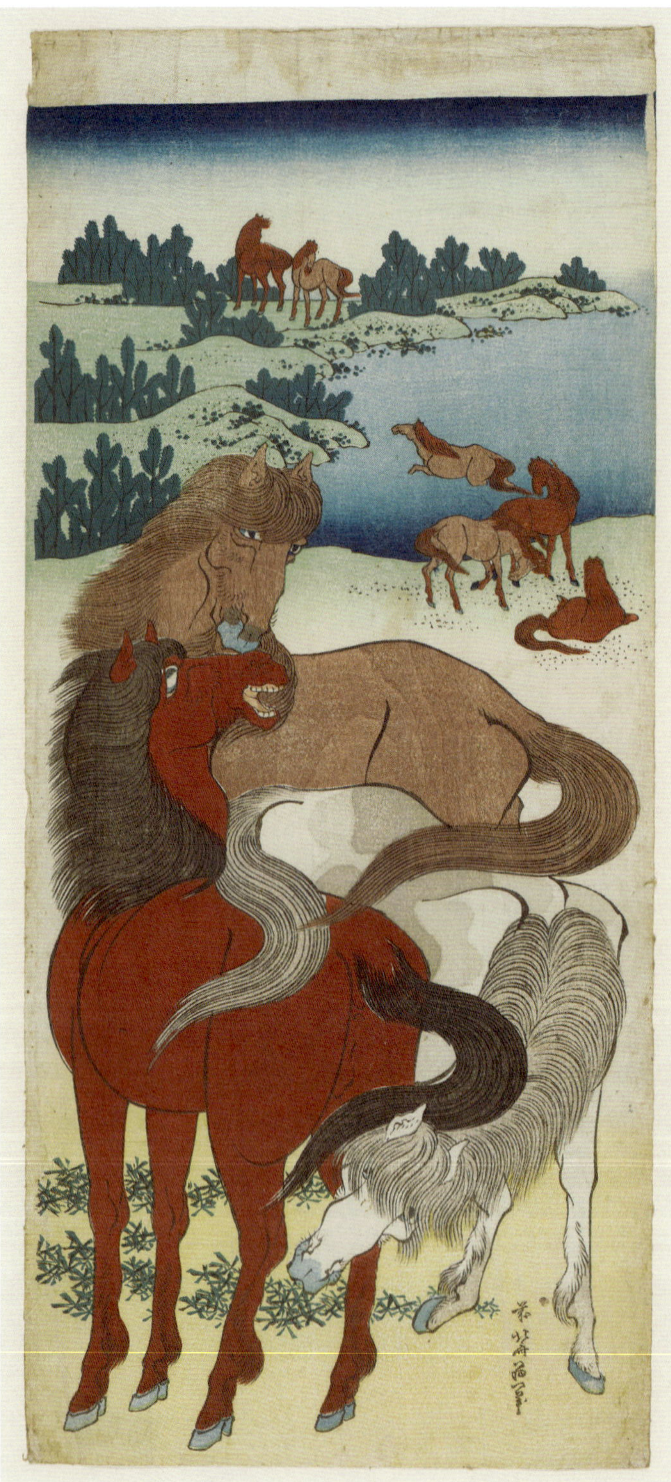

Katsushika Hokusai (1760–1849)
Horses in Pasture, c. 1834 (Tenpo 5)
Woodblock print (nishiki-e);
ink and color on paper
Vertical nagaban; 9¼ × 20½ in.
(23.4 × 52 cm)

Three horses of three different colors nuzzle each other companionably in the foreground; in the background, more horses roam freely through an idyllic equine paradise. The young pine shoots are a symbol of the New Year, and so this print and the group that includes it were probably made for the New Year of the Year of the Horse, 1834. No specific location is indicated, but Hokusai may have been thinking of the official horse farms in Shinano Province where fine steeds were bred for the shogun.

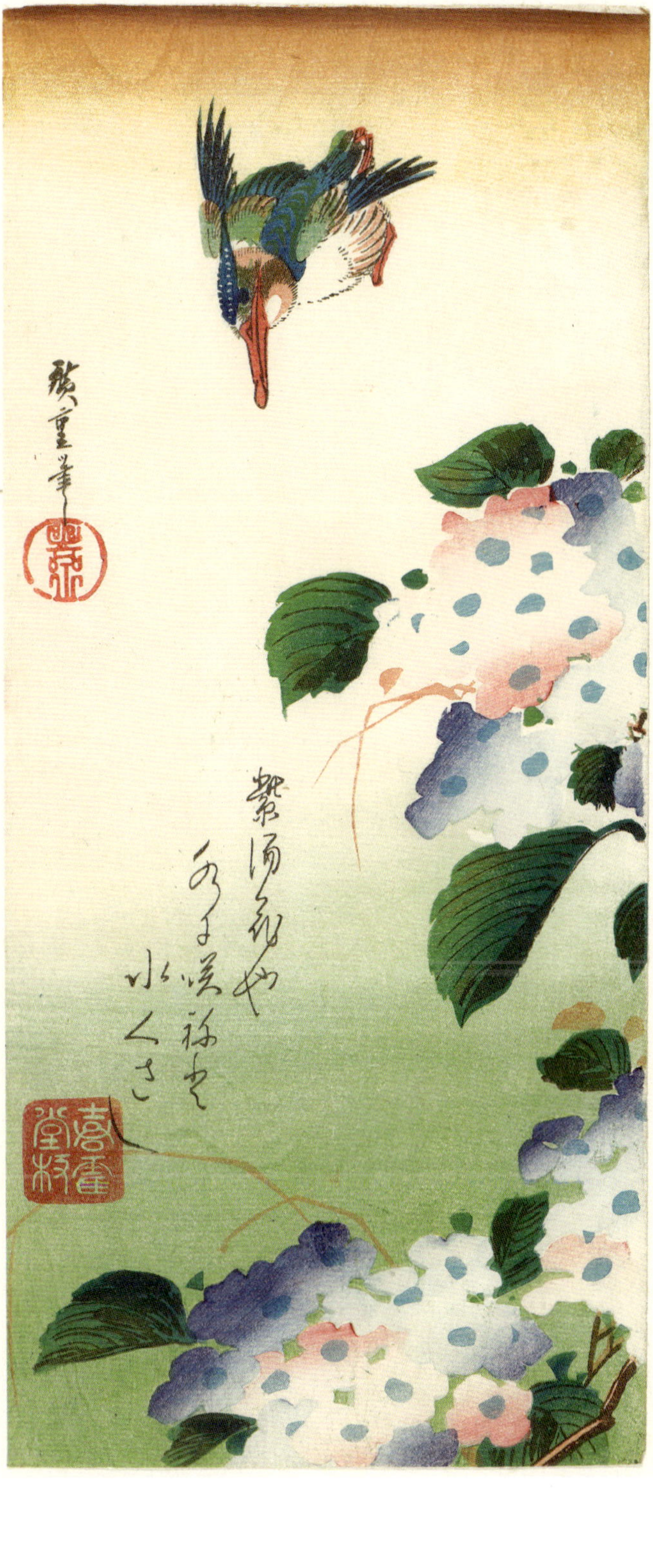

Utagawa Hiroshige I (1797–1858)
Publisher: Sanoya Kihei (Kikakudo)
Kingfisher and Hydrangea, c. 1832 (Tenpo 3)
Woodblock print (nishiki-e);
ink and color on paper
Otanzaku; 6¾ × 14¾ in. (17.1 × 37.5 cm)

In a technique derived from the Chinese painting style called "boneless," the flowers are depicted as masses of color, without outlines. Hydrangeas bloom during the rainy season in Japan and so are associated with water; there may be a humorous implication that the little kingfisher, whose feathers complement the blue and pink tones of the flowers, is mistaking the damp blossoms for the riverside environment that he prefers. The unsigned haikai poem reads: "Though hydrangeas / do not bloom in water, still / they are watery."

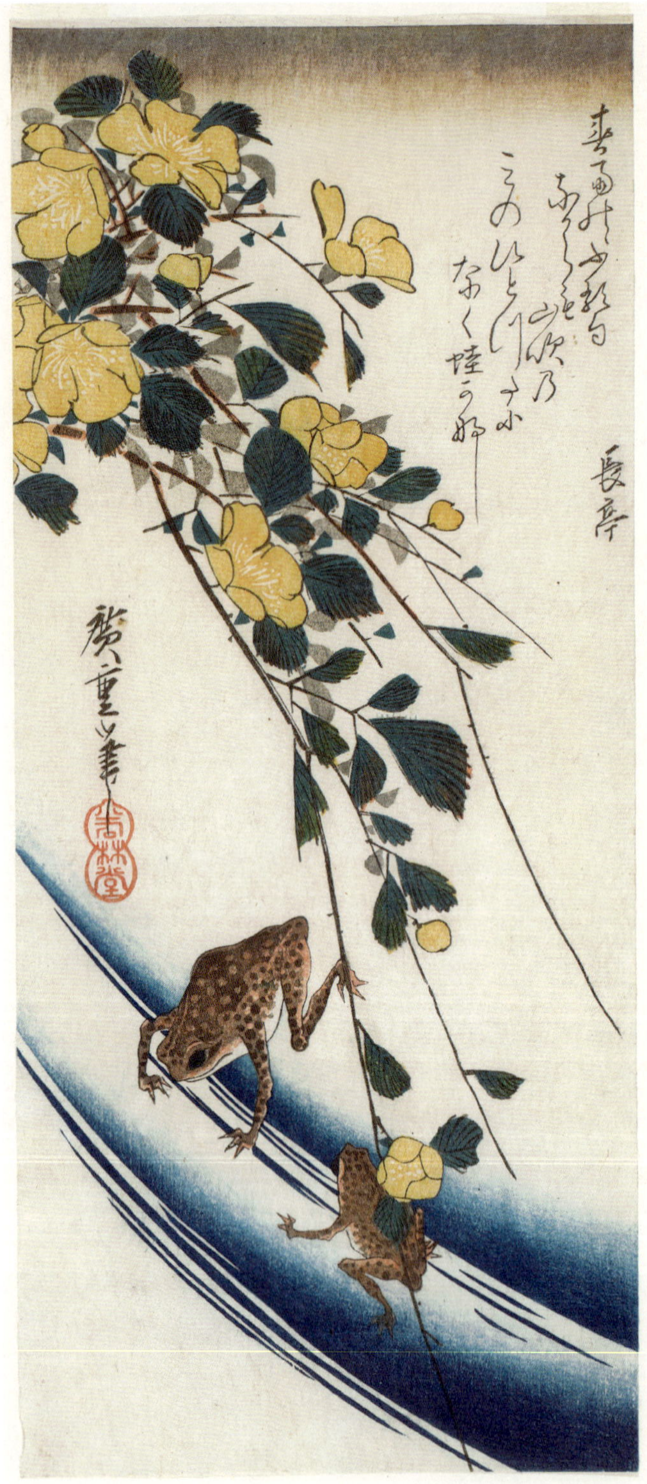

Utagawa Hiroshige I (1797–1858)
Publisher: Wakasaya Yoichi (Jakurindo)
Yellow Rose (Yamabuki) and Frogs, c. 1832 (Tenpo 3)
Woodblock print (nishiki-e); ink and color on paper
Otanzaku; 6½ × 14¾ in. (16.5 × 37.5 cm)

Inscribed on this charming scene of two small frogs under a spray of yellow kerria roses is a reference to a famous old story: a visitor who asked to borrow a raincoat was handed a spray of yellow roses instead—flowers with "no fruit," a pun on "no raincoat," as explained in an accompanying poem. The new kyoka poem by Chotei reads: "In the rains of spring / just as in the old poem / from yellow roses / even without a raincoat / a little frog comes chirping."

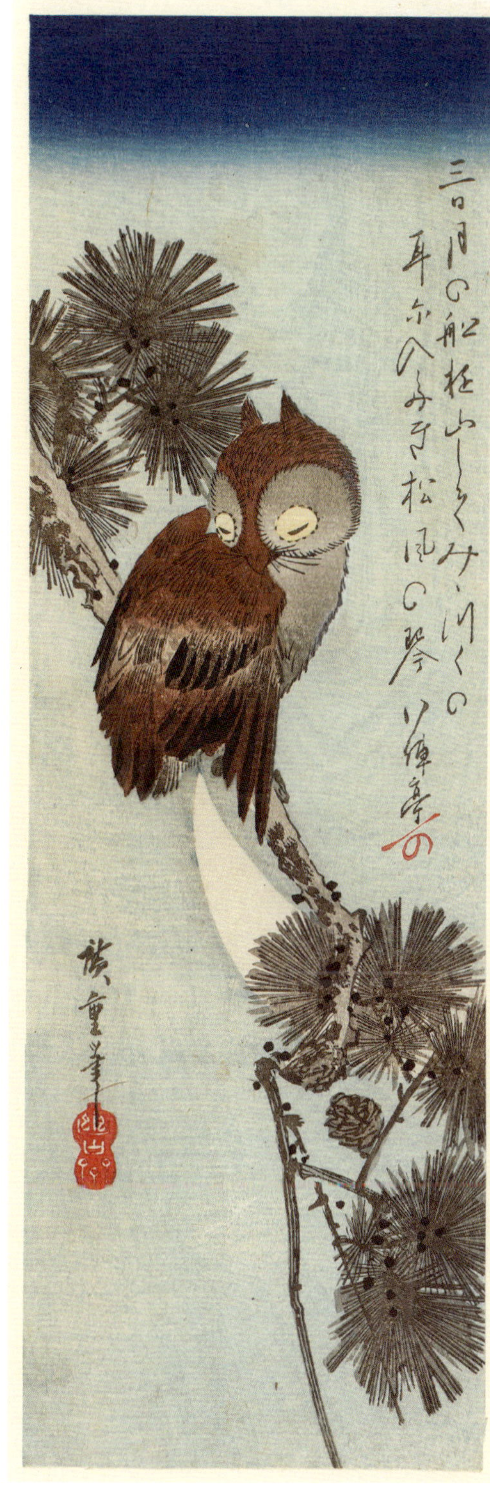

Utagawa Hiroshige I (1797–1858)
Small Horned Owl in a Pine Tree, c. 1835
Woodblock print (nishiki-e); ink and color on paper
Chutanzaku; 4¾ × 14½ in. (12 × 36.7 cm)

A drowsy owl naps on the branch of a pine tree as the crescent moon rises. The angle of the moon behind the pine bough creates an optical illusion, suggesting that the owl is perched on the curved prow of a boat, as if embarking on an excursion. The kyoka poem by Hajintei reads: "Into the ears of / the horned owl jaunting in / a crescent moon boat / enters the pleasant music / of the wind in the pine boughs."

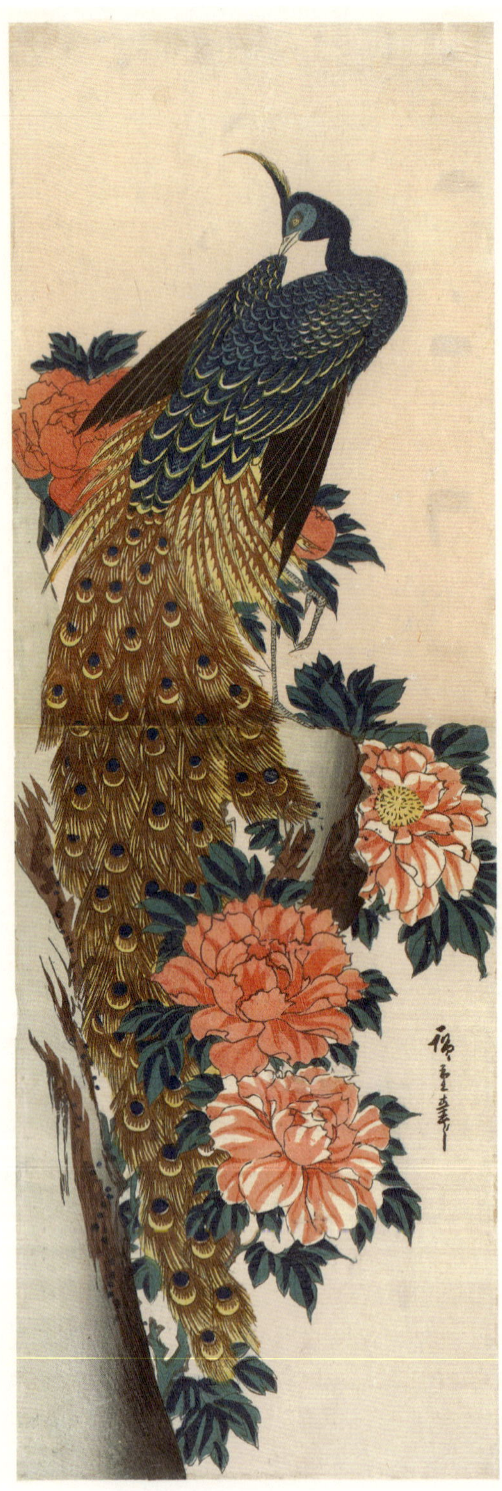

Utagawa Hiroshige I (1797–1858)
Peacock and Peonies, c. 1830
Woodblock print (nishiki-e);
ink and color on paper
Vertical oban, upright diptych;
9¾ × 28½ in. (24.7 × 72.4 cm)

Perched high on the side of a cliff, the peacock lets its splendid tail cascade down over the rocks, surrounded by gorgeous peony blossoms drawn even larger in scale than they really are. In Japan both peacocks and peonies were luxurious imports and thus symbols of wealth and elegance. This large composition, spread over two full-size sheets joined vertically, suggests the hanging scroll paintings that would be displayed in affluent settings; the print may also have been intended to be mounted in scroll form.

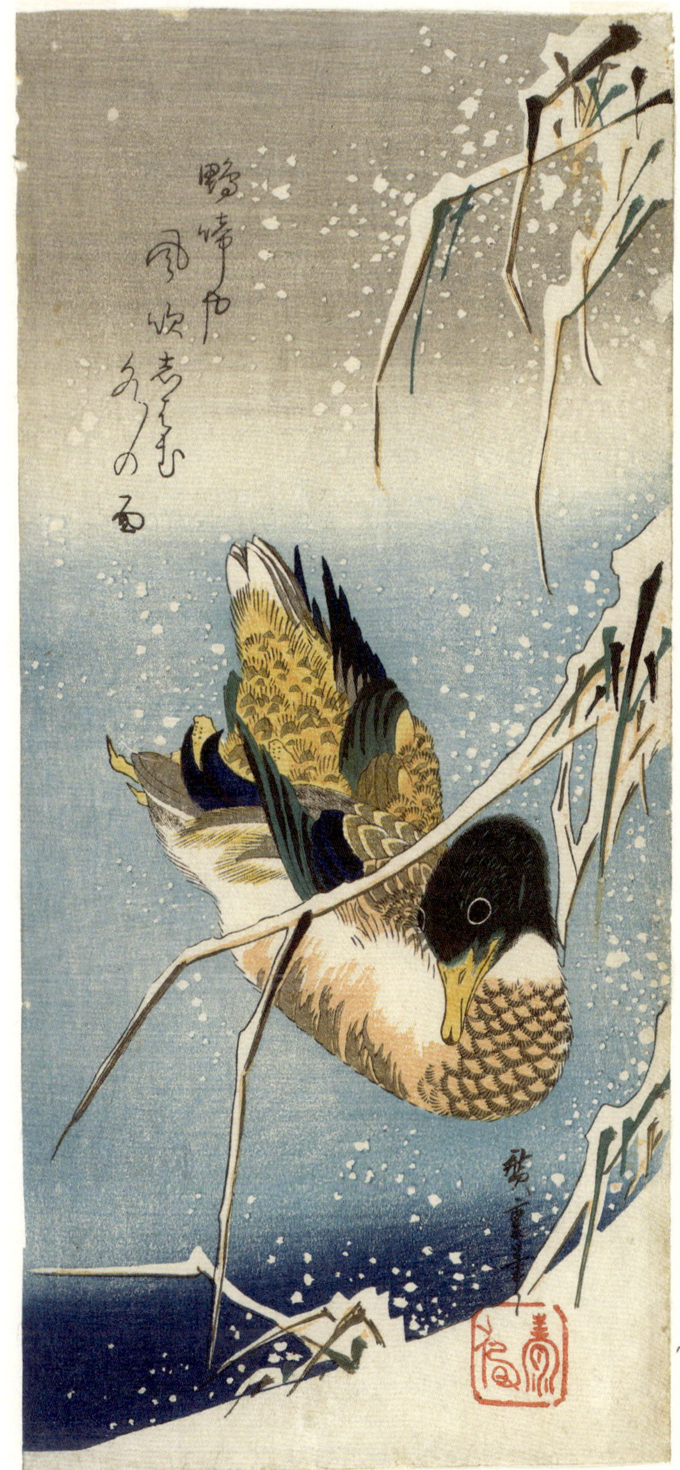

Utagawa Hiroshige I (1797–1858)
Mallard Ducks and Snow-covered Reeds, c. 1836 (Tenpo 7)
Woodblock print (nishiki-e); ink and color on paper
Otanzaku; 6⅞ × 15¼ in. (17.5 × 38.5 cm)

One of Hiroshige's most famous bird-and-flower designs, this print captures the chill beauty of a winter day. Under snow-covered branches, a male mallard duck drifts peacefully over the water. Behind it is the tail of a second duck, perhaps the mate of the first, that has upended itself to thrust its head underwater in search of food. The poem reads: "A mallard calls, and / the wind blows ripples over / the water's surface."

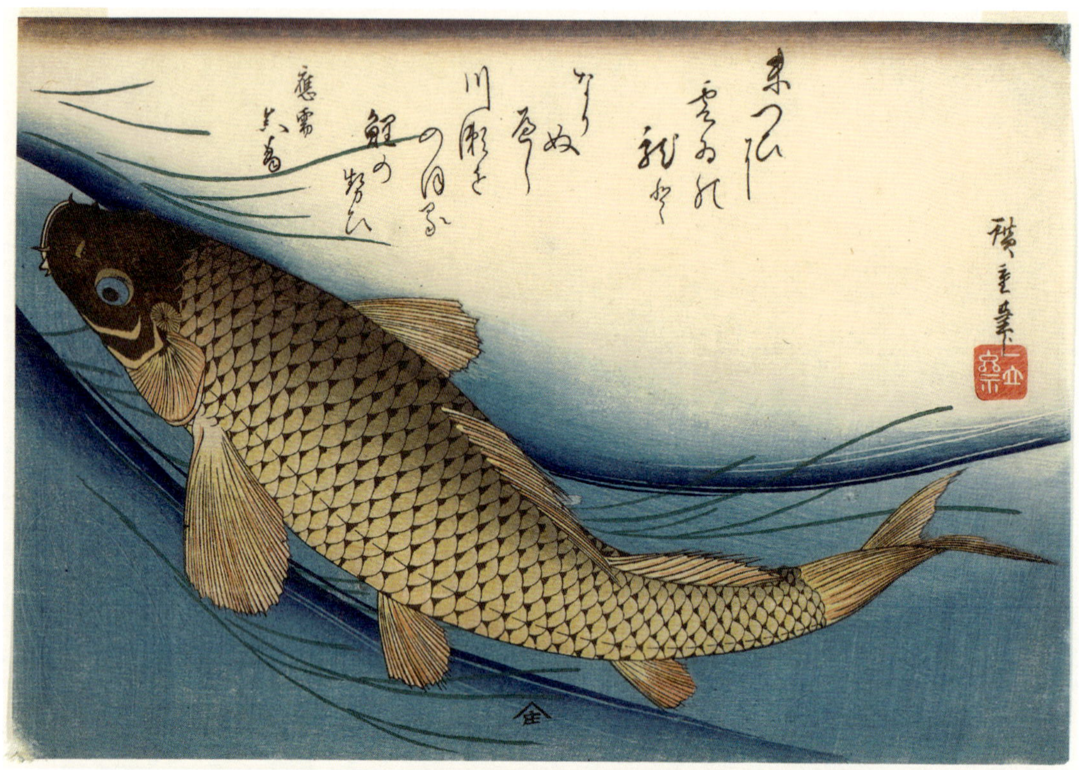

Utagawa Hiroshige I (1797–1858)
Publisher: Yamadaya Shojiro
Carp, from an untitled series known as Large Fish, c. 1840–42 (Tenpo 11–13)
Woodblock print (nishiki-e); ink and color on paper
Horizontal oban; 14½ × 9⅞ in. (36.8 × 25 cm)

The series known as Large Fish began with ten illustrations for a privately commissioned poetry album that were later reissued as commercial prints. Still later, ten more designs including this one were added to the set. The unsigned kyoka poem alludes to the ancient Chinese belief that carp who swam up the rapids at Longmen would be transformed into dragons. Carp were greatly admired for their bravery in swimming upstream to spawn, and they came to be seen as symbols of perseverance leading to success.

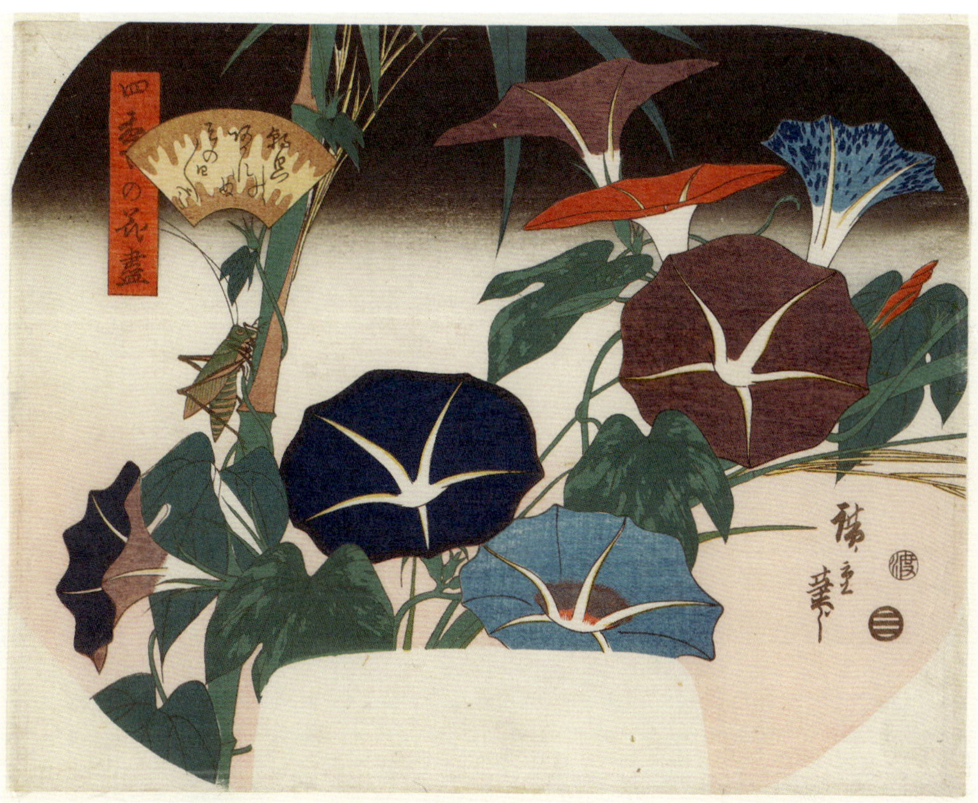

Utagawa Hiroshige I (1797–1858)
Publisher: Ibaya Senzaburo (Dansendo)
Morning Glories and Cricket, from the series A Compendium of Flowers of the Four Seasons (*Shiki no hana zukushi*), 1843–47 (Tenpo 14–Koka 4)
Woodblock print (nishiki-e); ink and color on paper
Uchiwa-e on horizontal aiban sheet; 11½ × 9 in. (29 × 22.7 cm)

The two known designs in this series both show summer scenes, appropriate for fans. The anonymous poem inscribed on the print—in a cartouche shaped like a folding fan as opposed to a flat fan—must have been a favorite of Hiroshige's, since it appears on many of his other depictions of morning glories. It emphasizes the importance of enjoying fleeting moments of beauty whenever they may occur: "Is it the day that / the morning glories open— / yes, that very day."

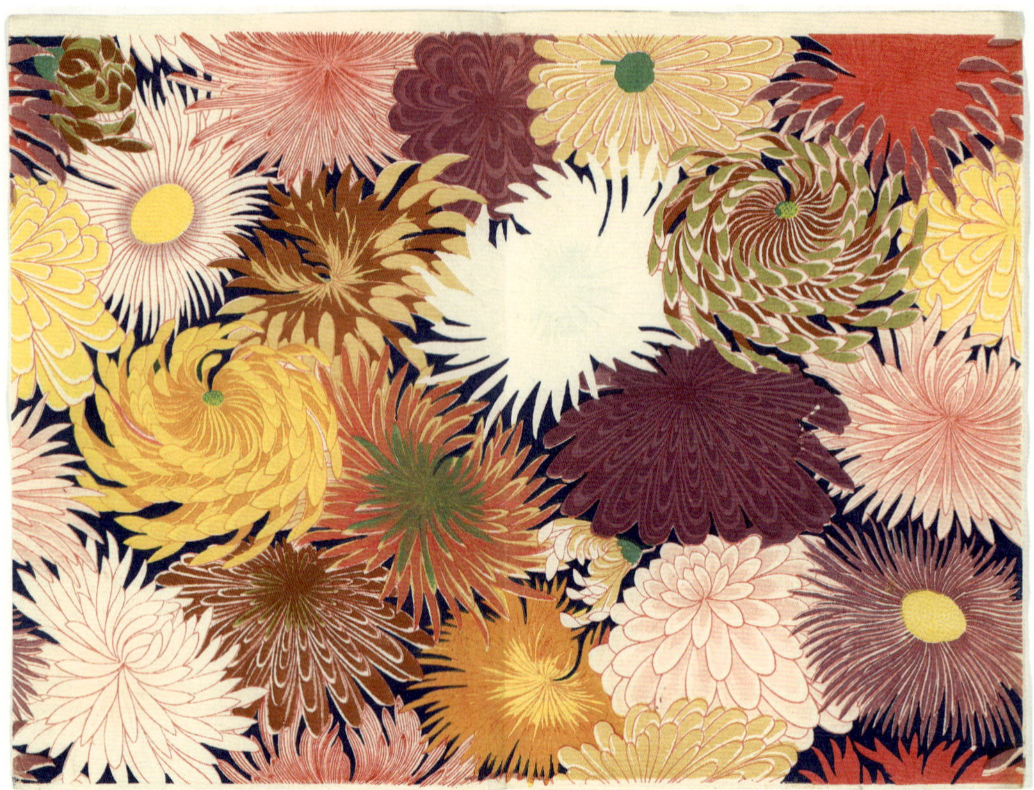

Attributed to Kawanabe Kyosai, 1831–1889
Decorative Paper with Design of Chrysanthemums, c. 1860–70
Woodblock print (nishiki-e); ink and color on paper
Horizontal oban;
20⅛ × 15 in. (51 × 38 cm)

The great popularity of chrysanthemums in Japan led to the cultivation of many different varieties. Over a dozen kinds are combined to form this colorful pattern, which is cleverly designed to repeat both vertically and horizontally. The printed paper might have been used as wrapping paper, as a wall covering with multiple sheets fitted together, or even as the prototype for a fabric pattern. Though unsigned, the composition may be the work of the ingenious Kawanabe Kyosai.

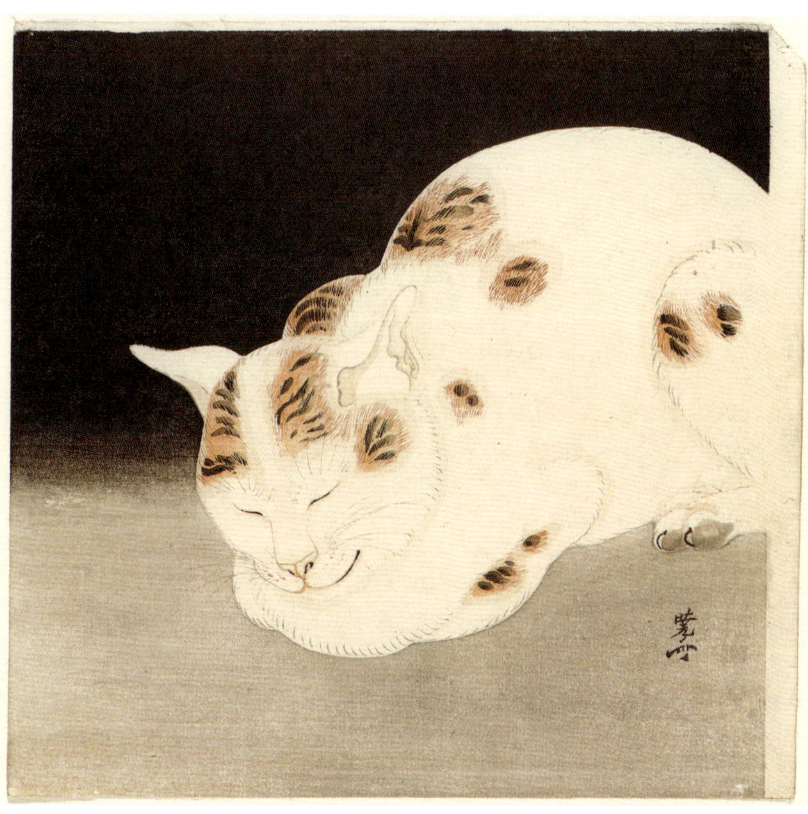

Kawanabe Kyosai (1831–1889)
Sleeping Cat, 1885–89 (Meiji 18–22)
Woodblock print (nishiki-e);
ink and color on paper
Shikishiban, 10⅛ × 9¾ in.
(25.5 × 24.8 cm)

Kyosai shared a love of cats with his first teacher, Utagawa Kuniyoshi. This portrait of a tortoiseshell cat smiling in its sleep must have been a popular design, since the MFA owns three different versions of it: a fan print, a reprint with a light background, and this one, its dark background contrasting with the embossed fur of the cat. Three-colored cats, with black and ginger markings on white fur, were considered auspicious animals that would bring good fortune to their owners.

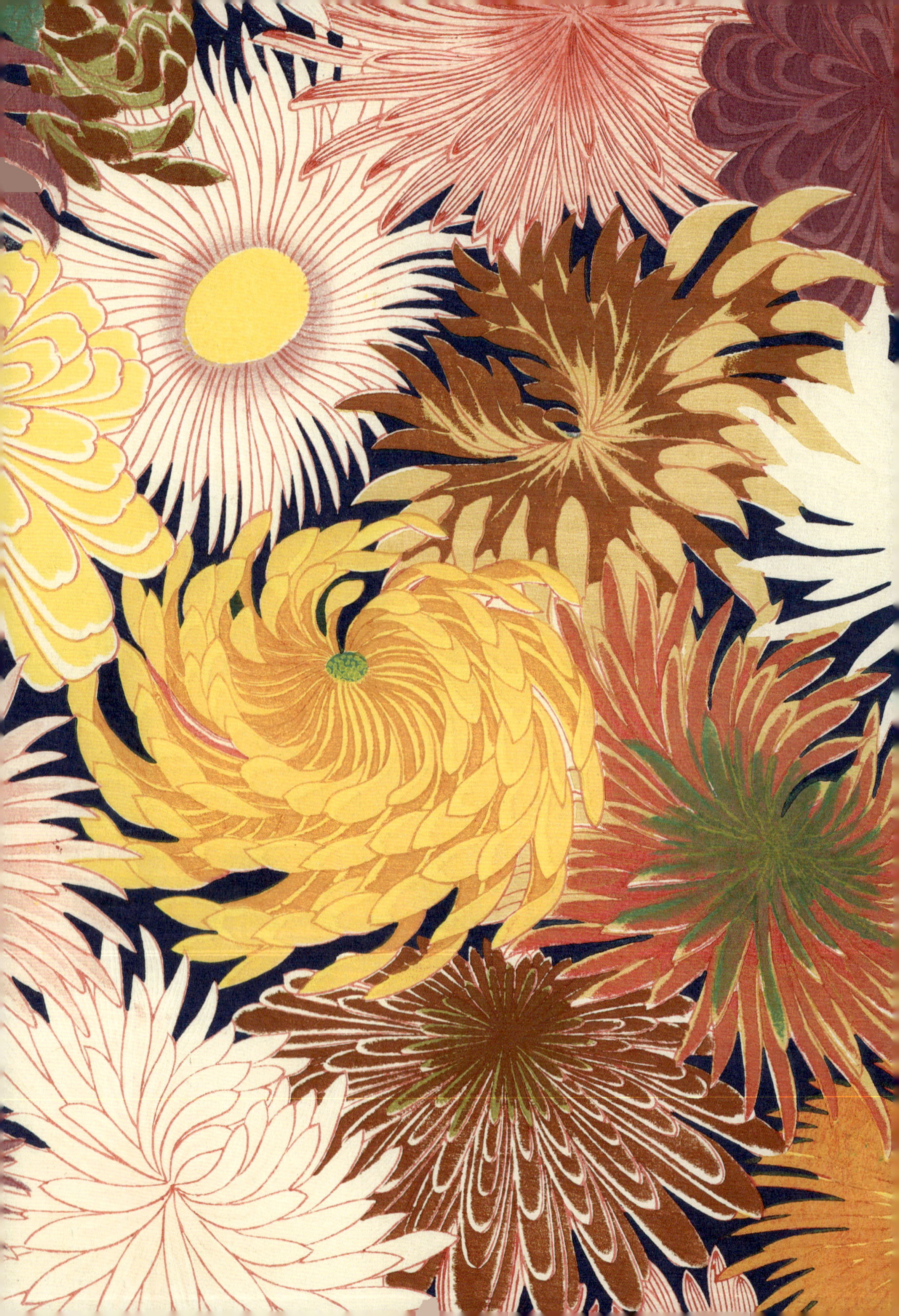

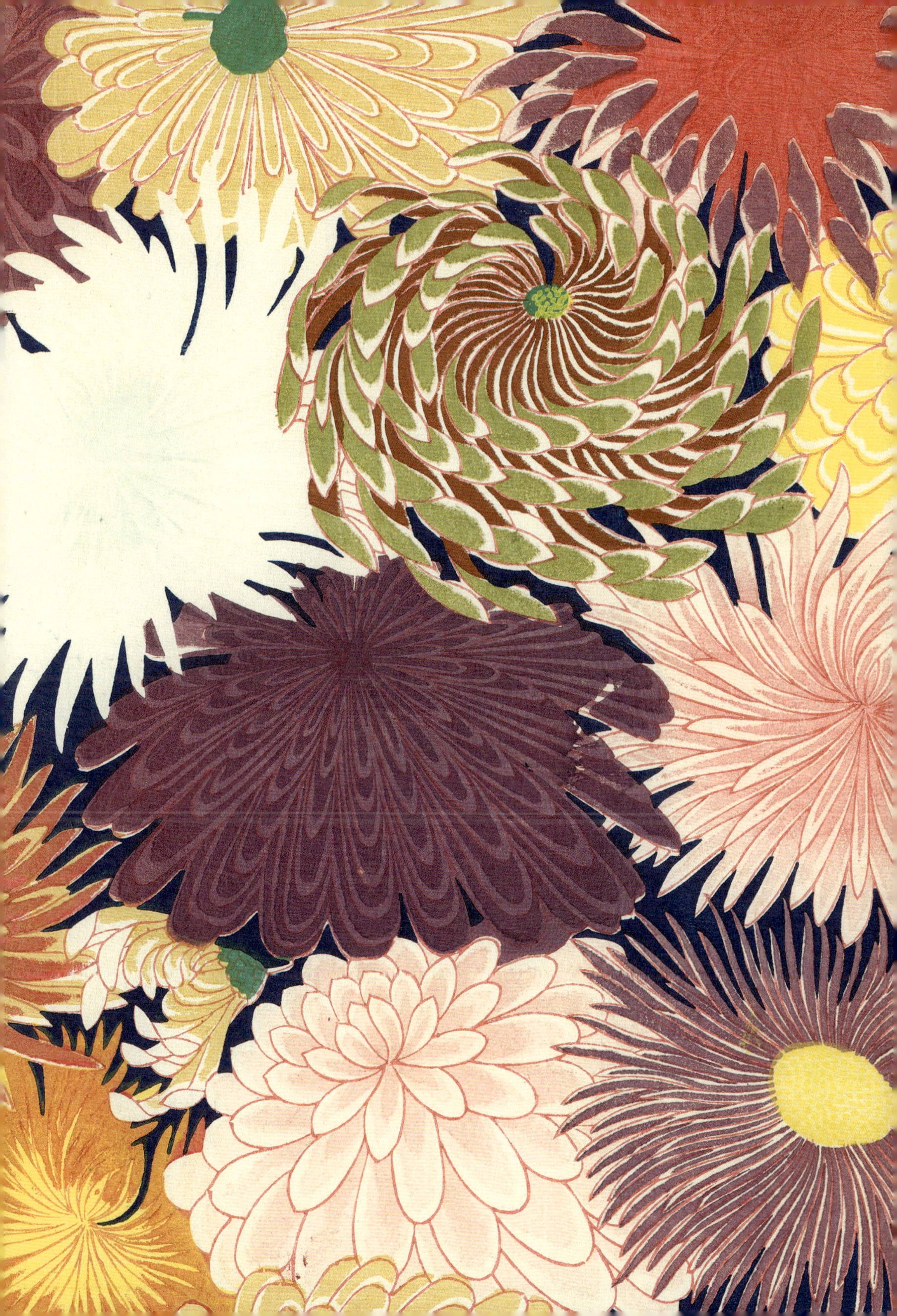

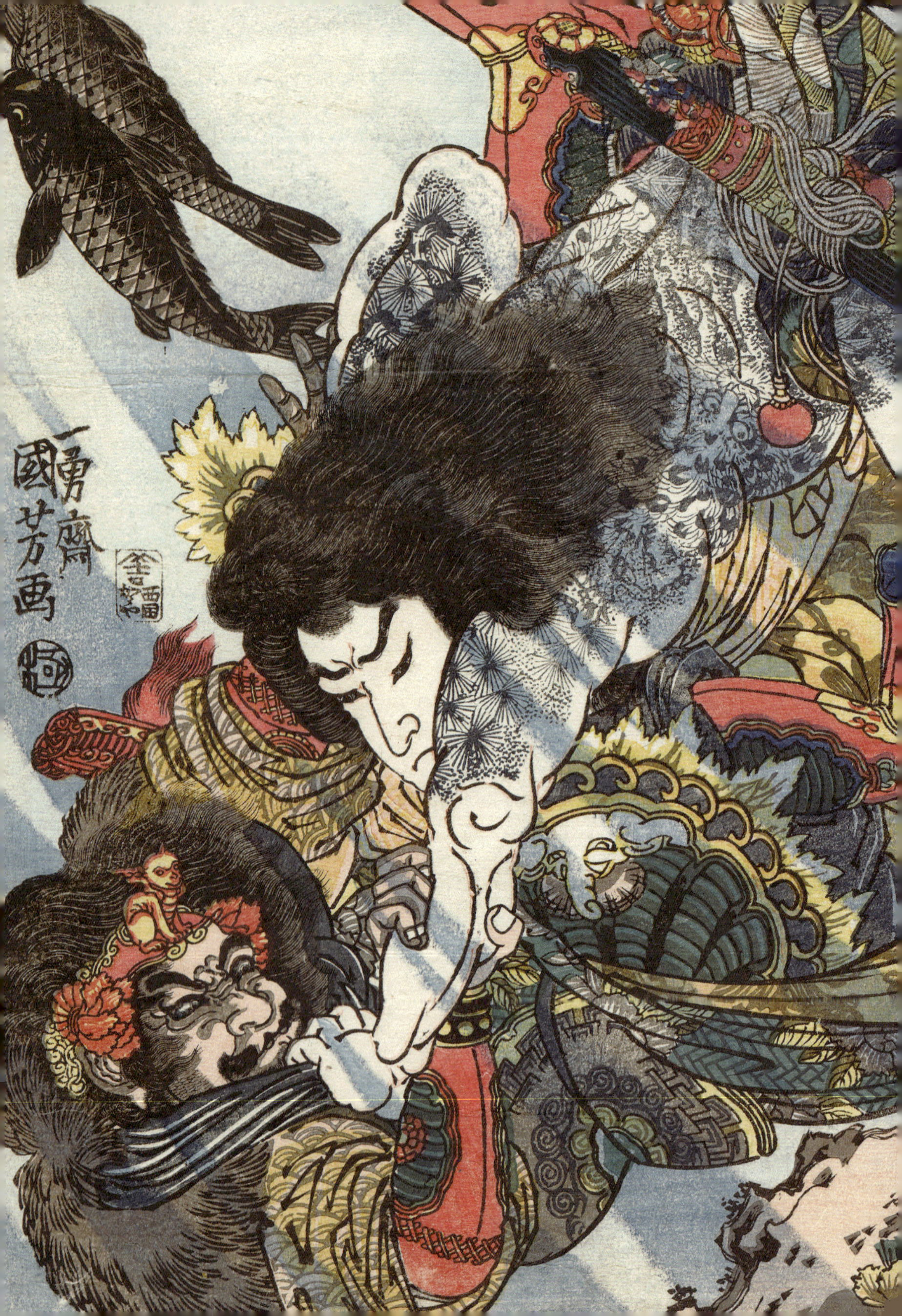
一勇齋
國芳画

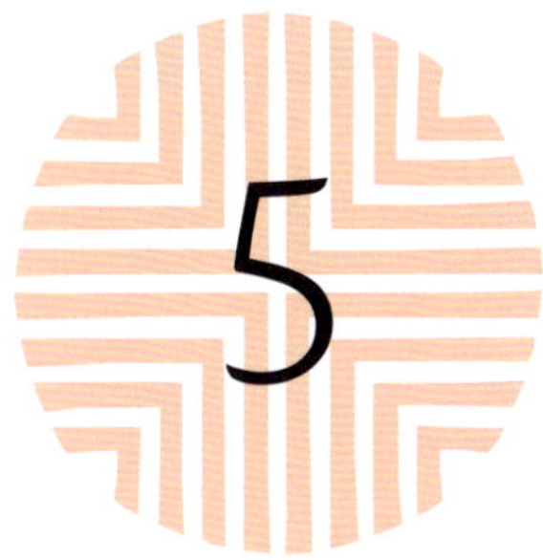

History and Literature

The illustrated printed books of the early Edo period that were the direct ancestors of ukiyo-e prints included many scenes from Japanese history and literature, and these subjects appeared occasionally in prints throughout the eighteenth century, although they did not achieve the same level of popularity as depictions of celebrated actors and fashionable beauties. In some cases, prints of modern beauties included witty parodic allusions to the heroes, poets, and lovers of classical literature, reworking the high culture to suit the tastes of the Floating World and thereby claiming it as the rightful heritage not only of the elite but of the entire nation.

The genre known as warrior prints (*musha-e*)—including not only scenes of combat but historical illustrations—became enormously popular from the late 1820s on, as a result of the success of Kuniyoshi's series of dynamic images depicting the heroes of China's greatest martial arts novel, *The Water Margin*, newly available in a Japanese translation. Kuniyoshi and his students designed many prints showing great warriors from the history of both Japan and China, either in single-sheet imaginary portraits or triptychs featuring complex combat scenes. The landscapes and nature subjects that also became popular subjects for prints in the 1830s were sometimes illustrations of classical poetry, another happy reminder that traditional Japanese literature was for everyone.

During the Meiji era, artists such as Kuniyoshi's pupil Yoshitoshi developed a hybrid, Western-influenced style that gave a new sense of realism to historical scenes. At the same time, the censorship regulations of the deposed Tokugawa shogunate were lifted. It had been forbidden to show activities of the ruling class since 1573, when the Tokugawa clan rose to power, but at this time artists could depict recent historical events and those of earlier centuries.

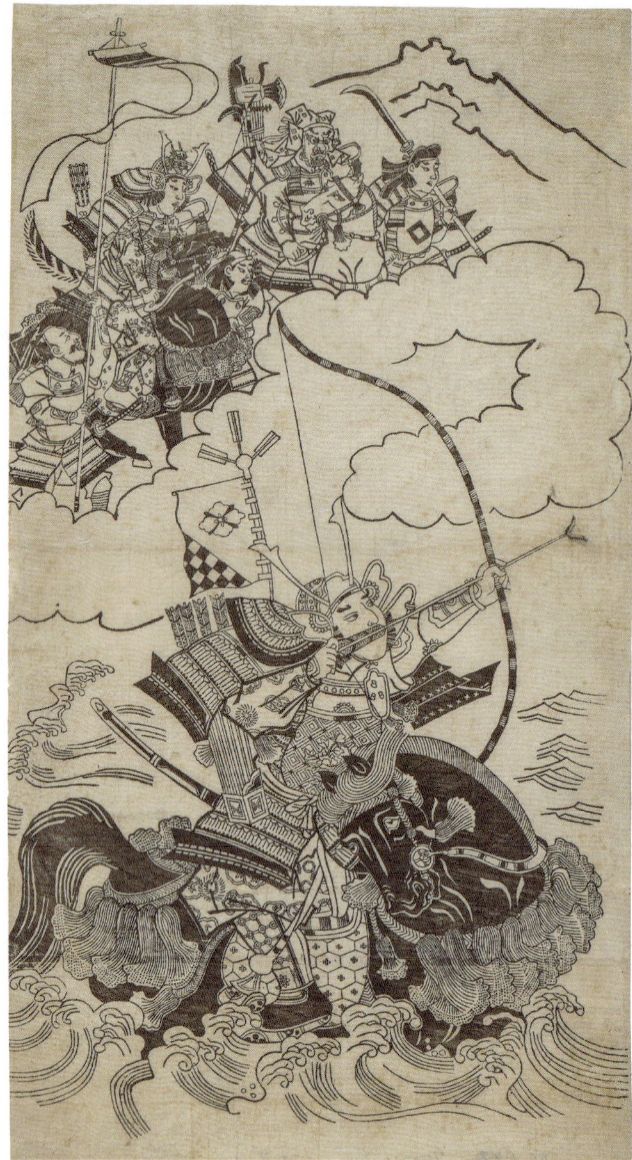

Attributed to Sugimura Jihei (active c. 1680–1698)
The Archer Nasu no Yoichi, c. 1684–1700 (Jokyo 1–Genroku 13)
Woodblock print (sumizuri-e); ink on paper
Vertical o-oban; 12¼ × 22 in. (30.9 × 56.3 cm)

This large print, the left half of a diptych, shows a famous scene from the Battle of Yashima in 1185, during the civil war between the Minamoto and Taira warrior clans. As the Taira retreated in their ships, taking with them the child emperor Antoku and his entourage of courtiers, a beautiful court lady tauntingly held up a fan. The young archer Nasu no Yoichi, observed by his commander Minamoto no Yoshitsune, rode out into the surf and loosed an arrow that knocked down the fan.

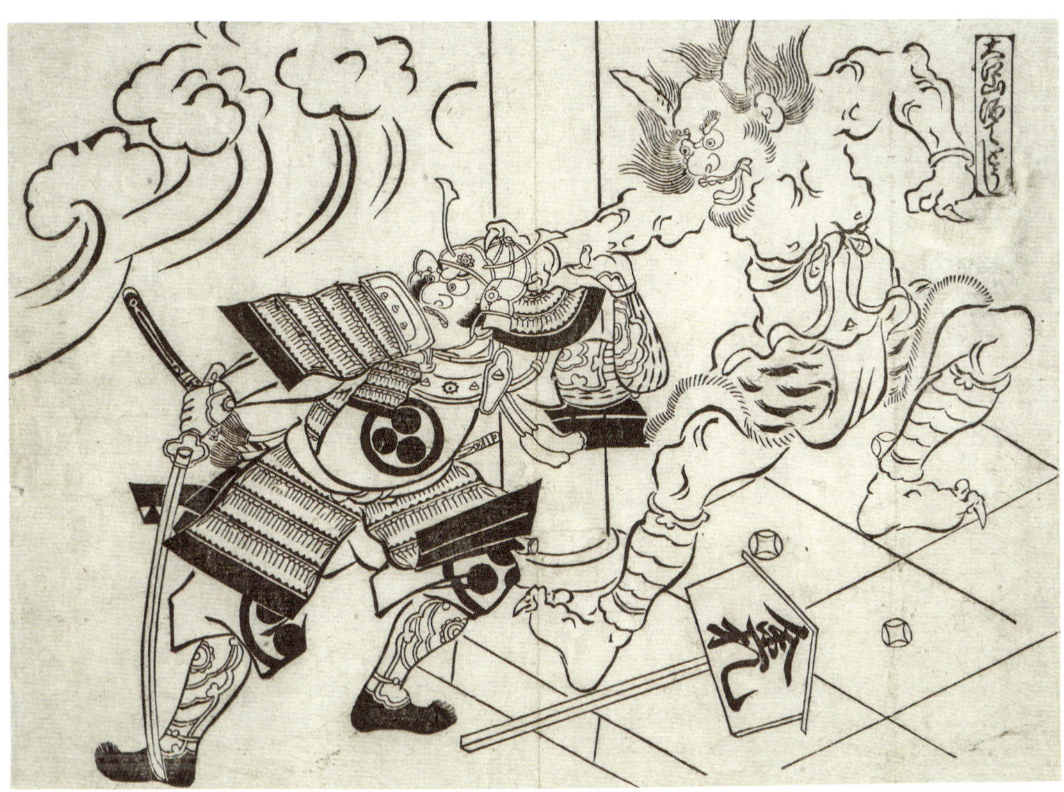

Okumura Masanobu (1686–1764)
Publisher: Sudo Gonbei
(Yamaguchiya)
*The Shuten-doji of Mount Oe
(oeyama Shuten-doji)*, from
the series Famous Scenes from
Japanese Puppet Plays *(Yamato
irotake)*, c. 1705–6 (Hoei 2–3)
Woodblock print
(sumizuri-e); ink on paper
Horizontal oban; 14½ × 10¼ in.
(36.9 × 26.2 cm)

The popularity of the puppet theater rivaled that of kabuki, especially in the early years of ukiyo-e. The play shown here dealt with the adventures of the tenth-century warrior Minamoto no Yorimitsu and his comrades. In this scene, Yorimitsu's retainer Watanabe no Tsuna battles a demon at Rashomon Gate in Kyoto, eventually managing to cut off its arm. The heroes then proceed in a group to Mount Oe to defeat another demon, the Shuten-doji of the play's title.

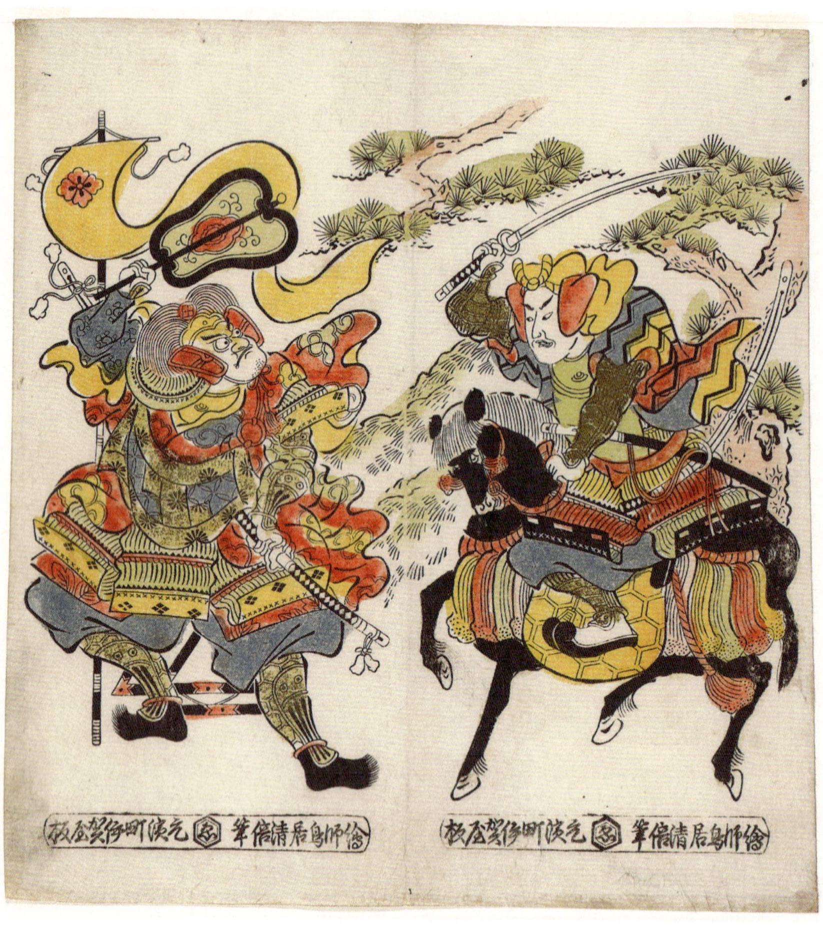

Torii Kiyomasu I (active c. 1696–1716)
Publisher: Igaya Kan'emon (Bunkido)
Uesugi Kenshin (R) and Takeda Shingen (L) at the Battle of Kawanakajima, c. 1710
Woodblock print (urushi-e); ink on paper, with hand-applied color, nikawa, and metallic powder
Uncut hosoban diptych; 12¾ × 13½ in. (32.4 × 34.3 cm)

This stunning hand-colored print, preserved in unusually good condition, depicts two of the greatest warriors from Japan's tumultuous sixteenth century. When Uesugi Kenshin made a surprise attack on the camp of rival warlord Takeda Shingen, Shingen calmly parried Kenshin's sword stroke with his iron battle fan. The print was intended to be cut in half and sold as two sheets, so that customers could purchase either the mounted warrior, the seated warrior, or both.

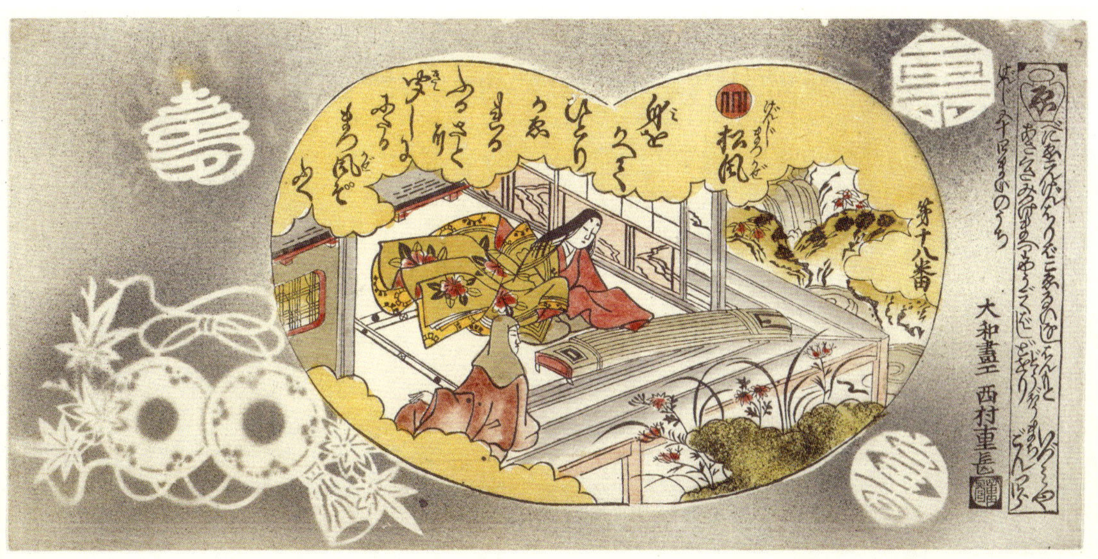

Nishimura Shigenaga (1697?–1756)
Publisher: Izumiya Gonshiro
The Tale of Genji: The Wind in the Pines (Genji Matsukaze), no. 18
from the series Genji in Fifty-Four Sheets *(Genji gojuyonmai no uchi)*, c. 1735 (Kyoho 20)
Woodblock print (beni-e);
ink on paper, with hand-applied and stenciled color and metallic powder
Horizontal hosoban;
13¼ × 6½ in. (33.8 × 16.5 cm)

Written by Lady Murasaki around the year 1000, *The Tale of Genji* is regarded by many as the world's first novel. It tells of the life and loves of Prince Genji, including the beautiful but lonely lady shown here, who plays the koto as she waits for Genji to visit her. This series shows one scene from each chapter of the book, drawn in a traditional style and lavishly hand-colored, with stenciled background designs.

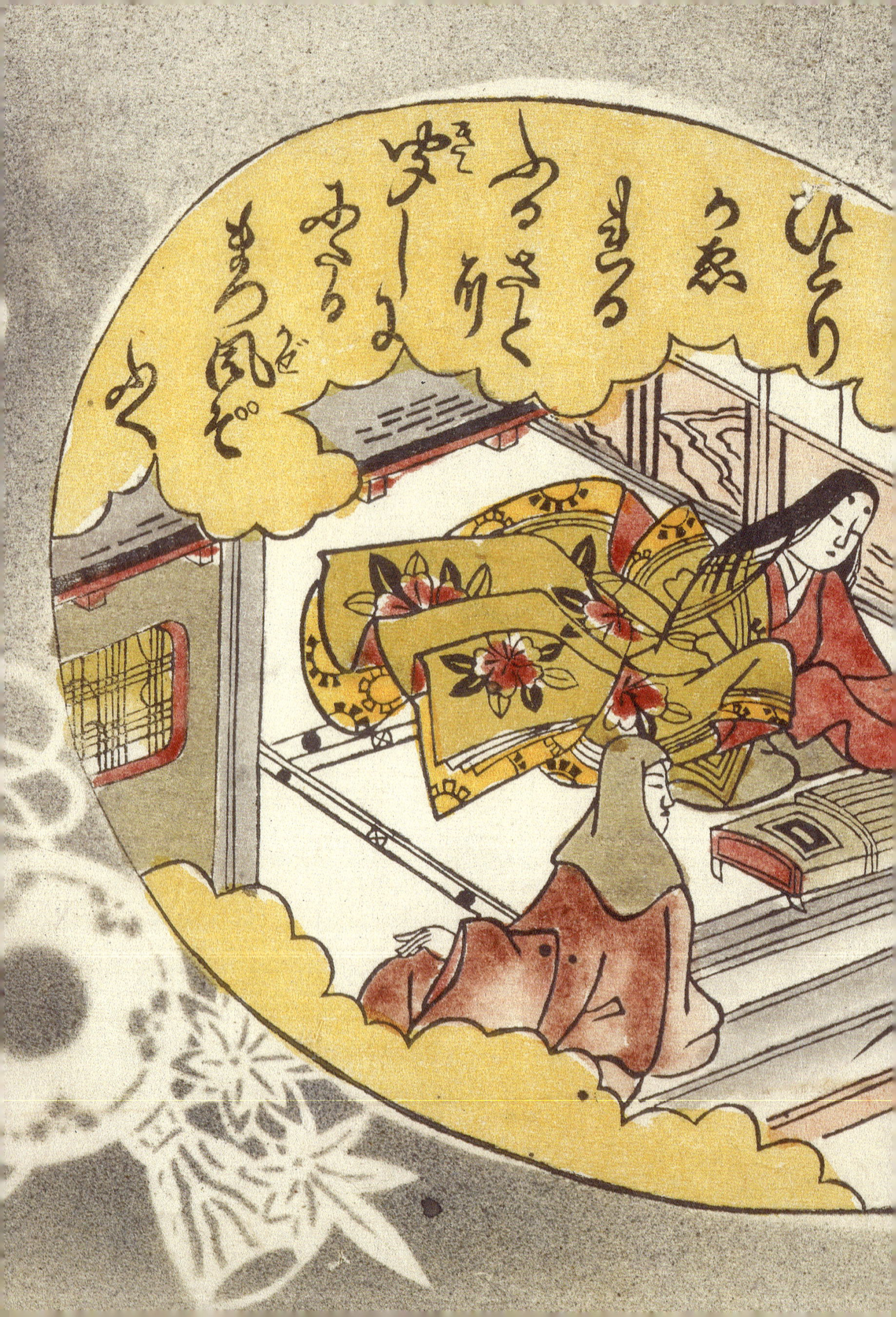

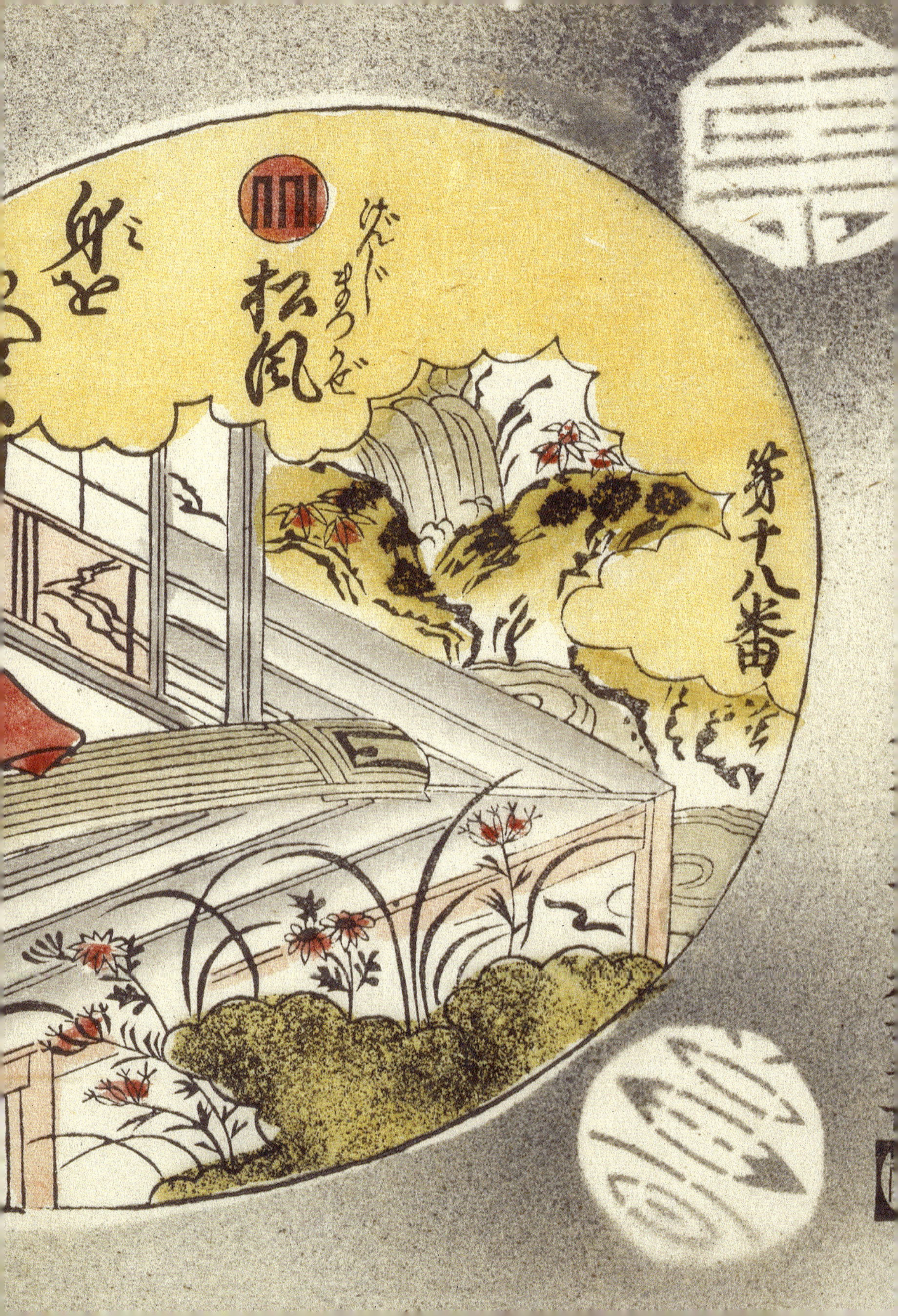

げんじまつかぜ
松風
第十八番

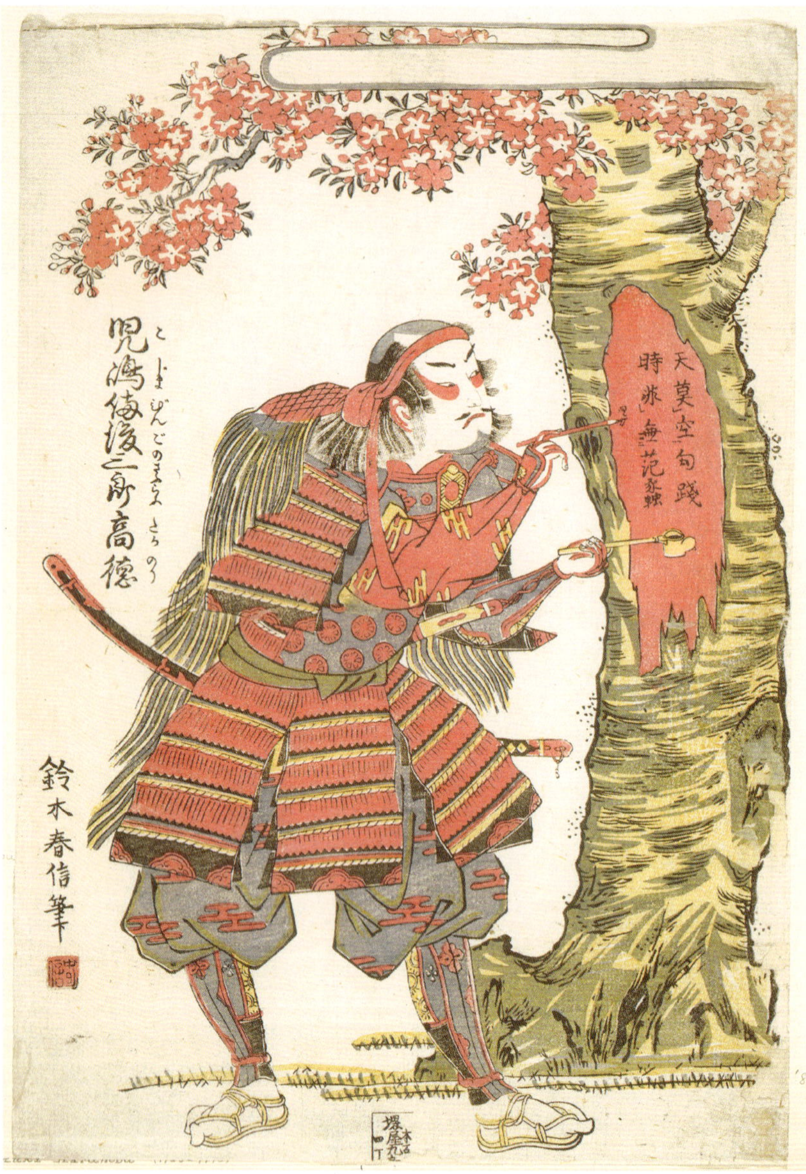

Suzuki Harunobu (1725–1770)
Publisher: Sakaiya Kurobei
Kojima Bingo no Saburo Takanori,
c. 1762–64 (Horeki 12–Meiwa 1)
Woodblock print (benizuri-e);
ink and limited color on paper
Vertical oban; 10⅞ × 15½ in.
(27.6 × 39.3 cm)

Shortly before he designed the first ukiyo-e prints to be produced in full color, Harunobu skillfully deployed just three printed colors—red, yellow, and blue—to create the effect of a much more complex color scheme in this unusually well-preserved print. The subject is a touching story from the civil wars of the fourteenth century, in which a loyal retainer leaves a message of hope for a captured emperor, a Chinese poem that only the emperor will be able to understand.

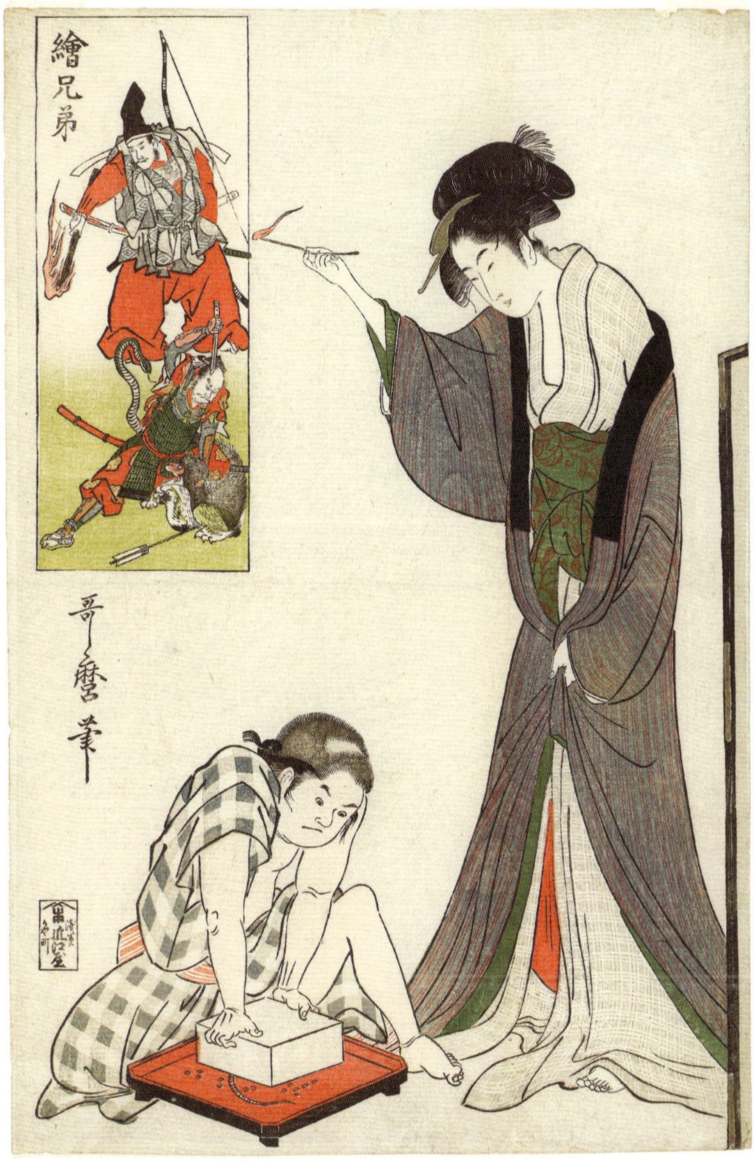

Kitagawa Utamaro I
(early 1750s–1806)
Publisher: Omiya Gonkuro
Parody of the Killing of the Nue,
from the series Picture Siblings
(*E-kyodai*), c. 1798 (Kansei 10)
Woodblock print (nishiki-e);
ink and color on paper
Vertical oban; 10⅛ × 15¼ in.
(25.6 × 38.7 cm)

Famous for his pictures of fashionable beauties, Utamaro enjoyed showing contemporary women in poses that parody older stories. One evening, a woman and a young boy use a boxlike trap to capture a rat. This feat is humorously compared to the brave deed of the warrior Minamoto no Yorimasa, who shot down a monster known as the *nue* as it flew over the imperial palace by night. The creature was then killed with a sword by Yorimasa's retainer I no Hayata, as shown in the inset picture.

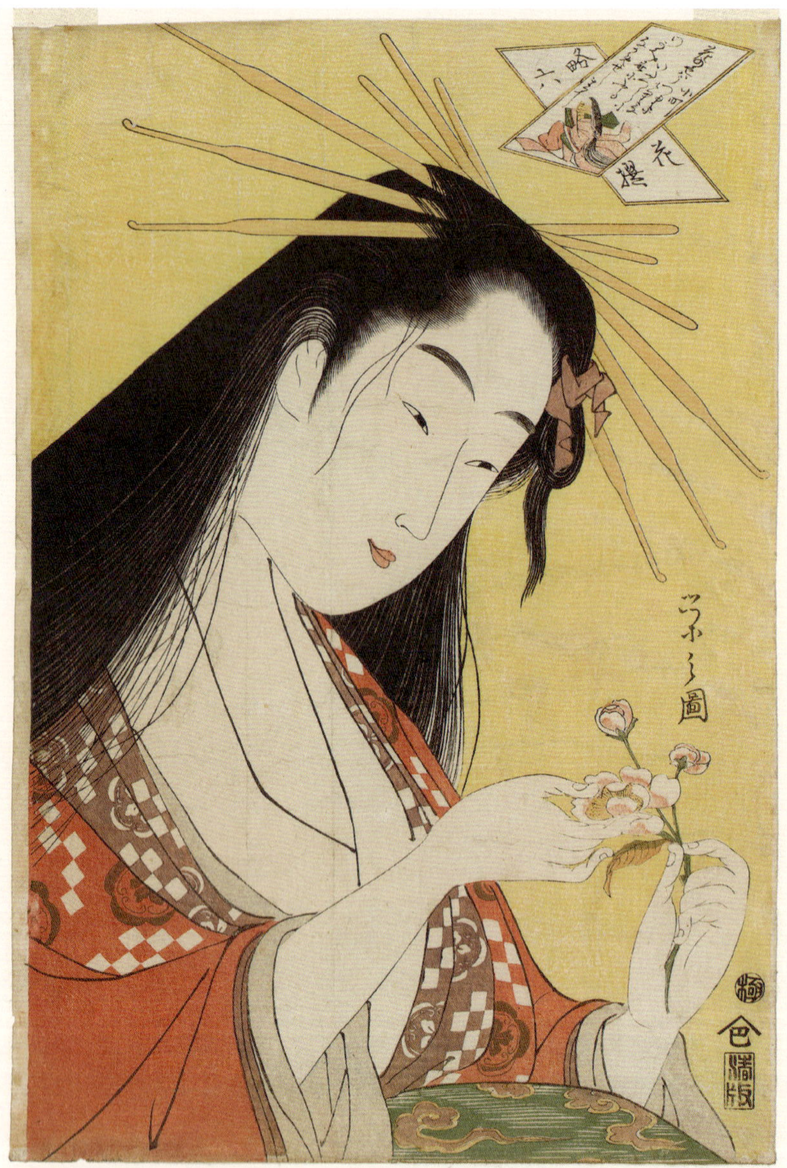

Chobunsai Eishi (1756–1829)
Publisher: Nishimuraya Yohachi (Eijudo)
Komachi, from the series Six Selected Flowers Imitating the Six Poetic Immortals (*Yatsushi Rokkasen*), c. 1796 (Kansei 8)
Woodblock print (nishiki-e); ink and color on paper
Vertical oban; 10¼ × 14¾ in. (26 × 37.3 cm)

Ono no Komachi, one of the greatest classical Japanese poets, was also said to have been the most beautiful woman in Japan during her lifetime in the ninth century. Eishi shows a contemporary courtesan with her hair loose after washing, not yet tied up into a fashionable style, to suggest the flowing floor-length hair of the beauties of Komachi's time. Komachi herself is shown, together with one of her poems, on a card for a New Year card game that forms the title inset at the upper right.

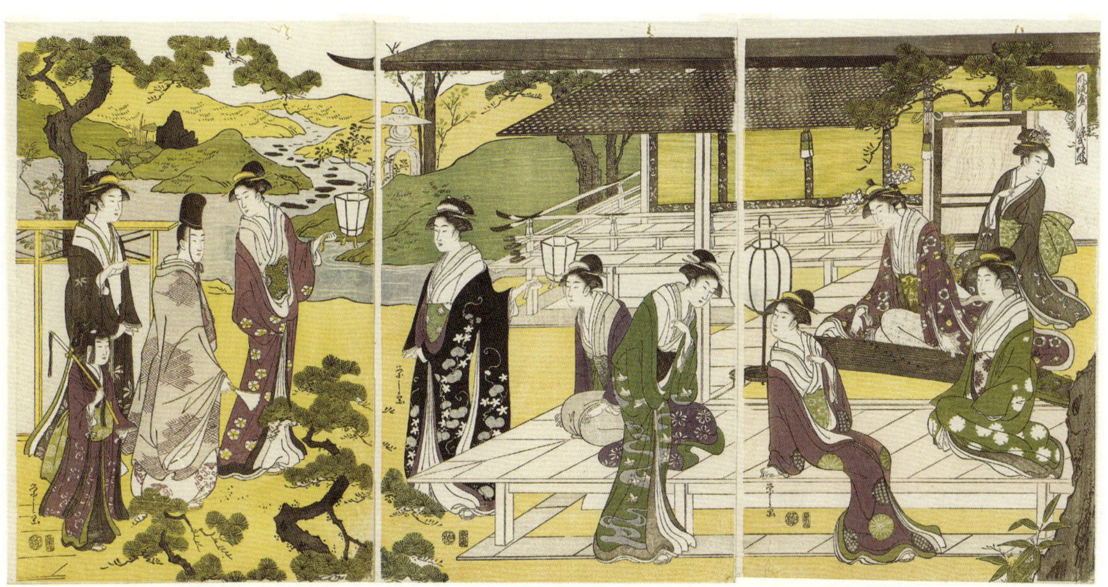

Chobunsai Eishi (1756–1829)
Publisher: Izumiya
Ichibei (Kansendo)
Matsukaze, from the series
Genji in Fashionable Modern
Guise (*Furyu yatsushi Genji*),
c. 1792–93 (Kansei 4–5)
Woodblock print (nishiki-e);
ink and color on paper
Vertical oban triptych;
30⅞ × 15½ in. (78.2 × 39.4 cm)

The same scene from the classic novel *The Tale of Genji* that was illustrated by Nishimura Shigenaga roughly sixty years earlier in a traditional style (pp. 127–29) is shown here in an elegant modernized parody. The lonely lady playing her koto to the sound of the wind in the pines (*matsukaze*) at last receives a visit from her lover Genji. Eishi made his version even more elegant by deliberately using a restricted color palette, focusing on purple and gray tones and avoiding red.

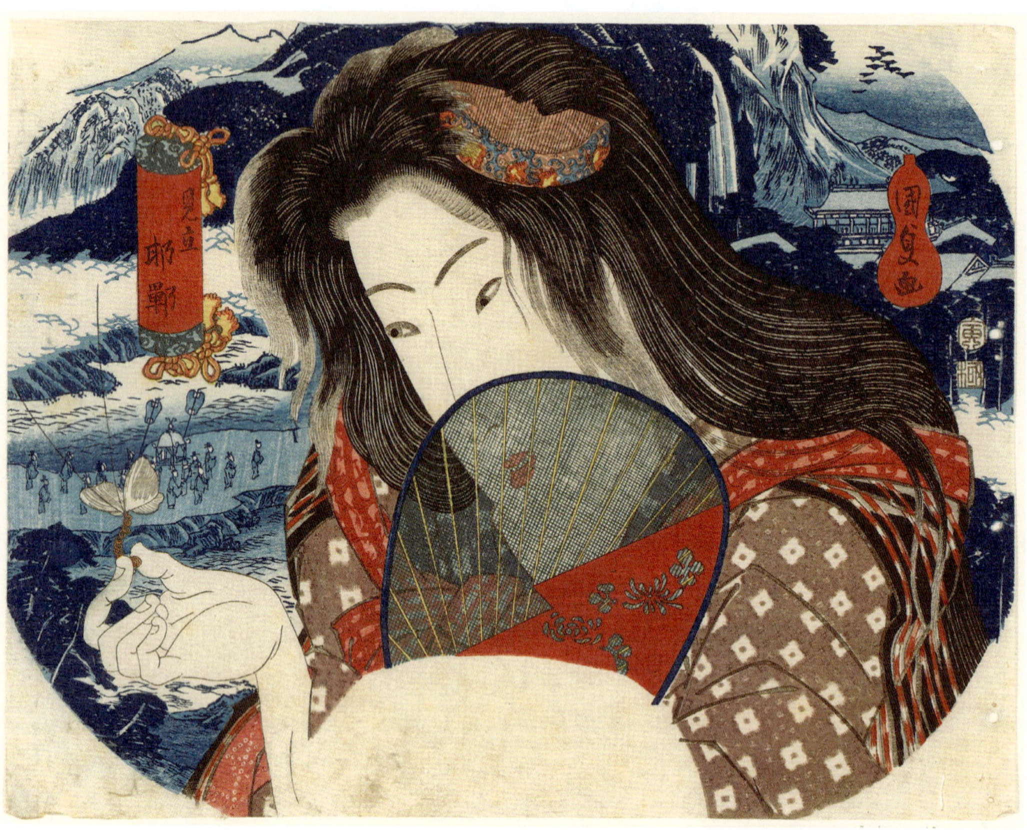

Utagawa Kunisada I (Toyokuni III) (1786–1864)
Parody of the Story of Kantan (Mitate Kantan),
1830 (Bunsei 13/Tenpo 1)
Woodblock print (nishiki-e); ink and color on paper
Uchiwa-e on horizontal aiban sheet; 11¾ × 9 in. (28.9 × 22.7 cm)

Intended to be cut out and pasted onto a bamboo framework to make a flat fan, this print shows a woman with her hair spread out to dry after washing, in front of a dreamlike Chinese landscape in shades of blue. The scene parodies the no play *Kantan*, in which a young man in ancient China goes to sleep on a magic pillow and dreams of a lifetime of future splendor that vanishes when he awakens.

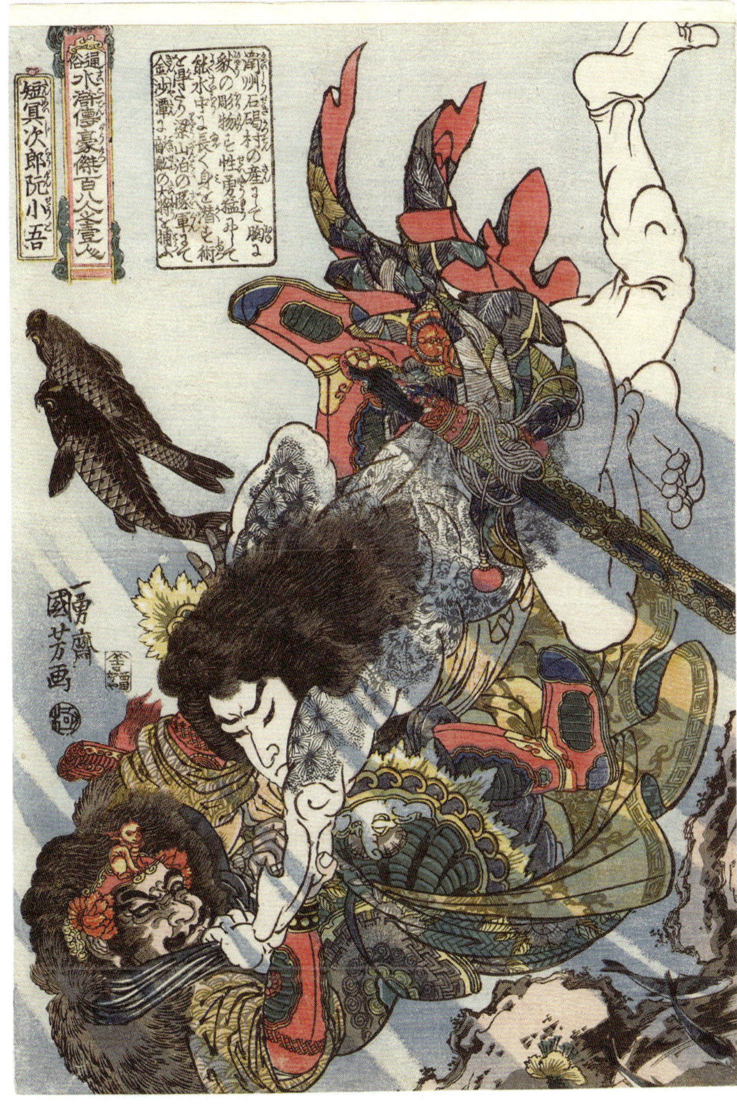

Utagawa Kuniyoshi (1797–1861)
Publisher: Kagaya Kichiemon (Kichibei)
Ruan Xiaowu, the Short-lived Second Son (Tanmeijiro Genshogo), from the series One Hundred and Eight Heroes of the Popular Shuihuzhuan (*Tsuzoku Suikoden goketsu hyakuhachinin no hitori*), c. 1827–30 (Bunsei 10–Tenpo 1)
Woodblock print (nishiki-e); ink and color on paper
Vertical oban; 10 × 14¼ in. (25.3 × 36.3 cm)

Kuniyoshi's best-selling series showing the characters of the great Chinese martial arts novel known in English as *The Water Margin* (*Shuihuzhuan* in the original Chinese, *Suikoden* in Japanese) not only made warrior prints a major genre but also strongly influenced the art of tattooing through the beautiful, complex designs that he drew for some of the heroic outlaws of the story, who band together to battle corrupt officials. Here, a tattooed hero fights an enemy soldier underwater.

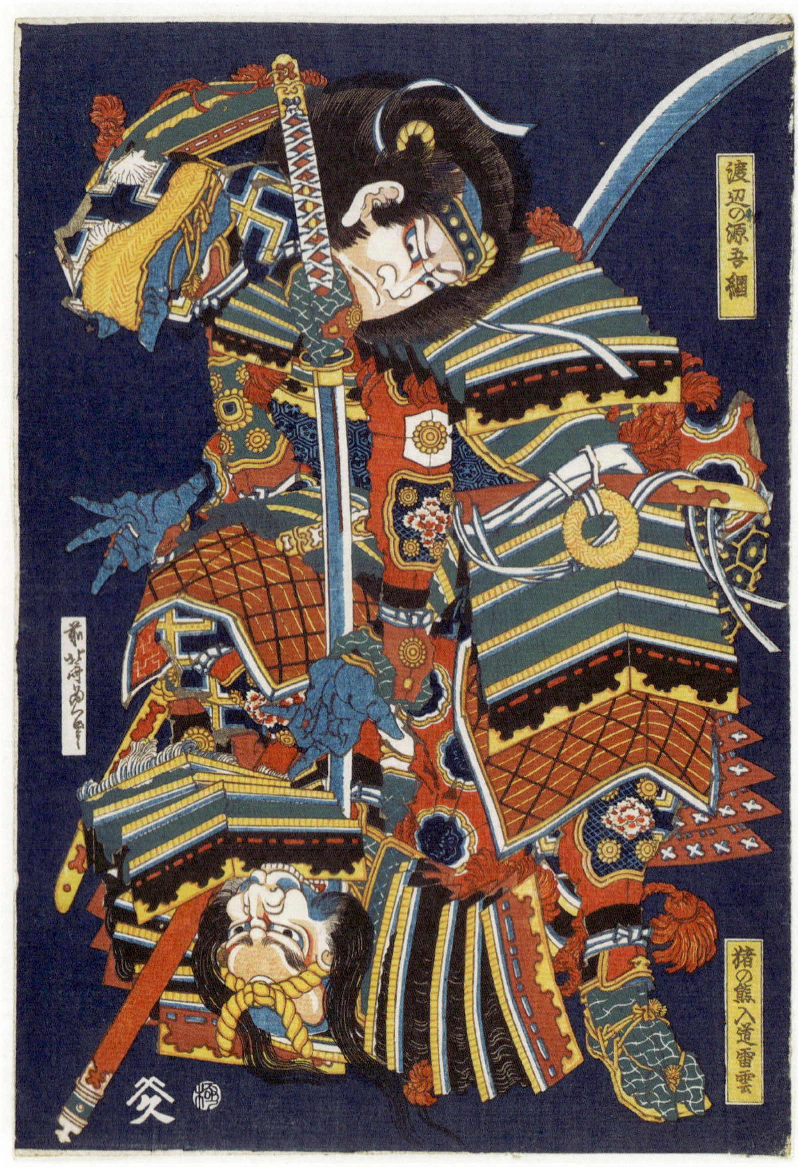

Katsushika Hokusai (1760–1849)
Publisher: Yamamotoya Heikichi (Eikyudo)
Watanabe no Gengo Tsuna and Inokuma Nyudo Raiun, from an untitled series of warriors in combat, c. 1833–35 (Tenpo 4–6)
Woodblock print (nishiki-e); ink and color on paper
Vertical oban; 10½ × 14¾ in. (26.5 × 37.4 cm)

Hokusai had already done many black-and-white book illustrations of warriors in combat when full-color prints of warriors became popular; in fact, his work was a major source of inspiration for Kuniyoshi. Hokusai himself later designed a few spectacular examples of warrior prints, such as this scene of a fierce struggle between the legendary tenth-century warrior Watanabe no Tsuna and a fictional enemy. The coloring of the armor on the intertwined bodies of the two warriors helps the viewer to decipher what is happening.

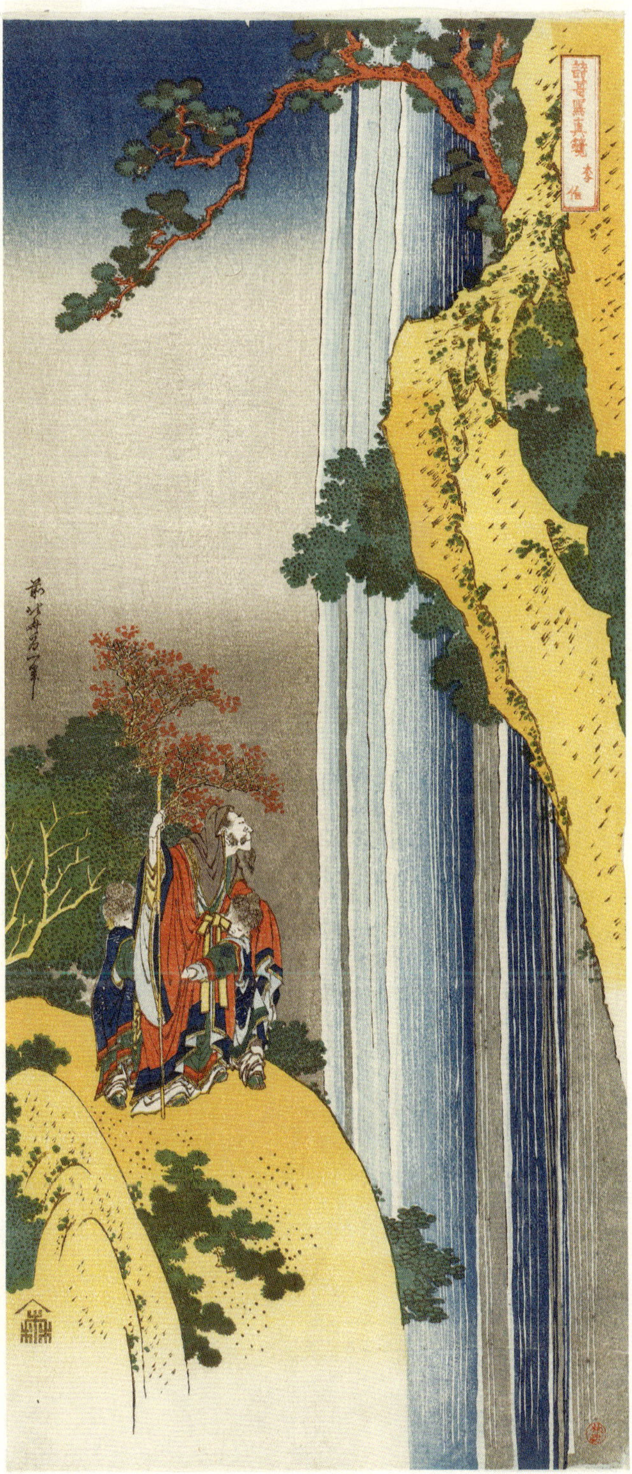

Katsushika Hokusai (1760–1849)
Publisher: Moriya Jihei (Kinshindo)
Li Bai (Ri Haku), from the series A True Mirror of Chinese and Japanese Poetry (*Shika shashin kyo*), also called Imagery of the Poets, c. 1833 (Tenpo 4)
Woodblock print (nishiki-e); ink and color on paper
Vertical nagaban; 8⅞ × 20⅛ in. (22.4 × 50.9 cm)

From a series of unusually large prints illustrating classical poetry from both China and Japan, this work depicts the Tang-dynasty Chinese poet Li Bai admiring the waterfall of Mount Lu, the subject of one of his most famous poems. Li Bai was also known for his love of wine, and so Hokusai added a humorous detail: the two little boys who hold the poet upright as he gazes in drunken rapture at the falls, to keep him from falling in.

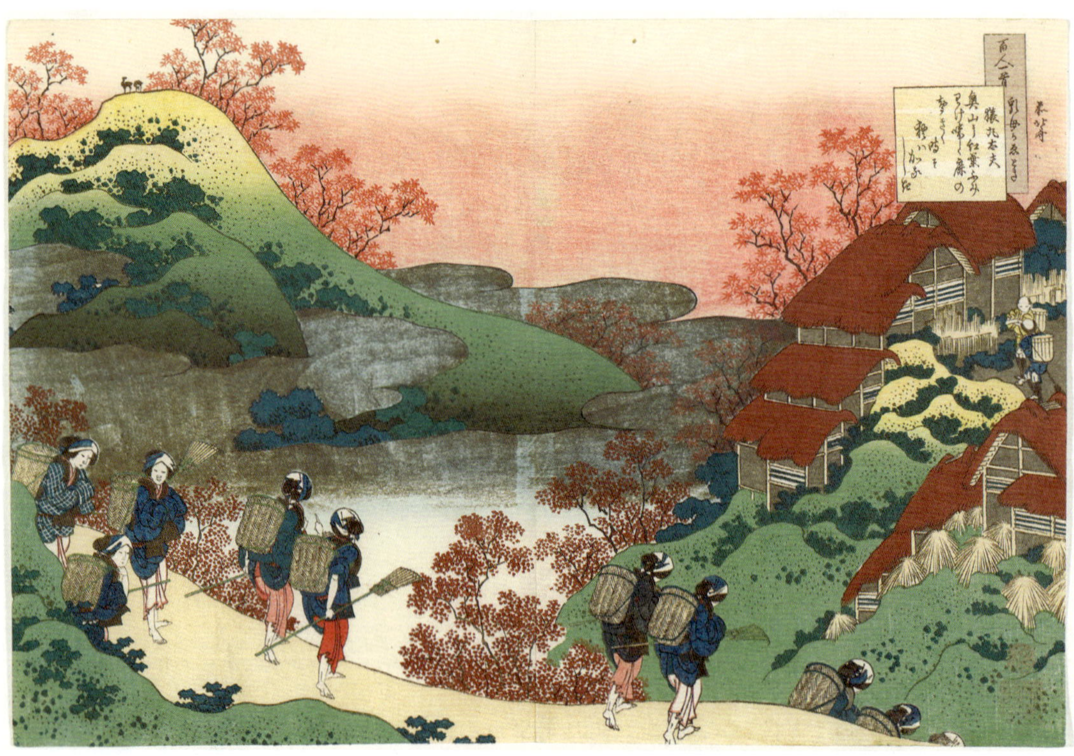

Katsushika Hokusai (1760–1849)
Publisher: Iseya Sanjiro (Eijudo)
Poem by Sarumaru Dayu,
from the series One Hundred Poems Explained by the Nurse (*Hyakunin isshu uba ga etoki*),
c. 1835–36 (Tenpo 6–7)
Woodblock print (nishiki-e); ink and color on paper
Horizontal oban; 14¾ × 9¾ in. (37.5 × 24.7 cm)

The twelfth-century anthology *One Hundred Poems by One Hundred Poets* was, and still is, the standard introduction to Japanese classical literature. In Hokusai's illustration for a poem describing the haunting melancholy of a deer calling for its mate on an autumn evening, the people who respond to the evocative sound are not ancient courtiers but humble mountain villagers returning home at the end of their day's work, underscoring the point that the emotions expressed in poetry are felt by everyone.

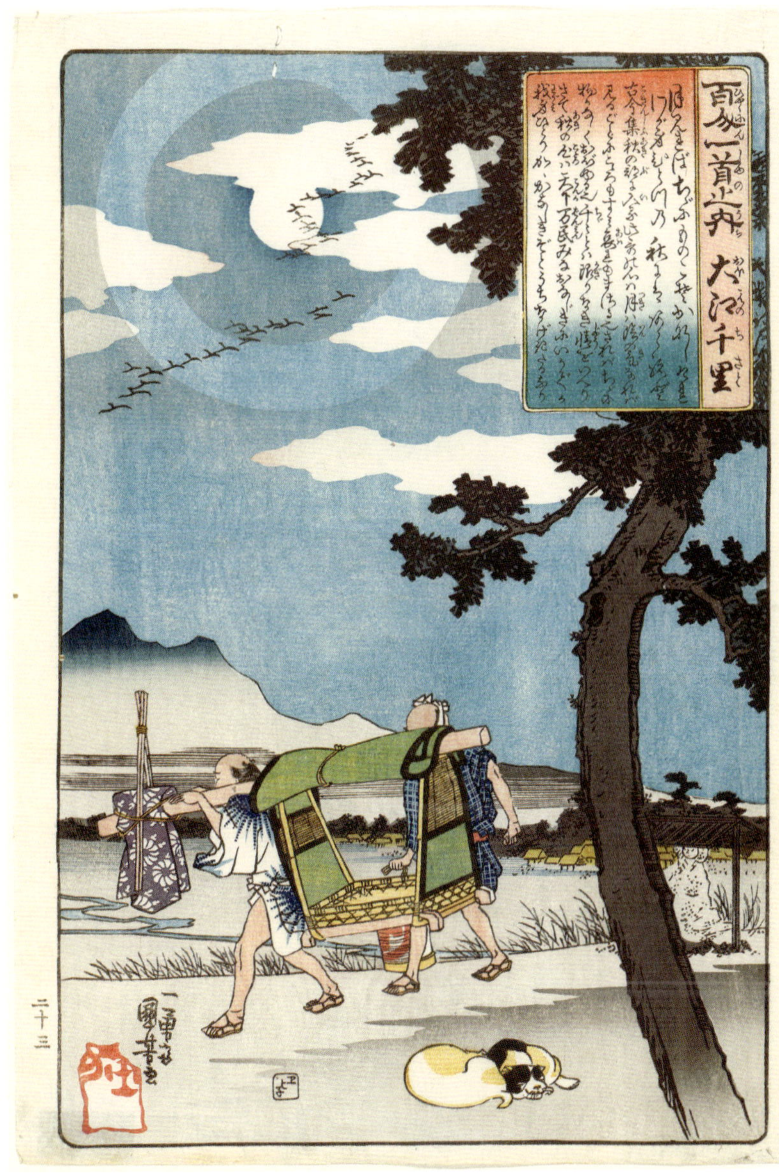

Utagawa Kuniyoshi (1797–1861)
Publisher: Ehiko
Poem by Oe no Chisato, from the series One Hundred Poems by One Hundred Poets (*Hyakunin isshu no uchi*), c. 1840–42 (Tenpo 11–13)
Woodblock print (nishiki-e); ink and color on paper
Vertical oban; 10¼ × 14¾ in. (25.9 × 37.5 cm)

Like the slightly earlier series by Hokusai on the same subject, Kuniyoshi's version of the *One Hundred Poems* theme includes both depictions of the long-ago courtiers who composed the poems and modern people of all social classes who appreciate their universal appeal. Here, two palanquin bearers returning home with their empty vehicle contemplate the chilly beauty of the autumn moon, reflecting the conclusion of the poem by an ancient nobleman: "It is not autumn for me alone."

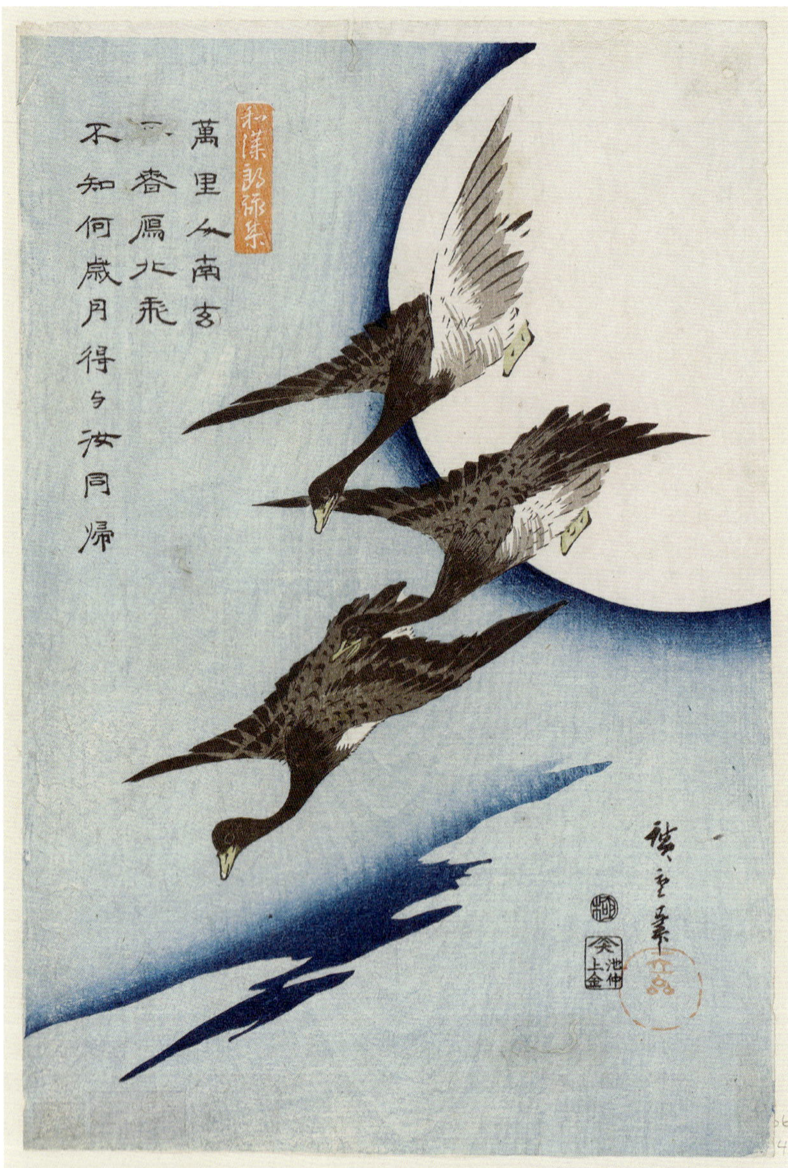

Utagawa Hiroshige I (1797–1858)
Publisher: Joshuya Kinzo
Flying Geese and Full Moon, from the series Japanese and Chinese Poems for Recitation (*Wakan roeishu*), c. 1842–43 (Tenpo 13–14)
Woodblock print (nishiki-e); ink and color on paper
Vertical oban; 10⅛ × 14¾ in. (25.6 × 37.5 cm)

Hiroshige designed a handful of especially fine images based on Chinese poems that had appeared in a classical bilingual anthology comparing them to similar works by Japanese poets. This poem, by the seventh-century Chinese government official Wei Chengqing, evokes the homesickness of a political exile as he gazes wistfully at the geese returning north in the spring. When, the poet wonders, will he himself be able to return from his exile in the south to his northern homeland?

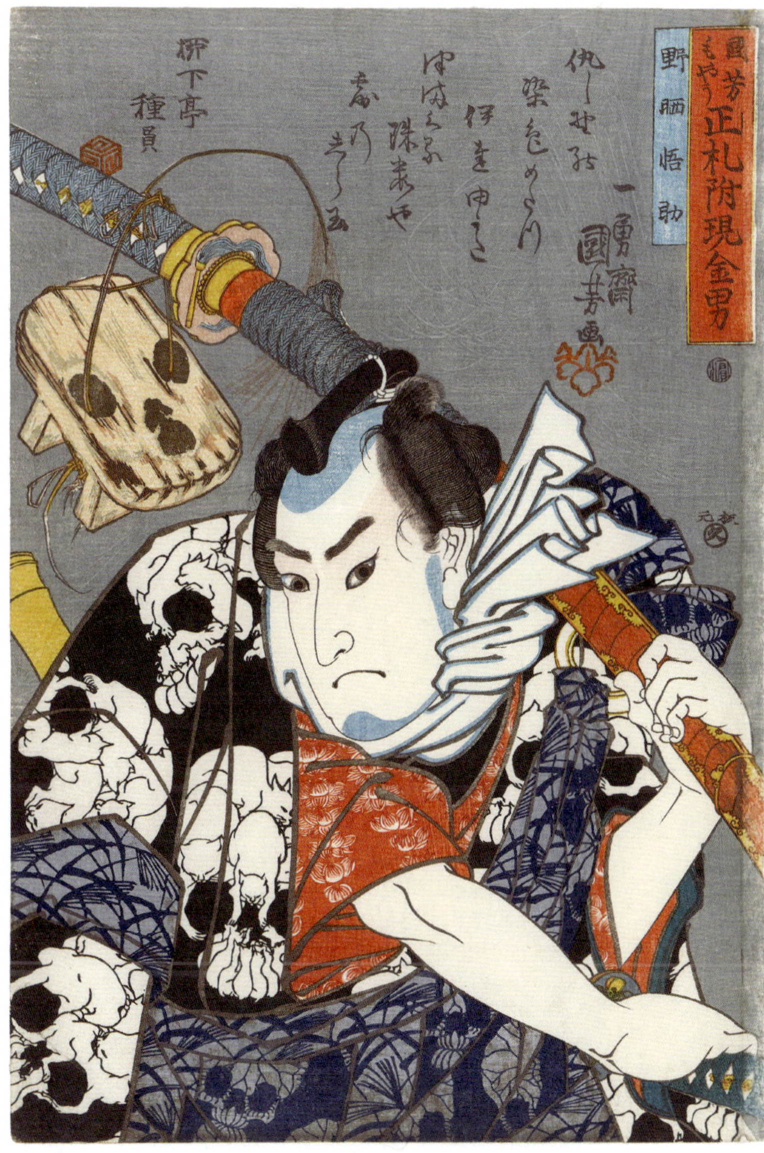

Utagawa Kuniyoshi (1797–1861)
Publisher: Ibaya Kyubei
Nozarashi Gosuke, from the series Men of Ready Money with True Labels Attached, Kuniyoshi Fashion (*Kuniyoshi moyo shofuda tsuketari genkin otoko*), c. 1845 (Koka 2)
Woodblock print (nishiki-e); ink and color on paper
Vertical oban; 9¾ × 14¼ in. (24.6 × 36 cm)

Kuniyoshi's close-up portrait of the fictional man-about-town Nozarashi Gosuke is full of visual puns. As Zen master Ikkyu was famous for carrying a skull on a stick as a symbol of the transience of human life, so Gosuke has an old wooden clog whose holes suggest a skull dangling from his sword. His kimono also has a pattern of skulls, but look closely—the skulls are made up of cats, a joke by the notorious cat-lover Kuniyoshi.

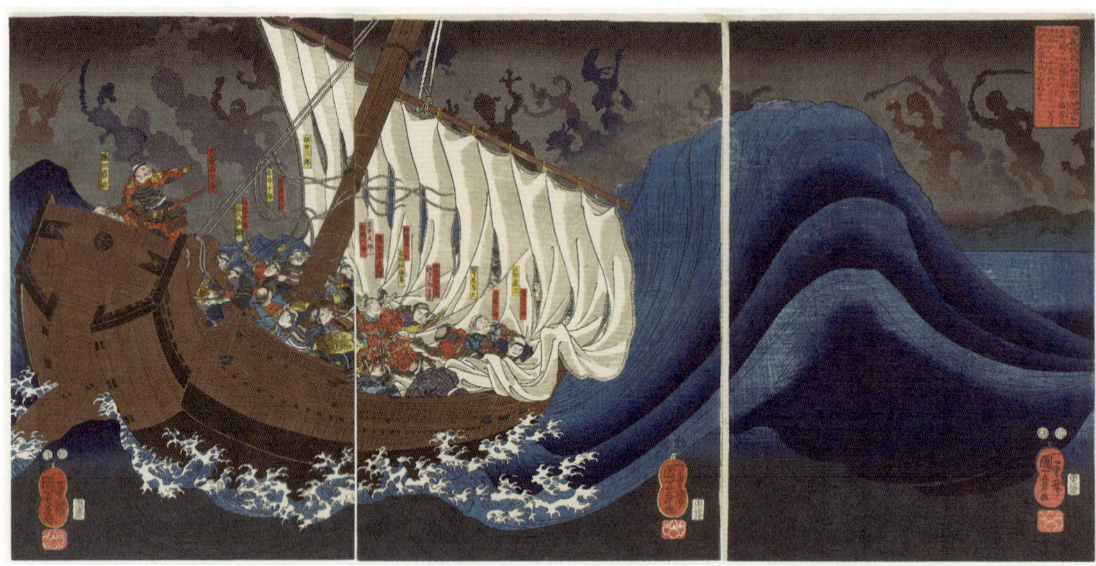

Utagawa Kuniyoshi (1797–1861)
Publisher: Enshuya Hikobei
The Ghosts of the Taira Attack Yoshitsune in Daimotsu Bay,
c. 1849–52 (Kaei 2–5)
Woodblock print (nishiki-e); ink and color on paper
Vertical oban triptych;
29¼ × 14½ in. (74.2 × 36.8 cm)

This exciting triptych shows the great twelfth-century general Minamoto no Yoshitsune attempting to escape by ship from enemies pursuing him. In a massive storm, his ship is attacked by the ghosts of his old foes, the Taira warrior clan, who had drowned themselves when Yoshitsune defeated them. Fortunately, Yoshitsune's chief retainer Benkei is a Buddhist priest as well as a warrior, and his prayers succeed in calming the ghosts.

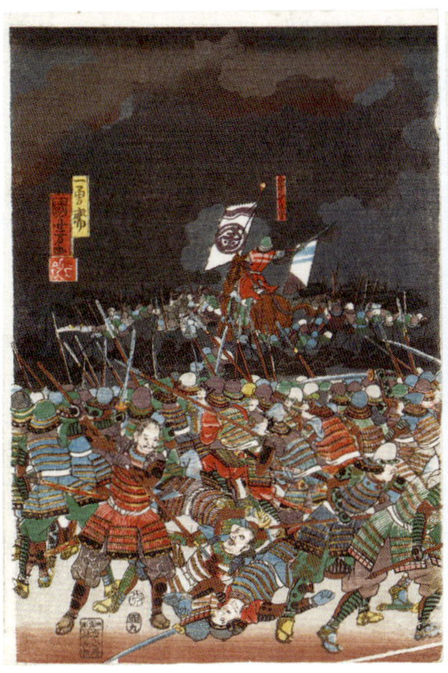
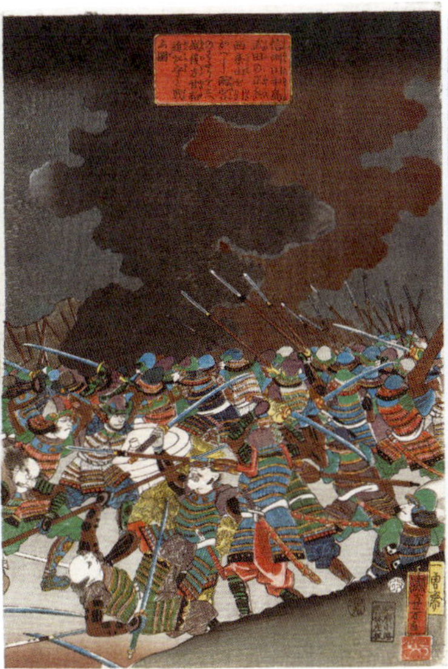
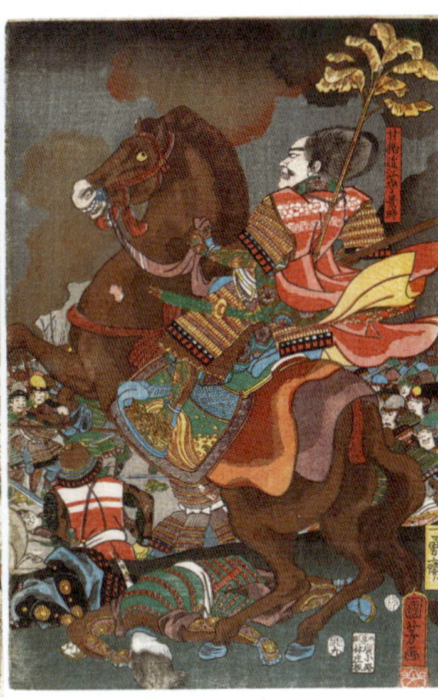

Utagawa Kuniyoshi (1797–1861)
Publisher: Hayashiya Shogoro
At Kawanakajima in Shinano Province, the Takeda Forces Crossed Mount Saijo and the Ford at Ame-no-Miya and Fought Amakasu Omi no Kami of the Echigo Side (Shinshu Kawanakajima Takeda no shohei Saijozan o hikikaeshi Ame no-Miya no watari o koe Echigo-gata), 1855 (Ansei 2), 9th month
Woodblock print (nishiki-e); ink and color on paper
Vertical oban triptych;
29¾ × 14¾ in. (75.6 × 37.5 cm)

For most of Kuniyoshi's lifetime, Japan was largely isolated from the outside world, with only a trickle of European goods coming in via the Dutch outpost at Nagasaki. Kuniyoshi, however, was very interested in Western art and is said to have collected European prints and book illustrations. In this triptych showing a battle between rival warlords in Japan's sixteenth-century civil wars, the rearing horse in the foreground is probably based on a European prototype.

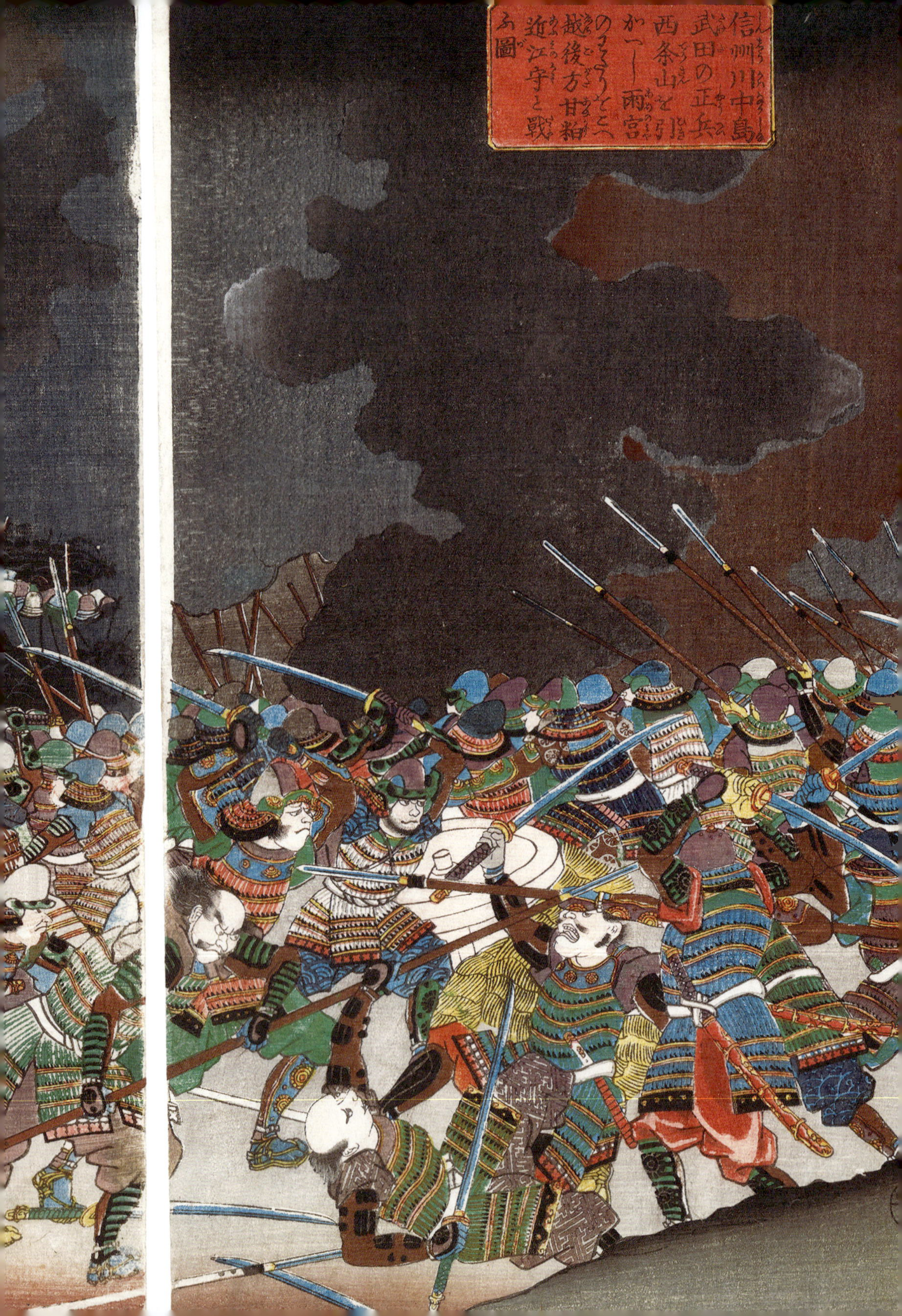

信州川中島
武田の正兵
西条山を引
かへし雨宮
越後方甘粕
近江守と戦
ふ図

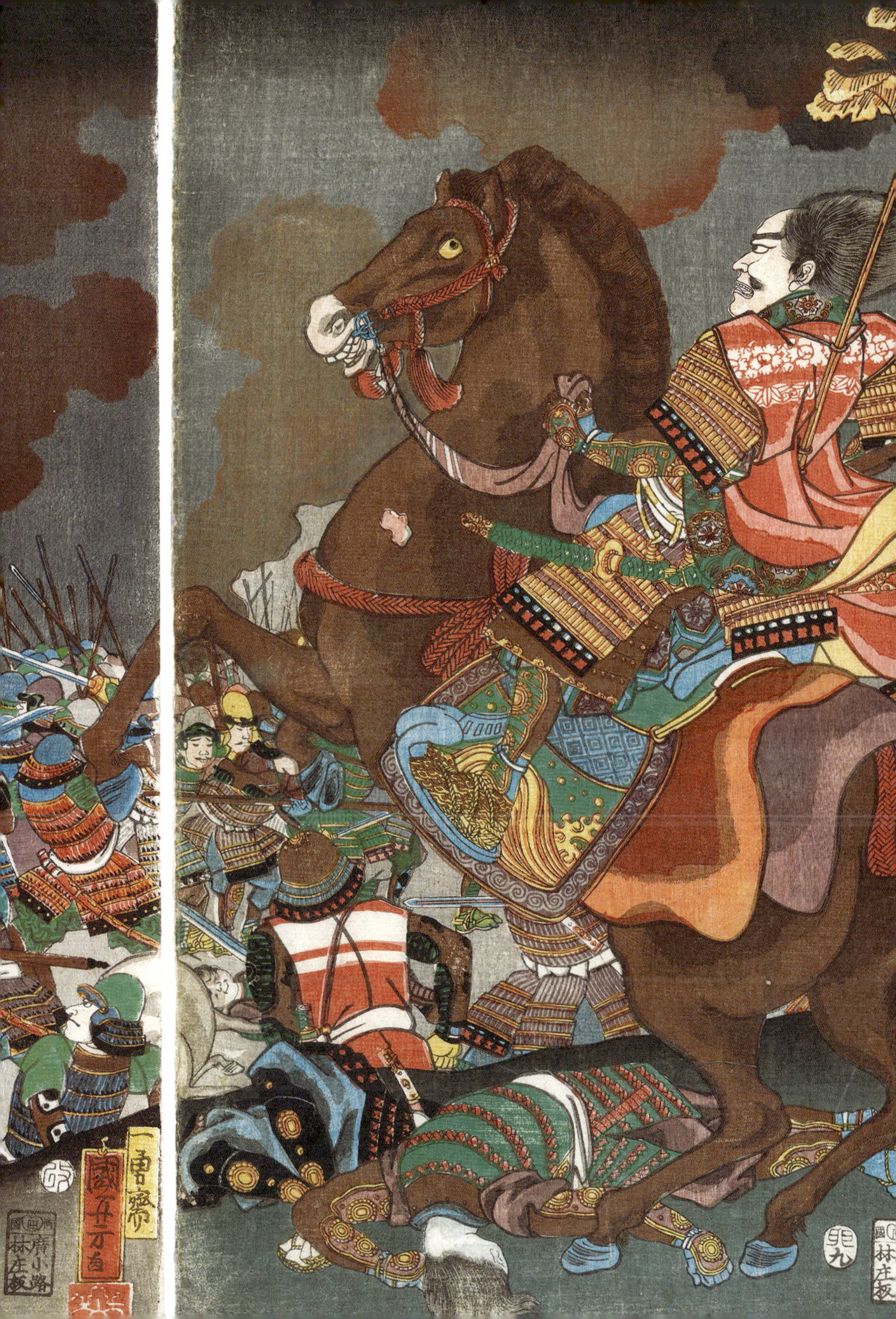
一勇齋
國芳画
廣小路
林庄板

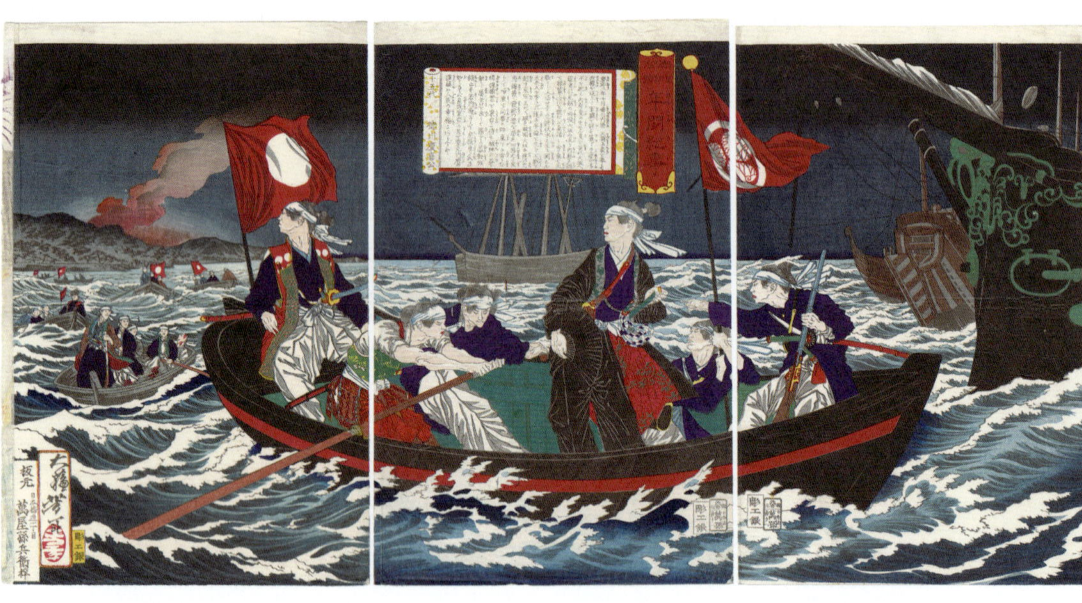

Tsukioka Yoshitoshi (1839–1892)
Publisher: Yorozuya Magobei
Blockcutter: Asai Ginjiro (Hori Gin), 1844–1894
The Fifteenth Shogun, Lord Tokugawa Yoshinobu (Jugodai, Tokugawa Yoshinobu ko), from the series Chronological Record of the Rule of the Tokugawas (*Tokugawa jiseki nenkan kiji*), c. 1874 (Meiji 7)
Woodblock print (nishiki-e); ink and color on paper
Vertical oban triptych;
28¾ × 14¾ in. (73.1 × 37.5 cm)

During the Edo period, it was strictly forbidden to depict the Tokugawa shoguns or any other members of the ruling class from 1573 on. But under the new Meiji government, the old rules were dropped, and artists could show both current events and recent historical scenes. Yoshitoshi used a Westernized style for this series portraying each of the fifteen Tokugawa shoguns, including the last, who is shown making his escape after losing a decisive battle in 1868.

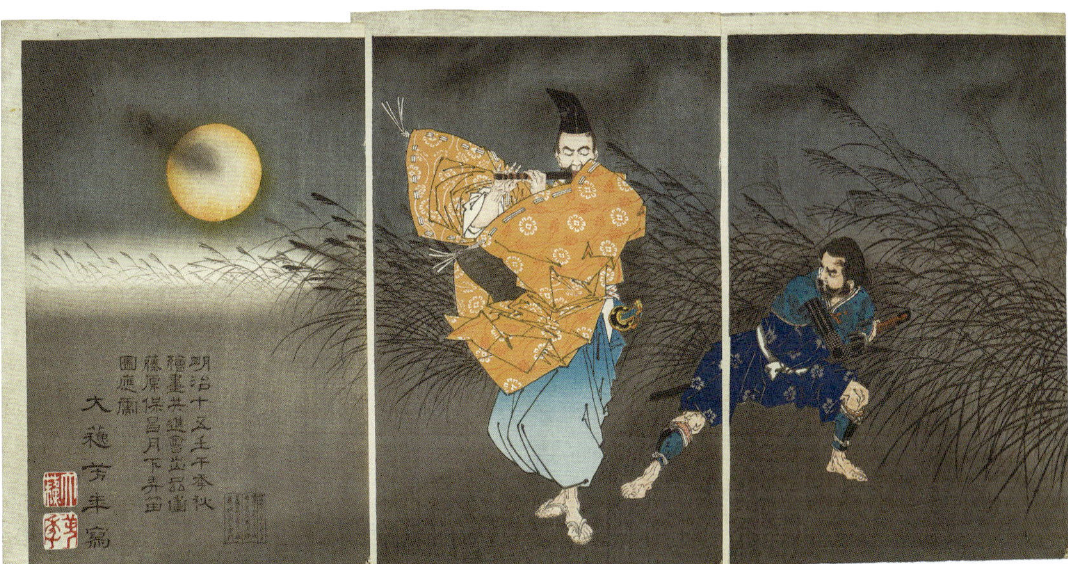

Tsukioka Yoshitoshi (1839–1892)
Publisher: Akiyama Buemon
Fujiwara no Yasumasa Playing the Flute by Moonlight, a Painting Shown at the Exhibition for the Advancement of Painting in Autumn 1882 (Meiji jugo mizunoe uma kishu Kaiga Kyoshinkai shuppinga Fujiwara no Yasumasa gekka fue o moteasobu zu, oju),
1883 (Meiji 16), February 12
Woodblock print (nishiki-e);
ink and color on paper
Vertical oban triptych;
29 × 14¾ in. (73.5 × 37.5 cm)

The twelfth-century courtier Fujiwara no Yasumasa was known for his skills in both martial arts and music. One night as he wandered in the moonlight playing his flute, he was stalked by a bandit who planned to rob him, but in the end, the would-be mugger was so smitten with the beauty of the music that he refrained. The printed triptych was based on a painting that Yoshitoshi had submitted to an exhibition intended to support and promote traditional Japanese-style painting.

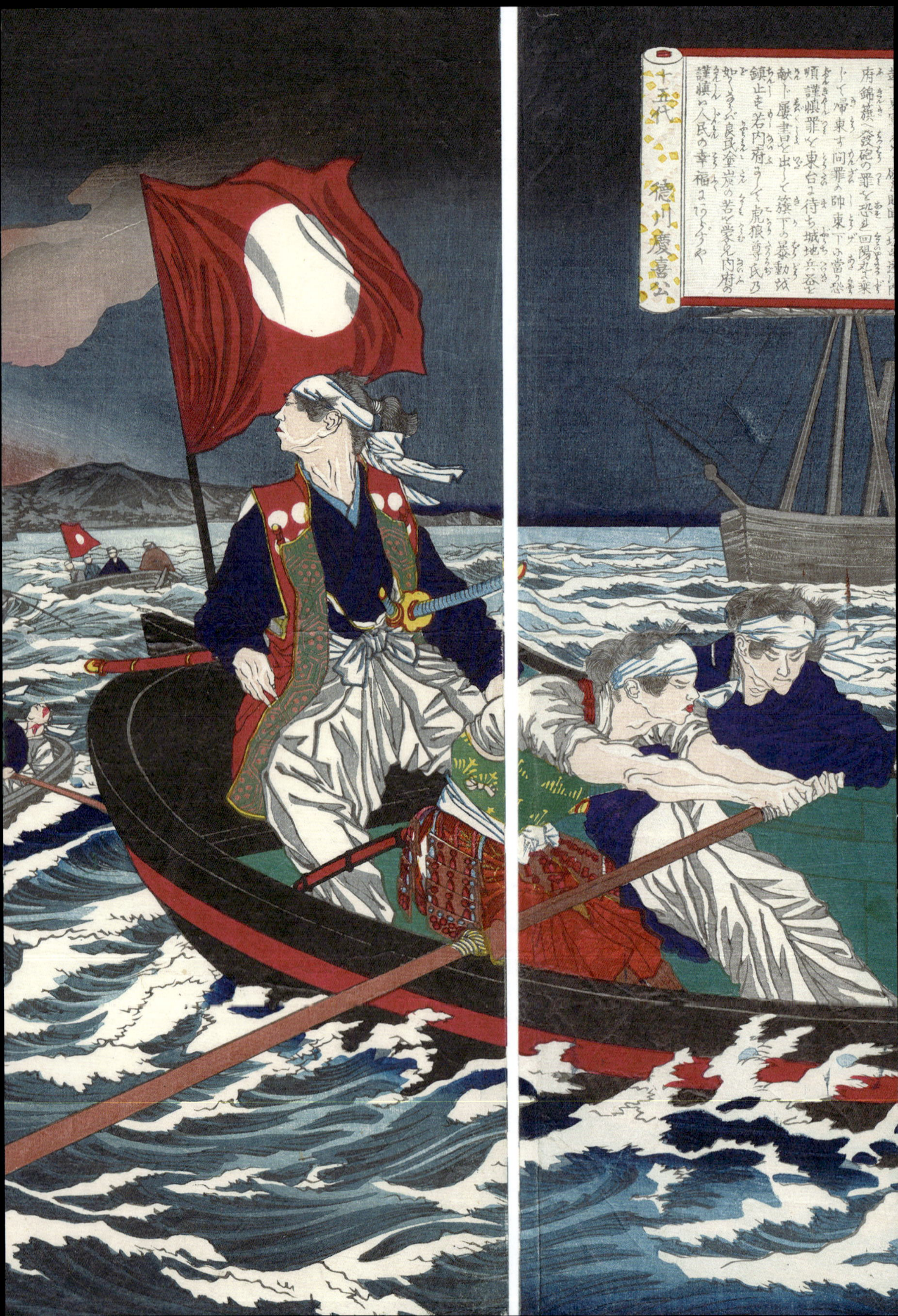
十五代 徳川慶喜公
府錦旗へ發砲の罪を恐れ回陽丸に乗
じて歸東す同罪の師東下に當り恐
頓謹慎罪を東台に待ち城地兵器を
献じ屢書を出して旗下の暴動を
鎮止む若内府をして虎狼尊氏乃
如くならバ良民塗炭の苦を蒙ん内府の
謹慎ハ人民の幸福ならずや

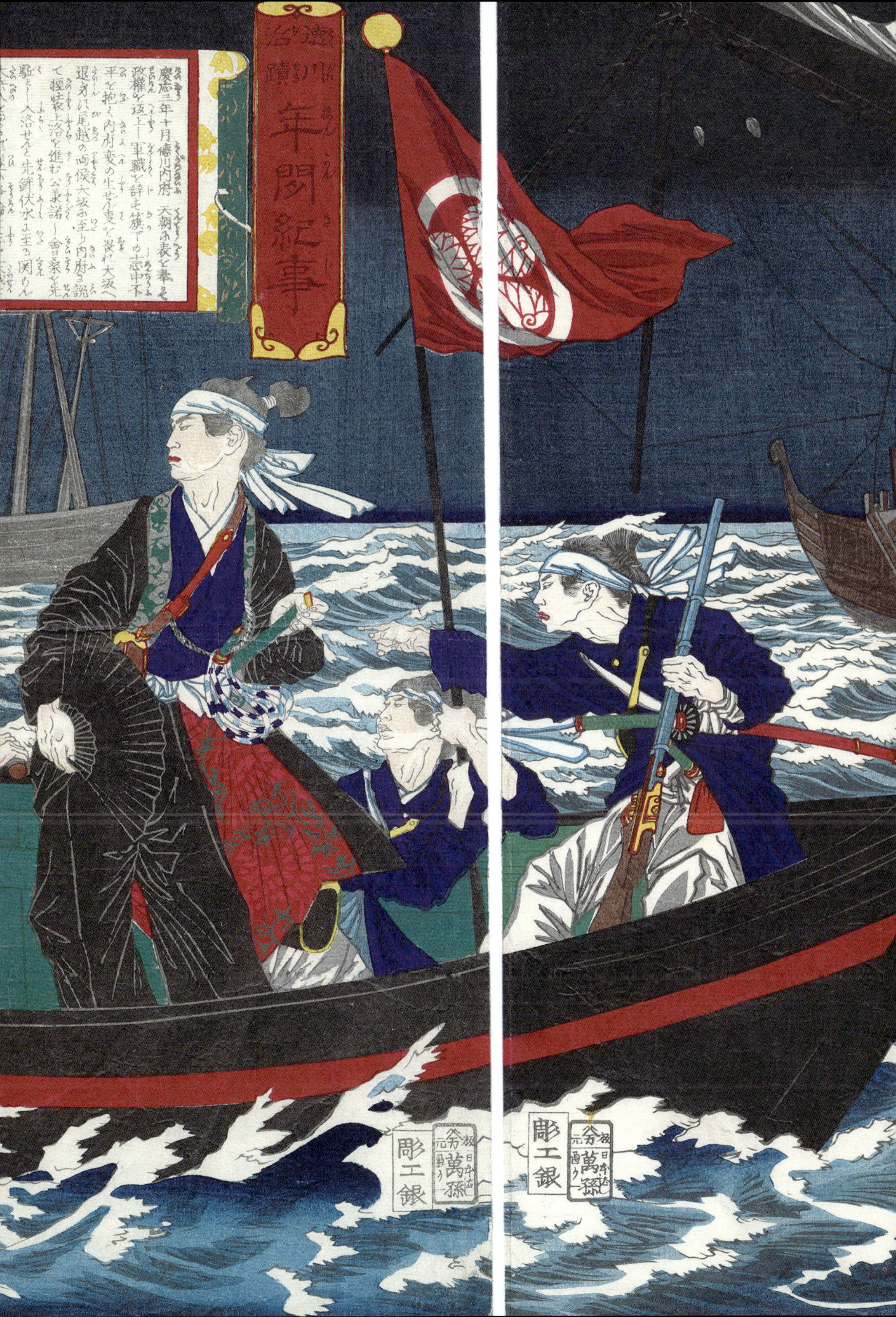
徳川治績
年間紀事
慶応三年十月徳川内府 天朝に表を奉て
政権を返上し軍職を辞さ旗下の志中不
平を抱く内府変の生ぜん事を畏れ大坂へ
退身に尾越の両侯大坂に至り内府に説
て軽装上洛を進む公承諾し會桑を先
駈とし入洛せんと先鋒伏水に至る関めん
萬孫
彫工銀
萬孫
彫工銀

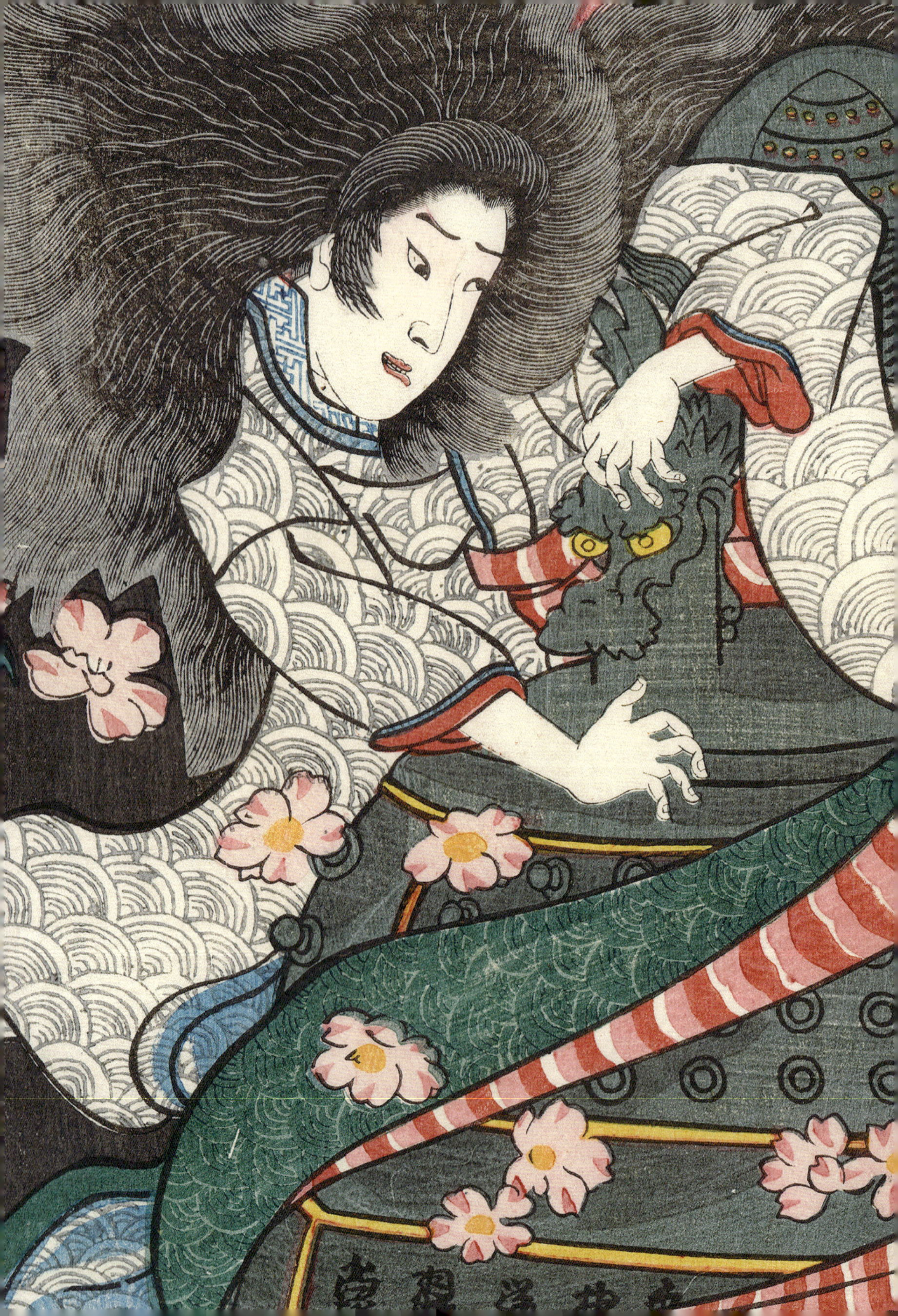

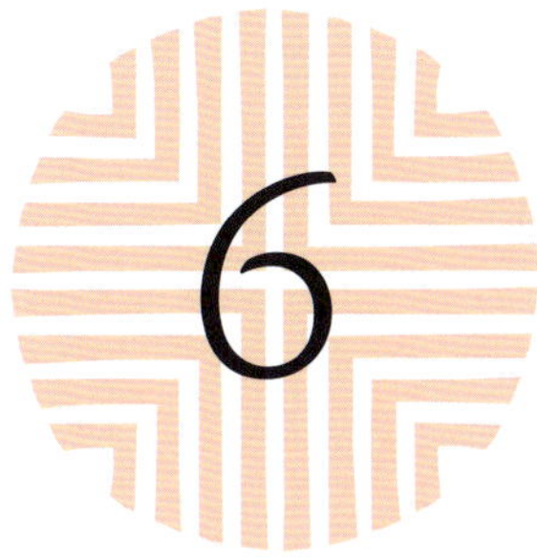

Fantasy

The rich heritage of tales of supernatural beings in Japanese culture—supplemented with stories imported from China—is well represented in ukiyo-e prints. Ghosts, monsters, superheroes, mischievous demons, shapeshifters, and magical creatures that bring good luck all appear in prints from the earliest days of ukiyo-e, but these themes became especially popular from the 1830s on, as a part of the enthusiasm for historical warrior prints. In addition to scenes of historical battles, warriors are shown fighting ghosts or monsters in episodes drawn either from the classical war stories—which frequently embellish their accounts of Japan's civil wars with anecdotes of supernatural events—or from the historical novels that became popular in the early nineteenth century. In popular publishing, lengthy action-adventure stories, often with supernatural elements, largely replaced the earlier tales of the amorous adventures in the Floating World in response to the government crackdown of the 1790s known as the Kansei Reforms. Adventure stories set "long ago" were safely distant from any mention of contemporary problems that might be construed as critical of the government, with the bonus that they emphasized officially approved samurai virtues such as bravery and loyalty. The books were heavily illustrated by leading artists such as Hokusai and Toyokuni, but the one most famous for color prints of the supernatural was Kuniyoshi, who loved to draw monsters as well as heroes fighting them. His students, such as Yoshitsuya and Yoshitoshi, also enjoyed drawing imaginary beings in ingenious ways.

Toward the end of the Edo period, from the 1840s to the 1860s, works appeared that hinted at mysterious hidden meanings, and possibly forbidden political messages. Kuniyoshi was especially well-known for these ambiguous, tantalizing puzzle pictures, and some of his students also designed them.

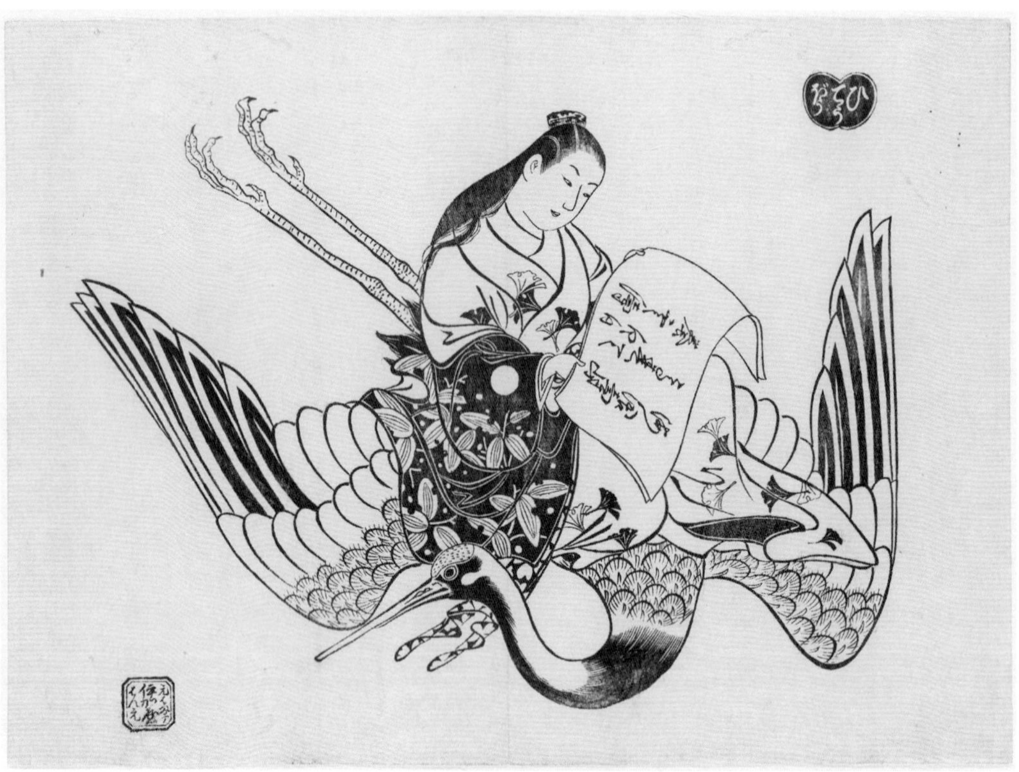

Okumura Masanobu (1686–1764)
Publisher: Igaya Kan'emon (Bunkido)
Courtesan as Fei Zhangfang (Hi Chobo), from a series of courtesans imitating Taoist immortals, c. 1706–8 (Hoei 3–5)
Woodblock print (sumizuri-e); ink on paper
Horizontal oban; 15⅞ × 11½ in. (40 × 29.2 cm)

In the Chinese religion of Taoism (also spelled Daoism), immortals are supernatural beings with magical powers; some of them were originally human beings who achieved immortality through alchemy. Chinese paintings imported into Japan, and Japanese works in the Chinese style, often depicted them riding through the air on birds such as cranes. Okumura Masanobu created this witty parody by substituting a beautiful Japanese courtesan for the original Chinese sage, implying that her lovers will be transported into the heavens.

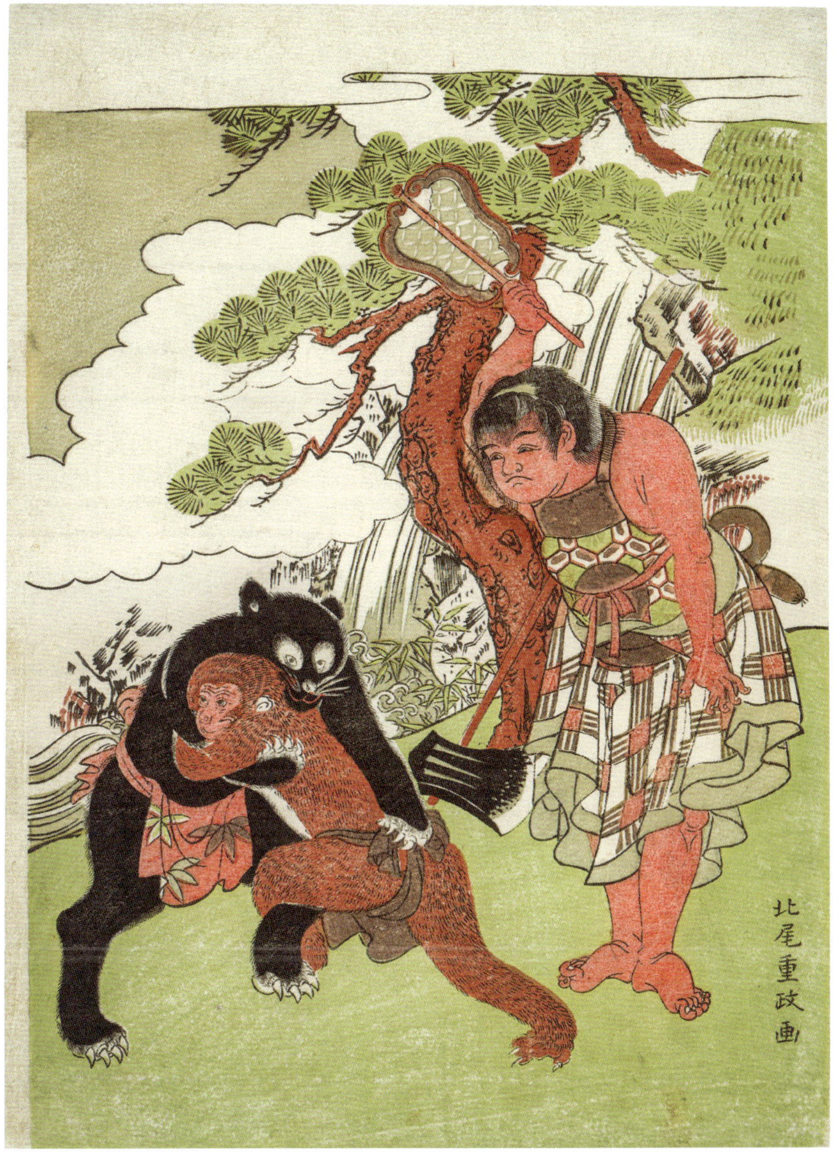

Kitao Shigemasa (1739–1820)
Kintaro Judging the Wrestling Match of a Monkey and a Bear, c. 1772–74 (An'ei 1–3)
Woodblock print (nishiki-e); ink and color on paper
Vertical chuban; 7¾ × 10¼ in. (19.7 × 26.2 cm)

The child superhero known as Kintaro (Golden Boy) was brought up by his mother, the Mountain Witch, deep in the mountains far from human beings with animals as his playmates. He is always shown with red or orange skin to symbolize his superhuman strength. Kintaro grew up to be a mighty warrior and became one of the four most trusted retainers of the demon-fighter Minamoto no Yorimitsu, taking the adult name Sakata no Kintoki.

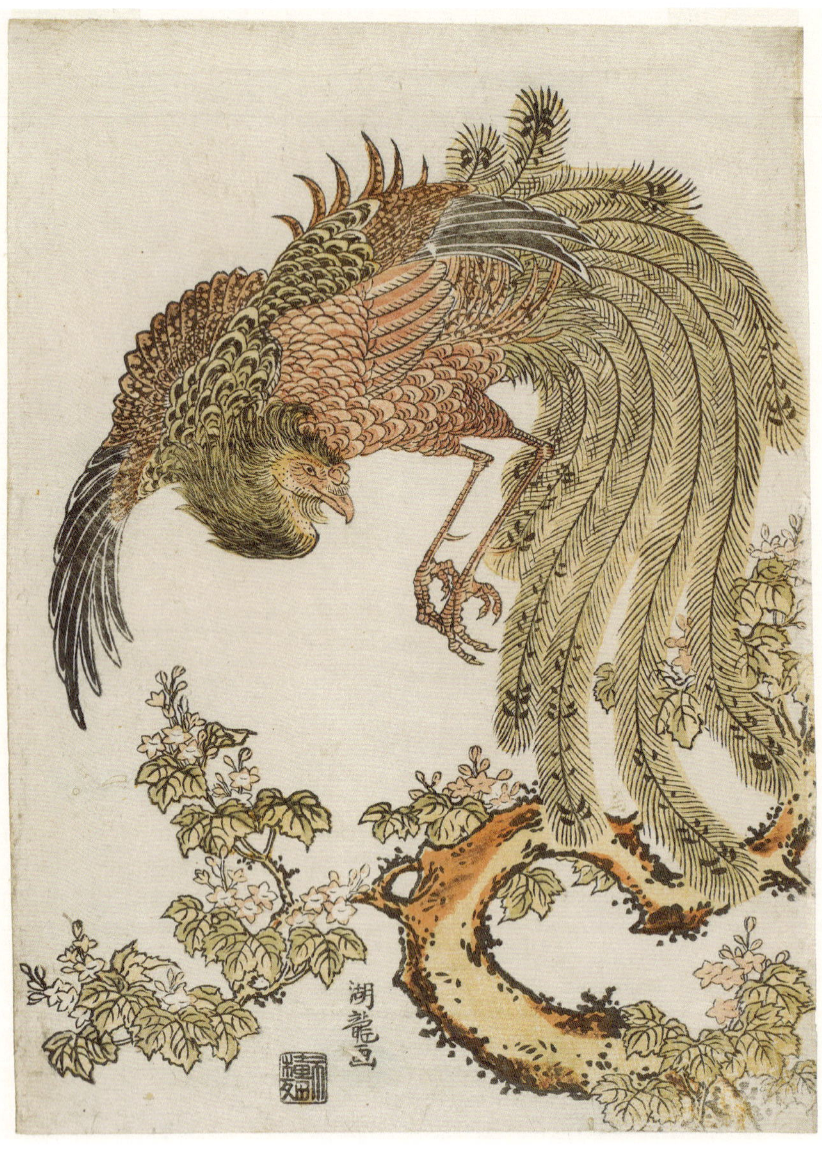

Isoda Koryusai (1735–1790)
Publisher: Nishimuraya Yohachi (Eijudo)
Phoenix and Paulownia Tree, c. 1770
Woodblock print (nishiki-e); ink and color on paper
Vertical chuban; 7½ × 10 in. (19 × 25.5 cm)

The fabulous bird known in English as a phoenix—although its mythological attributes are somewhat different from those of its Western namesake—has a long history in East Asian art. In ancient China, it was believed to appear only in times of good government, and so it became a symbol of prosperity and good fortune as well as benevolent power. In Japan, it appeared in paintings, sculpture, and textile designs, often paired with the auspicious paulownia tree in which it was said to roost.

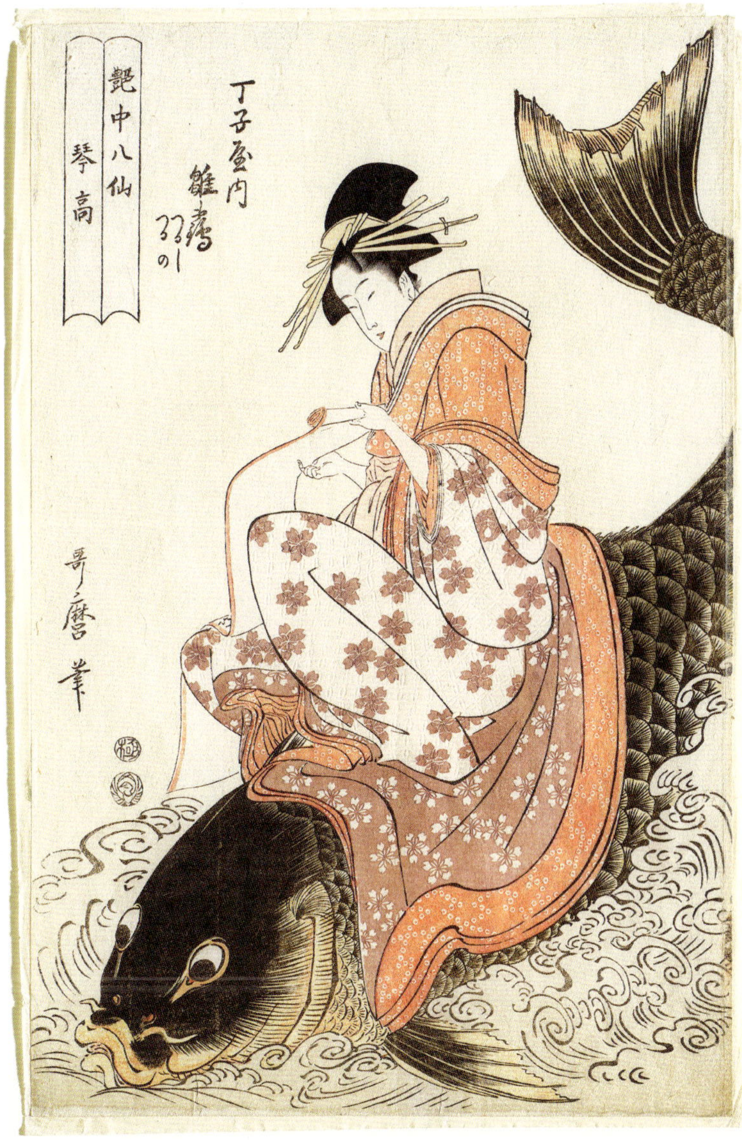

Kitagawa Utamaro I (c. 1750–1806)
Publisher: Tsuruya
Kiemon (Senkakudo)
The Immortal Qin Gao, represented by Hinazuru of the Chojiya, kamuro Tsuruji and Tsuruno (Kinko, Chojiya uchi Hinazuru, Tsuruji, Tsuruno), from the series Eight Immortals in the Art of Love (*Enchu hassen*), c. 1793–94 (Kansei 5–6)
Woodblock print (nishiki-e); ink and color on paper
Vertical oban; 9⅞ × 14¾ in. (25 × 37.5 cm)

Taoist immortals not only soar through the air riding birds—or under their own power—they also sometimes ride through the waves on the backs of fish. The carp-riding Qin Gao, a frequent subject for paintings in both China and Japan, is imitated by a high-ranking courtesan in this series by the leading designer of prints of women. Perched on a fish that is a symbol of courage and success because of its bravery in swimming upstream, Hinazuru calmly peruses a love letter.

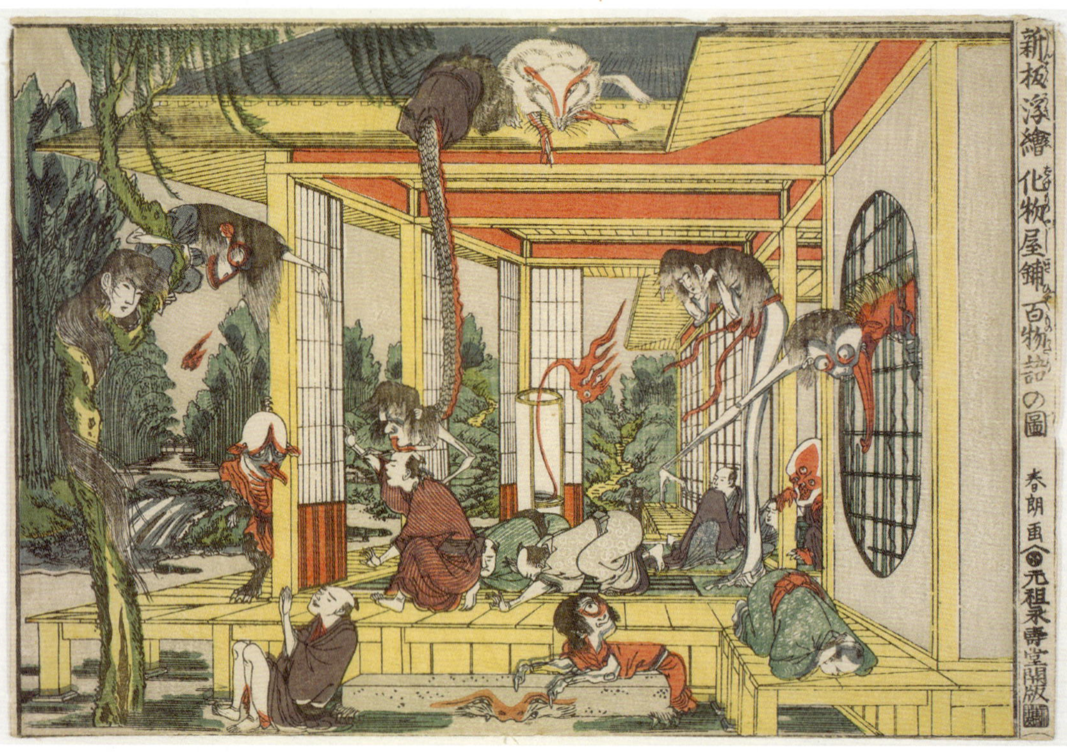

Katsushika Hokusai (1760–1849)
Publisher: Nishimuraya Yohachi (Eijudo)
Newly Published Perspective Picture: One Hundred Ghost Stories in a Haunted House (Shinpan uki-e bakemono yashiki hyaku monogatari no zu), c. 1790
Woodblock print (nishiki-e); ink and color on paper
Horizontal oban; 14 × 9¼ in. (35.4 × 23.7 cm)

Early in his career Hokusai designed many perspective prints (*uki-e*), which used Western-style vanishing point perspective to create a startlingly realistic effect. In this design he combines realism with fantasy, showing the monsters who have appeared to haunt a mansion where a group of men were playing the "Hundred Stories" game by telling scary ghost stories at night, putting out one of the lights as each story was finished. Little did they know what creatures they were summoning!

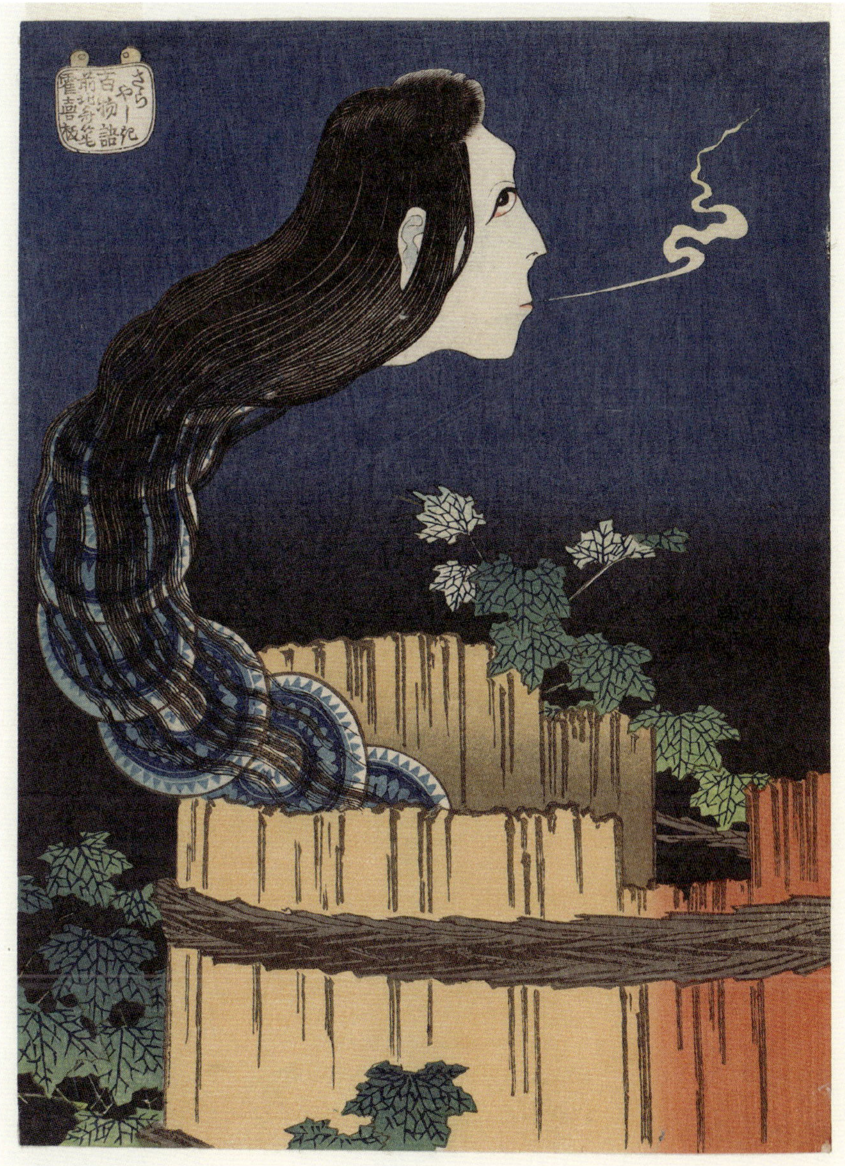

Katsushika Hokusai (1760–1849)
Publisher: Tsuruya Kiemon (Senkakudo)
The Mansion of the Plates (Sara yashiki), from the series One Hundred Ghost Stories (*Hyaku monogatari*), c. 1831–32 (Tenpo 2–3)
Woodblock print (nishiki-e); ink and color on paper
Vertical chuban; 7 × 9¼ in. (17.6 × 23.7 cm)

In an urban legend retold in several kabuki plays, a mansion was haunted by the ghost of a serving woman who had broken a precious porcelain plate and then either drowned herself in remorse or was murdered by the master of the house in a fit of rage. Every night her ghost rose from the well where her body was found and counted the plates, moaning over the missing one. Hokusai cleverly used the plates themselves to construct the body of the ghost.

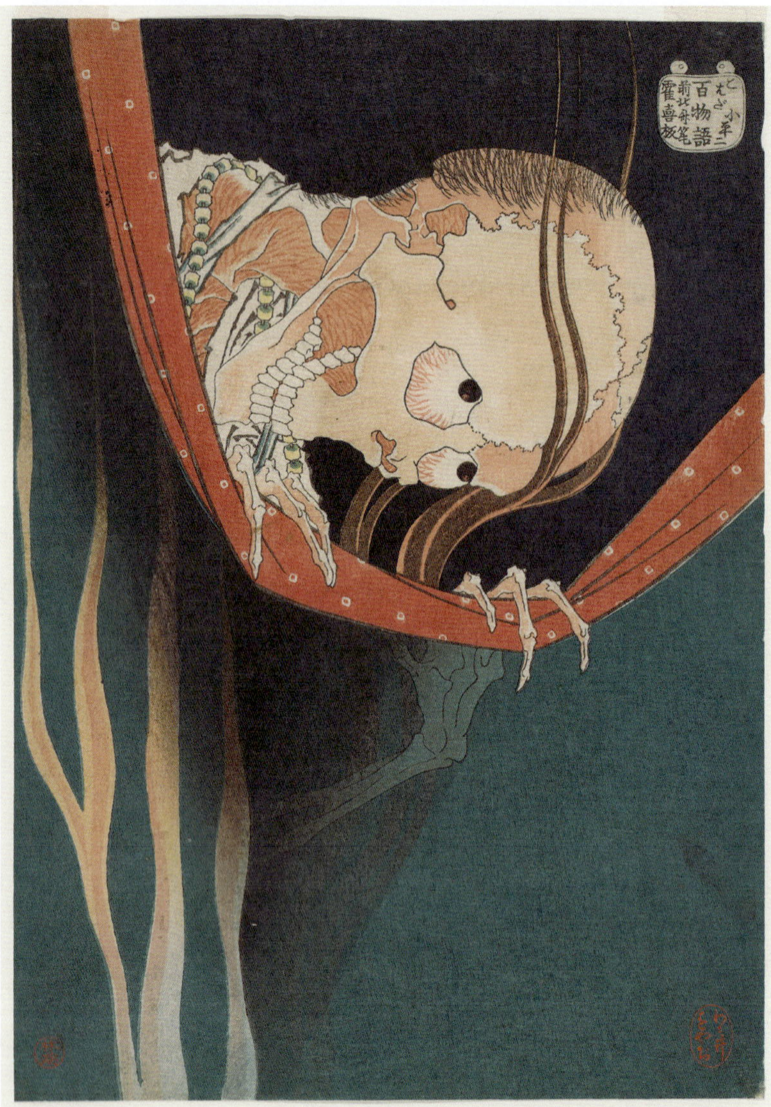

Katsushika Hokusai (1760–1849)
Publisher: Tsuruya
Kiemon (Senkakudo)
The Ghost of Kohada Koheiji, from the series One Hundred Ghost Stories (*Hyaku monogatari*), c. 1831–32 (Tenpo 2–3)
Woodblock print (nishiki-e); ink and color on paper
Vertical chuban; 7¼ × 10⅛ in. (18.5 × 25.7 cm)

The title “One Hundred Ghost Stories” comes from the name of a popular story-telling game, but only five prints in the series are known. The unfortunate Kohada Koheiji was murdered by his wife and her lover, but he returned to take revenge on them. On a summer night, as the guilty couple are sleeping under a tentlike gauze mosquito net, the rotting corpse of their victim appears. The ghost claws down the edge of the mosquito net and glares balefully over it.

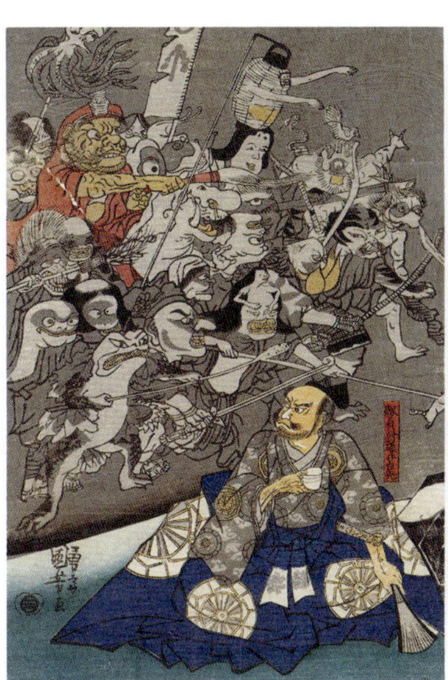
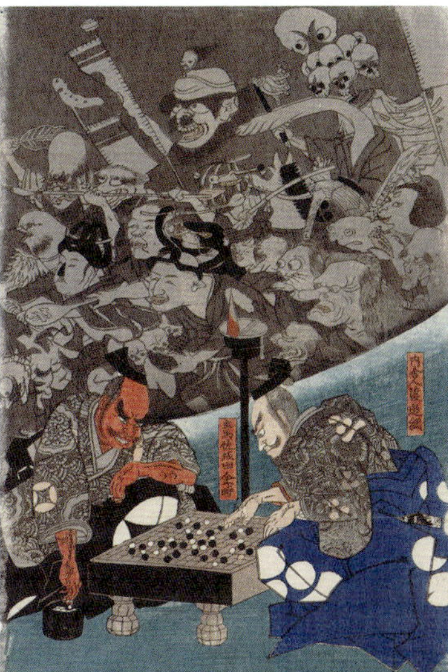
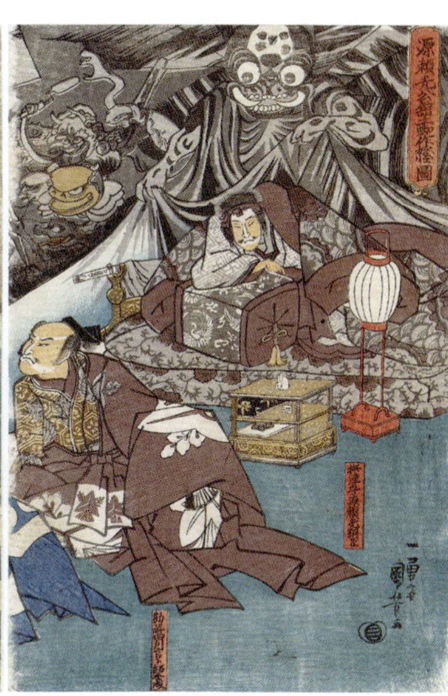

Utagawa Kuniyoshi (1797–1861)
Publisher: Ibaya Senzaburo (Dansendo)
The Earth Spider Generates Monsters at the Mansion of Lord Minamoto no Yorimitsu (Minamoto Yorimitsu [Raiko] ko no yakata ni tsuchigumo yokai o nasu zu), 1843 (Tenpo 14)
Woodblock print (nishiki-e); ink and color on paper
Vertical oban triptych; 28¾ × 14⅛ in. (73.1 × 35.8 cm)

Perhaps the most controversial of all ukiyo-e prints, this work may have been a covert, illegal political cartoon. The four retainers of the demon-fighting hero Minamoto no Yorimitsu play go while their master sleeps uneasily, tormented by a nightmare sent by the evil Earth Spider. Rumors spread that the battling demons in Yorimitsu's dream represented citizens upset about new, stricter regulations on the Floating World. However, Kuniyoshi and his publisher escaped punishment by claiming that it had all been a misunderstanding.

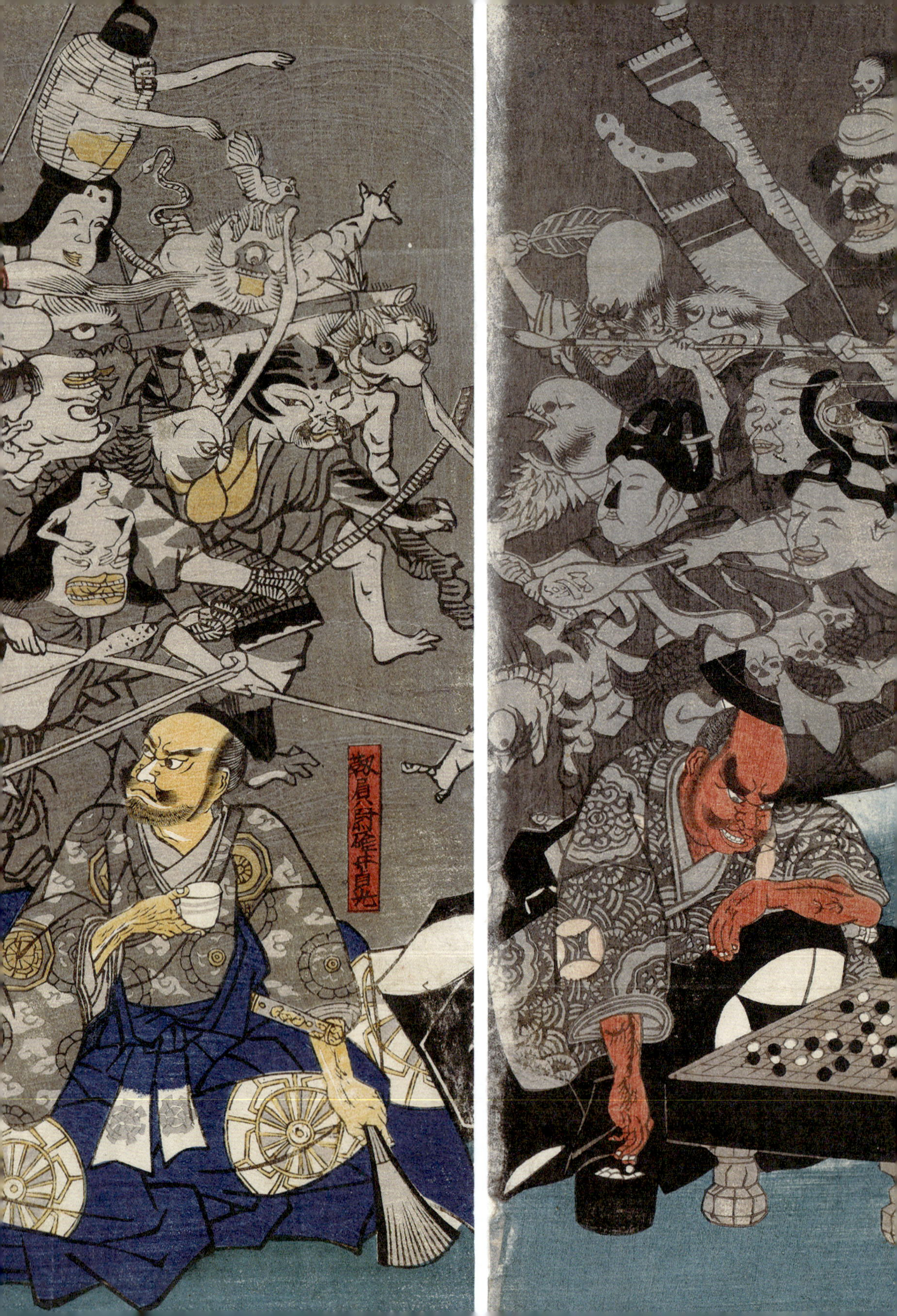

靫負尉碓井貞光

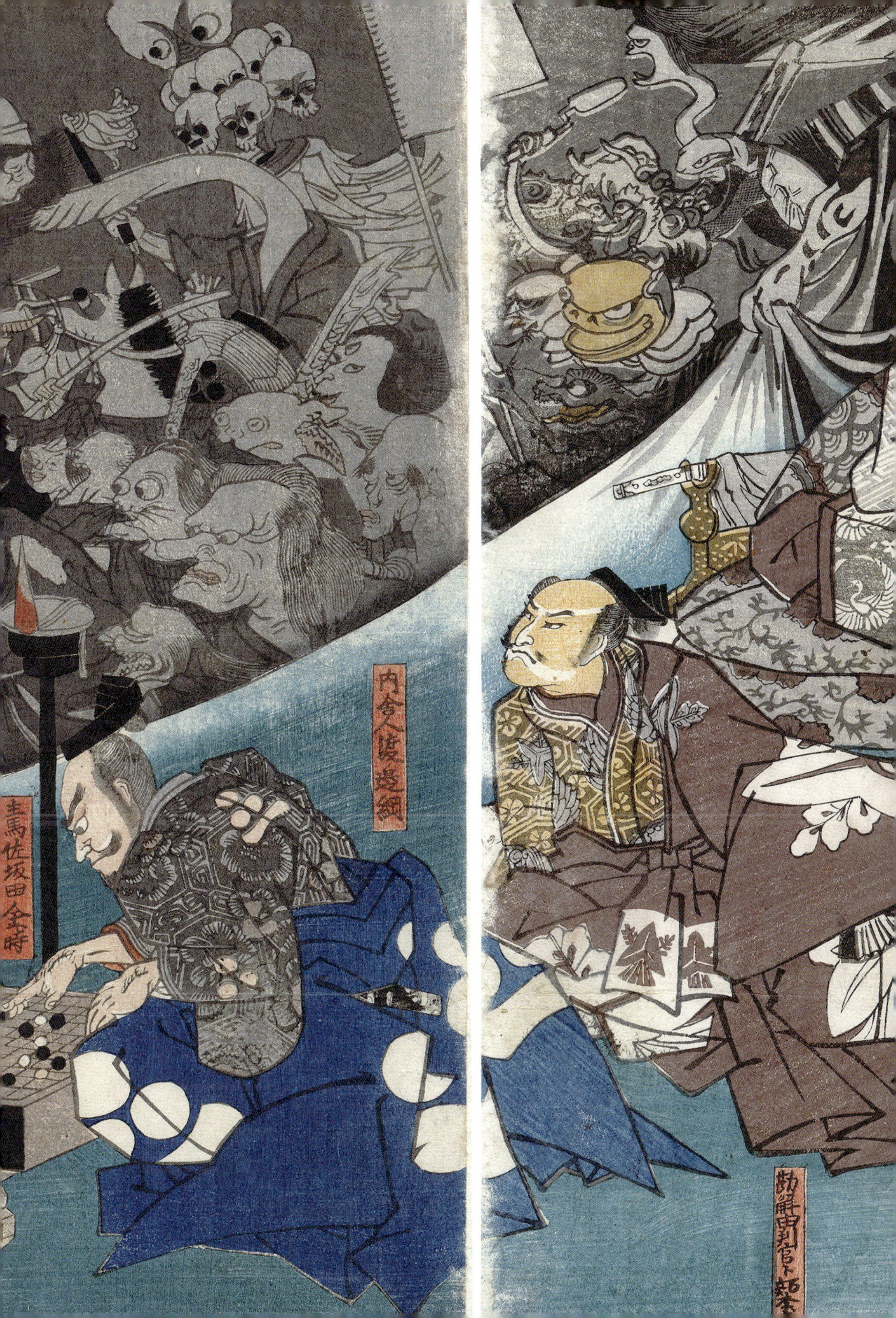

内舎人渡辺綱
主馬佐坂田金時
勘解由判官卜部季

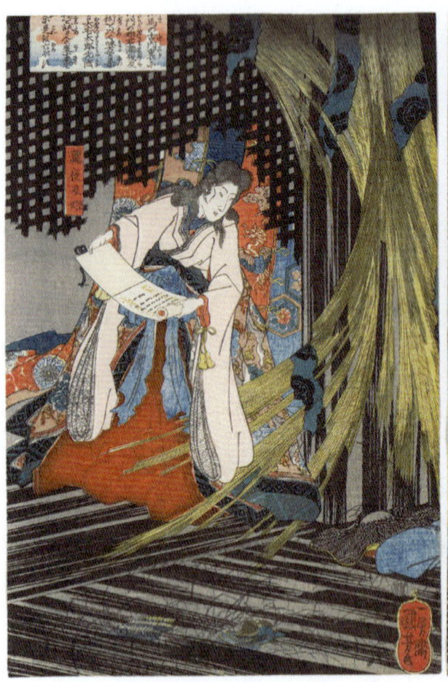
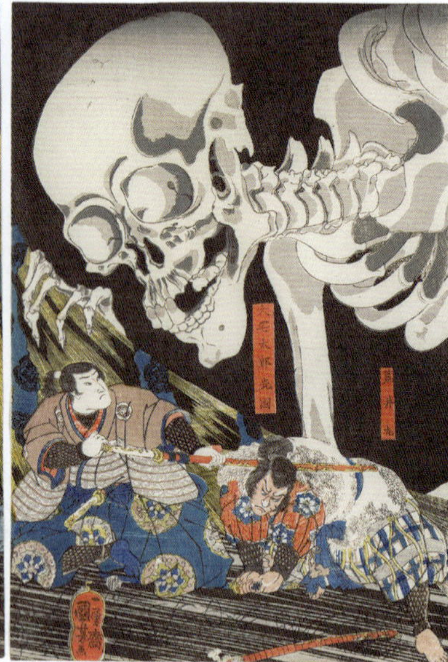
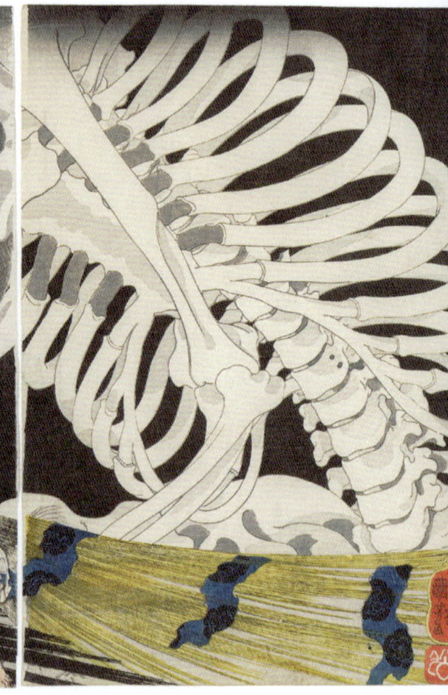

Utagawa Kuniyoshi (1797–1861)
In the Ruined Palace at Soma, Masakado's Daughter Takiyasha Uses Sorcery to Gather Allies; Oya no Taro Mitsukuni Comes Here to Investigate the Monsters and Finally Destroys Them (Soma no furudairi ni Masakado himegimi Takiyasha yojutsu o motte mikata o a), c. 1844 (Tenpo 15/Koka 1)
Woodblock print (nishiki-e); ink and color on paper
Vertical oban triptych;
29¼ × 14¼ in. (74.1 × 36.2 cm)

The beautiful but evil sorceress Takiyasha, who is plotting to continue her late father's rebellion, reads from a scroll of magic spells to summon a gigantic skeleton, which looms menacingly over the young samurai sent to stop her. The scene is from a fantasy novel that was also dramatized as a kabuki play, but since theatrical prints were technically illegal at the time, Kuniyoshi presents it as history instead. The skeleton is probably based on a European prototype.

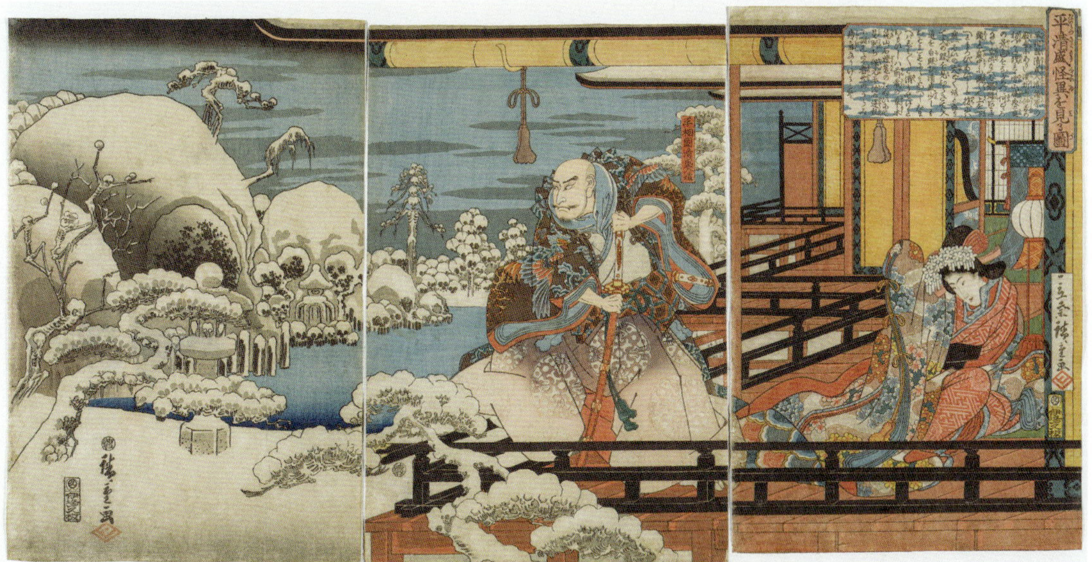

Utagawa Hiroshige I (1797–1858)
Publisher: Ibaya Kyubei
Taira no Kiyomori Haunted by Strange Sights (Taira Kiyomori kaii o miru zu), c. 1844–45 (Koka 1–2)
Woodblock print (nishiki-e); ink and color on paper
Vertical oban triptych; 29⅛ × 14¾ in. (74 × 37.5 cm)

Hiroshige's skill in designing landscapes takes a different turn in this warrior triptych. Kiyomori, the head of the Taira clan, was the de facto ruler of Japan for several decades in the twelfth century. One morning he awakened to find that the shapes of the snow-covered bushes in his garden had taken on the appearance of skulls—a gruesome reminder of the many people who had died in his rise to power. Kiyomori was unfazed by the ghostly vision, and presently it vanished away.

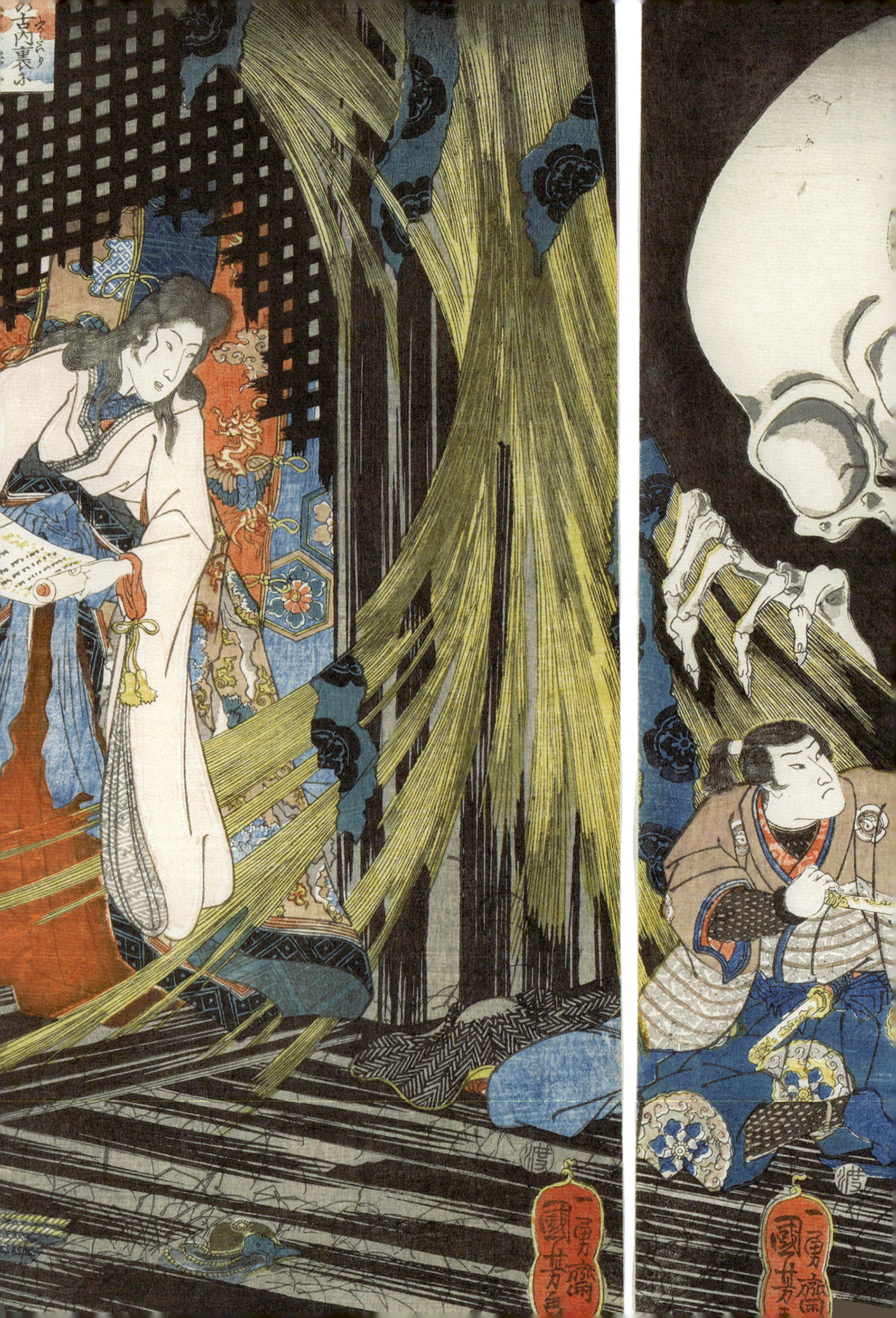
古内裏
一勇齋國芳画
一勇齋國芳

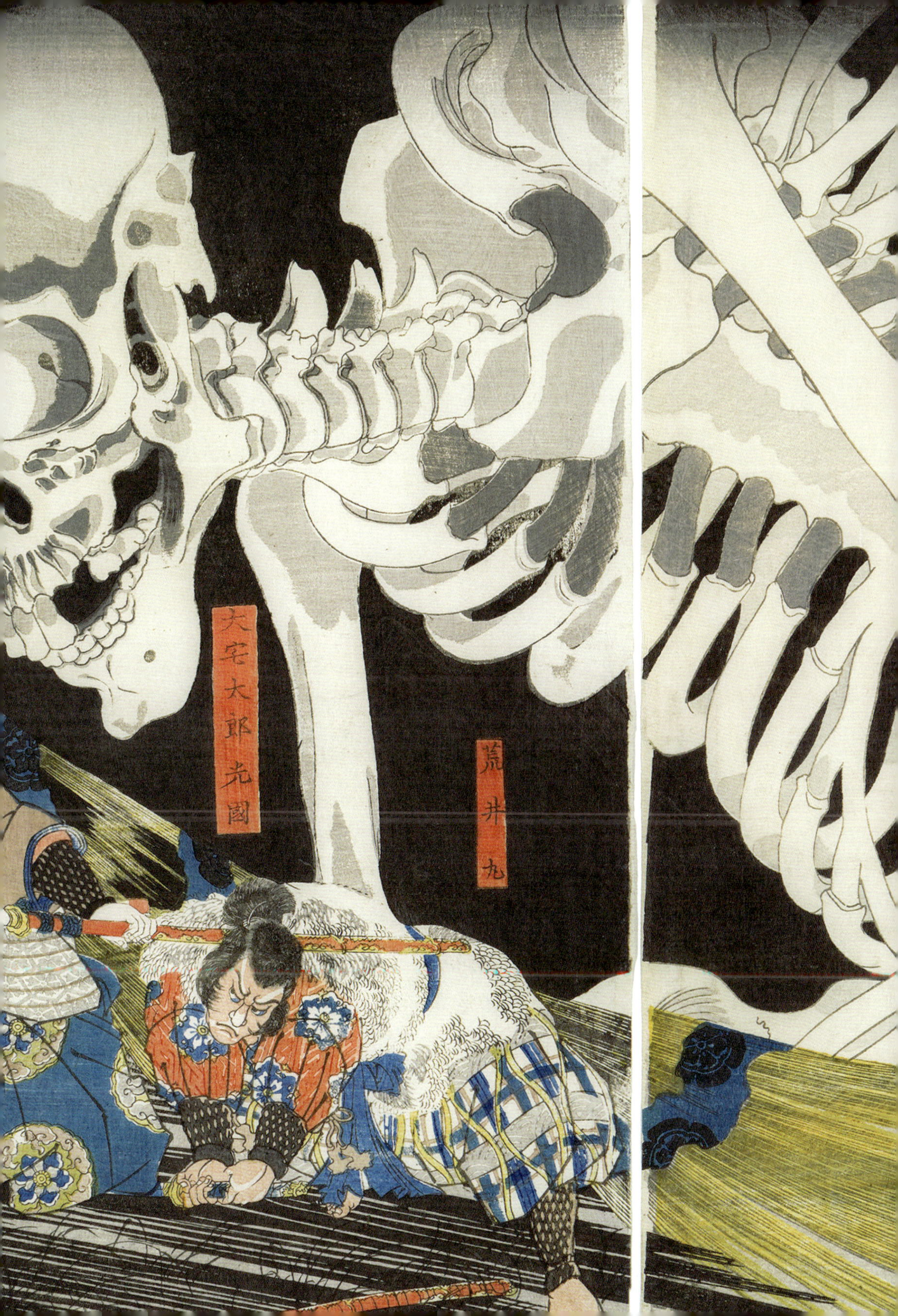
大宅太郎光圀
荒井丸

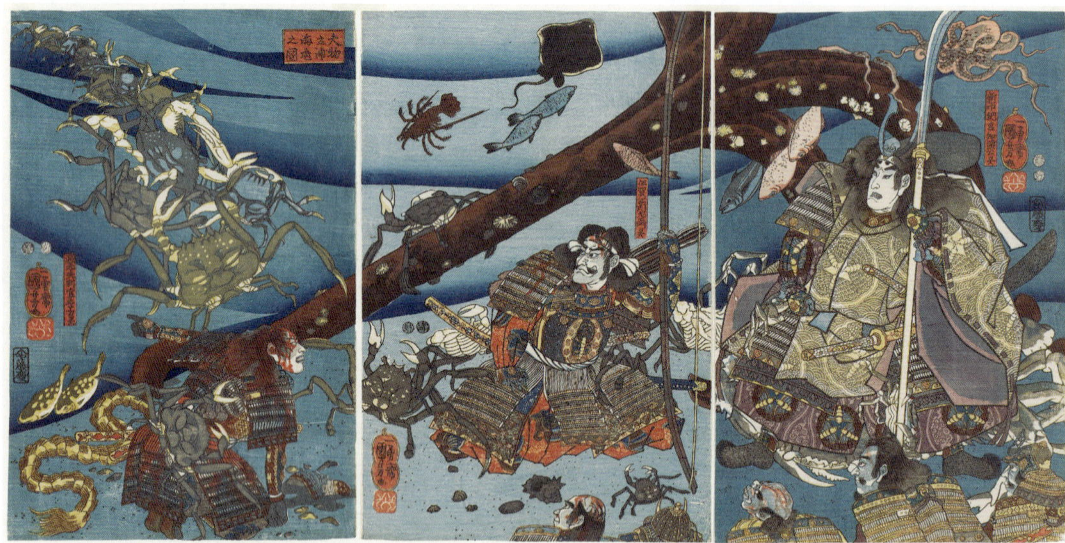

Utagawa Kuniyoshi (1797–1861)
Publisher: Fujiokaya Keijiro (Shorindo)
At the Bottom of the Sea in Daimotsu Bay (Daimotsu no ura kaitei no zu), c. 1851–52 (Kaei 4–5)
Woodblock print (nishiki-e); ink and color on paper
Vertical oban triptych; 29⅛ × 14¼ in. (73.9 × 36 cm)

Far beneath the waves, the ghosts of the Taira warrior clan who were defeated by Minamoto no Yoshitsune in 1185—and drowned themselves so as not to be taken alive—gather to plot revenge against their great enemy. When Yoshitsune and his followers set sail from Daimotsu Bay, the ghosts raise a massive storm in an unsuccessful attempt to sink the ship. Their spirits have possessed the local crabs, which now bear the mark of a scowling face on their shells.

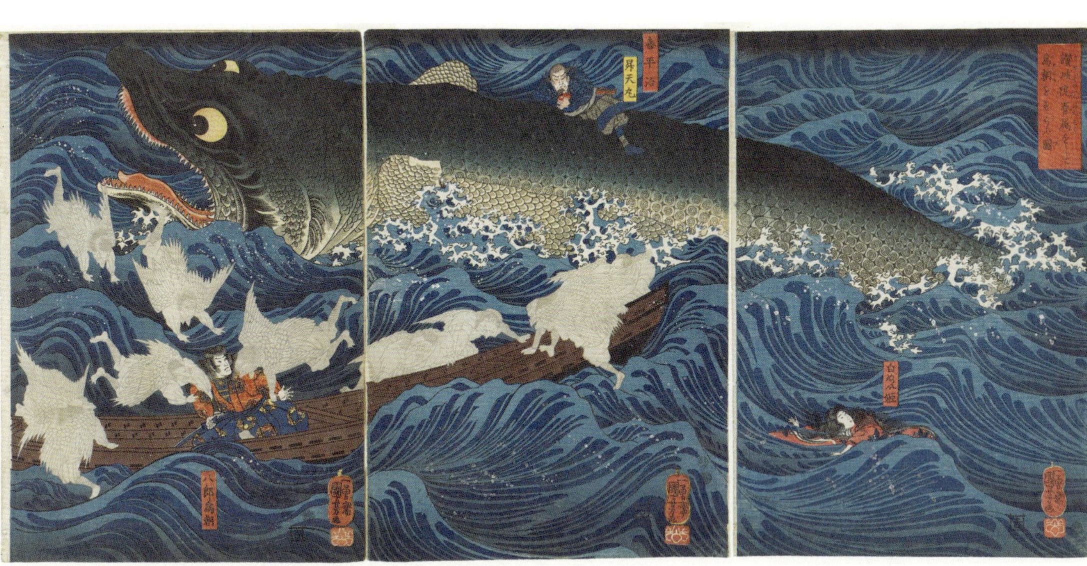

Utagawa Kuniyoshi (1797–1861)
Publisher: Sumiyoshiya Masagoro
The Former Emperor [Sutoku] from Sanuki Sends His Retainers to Rescue Tametomo (Sanuki no in kenzoku o shite Tametomo o sukuu zu), c. 1851–52 (Kaei 4–5)
Woodblock print (nishiki-e); ink and color on paper
Vertical oban triptych; 30 × 14¼ in. (76 × 36 cm)

The real-life warrior Minamoto no Tametomo, who died in exile after his faction lost the Hogen Rebellion of 1156, became the hero of the best-selling nineteenth-century fantasy novel *The Crescent Moon Bow*. In the book, Tametomo escaped and, after many adventures, made his way to the kingdom of the Ryukyu Islands (modern Okinawa Prefecture). When his ship was sunk by a sea monster, he was rescued by winged demons known as *tengu* sent by the ghost of his onetime lord, the former emperor Sutoku.

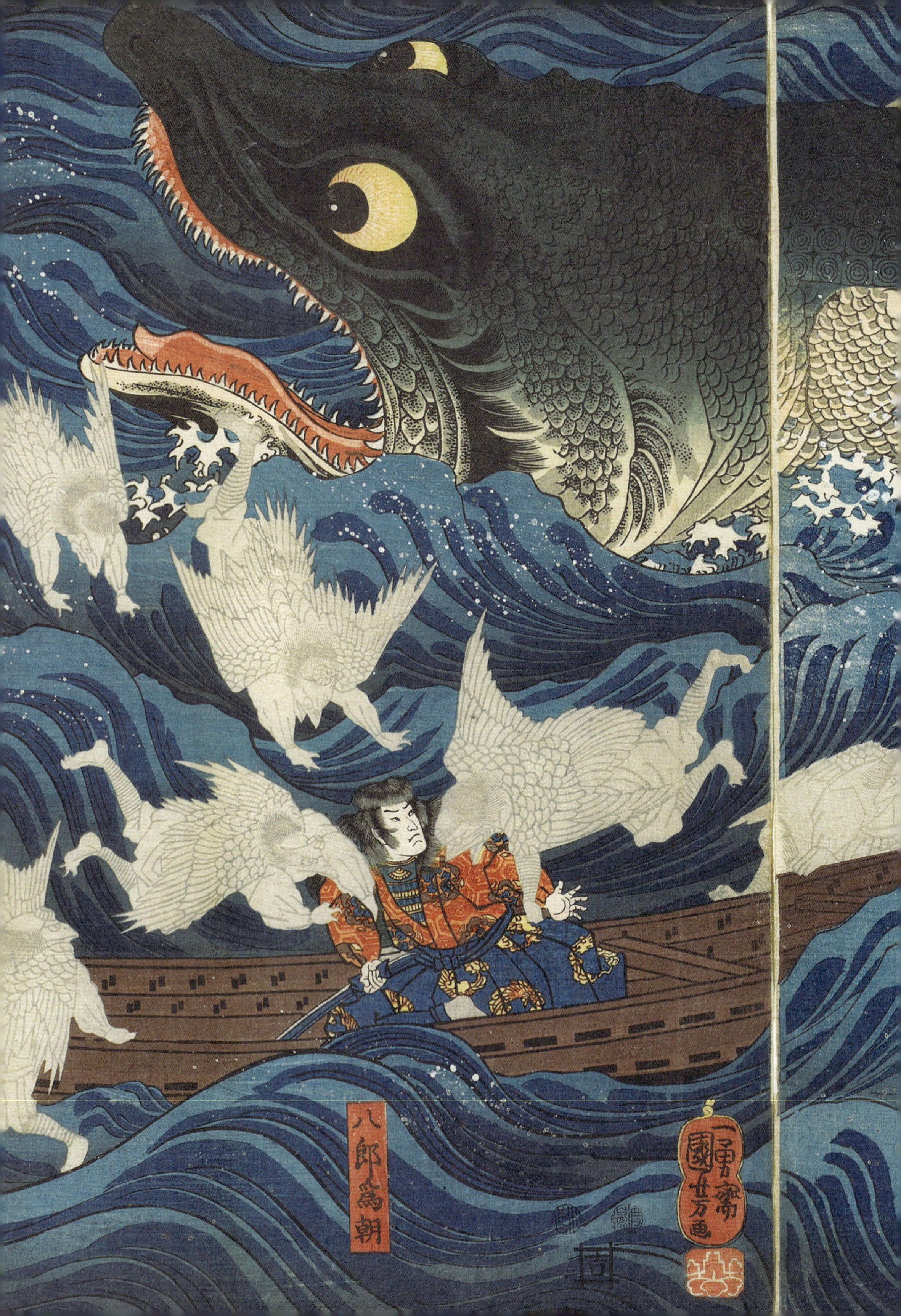
八郎為朝
一勇斎
國芳画

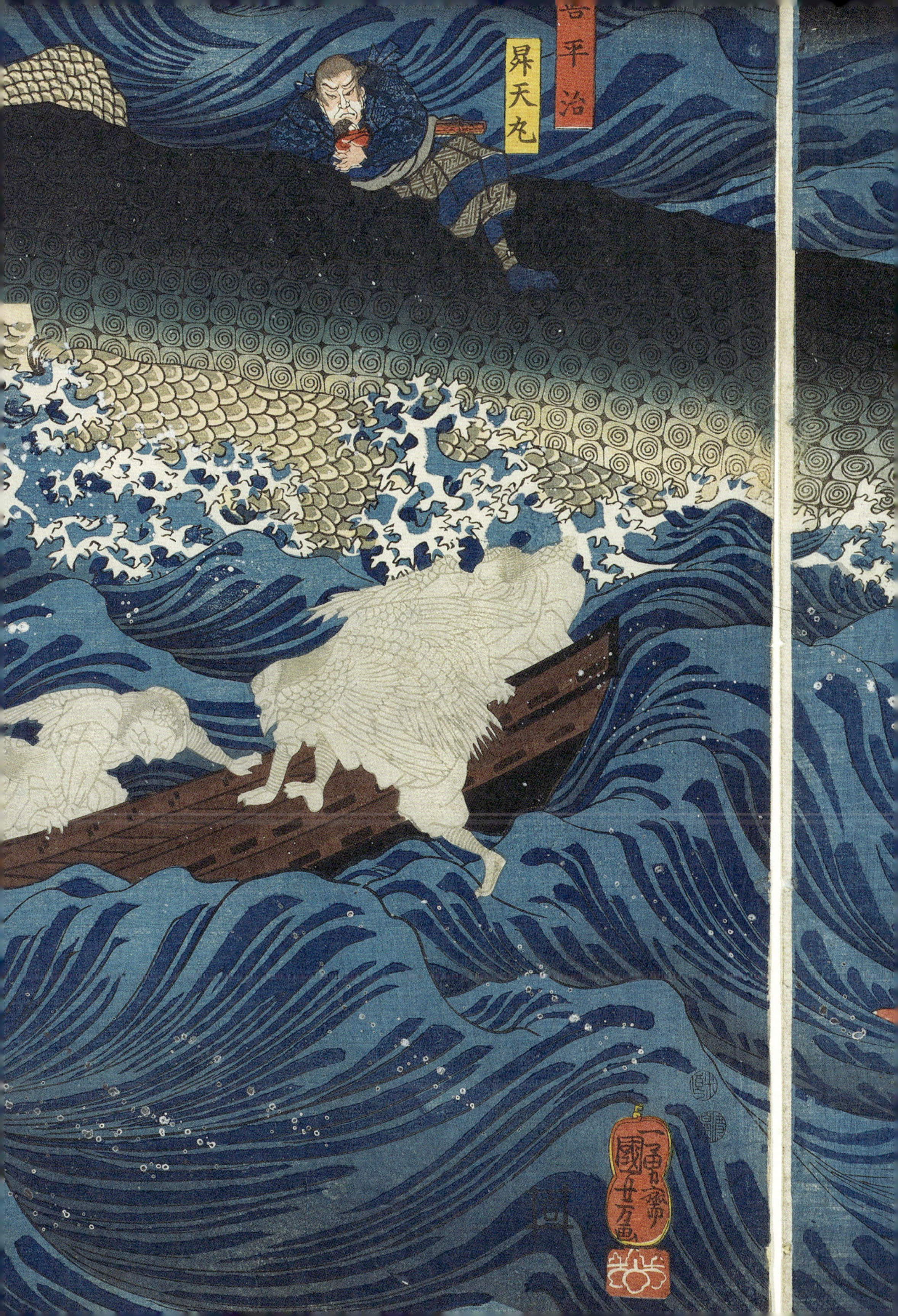
平治
昇天丸
一勇斎國芳画

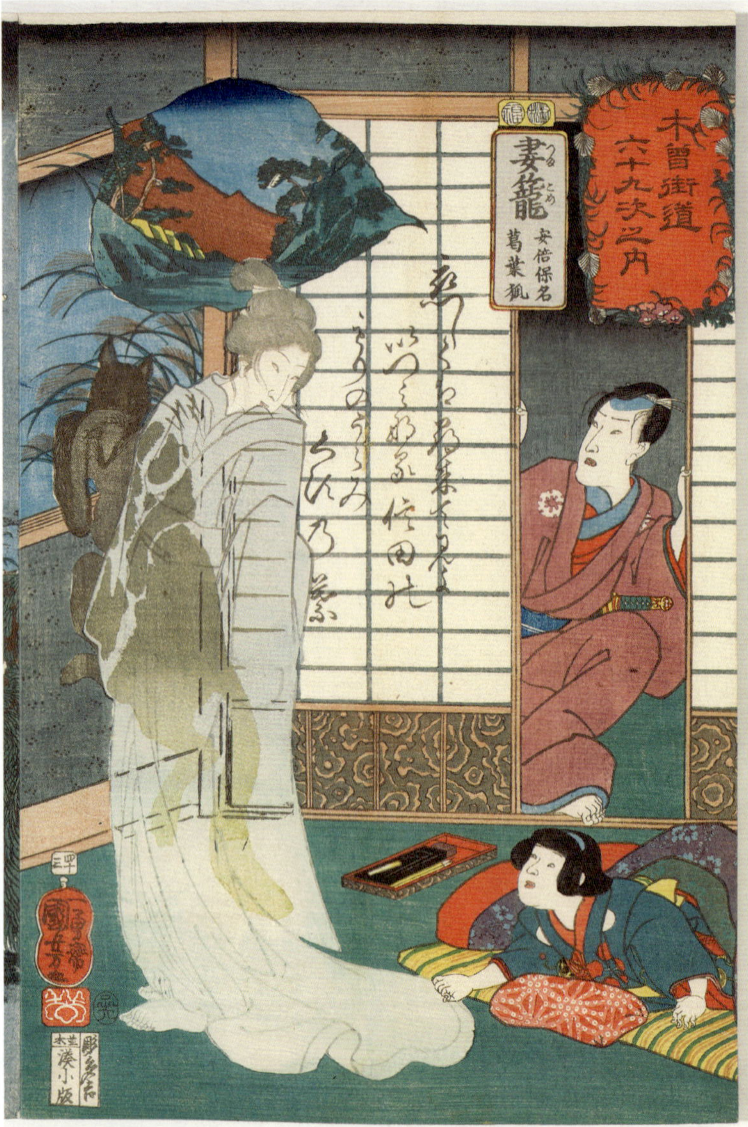

Utagawa Kuniyoshi (1797–1861)
Publisher: Minatoya Kohei
Blockcutter: Otaya Takichi (Hori Takichi)
Tsumagome: Abe no Yasuna and the Fox Kuzunoha, from the series Sixty-nine Stations of the Kisokaido Road (*Kisokaido rokujukyu tsugi no uchi*), 1852 (Kaei 5), 6th month
Woodblock print (nishiki-e); ink and color on paper
Vertical oban; 10⅛ × 14⅞ in. (25.5 × 37.8 cm)

The fox Kuzunoha fell in love with a human man and took human form so that she could marry him and bear his child, but eventually she had to abandon her family and go back to the forest. In Kuniyoshi's series based on the Kisokaido Road, the highway that ran between Edo and Kyoto along the interior mountain route, the landscapes are relegated to small insets and the main pictures are stories loosely linked to the place-names. The *tsuma* in Tsumagome means "wife."

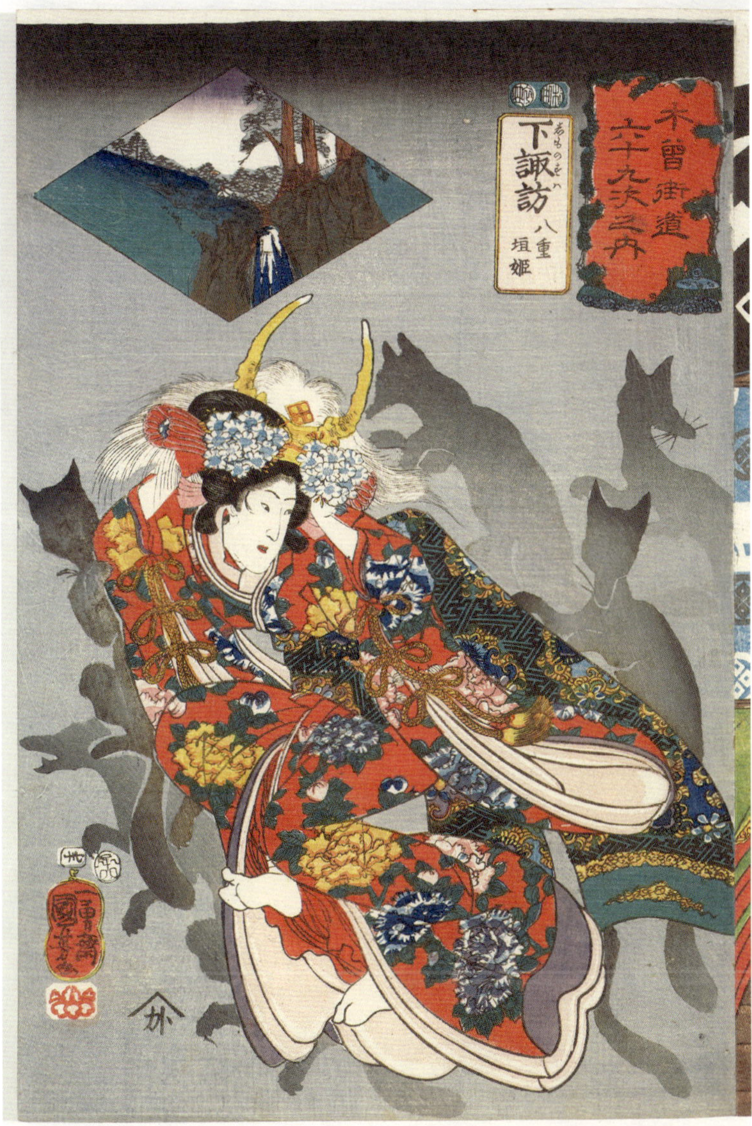

Utagawa Kuniyoshi (1797–1861)
Publisher: Yawataya Sakujiro
Shimosuwa: Yaegaki-hime, from the series Sixty-nine Stations of the Kisokaido Road (*Kisokaido rokujukyu tsugi no uchi*), 1852 (Kaei 5), 8th month
Woodblock print (nishiki-e); ink and color on paper
Vertical oban; 10⅛ × 14⅞ in. (25.5 × 37.8 cm)

A kabuki play set in Shimosuwa tells the story of Yaegaki-hime, who is torn between her loyalty to her warlord father and her love for her fiancé, the son of a rival warrior clan. The god of Suwa helps her to make a choice by instructing her to return the heirloom helmet stolen by her father from her fiancé's family, telling her to carry it across frozen Lake Suwa and sending magical foxes to show her the way. Holding the helmet, she dances with the foxes.

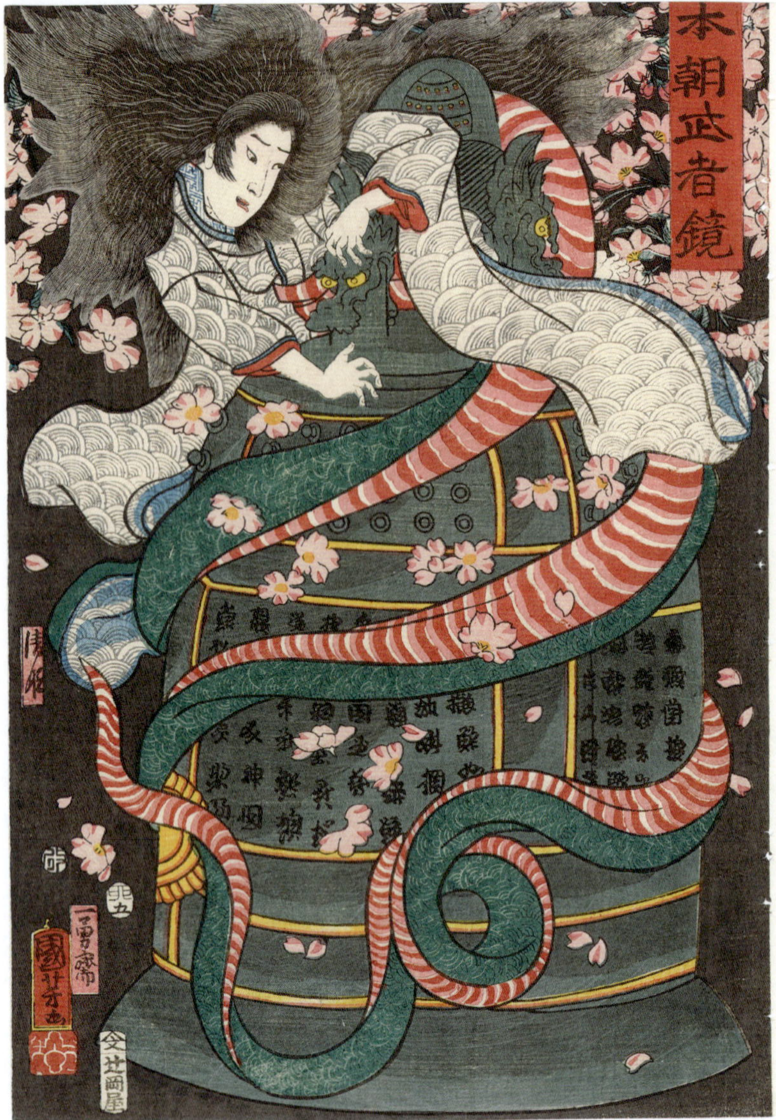

Utagawa Kuniyoshi (1797–1861)
Publisher: Tsujiokaya Bunsuke (Kinshodo)
Kiyo-hime, from the series Mirror of Warriors of Our Country (*Honcho musha kagami*), 1855 (Ansei 2), 5th month
Woodblock print (nishiki-e); ink and color on paper
Vertical oban; 10 × 14¼ in. (25.3 × 36 cm)

A legend of the Dojo-ji temple, dramatized in both no and kabuki plays, tells how Kiyo-hime fell in love with a priest who passed by her home on a pilgrimage. When she realized that he had trifled with her affections, she became so angry that she transformed into a dragon. The terrified priest hid under the great bell of the temple, but the dragon-woman's rage heated the metal bell red-hot and burned him to death.

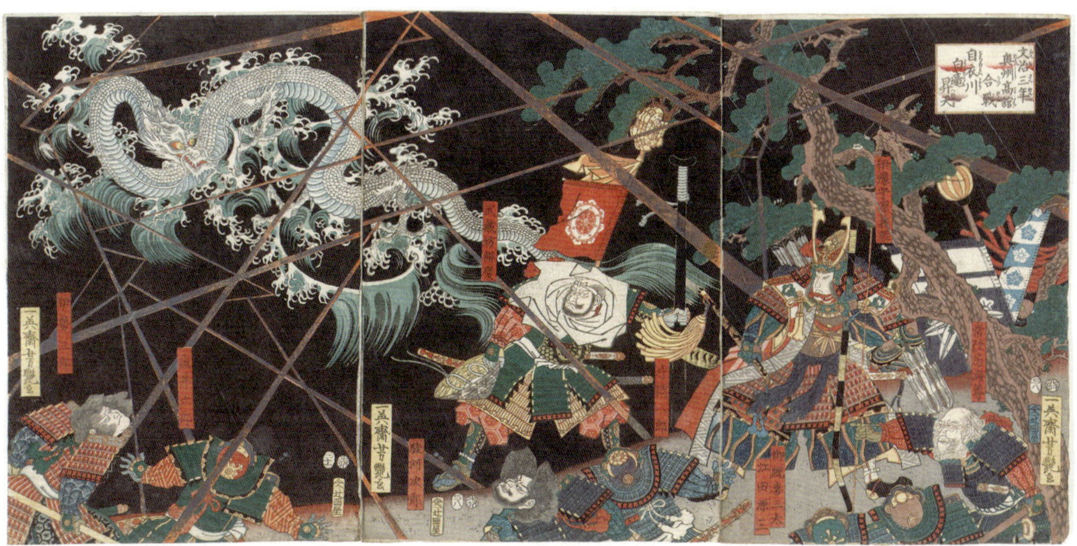

Utagawa Yoshitsuya (1822–1866)
Publisher: Tsujiokaya Bunsuke (Kinshodo)
At the Battle of Takadachi in Oshu Province in 1187, a White Dragon Ascends to Heaven from the Koromo River (Bunji sannen oshu Takadachi kassen Koromogawa yori hakuryu ten e noboru),
1857 (Ansei 4), 11th month
Woodblock print (nishiki-e); ink and color on paper
Vertical oban triptych;
29⅞ × 14¾ in. (75.9 × 37.5 cm)

There is a small mistake in the title inscribed on the print, since the Battle of Takadachi—the last stand of the great general Minamoto no Yoshitsune—actually took place in 1189. Yoshitsune had found temporary safety with allies in Oshu Province in the far north, but eventually his enemies attacked and he was hopelessly outnumbered. A much later legend claimed that a white dragon rose up from the Koromo River, foreshadowing the tragic but noble deaths of Yoshitsune and his chief retainer, the warrior-priest Benkei.

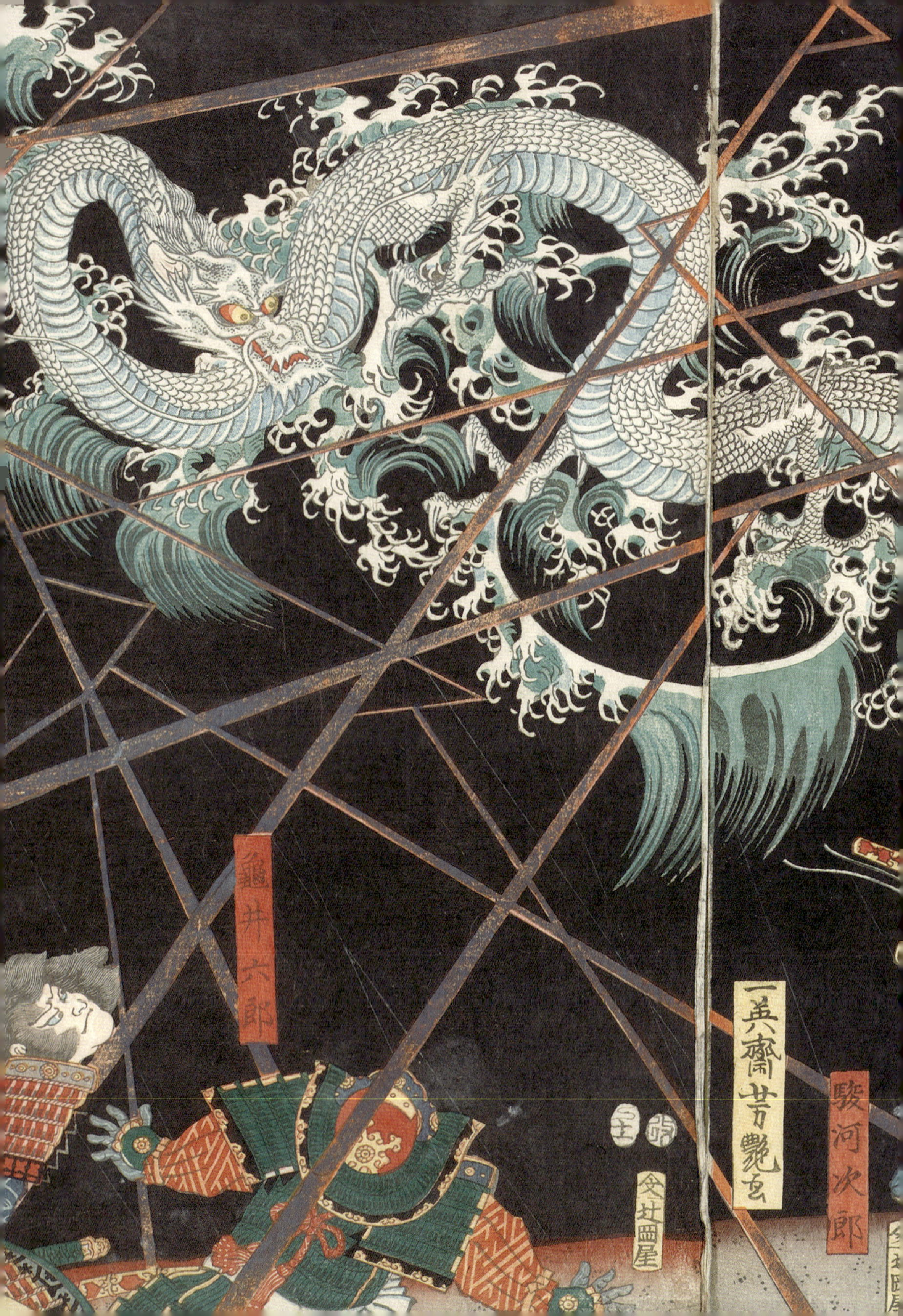
亀井六郎
一勇齋芳艶画
駿河次郎

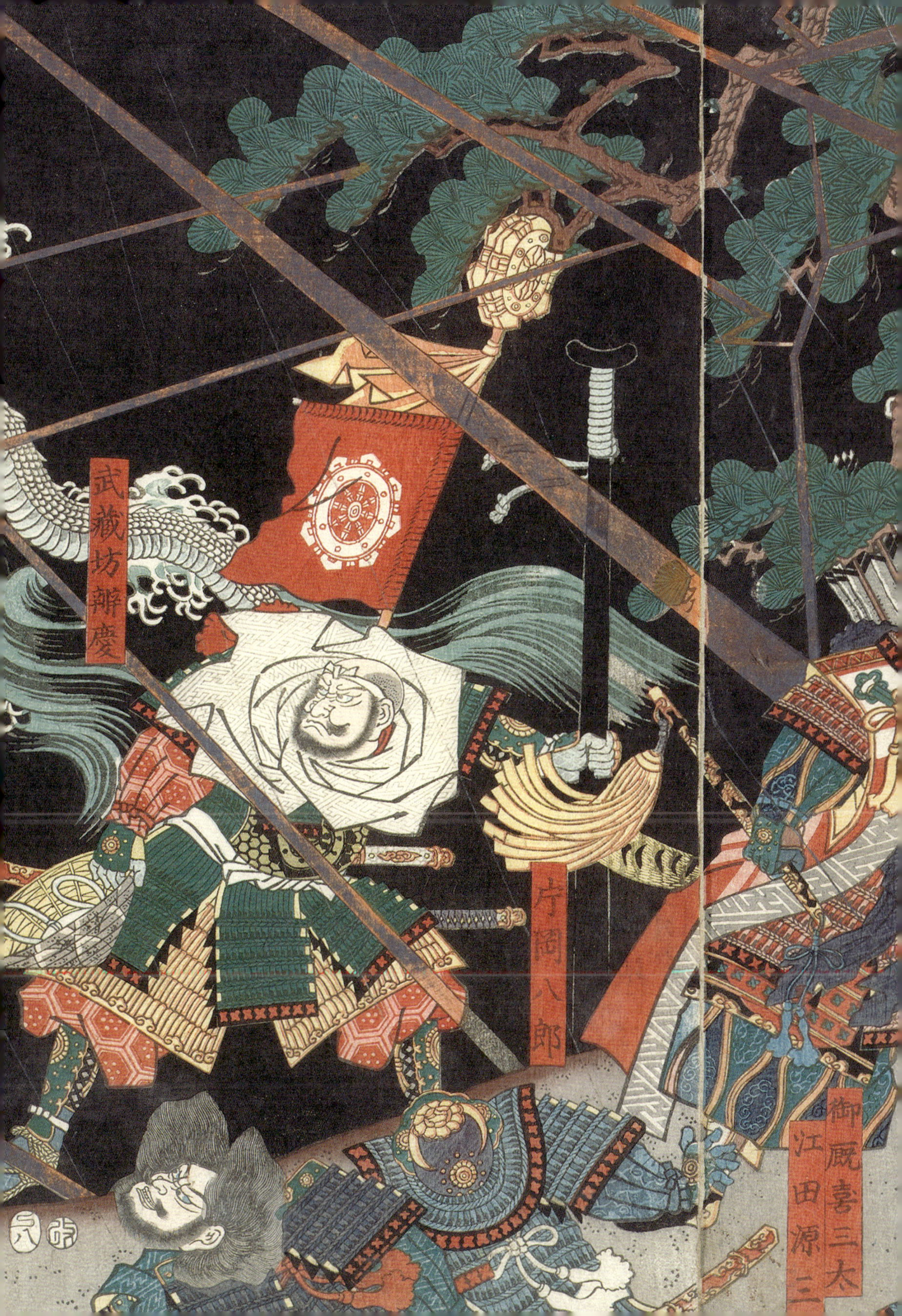
武藏坊辨慶
片岡八郎
御厩喜三太
江田源三

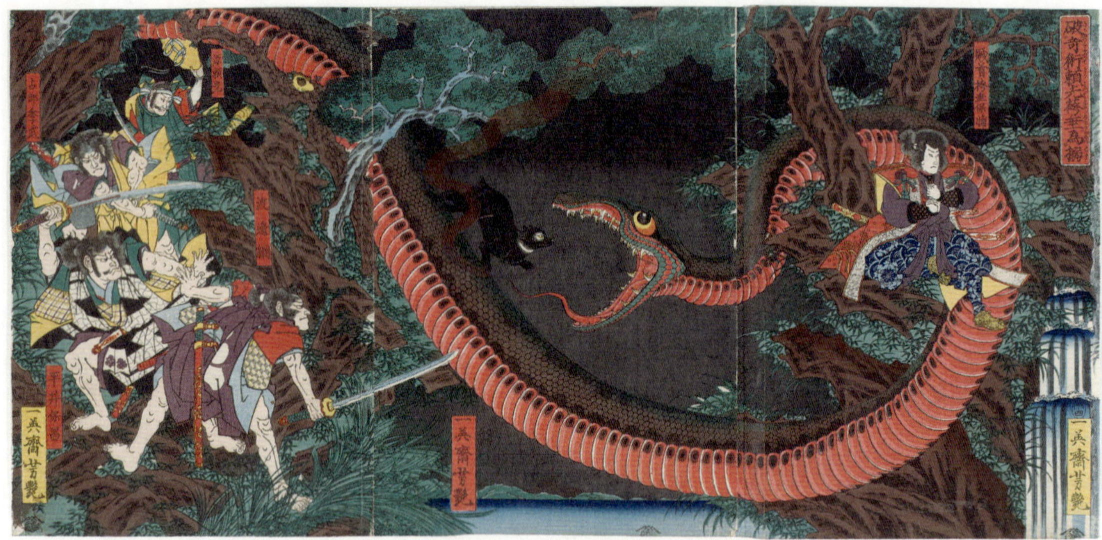

Utagawa Yoshitsuya (1822–1866)
Publisher: Tsutaya Kichizo (Koeido)
Yorimitsu Tries to Capture Hakamadare by Destroying His Magic (Kijutsu o yabutte Yorimitsu Hakamadare o karamen to su), 1858 (Ansei 5), 4th month
Woodblock print (nishiki-e); ink and color on paper
Vertical oban triptych;
29¾ × 14 in. (75.6 × 35.4 cm)

In a scene from a fantasy novel published in 1806, Minamoto no Yorimitsu and his four retainers pursue the master thief Hakamadare, who uses his magical powers to create an illusion of a fight between a bear and a giant snake. While the warriors are distracted, Hakamadare steals their baggage. This print seems to have been very popular, not only because of its striking composition, but also because it was suspected of being a political cartoon referring to a succession dispute in the shogunate.

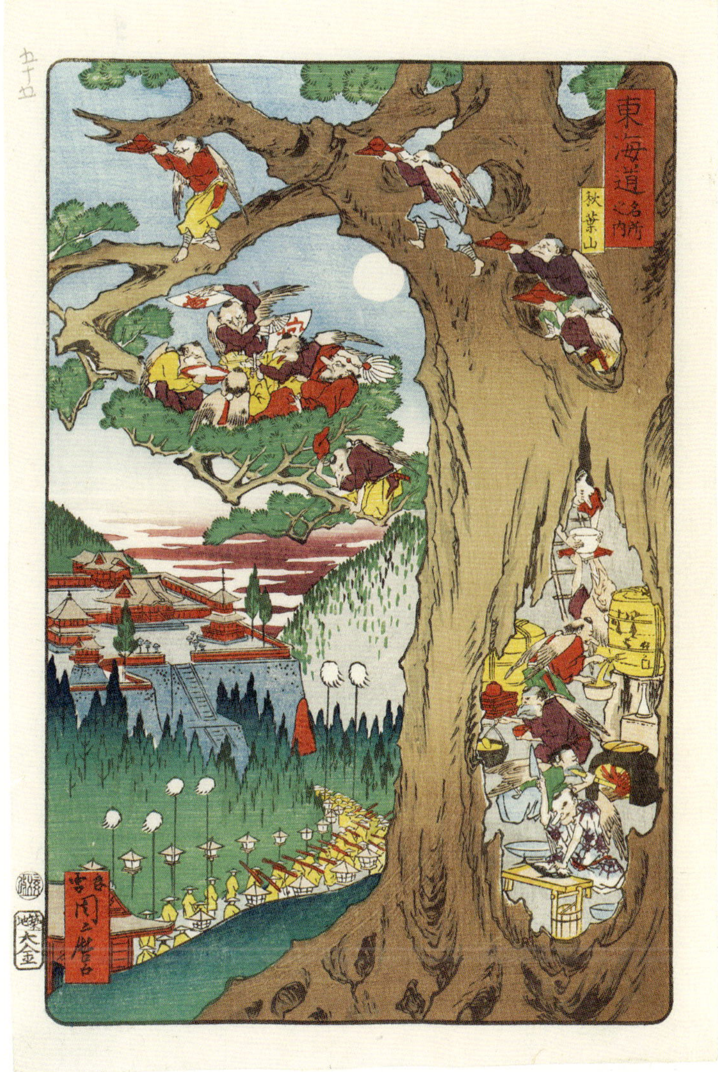

Kawanabe Kyosai (1831–1889)
Publisher: Daikokuya
Kinnosuke (Kinjiro)
Mount Akiba (Akiba-san), from the series Scenes of Famous Places along the Tokaido Road (*Tokaido meisho fukei*), also known as the Processional Tokaido (*Gyoretsu Tokaido*), here called *Tokaido meisho no uchi*, 1863 (Bunkyu 3), 5th month
Woodblock print (nishiki-e); ink and color on paper
Vertical oban; 9¾ × 14¼ in. (24.7 × 36 cm)

The largest Tokaido series ever made, this collaborative set of over 150 prints by multiple artists and publishers was issued on the occasion of the shogun's historic trip to Kyoto to confer with the emperor. Most of the designs are straightforward landscapes, but Kyosai included some fantasy scenes, such as this view of a side trip to the Akiba (or Akiha) shrine near modern Shizuoka. The local *tengu* (winged mountain demons) gather at a treetop restaurant to celebrate while watching the shogun's procession from a polite distance.

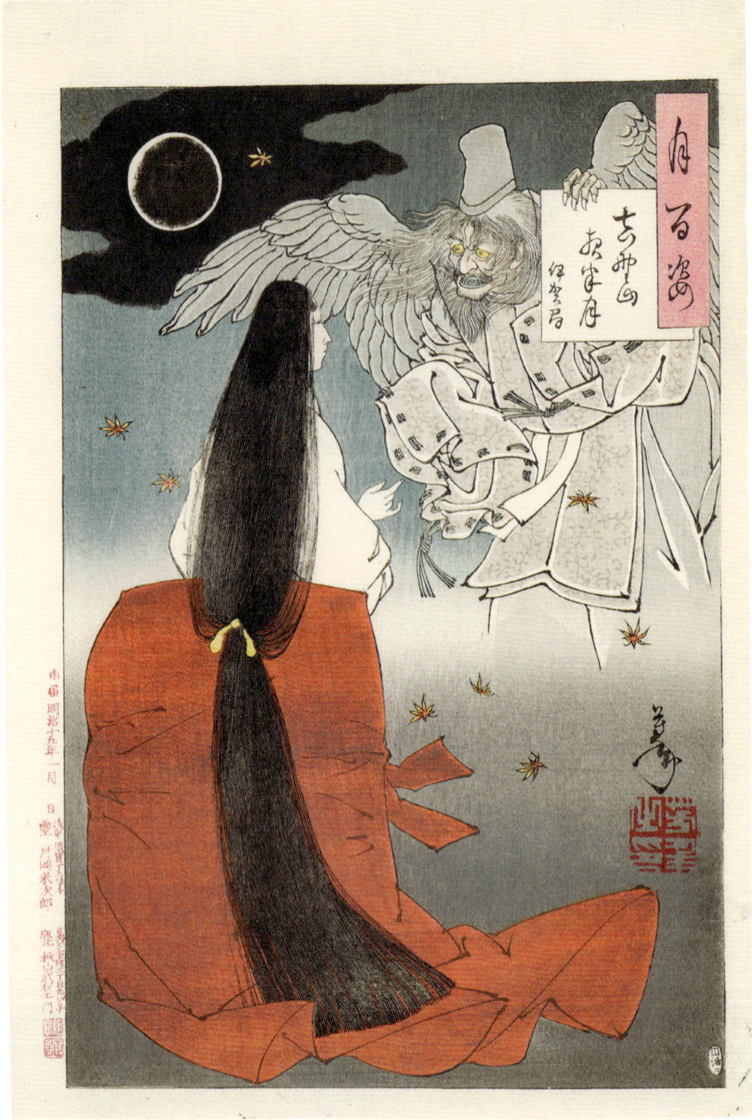

Tsukioka Yoshitoshi (1839–1892)
Publisher: Akiyama Buemon
Midnight Moon at Mount Yoshino: Iga no tsubone (Yoshinoyama yahan tsuki, Iga no tsubone), from the series One Hundred Aspects of the Moon (*Tsuki hyakushi*), 1886 (Meiji 19), January
Woodblock print (nishiki-e); ink and color on paper
Vertical oban; 9⅞ × 14½ in. (25 × 36.8 cm)

In the fourteenth century, when Japan had two rival imperial courts, Iga no tsubone was a lady-in-waiting serving the former empress at the southern court in Yoshino. One night in the palace garden, she encountered a ghost in the form of a *tengu* (winged demon) who told her that he could not rest in peace because of his unrequited love for the empress. The brave lady told him that she and the empress would visit his grave, and the ghost disappeared.

Tsukioka Yoshitoshi (1839–1892)
Publisher: Matsui Eikichi
Blockcutter: Negishi Chokuzan
Taira no Koremochi Vanquishes a Female Demon at Togakushi Mountain (Taira Koremochi Togakushiyama kijo taiji no zu), 1887 (Meiji 20)
Woodblock print (nishiki-e); ink and color on paper
Vertical oban, upright diptych; 9¾ × 28¾ in. (24.8 × 73 cm)

The no play *Momijigari* (Maple-leaf Viewing) tells how the warrior Taira no Koremochi encountered a group of noblewomen enjoying an autumn leaf-viewing picnic. When they invited him to join their party, he drank so much that he fell asleep. A god appeared in a dream to warn him that the ladies were actually demons, and he awoke and fought them off. In the print, the reflection in the stream shows the true face of the beautiful lady behind Koremochi.

Artist Biographies

A NOTE ABOUT NAMES: In standard Japanese word order, the family name comes first and the personal name second. For artists of the Edo period and Meiji era, this order is usually retained even in English-language publications. The artists are almost always referred to by their art pseudonyms rather than their legal names—which in some cases are not even known. For short references, they are generally called by their personal names, which are printed here in boldface. The surname usually indicates the school to which the artist belongs, but sometimes a studio name ending in *-sai*—for example, Hokusai, which means "Northern Studio"—may be substituted for either the surname or the personal name. The artists are arranged here in historical, rather than alphabetical, order.

Hishikawa **Moronobu** (died 1694)

Moronobu is the first artist of the ukiyo-e school whose name is recorded. He came from an artisan family in Awa Province on Shikoku who specialized in dyeing and embroidering fine textiles, but he took his talent for design in a different direction by moving to the great city of Edo and becoming involved in the publishing business. During the 1670s and early 1680s, he illustrated about a hundred woodblock printed books, at first creating printed versions of earlier painted illustrations and then developing a distinctive style that emphasized current fashions depicted with expressive black lines well suited to the medium. In the early 1680s, he designed around 120 single-sheet prints in this new ukiyo-e style. For the final decade of his life, he concentrated on painting; this pattern was also followed by some later ukiyo-e artists including Shunsho and Hokusai.

Sugimura **Jihei** (active c. 1680–1698)

Although the birth dates of both artists are unknown, Sugimura Jihei was probably a little younger than Moronobu. Like a handful of other ukiyo-e artists including Koryusai, Eishi, and Hiroshige, he came from the elite samurai class but was attracted to the pleasures of the Floating World. In the 1690s, when Moronobu was concentrating on paintings, Jihei became the leading designer of book illustrations and prints. His style is similar to that of Moronobu but tends to be more dynamic; his output includes works with a clear signature, works with a hidden signature worked into the design, and still others that are not signed but are attributed to him because they are so similar to the signed works.

Torii **Kiyonobu I** (1664–1729)

Kiyonobu I was the founder of the Torii school, which dominated the field of actor prints from the late 1690s to the early 1760s. He and his fellow Torii artists also drew images of beautiful women, especially notable courtesans, and occasionally other subjects as well. The head of the school was expected to paint billboards advertising current plays to be displayed on the marquees of the kabuki theaters, but no early examples of these paintings have survived. At some point in the late 1720s Kiyonobu I was succeeded by another artist of the same name, now called Kiyonobu II, but the time of the transition is unclear; publishers may have obscured it deliberately in order to maintain the selling power of the famous signature.

Torii **Kiyomasu I** (active c. 1696–1716)

The relationship between Kiyomasu I and Kiyonobu I is uncertain. He may have been the son or younger brother of the founder of the school, or simply another artist affiliated with the school who took the family name as part of his own art name even though he was not a blood relative. He was an especially versatile artist, producing large portraits of statuesque beauties in gorgeous kimono as well as actor prints and scenes of famous historical warriors. Like Kiyonobu I, he was succeeded by another artist who used the same name; but the relationship between these two artists and the exact time of the shift from Kiyomasu I to Kiyomasu II is not definitely known.

Okumura **Masanobu** (1686–1764)

Okumura Masanobu was an enormously versatile and inventive artist and publisher active throughout the first half of the eighteenth century, beginning in 1701 when he was only fifteen. He claimed to be the originator of three major innovations of the 1740s: pillar prints, the tall, narrow works suitable for hanging on one of the pillars of a room in a Japanese house; perspective prints utilizing Western-style vanishing point perspective; and early color printing, with red and green color blocks in addition to the main black outline block. These claims may have been exaggerated for the sake of publicity, but at the very least he was one of the pioneers in producing such prints. He was also known for clever parodies that modernized classical themes—early examples of the kind of humor later called *mitate* (literally "selection," i.e., humorous comparison of two different concepts).

Nishimura **Shigenaga** (1697?–1756)

The self-taught artist Nishimura Shigenaga, who is said to have operated a bookshop, was a rival—and sometimes an imitator—of Okumura Masanobu. Like Masanobu's prints, his works show a wide range of subjects, including not only kabuki actors and fashionable women, but also bird-and-flower images, cityscapes in Western-style perspective, and illustrations of classical literature in a traditional style. Many of his works of the 1730s have elaborate hand coloring, often including such special features as sprinkled metal filings to suggest the gold used similarly in paintings, or black mixed with glue to produce a shiny, lacquer-like effect. Later, in the 1740s, he designed early color prints (*benizuri-e*) of women and actors. He may have been the teacher of Suzuki Harunobu.

Torii **Kiyoshige** (active 1720–1760)

The Torii school of artists dominated the field of actor prints from its beginning in the 1690s until the late 1760s. Kiyoshige was said to have been a pupil of Kiyonobu I, the founder of the school. Most of his works are actor prints in the standard *hosoban* format, with a few pillar prints. His eye-catching designs, typical of the Torii school artists, span the period from hand-colored prints to early color printing. The depictions of actors show the early stages of the eighteenth-century trend toward greater realism in portraiture, with increased emphasis on their individual facial features.

Suzuki **Harunobu** (1725–1770)

One of the most important of all ukiyo-e artists was Harunobu, the first to design prints that were produced in full color (defined as five or more colors in addition to the black outlines) on a large scale (as opposed to earlier, more limited experiments). His work ushered in an age of popular, affordable color printing that lasted until the early twentieth century. The first of these full-color prints, called *nishiki-e* or "brocade pictures," were calendars for the year 1765, privately printed for special customers who financed the development of the new printing method. But canny publishers later issued mass-market editions of the pictures with the calendrical information removed. Harunobu's prints typically show sweet, almost childlike young people, often in romantic situations. Since he died in 1770, just five years after the development of full-color printing, his color prints can be dated within this period.

Katsukawa **Shunsho** (1726–1792)

Thanks to Shunsho's gift for capturing likenesses, the Katsukawa school founded by his teacher Shunsui overtook the Torii school to become the leading designers of actor prints in the late eighteenth century. Printed in full color in the *hosoban* format, Shunsho's prints were often made in sets showing several actors from a particular play, one per sheet, posing against a continuous background. These could then be rearranged in any order so that theater fans could purchase the entire cast or just their personal favorites. In the last decade of his life, he turned over most of the print-designing business to his students and devoted himself to luxurious paintings of beautiful women in high-fashion kimono. The most famous of his many students was the young Hokusai.

Isoda **Koryusai** (1735–1790)

After the death of Harunobu in 1770, Koryusai became the leading designer of prints of women, while Shunsho maintained his position as the top artist of actor prints. Koryusai was originally a samurai, but after the death of the lord he served, he became an ukiyo-e artist when he was in his late thirties. His early works are very similar in style to Harunobu's, but he gradually shifted to drawing taller figures, the better to show off the fabric of their elaborate kimono. For his most famous series—portraits of Yoshiwara courtesans in their New Year finery—he switched from the smaller *chuban* format (roughly the size of one sheet of printer paper) favored by Harunobu to the larger *oban*

format (twice as big) that became standard from that time on. In addition to his images of beautiful women, he was also known for his elegant bird-and-flower designs.

Kitao **Shigemasa** (1739–1820)

Kitao Shigemasa was the son of a publisher and bookseller, and much of his artistic output was book illustrations. He designed several noteworthy picture books in collaboration with Katsukawa Shunsho. He was partly self-taught but also studied under Nishimura Shigenaga, later founding his own Kitao school. He is best known for his depictions of women, similar in style to the work of Harunobu and Shunsho. He also drew scenes from classical literature, history, and legend, generally in the *chuban* format favored by Harunobu, as well as some kabuki prints and a few cityscapes using vanishing point perspective.

Torii **Kiyonaga** (1752–1815)

During the 1780s Kiyonaga became the leading designer of prints of fashionable women, drawing both Yoshiwara courtesans and ordinary middle-class women in an elegant, elongated style. He was trained in the Torii school, which specialized in actor prints, and eventually became the head of the school. But it was his images of women that made him the favorite artist of early Western connoisseurs such as Ernest Fenollosa. Some of his more spectacular designs consisted of multiple vertical *oban* sheets combined into diptychs or triptychs to form a larger image, often with landscapes using Western perspective as backgrounds to set off the figures. His actor prints typically showed complex stage scenes with multiple figures. In the last decade of his life, he designed few color prints and concentrated on paintings and black-and-white theatrical programs.

Kitagawa **Utamaro I** (early 1750s–1806)

As the most prominent designer of prints of women in the 1790s, Utamaro developed the elongated body type favored by Kiyonaga into an even more extreme form. His attenuated beauties with their air of languorous sensuality made him enormously popular both during his lifetime and later with collectors in Japan and abroad, although early Western critics occasionally described him as "decadent." He also became known for bust portraits of women, known as *okubi-e* (literally "big head pictures"), occasionally embellished with backgrounds of sparkling mica. In addition to generic beauties, he sometimes experimented with portraits of actual women that indicated their individual facial features. In 1805 he ran afoul of the censorship laws for prints depicting great samurai of the past in suggestive situations and was briefly imprisoned. The punishment of such a prominent artist was a shock to the world of ukiyo-e prints, which became more discreet as a result.

Chobunsai **Eishi** (1756–1829)

Born into a high-ranking samurai family, Eishi may have been the ukiyo-e print designer with the highest social status, but he retired from his government position directly under the shogun in order to become a full-time artist. Second only to Utamaro as a popular artist depicting women in the 1790s, he drew figures with the same elongated body type, which was very beautiful if not strictly realistic. In contrast to the more sensual look of Utamaro's figures, Eishi's beauties have a cool elegance reflecting the artist's upper-class background. He also drew on his elite education with numerous references to classical literature, comparing modern women to fictional or legendary beauties of the past. He had several very talented students who followed his style. After about 1800, he gave up print design and concentrated on painting instead.

Eishosai **Choki** (active c. 1780–1810)

There is little biographical information about Choki, who worked during the same periods as Kiyonaga and Utamaro and used styles similar to theirs. Like Utamaro, he was a student of Toriyama Sekien, and he may have been Sekien's adopted son. Most of his works are depictions of women, with a few examples of landscapes and cityscapes. His most famous works are half-length portraits of women made during the late 1790s, often with the shiny mica backgrounds also seen in prints by Utamaro and Sharaku.

Toshusai **Sharaku** (active 1794–1795)

The mysterious Sharaku is known only by his pen name, which appeared on a group of about 150 spectacular theatrical prints produced over a period of less than one year in 1794–95. There are many theories about his true identity, but none have been definitely proven. In his work, the trend toward increasing realism in actor portraits is taken to its ultimate extreme and becomes caricature, with results that are strikingly modern in appearance and still cherished by collectors today. The most highly prized of all his works are the close-up portraits (*okubi-e*), which have shiny backgrounds of ground mica added by hand as a final, deluxe touch after the color printing was completed. Sharaku's distinctive style strongly influenced other ukiyo-e artists, especially Utagawa Toyokuni and his students.

Katsushika **Hokusai** (1760–1849)

Today Hokusai is by far the most famous of all Japanese artists and indeed one of the best-known artists in the world, associated with iconic images based on his color prints nicknamed *The Great Wave* and *The Red Fuji*, which were designed when he was already over seventy years old. He began drawing at the age of six, became a professional ukiyo-e artist in his late teens, and continued working until his death at almost ninety, referring to himself in later years as the "old man mad about painting." The beauty and ingenuity of his print designs elevated both landscape and nature studies from minor subjects to major genres comparable in popularity to prints of actors and beautiful women. He was known for his great versatility and did prints, book illustrations, and one-of-a-kind paintings on many different subjects, including the history and literature of both China and Japan and highly imaginative scenes of supernatural events.

Shotei **Hokuju** (1763–1824)

Little is known about Hokuju, an early pupil of Hokusai who was actually the first artist to design landscape prints in the full-size *oban* format, even preceding his teacher, since Hokusai's earliest landscapes were smaller. Hokuju's works of the 1810s and early 1820s, like Hokusai's later works of the 1830s, utilize Western-style vanishing point perspective and low horizons. Hokuju also has a very interesting and distinctive drawing style, rendering his landscapes in geometric shapes with a kind of proto-Cubist flavor. His works seem to have been successful, to judge by their many reprintings, but he did not quite manage to make the breakthrough that Hokusai eventually did in raising landscape prints to best-seller status.

Utagawa **Toyokuni I** (1769–1825)

In his early years Toyokuni designed many elegant prints of beautiful women, following the styles set by Kiyonaga and Utamaro, and even a few prints of historical warriors, but most of his prolific output was actor portraits. His skill in portraying kabuki actors made the Utagawa school, founded by his teacher Utagawa Toyoharu, the leader in theatrical prints throughout the nineteenth century. Toyokuni designed some striking bust portraits similar to those of Sharaku as well as full-length images that also emphasized the individuality of the actors; later, he set his figures against detailed backgrounds showing actual scenes from plays. He maintained a large studio workshop with many pupils, among them Kunimasa, Kunisada, and Kuniyoshi.

Utagawa **Kunimasa** (1773–1810)

Kunimasa is generally considered second only to Sharaku in the power and expressiveness of his bust portraits of kabuki actors. He may have been the very first pupil of Utagawa Toyokuni, just a few years older than himself, who later taught the two stars of nineteenth-century figure prints—Kunisada and Kuniyoshi. In addition to the close-up portraits, Kunimasa also designed outstanding full-length images of women and actors and illustrated several books, but toward the end of his life, he is said to have given up print design and applied his interest in portraiture to carving three-dimensional masks of the actors. We will never know whether he might have gone back to prints later, since his career was cut short by an early death.

Totoya **Hokkei** (1780–1850)

Hokkei had been a fishmonger—the meaning of his art surname—before he became an artist, studying first under a painter of the Kano school—the official painters to the shogun—and then under Hokusai. Most of his works were *surimono*, privately commissioned prints usually made to illustrate the poems written by members of amateur poetry clubs, which was a popular intellectual hobby, and often beautifully printed at the expense of the affluent patrons. Hokkei became one of the top *surimono* designers of the 1810s and 1820s and was the teacher of Yashima Gakutei, another very successful *surimono* artist. Hokkei also designed a number of illustrations for poetry books and a few com-

mercial single-sheet prints featuring striking landscape compositions, such as the series Famous Places in the Provinces with its unusual narrow horizontal format.

Utagawa **Kunisada I (Toyokuni III)** (1786–1864)

Kunisada, the star pupil of Toyokuni, was the most prolific and financially successful of all ukiyo-e artists, producing tens of thousands of designs—primarily of actors and women. In the days before photography, his ability to capture a likeness made his theatrical portraits must-haves for kabuki fans; he became a best-selling artist in his teens and held on to that status for the rest of his long life. Kunisada was born into a wealthy merchant family operating a ferry service in Edo. Through talent, hard work, and good money management, he turned his modest family fortune into a much bigger one and died a very rich man. He operated a large workshop with many pupils, producing prints, book illustrations, and paintings. In 1844, almost twenty years after the death of his teacher Toyokuni, Kunisada changed his own art name to Toyokuni, becoming the third artist to use the name.

Keisai **Eisen** (1790–1848)

The versatile and prolific Eisen designed prints of fashionable women similar in style to the works of Kunisada and landscapes that resembled those of Hiroshige. His father was a samurai and a noted calligrapher, but after his father died, young Eisen had to support himself with a variety of jobs before establishing himself as an artist. He probably studied under the ukiyo-e artist Kikukawa Eizan, but he was not affiliated with any one school. His most famous work is a landscape series designed partly by him and partly by Hiroshige: The Sixty-nine Stations of the Kisokaido Road. He also wrote a valuable supplement to the standard history of the ukiyo-e field, incorporating his own research on the great artists of the past, and even tried his hand at writing popular fiction.

Utagawa **Hiroshige I** (1797–1858)

The great landscape artist Hiroshige was originally a low-ranking samurai who inherited his father's position as a fire warden in the city of Edo. He studied under Utagawa Toyohiro, a pupil of the Utagawa school founder Toyoharu. Inspired by the success of Hokusai's pioneering landscape series Thirty-six Views of Mount Fuji, Hiroshige designed The Fifty-three Stations of the Tokaido Road, showing scenes of the much-traveled highway between Edo and Kyoto. The huge success of this series—still often reproduced and referred to by artists today—catapulted him to stardom as an artist rivaling Hokusai in the design of landscapes. Hiroshige continued to produce large numbers of outstanding landscape prints and nature studies until his sudden death in a cholera epidemic. His final masterpiece, the series One Hundred Views of Edo, is noted for its unusual compositions, which became a source of inspiration for European artists in the late nineteenth century.

Utagawa **Kuniyoshi** (1797–1861)

In recent years Kuniyoshi has become enormously popular because his action-packed depictions of warriors and monsters are very similar to modern manga and anime. His father is said to have been a textile dyer, which might account for Kuniyoshi's love of brilliant colors and bold designs. A pupil of Toyokuni, he became one of the stars of ukiyo-e in the late 1820s with a series showing the 108 heroes of a beloved Chinese martial arts novel. He and his students followed up on the success of this series with many other designs showing heroes from the history and literature of both Japan and China. Kuniyoshi often drew heroes with magnificent tattoos, an ongoing source of inspiration for tattoo artists even today. In addition to the warrior prints (*musha-e*) that he popularized, he designed numerous prints of kabuki actors and fashionable women, as well as landscapes.

Ryusai **Shigeharu** (1803–1853)

When full-color prints first appeared in the 1760s, they were considered a specialty of the city of Edo, but from the 1790s on, they were published in Osaka as well. Unlike the Edo prints with their wide range of subjects, the Osaka prints focused primarily on the kabuki theater. The artist Shigeharu came originally from Nagasaki but was designing prints in Osaka, under the name Kunishige, while still in his teens. He may have studied under Hokusai's pupil and son-in-law Shigenobu, who lived in Osaka during the early 1820s. In 1826, he took the new name Ryusai Shigeharu and soon became one of the leading designers of

Osaka actor portraits. He seems to have gone back to Nagasaki in the late 1830s, but there is also a possibility that he returned in the late 1840s and designed some excellent actor prints that appeared at that time under his old name Kunishige.

Utagawa **Yoshitora** (active c. 1836–1887)

Little is known about the life of Yoshitora, but he was one of Kuniyoshi's oldest and best students. He designed numerous warrior triptychs in the same style as his teacher, as well as humorous prints and scenes from kabuki plays. He was one of the main artists designing the so-called Yokohama prints—images of the exotic foreigners who were coming into Japan in large numbers as a result of the opening of this port to outlanders in 1860. In the early 1860s, he collaborated with Kunisada and contributed some striking designs to a series of close-up actor portraits.

Utagawa **Yoshitsuya** (1822–1866)

Like his teacher Kuniyoshi, Yoshitsuya specialized in warrior prints, and it is suspected that he, too, occasionally inserted hidden political commentary into his designs. In addition to warrior prints, he sometimes did actor portraits, Yokohama prints, landscapes, and "toy prints" (*asobi-e*) featuring games and puzzles for children, as well as designs for tattoos. He joined Kuniyoshi's studio at the age of fifteen and soon became known for his excellent depictions of warriors, but when he was around thirty, he left the studio for several years because other students had complained about his gambling habit. In about 1856 he returned to the field of print design and produced still more outstanding compositions.

Kawanabe **Kyosai** (1831–1889)

Kyosai's father, like Hiroshige's, was a low-ranking samurai who worked as a fire warden. As a young child, Kyosai studied for three years with Kuniyoshi, but his later art training was under painters of the official Kano school. Even as a student in his teens, he loved drinking and partying. His paintings, prints, and book illustrations show an eclectic drawing style and a zany sense of humor, which sometimes included covert political satire. Eventually, in 1870–71, he was sentenced to a jail term for a painting—a performance piece at a raucous party—that criticized the new Meiji government, and he was more cautious thereafter. In the 1870s and '80s his paintings were among the Japanese goods displayed at major international expositions, and he was on friendly terms with visiting foreigners, particularly the British architect Josiah Conder.

Toyohara **Kunichika** (1835–1900)

Kunichika, whose family operated a public bathhouse, became a pupil of Utagawa Kunisada after first studying under an obscure artist named Toyohara Chikanobu (not to be confused with the later, more famous artist Chikanobu, Kunichika's own pupil, whose name has the same pronunciation but is composed of different Japanese characters). He took an art name consisting of the family name of his first teacher and a personal name that combined elements from both of his teachers. Following in the footsteps of Kunisada as a designer of actor portraits, Kunichika became the preeminent artist of kabuki prints from Kunisada's death until his own. Although he did not use the Utagawa name, he continued to work in the traditional Utagawa school style even while other artists of his time experimented with Westernized styles. Most of his prolific output was theatrical scenes, but he also occasionally drew women, landscapes, or scenes from history and literature.

Tsukioka **Yoshitoshi** (1839–1892)

Yoshitoshi was the most talented student of Kuniyoshi, and his early works are very similar in style to those of his teacher. He suffered episodes of mental illness throughout his life, which may have influenced the extreme violence seen in some of his prints. In the Meiji era, when Japan once again had extensive interactions with the rest of the world, Yoshitoshi developed a new hybrid style influenced by the realism of Western art that made his work very popular. In addition to color prints, he also did paintings and book illustrations, as well as illustrations for serialized fiction published in a form new to Japan: the newspaper. He shared Kuniyoshi's love of the supernatural, designing numerous scenes of ghosts and monsters. Many of his prints were issued in lengthy series, the most famous of which is One Hundred Aspects of the Moon, published from 1885 to 1891.

Glossary

aiban: a size of print that is about halfway between *oban* and *choban,* roughly 13 × 9 inches (33 × 23 cm).

beni: a bright, pinkish-red pigment derived from safflower.

beni-e: hand-colored prints utilizing *beni* as well as vegetal blues, yellows, and sometimes greens.

benizuri-e: a type of printing utilizing blocks with a limited number of colors, usually red and green, and possibly yellow or blue.

bijin-ga: literally "pictures of beautiful people"; prints showing the theme of lovely women—often courtesans or geisha—or sometimes attractive young men.

chuban: a size of print that is half an *oban* or roughly 10 × 7 inches (25 × 18 cm).

chutanzaku: a long print that is half the size of an *oban,* roughly 15 × 5 inches (38 × 13 cm).

fukei-ga: literally "views"; prints that depict landscapes and cityscapes.

hashira-e: literally "pillar print"; this format is particularly tall and narrow, suitable for hanging on the pillars of a room in a Japanese house.

hosoban: a narrow print size, roughly 13 × 6 inches (33 × 15 cm).

Japanese era names (nengo): The Japanese calendar system is broken up into era names. In modern times, these have corresponded to the reign of an emperor, but prior to the Meiji era, a single reign could encompass more than one era, with a new name chosen as a kind of reset after an inauspicious event—or in celebration of an auspicious one. As Japan only adopted the Gregorian calendar in 1873, the beginning and end of each year according to the lunar calendar may not correspond precisely to the Gregorian system. The era years covered in this book (organized by first year of the Gregorian calendar) are:

1673	Enpo
1681	Tenna
1684	Jokyo
1688	Genroku
1704	Hoei
1711	Shotoku
1716	Kyoho
1736	Genbun
1741	Kanpo
1744	Enkyo
1748	Kan'en
1751	Horeki
1764	Meiwa
1772	An'ei
1781	Tenmei
1789	Kansei
1801	Kyowa
1804	Bunka
1818	Bunsei
1830	Tenpo
1844	Koka
1848	Kaei
1854	Ansei
1860	Man'en
1861	Bunkyu
1864	Genji
1865	Keio
1868	Meiji

kacho-ga (or kacho-e): literally "bird-and-flower pictures"; prints depicting any kind of flora or fauna, whether on land or in water.

musha-e: warrior prints, which include not only themes of combat but also historical illustrations of all kinds.

nagaban: a large print format, roughly 22 × 10 inches (56 × 25 cm).

nikawa: a glue made from animal skin with many uses in Japanese art; in early hand-colored prints it was sometimes mixed with ink to create a pigment that would simulate the glossy veneer of lacquer once dried.

nishiki-e: literally "brocade pictures"; prints in full color (defined as five or more colors in addition to the black outlines) made with multiple blocks.

oban: most common size used in ukiyo-e, roughly 15 × 10 inches (38 × 25 cm).

okubi-e: literally "big head pictures"; i.e., close-up bust portraits.

o-oban: literally "large oban"; a print size roughly 23 × 12 inches (58 × 31 cm).

otanzaku: a long print size, roughly 15 × 7 inches (38 × 18 cm).

shikishiban: a square print format, roughly 10 × 9 inches (25 × 23 cm).

sumizuri-e: a print rendered in black and white, the earliest format for ukiyo-e.

surimono: literally "printed things"; privately commissioned prints, usually made to illustrate poems written by members of amateur poetry clubs, often beautifully printed at the expense of affluent patrons.

tan: a bright orange-red pigment made from lead.

tan-e: hand-colored prints utilizing *tan*, as well as yellow and green pigments, in which the color is applied here and there as accents.

uchiwa-e: prints formatted to be mounted on a flat fan (*uchiwa*).

uki-e: literally "floating pictures"; this is the term used for perspective prints rendered with a Western-style vanishing point.

ukiyo-e: literally "Floating World pictures"; prints, paintings, and book illustrations depicting the urban entertainment culture of Edo Japan, and later other subjects as well.

urushi-e: literally "lacquer pictures"; these prints employ a black ink mixed with glue (*nikawa*) to create a shiny finish resembling lacquer once the ink/glue mixture dried.

Yokohama print: a print depicting foreigners, either arriving in Japan or as imagined in their home countries, after the city of Yokohama became a treaty port for foreign trade in 1860.

Further Reading

Clark, Timothy, Anne Nishimura Morse, and Louise E. Virgin, with Allen Hockley. *The Dawn of the Floating World, 1650–1765: Early Ukiyo-e Treasures from the Museum of Fine Arts, Boston*. London: Royal Academy of Arts, 2001.

Guth, Christine. *The Art of Edo Japan: The Artist and the City, 1615–1868*. New York: Harry N. Abrams, 1996.

Marks, Andreas. *Japanese Woodblock Prints: Artists, Publishers, and Masterworks, 1680–1900*. Tokyo; Rutland, Vermont; and Singapore: Tuttle Publishing, 2010.

Meech, Julia, and Jane Oliver, eds. *Designed for Pleasure: The World of Edo Japan in Prints and Paintings, 1680–1860*. New York: Asia Society and Japanese Art Society of America, 2008.

Newland, Amy, ed. *The Hotei Encyclopedia of Japanese Woodblock Prints*. Amsterdam: Hotei Publishing, 2005.

Salter, Rebecca. *Japanese Woodblock Printing*. Honolulu: University of Hawai'i Press, 2001.

Tinios, Ellis. *Japanese Prints: Ukiyo-e in Edo, 1700–1900*. London: The British Museum Press, 2010.

Index of Artists and Titles

Italic page numbers indicate an image.

Toyohara **Chikanobu**, 185

Eishosai **Choki**, 14, *34*, 182
biography, 182
Sunrise on New Year's Morning, *14* (detail), *34*

Keisai **Eisen**, 15, *39*, *85*, 88, 184
biography, 184
Hanaogi of the Ogiya, *39*
Toeizan Temple Seen from Shinobazu Benten Shrine in Edo (Edo Shinobazu Benten yori Toeizan o miru zu), from a series of famous places in Edo with frames of Western letters, *85*

Chobunsai **Eishi**, 14, 19, *30*, *132*, *133*, 182
biography, 182
Five Teahouse Waitresses as the Five Men of the Karigane Gang, *30*
Komachi, from the series Six Selected Flowers Imitating the Six Poetic Immortals (*Yatsushi Rokkasen*), *132*
Matsukaze, from the series Genji in Fashionable Modern Guise (*Furyu yatsushi Genji*), *133*

Kikukawa **Eizan**, 184

Yashima **Gakutei**, 183

Suzuki **Harunobu**, *10*, 14, 23, 97, *130*, 181, 182
biography, 181
Kojima Bingo no Saburo Takanori, *10* (detail), *130*
Koto Player, The, *23*

Utagawa **Hiroshige I**, 9, 69, *86*, *87*, *88*, *89*, *90–91*, *92*, *93*, *94*, *96*, 97, *111*, *112*, *113*, *114*, *115*, *116*, *117*, *140*, *163*, 180, 184
biography, 184
Carp, from an untitled series known as Large Fish, *116*
Chiryu: Early Summer Horse Fair (Chiryu, shuka uma ichi), second (?) state, from the series Fifty-three Stations of the Tokaido Road (*Tokaido gojusan tsugi no uchi*), also known as the First Tokaido or Great Tokaido, *87*
Eight Views of Kanazawa at Night (Buyo Kanazawa hassho yakei), from an untitled set of three triptychs, *93*
Flying Geese and Full Moon, from the series Japanese and Chinese Poems for Recitation (*Wakan roeishu*), *140*
Kanbara: Night Snow (Kanbara, yoru no yuki), second state, from the series Fifty-three Stations of the Tokaido Road (*Tokaido gojusan tsugi no uchi*), also known as the First Tokaido or Great Tokaido, *86*
Kingfisher and Hydrangea, *96*, *111*
Mallard Ducks and Snow-covered Reeds, *115*
Mariko, from the series Fifty-three Stations of the Tokaido Road (*Tokaido gojusan tsugi no uchi*), also known as the First Tokaido or Great Tokaido, 9 (detail)
Morning Glories and Cricket, from the series A Compendium of Flowers of the Four Seasons (*Shiki no hana zukushi*), *117*
Night View of Saruwaka-machi (Saruwaka-machi yoru no kei), from the series One Hundred Famous Views of Edo (*Meisho Edo hyakkei*), *89*, *90–91*
No. 12, Shinmachi, from the series Sixty-nine Stations of the Kisokaido Road (*Kisokaido rokujukyu tsugi no uchi*), *88*
Peacock and Peonies, *114*
Plum Estate, Kameido (Kameido Umeyashiki), from the series One Hundred Famous Views of Edo (*Meisho Edo hyakkei*), *92*
Sea off Satta in Suruga Province, The (Suruga Satta kaijo), from the series Thirty-six Views of Mount Fuji (*Fuji sanjurokkei*), *94*
Small Horned Owl in a Pine Tree, *113*
Taira no Kiyomori Haunted by Strange Sights (Taira Kiyomori kaii o miru zu), *163*
Yellow Rose (Yamabuki) and Frogs, *112*

Totoya **Hokkei**, *2*, 15, *84*, 183–84
biography, 183–84
Musashi Plain (Musashino), from the series Famous Places in the Provinces (*Shokoku meisho*), *2*, *84*

Shotei **Hokuju**, 12, *74*, 183
biography, 183
True Depiction of the Fuji River (Fujikawa shinsha no zu), from the series The Tokaido Road (*Tokaido*), *74*

Katsushika **Hokusai**, *8*, 15, 69, *74*, *78*, *79*, *80*, *81*, *82*, *83*, *84*, 86, *94*, 97, *100*, *101*, *102–3*, *104*, *105*, *106*, *107*, *108*, *109*, *110*, *136*, *137*, *138*, *139*, *151*, *156*, *157*, *158*, 180, 181, 183, 184
Amida Falls in the Far Reaches of the Kiso Road, The (Kisoji no oku Amida-ga-taki), from the series A Tour of Waterfalls in Various Provinces (*Shokoku taki meguri*), *83*
Bellflower and Dragonfly, from an untitled series known as Large Flowers, *101*
biography, 183
Bullfinch and Weeping Cherry (Uso, shidarezakura), from an untitled series known as Small Flowers, *105*
Chrysanthemums and Horsefly, from an untitled series known as Large Flowers, *100*, *102–3*
Cranes on a Snow-covered Pine Tree, *109*
Falling Mist Waterfall at Mount Kurokami in Shimotsuke

Province, The (Shimotsuke Kurokamiyama Kirifuri no taki), from the series A Tour of Waterfalls in Various Provinces (*Shokoku taki meguri*), *82*
Fine Wind, Clear Weather (Gaifu kaisei), also known as *Red Fuji*, from the series Thirty-six Views of Mount Fuji (*Fugaku sanjurokkei*), *79*, 185
Flock of Chickens, *108*
Fuji View Plain in Owari Province (Bishu Fujimi-ga-hara), from the series Thirty-six Views of Mount Fuji (*Fugaku sanjurokkei*), *81*
Ghost of Kohada Koheiji, The, from the series One Hundred Ghost Stories (*Hyaku monogatari*), *158*
Hodogaya on the Tokaido (Tokaido Hodogaya), from the series Thirty-six Views of Mount Fuji (*Fugaku sanjurokkei*), *80*
Horses in Pasture, *110*
Hundred Views of Mount Fuji (book), 94
Kingfisher with Iris and Wild Pinks (Kawasemi, shaga, nadeshiko), from an untitled series known as Small Flowers, *106*
Li Bai (Ri Haku), from the series A True Mirror of Chinese and Japanese Poetry (*Shika shashin kyo*), also called Imagery of the Poets, *137*
Mansion of the Plates, The (Sara yashiki), from the series One Hundred Ghost Stories (*Hyaku monogatari*), *157*
Newly Published Perspective Picture: One Hundred Ghost Stories in a Haunted House (Shinpan uki-e bakemono yashiki hyaku monogatari no zu), *156*
Peonies and Canary (Shakuyaku, kanaari), from an untitled series known as Small Flowers, *104*
Poem by Sarumaru Dayu, from the series One Hundred Poems Explained by the Nurse (*Hyakunin isshu uba ga etoki*), *138*
Print and Book Store (Ezoshi ten): The Store of Tsutaya Juzaburo, from the book Illustrated Pleasures of the East (*Ehon Azuma Asobi*), *8*
Under the Wave off Kanagawa (Kanagawa-oki nami-ura), also known as The Great Wave, from the series Thirty-six Views of Mount Fuji (*Fugaku sanjurokkei*), *78*, *79*, 94, 185
Watanabe no Gengo Tsuna and Inokuma Nyudo Raiun, from an untitled series of warriors in combat, *136*
Wisteria and Wagtail (Fuji, sekirei), from an untitled series known as Small Flowers, *107*

Sugimura **Jihei**, 11, *124*, 180
Archer Nasu no Yoichi, The, *124*
biography, 180

Torii **Kiyomasu I**, *11*, *21*, *48*, *126*, 180
Actor Fujimura Handayu II as Oiso no Tora, *48*
biography, 180
Standing Courtesan, *11* (detail), *21*
Uesugi Kenshin (R) and Takeda Shingen (L) at the Battle of Kawanakajima, *126*

Torii **Kiyonaga**, 14, *26*, *27*, *28–29*, *52*, *71*, 182, 183
Actors Sawamura Sojuro III as the Fox Tadanobu, Nakayama Tomisaburo I as Shizuka, and Ichikawa Danjuro V as Yokawa Kakuhan, *52*
biography, 182
Courtesans Viewing Cherry Blossoms: Nioteru of the Ogiya, kamuro Namiji and Omi (R); Utahime of the Matsubaya, kamuro Kanomo and Konomo (C); Senzan of the Chojiya, kamuro Yasono and Yasoji (L), *27*, *28–29*
Pilgrimage to Enoshima, A, *71*
Woman in Bathrobe and Mother Playing with Baby, from the series Current Manners in Eastern Brocade (*Fuzoku Azuma no nishiki*), *26*

Torii **Kiyonobu I**, 11, *47*, 180, 181
Actor Tsutsui Kichijuro in the Spear Dance, *47*
biography, 180

Torii **Kiyonobu II**, 180

Torii **Kiyoshige**, 12, *50*, 181
Actor Ichikawa Ebizo II as Bunshin Yanone Goro, *12* (detail), *50*
biography, 181

Isoda **Koryusai**, 14, *24*, *25*, 97, *99*, *154*, 180, 181–82
biography, 181–82
Eagle on a Pine Branch in the Rain, *99*
Kaoru and Eguchi of the Shin-Kanaya, from the series Models for Fashion: New Year Designs as Fresh as Young Leaves (*Hinagata wakana no hatsu moyo*), *24*
Phoenix and Paulownia Tree, *154*
Young Woman Holding a Cat, *25*

Toyohara **Kunichika**, 15, *66*, *67*, 185
Actor Ichikawa Danjuro IX as Musashibo Benkei in The Subscription List (Kanjincho), one of the Eighteen Great Kabuki Plays (Kabuki juhachiban no uchi), *67*
Actors Kawarazaki Gonjuro as Takaramusubi no Gon (R), Ichimura Uzaemon XIII as Tachibana Hishizo (C), and Nakamura Shikan IV as Sanba Jafuku (L), in Unity of Three Happinesses: Favorite Actors Before a White Waterfall (Sanpuku soroe shiiki no shirataki), *66*
biography, 185

Utagawa **Kunimasa**, 14, *44*, *56*, *57*, 183
Actor Ichikawa Ebizo as Usui Arataro Sadamitsu in a Shibaraku Scene, *44*, *57*
Actor Nakamura Noshio II as Sakuramaru, *56*
biography, 183

Utagawa **Kunisada I** (Toyokuni III), 15, *38*, *42*, *58*, *64*, *65*, *134*, 183, 184, 185
Actor Bando Mitsugoro III as Kajiwara Genta, from

the series Great Hit Plays (*Oatari kyogen no uchi*), 58
Actors Arashi Kichisaburo III as Akabori Mizuemon, with Matsumoto Kunigoro and Arashi Kangoro (R); Arashi Rikan III as Nakano Tobei (C); and Kataoka Gado II as Miki Juzaemon, with Naritaya Sobei II (?) and Otani Tokuji II (L), 64
biography, 184
In-demand Type, The (Yoku ureso), from the series Thirty-two Physiognomic Types in the Modern World (*Tosei sanjuni so*), 38
Parody of the Story of Kantan (Mitate Kantan), 134
Wisteria in Full Bloom at Kameido (Kameido fuji no shinsei), 42

Utagawa **Kuniyoshi**, 15, 40, 41, *60, 61, 62–63, 75, 76–77*, 119, *122*, 123, 135, 136, *139*, 141, 142, *143, 144–45*, 150, 151, 159, *160–61, 162, 164–65, 166, 167, 168–69, 170, 171, 172*, 183, 184, 185
Actor Caricatures: Matsumoto Kinsho I (TR), Ichimura Uzaemon XII (TC), Ichikawa Shinsha I (TL), Nakamura Utaemon IV (BR), Bando Shuka I (BC), Sawamura Ujuro II (?) (BL), from the series Scribbles on a Storehouse Wall (*Nitakaragura kabe no mudagaki*), *61*
At Kawanakajima in Shinano Province, the Takeda Forces Crossed Mount Saijo and the Ford at Ame-no-Miya and Fought Amakasu Omi no Kami of the Echigo Side (Shinshu Kawanakajima Takeda no shohei Saijozan o hikikaeshi Ame-no-Miya no watari o koe Echigo-gata), 143, *144–45*
At the Bottom of the Sea in Daimotsu Bay (Daimotsu no ura kaitei no zu), *166*
biography, 184
Catching Fireflies in the Cool of the Evening (Suzumi no hotaru), from the series Excursions in the Four Seasons (*Shiki yukan*), *40*
Earth Spider Generates Monsters at the Mansion of Lord Minamoto no Yorimitsu, The (Minamoto Yorimitsu [Raiko] ko no yakata ni tsuchigumo yokai o nasu zu), 159, *160–61*
Former Emperor [Sutoku] from Sanuki Sends His Retainers to Rescue Tametomo, The (Sanuki no in kenzoku o shite Tametomo o sukuu zu), *167, 168–69*
Ghosts of the Taira Attack Yoshitsune in Daimotsu Bay, The, 142
In the Ruined Palace at Soma, Masakado's Daughter Takiyasha Uses Sorcery to Gather Allies; Oya no Taro Mitsukuni Comes Here to Investigate the Monsters and Finally Destroys Them (Soma no furudairi ni Masakado himegimi Takiyasha yojutsu o motte mikata o a), *162, 164–65*
Kiyo-hime, from the series Mirror of Warriors of Our Country (*Honcho musha kagami*), 150, *172*
Nichiren in the Snow at Tsukahara on Sado Island (Sashu Tsukahara setchu), from the series Sketches of the Life of Nichiren (*Koso goichidai ryakuzu*), *75, 76–77*
Nozarashi Gosuke, from the series Men of Ready Money with True Labels Attached, Kuniyoshi Fashion (*Kuniyoshi moyo shofuda tsuketari genkin otoko*), 141
Origin Story of the Cat Stone at Okabe, The, Representing One of the Fifty-three Stations of the Tokaido Road (Mitate Tokaido gojusan tsugi Okabe neko ishi no yurai): Actors Sawamura Sojuro V as Teranishi Kanshin (R), Onoe Kiku-goro III as the Cat Monster (C), and Ichimura Uzaemon XII as Oe Inabano-suke (L), *60, 62–63*
Poem by Oe no Chisato, from the series One Hundred Poems by One Hundred Poets (*Hyakunin isshu no uchi*), *139*
Ruan Xiaowu, the Short-lived Second Son (Tanmeijiro Genshogo), from the series One Hundred and Eight Heroes of the Popular Shuihuzhuan (*Tsuzoku Suikoden goketsu hyakuhachinin no hitori*), *122*, 135
Shimosuwa: Yaegaki-hime, from the series Sixty-nine Stations of the Kisokaido Road (*Kisokaido rokujukyu tsugi no uchi*), *171*
Takeout Sushi Suggesting Ataka, from the series Women in Benkei-checked Fabrics (*Shimazoroi onna Benkei*), *41*
Tsumagome: Abe no Yasuna and the Fox Kuzunoha, from the series Sixty-nine Stations of the Kisokaido Road (*Kisokaido rokujukyu tsugi no uchi*), *170*

Kawanabe **Kyosai**, 15, *16*, *118, 119, 120–21*, 177, 185
biography, 185
Decorative Paper with Design of Chrysanthemums, *118, 120–21*
Mount Akiba (Akiba-san), from the series Scenes of Famous Places along the Tokaido Road (*Tokaido meisho fukei*), also known as the Processional Tokaido (*Gyoretsu Tokaido*), here called *Tokaido meisho no uchi*, *177*
Sleeping Cat, *16* (detail), *119*

Okumura **Masanobu**, 11, *22, 49*, *70, 72–73*, 125, *152*, 180–81
Actor Onoe Kikugoro I as Soga no Goro dressed as a Komuso, *49*
biography, 180–81
Courtesan as Fei Zhangfang (Hi Chobo), from a series of courtesans imitating Taoist immortals, *152*
Large Perspective Picture of the Kabuki Theater District in Sakai-cho and Fukiya-cho, *70, 72–73*
Shuten-doji of Mount Oe, The (oeyama Shuten-doji), from the series Famous Scenes from Japanese Puppet Plays (*Yamato irotake*), *125*
Woman with Umbrella and Dog on Leash, *22*

Hishikawa **Moronobu**, 11, 20, 180
biography, 180
Young Man Dallying with a Courtesan, A, from an untitled series of twelve erotic prints, *20*

Toriyama **Sekien**, 182

Toshusai **Sharaku**, 14, 53, 54, 56, 58, 182–83
Actor Segawa Tomisaburo II as Yadorigi, Wife of Ogishi Kurando, 53
Actors Sawamura Yodogoro II as Kawatsura Hogen and Bando Zenji as Oninosadobo, 54
biography, 182–83

Ryusai **Shigeharu**, 59, 184–85
Actors Onoe Kikugoro III as Shizuka Gozen (R) and Nakamura Utaemon III as the Fox Tadanobu (L), 59
biography, 184–85

Kitao **Shigemasa**, 14, 153, 182
biography, 182
Kintaro Judging the Wrestling Match of a Monkey and a Bear, 153

Nishimura **Shigenaga**, *11*, 98, *127*, 128–29, 133, 181, 182
biography, 181
Cranes and Chrysanthemums, from a bird-and-flower series with the title Kashinsai (?), *11* (detail), 98
Tale of Genji, The: The Wind in the Pines (Genji Matsukaze), no. 18 from the series Genji in Fifty-Four Sheets *(Genji gojuyonmai no uchi), 127, 128–29*

Yanagawa **Shigenobu**, 184

Katsukawa **Shunsho**, 14, 51, 180, 181, 182
Actors, from right: Nakamura Riko I as Agemaki, Nakamura Nakazo I as Hige no Ikyu, and Ichikawa Danjuro V as Sukeroku, 51
biography, 181

Miyagawa **Shunsui**, 181

Utagawa **Toyoharu**, 183, 184

Utagawa **Toyohiro**, 184

Utagawa **Toyokuni I**, 14, *35*, *36–37*, 55, 56, 58, 151, 183, 184
biography, 183
Chofu Jewel River, The (Chofu no Tamagawa), 35, 36–37
Shogatsuya (Actor Sakata Hangoro III as Abe no Muneto), from the series Portraits of Actors on Stage *(Yakusha butai no ugata-e), 55*

unattributed works
Young Kabuki Actor Playing a Shamisen, 46

Kitagawa **Utamaro I**, *8*, 14, *18*, 19, *31*, *32*, *33*, 101, *131*, 155, 182, 183
biography, 182
Couple with a Standing Screen, 33
Immortal Qin Gao, The, represented by Hinazuru of the Chojiya, kamuro Tsuruji and Tsuruno (Kinko, Chojiya uchi Hinazuru, Tsuruji, Tsuruno), from the series Eight Immortals in the Art of Love *(Enchu hassen), 155*
Kitchen Scene, 32
Parody of the Killing of the Nue, from the series Picture Siblings *(E-kyodai), 131*
Selected Insects (Mushi erabi) (poetry album), 101
Three Beauties of the Present Day (Toji san bijin): Tomimoto Toyohina, Naniwaya Kita, Takashima Hisa, 18, 31
Woodblock Printer (Suriko), Print Shop, Distributing New Prints (Shinpan kubari), from the series the Cultivation of Brocade Prints, a Famous Product of Edo *(Edo meibutsu nishiki-e kosaku), 8*

Utagawa **Yoshitora**, 15, *16*, *65*, *95*, 185
Actor Bando Hikosaburo V as Jigoku Dayu, from an untitled series of actors, *65*
biography, 185
City of Paris, France, The (Furansu Parisu no fu), 16 (detail), *95*

Tsukioka **Yoshitoshi**, 15, *43*, 123, *146*, *147*, *148–49*, 151, *178*, *179*, 185
biography, 185
Fifteenth Shogun, The, Lord Tokugawa Yoshinobu (Jugodai, Tokugawa Yoshinobu ko), from the series Chronological Record of the Rule of the Tokugawas *(Tokugawa jiseki nenkan kiji), 146, 148–49*
Fujiwara no Yasumasa Playing the Flute by Moonlight, a Painting Shown at the Exhibition for the Advancement of Painting in Autumn 1882 (Meiji jugo mizunoe uma kishu Kaiga Kyoshinkai shuppinga Fujiwara no Yasumasa gekka fue o moteasobu zu, oju), 147
Looking as if She Wants to Go for a Walk: The Fashion of a Married Woman of the Meiji Era (Yuho ga shitaso, Meiji nenkan saikun no fuzoku), from the series Thirty-two Appearances of Fashion *(Fuzoku sanjuni so), 43*
Midnight Moon at Mount Yoshino: Iga no tsubone (Yoshinoyama yahan tsuki, Iga no tsubone), from the series One Hundred Aspects of the Moon *(Tsuki hyakushi), 178*
Taira no Koremochi Vanquishes a Female Demon at Togakushi Mountain (Taira Koremochi Togakushiyama kijo taiji no zu), 179

Utagawa **Yoshitsuya**, 15, 151, *173*, *174–75*, *176*, 185
At the Battle of Takadachi in Oshu Province in 1187, a White Dragon Ascends to Heaven from the Koromo River (Bunji sannen oshu Takadachi kassen Koromogawa yori hakuryu ten e noboru), 173, 174–75
biography, 185
Yorimitsu Tries to Capture Hakamadare by Destroying His Magic (Kijutsu o yabutte Yorimitsu Hakamadare o karamen to su), 176

Image Credits

Listings are alphabetized by donor's last name; numbers in parentheses are the Museum's accession numbers; numbers following accession numbers are page numbers.

Gift of Miss Lucy T. Aldrich: (47.48), 16 (detail), 119; (47.21), 96 (detail), 111

Asiatic Curator's Fund: (49.558), 85; (55.380), 124

William Sturgis Bigelow Collection: (11.14676), front cover (detail), 54; (11.14539-41), 8; (11.19633), 10 (detail), 130; (11.13253), 11 (detail), 21; (11.30416-8), 16 (detail), 95; (11.13338), 22; (11.14621), 24; (11.14007-9), 27, 28–29 (detail); (11.24991-3), 35, 36–37 (detail); (11.17936), 39; (11.30394-6), 40; (11.36360), 41; (11.43604a-c), 42; (11.14981), 44 (detail), 57; (11.13156), 46; (11.13339), 49; (11.13913), 52; (11.14682), 53; (11.15741), 58; (11.36220a-b), 59; (11.41806a-c), 60, 62–63 (detail); (11.27004), 61; (11.44182a-c), 64; (11.16281), 65; (11.41572a-c), 66; (11.2636), 68 (detail), 94; (11.19687), 70, 72–73 (detail); (11.17649), 81; (11.19528), 99; (11.19646), 109; (11.19649), 110; (21.6793), 112; (21.7943), 113; (11.39402), 118, 120–21 (detail); (21.6891), 114; (21.7929), 115; (21.9616), 116; (21.10125), 117; (11.13190), 125; (11.19132), 127, 128–29 (detail); (11.17552), 136; (11.30181), 138; (11.16029), 139; (11.28900), 141; (11.30566a-c), 142; (11.38244a-c), 143, 144–45 (detail); (11.37579a-c), 146, 148–49 (detail); (11.20238-40), 147; (11.19596), 153; (11.14262), 155; (11.39572a-c), 159, 160–61 (detail); (11.30468-70), 162; (11.26797-9), 163, 164–65; (11.30560-2), 166; (11.26999-7001), 167, 168–69 (detail); (11.38972.44), 170; (11.38972.31), 171; (11.38116), 172; (11.37940a-c), 173, 174–75 (detail); (11.22917-9), 176; (11.16606), 177; (11.22592), 178; (11.16272; 11.16274), 179

Nellie Parney Carter Collection—Bequest of Nellie Parney Carter: (34.489), 38

Bequest of Maxim Karolik: (64.800), 122 (detail), 135

Gift of the Anne Gordon Keidel Trust of June 2016: (2016.1478), 43

Gift of L. Aaron Lebowich: (53.505), 134

Gift of Mrs. Jared K. Morse in memory of Charles J. Morse: (RES.53.252), 8; (53.2923), 152

Denman Waldo Ross Collection: (06.1359), 74; (06.1224), 140

Gift of C. Adrian Rübel: (46.1417), 156

William S. and John T. Spaulding Collection: (21.6680), slipcase (detail), 101; (21.5344), 2 (detail), 84; (21.10436), 6 (detail), 89; (21.9328), 9; (21.5878), 11 (detail), 98; (21.5669), 12 (detail), 50; (21.4780), 14 (detail), 34; (21.6382), 18 (detail), 31; (21.5813), 20; (21.4439), 23; (21.8334), 25; (21.5601), 26; (21.7407-8), 32; (21.6610), 33; (21.5644), 47; (21.7149-51), 51; (21.6850), 55; (21.7008), 56; (21.7344-6), 71; (21.8174), 75, 76–77 (detail); (21.6765), 78; (21.6756), 79; (21.53610), 80; (21.6685), 82; (21.6687), 83; (21.5032), 86; (21.5065), 87; (21.5158), 88, 90–91 (detail); (21.10421), 92; (21.7615-7), 93; (21.6681), 100, 102–3 (detail); (21.10228), 104; (21.10229), 105; (21.10221), 106; (21.10219), 107; (21.10192), 108; (21.7169), 126; (21.6478), 131; (21.4921), 132; (21.7371-3), 133; (21.6669), 137; (21.8241), 154; (21.10236), 157; (21.10235), 158

Source unidentified: (RES.52.18-20), 67

Worcester Art Museum exchange, made possible through the Special Korean Pottery Fund, Museum purchase with funds donated by contribution, and Smithsonian Institution—Chinese Expedition, 1923–24: (54.338), 30; (54.216), 48

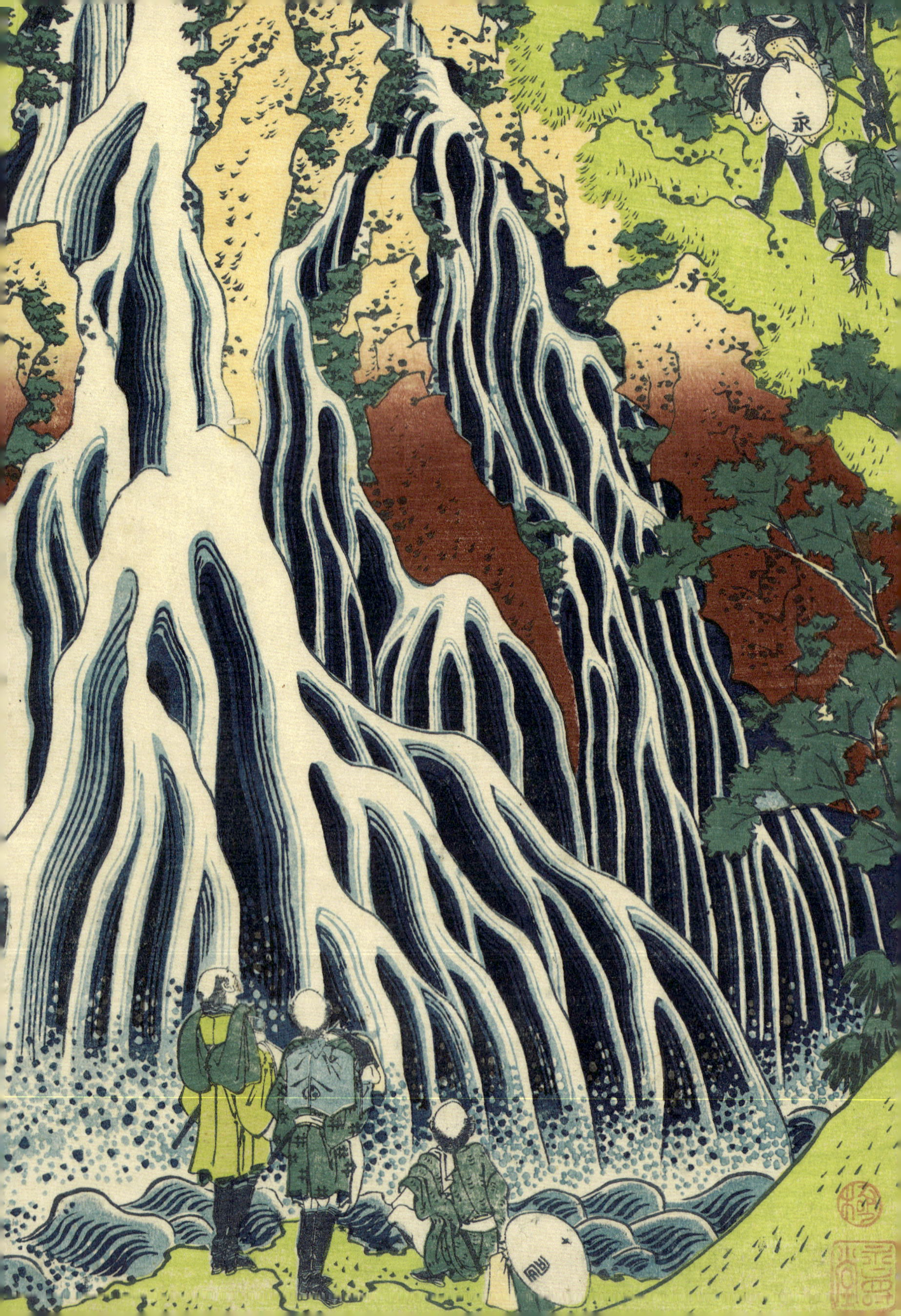